ENOUGH ROPE

ENOUGH ROPE

The inside story of the censure of Senator Joe McCarthy by his colleagues–the controversial hearings that signaled the end of a turbulent career and a fearsome era in American public life.

by Arthur V. Watkins

Former Senator from Utah and Chairman of The Select Committee to Study Censure Charges Against the Senator from Wisconsin, Mr. McCarthy

PRENTICE-HALL, INC., ENGLEWOOD CLIFFS, N. J.
UNIVERSITY OF UTAH PRESS, SALT LAKE CITY

Permission has been received from the following sources to use and/or reprint letters and other material:

Quotation from James Reston's column, November 11, 1954 issue of *The New York Times,* © 1954 by the New York Times Company. Reprinted by permission.

Letter quoted by permission of Dr. Harry Emerson Fosdick.

Letter quoted by permission of David O. McKay.

To the many thousands of Americans who by their communications to me indicated they did not have a full and correct understanding of the issues involved in the censure proceedings against Senator Joseph R. McCarthy; and to the millions of others who were undoubtedly confused, even distressed, because they were without sufficient information on these proceedings to enable them to make a valid judgment on the merits or demerits of the charges against the late Senator McCarthy, and;

For the guidance of future generations who will have, mayhap, a practical interest in the McCarthy episode, and precedents established—precedents which should be soundly based on a truthful record of facts, and a correct application of constitutional principles to those facts, and;

To my colleagues on the Select Committee: Senators Edwin C. Johnson, John C. Stennis, Frank Carlson, the late Senator Francis Case, and Sam J. Ervin, Jr., and to my former colleague, Senator Wallace F. Bennett, of Utah.

To Committee staff personnel: Honorable E. Wallace Chadwick, Counsel; Guy G. DeFuria, Assistant Counsel; John M. Jex, Clerk; and

To staff members: John W. Wellman, Frank I. Ginsberg, R. Ray McGuire; and

To political science students everywhere.

To all of the above this book is respectfully dedicated.

Acknowledgments

I would like to express my gratitude to a number of friends and wellwishers who encouraged me to write this book; or who have been active in gathering material and assisting in the preparation of the text; or who have given helpful suggestions as the writing proceeded. They are—

The late Henry R. Luce, co-founder of Time *and* Life *magazines;*

Richard Y. Thurman, Director of the University of Utah Press;

Carlos Whiting, researcher and my assistant, formerly with the U. S. Bureau of Reclamation and the National Parks Administration;

Cecil Holland, recently of the Washington Star *reportorial staff;*

Beverly Stoven, special clerk and typist for the Select Committee in 1954 and now on the staff of the University of Utah;

Keith Jacques, Washington staff assistant to Senator Wallace F. Bennett of Utah;

Judy McNamara, typist, of Arlington, Virginia;

Georgina Wibert, researcher, Arlington, Virginia;

And also the Washington staffs of the members of the Select Committee in 1954. These staffs rendered a great deal of assistance to the Committee and deserve special mention. With their help the Committee was enabled to carry on its activities with a very small budget.

Introduction

IN THE SUMMER OF 1954 THE UNITED STATES SENATE—AND MORE disquieting, the entire Nation—was embroiled in an alarming controversy which concerned the very foundations of American democracy.

Senator Joseph R. McCarthy, the initiator of the fierce debate, called it: "McCarthyism, the Fight for America." But a modern college dictionary * defines this same McCarthyism: "1. The practice of making public and sensational accusations of disloyalty or corruption, usually with little or no proof or with doubtful evidence. 2. The practice of conducting inquisitorial investigations, ostensibly to expose pro-communist activity." Thousands of Americans merely called it "The McCarthy Issue."

Seldom in the Nation's history has there been an issue which has been so divisive and has aroused such unreasoning emotions. Depths as dark and fetid as ever stirred on this continent came to public attention.

As the controversy grew, it challenged the integrity, dignity, and effectiveness of the Senate, and of the entire Federal establishment aside from the courts.

And as the voices became increasingly shrill the overriding concern was, "What shall we do about it?"

An answer to this bitter question seemed imminent in late summer of 1954 when Senator Ralph Flanders of Vermont offered a resolution on the floor of the Senate that the conduct of Senator McCarthy was unbecoming a member of the United States Senate and contrary to its traditions and should be condemned. Senator J. William Fulbright of Arkansas, Senator Wayne Morse of Oregon, and others further developed the charges in amendments to the Flanders resolution.

While I had felt a momentary apprehension that I might be appointed to a censure committee, a job for which I had not the least ambition, I was actually surprised to be selected as one of the three Republicans and three Democrats to investigate the censure charges, and to be named the Committee's Chairman. Reluctant as I was to accept the assignment, I felt compelled to do so. Service in the United States Senate is one of the highest honors which can come to any citizen, and it has corresponding responsibilities and obligations.

The proceedings, which resulted in the censure of McCarthy, were exhausting and nerve-racking. In my more than 80 years, with daily encounters and exchanges with people of diverse opinion, I have never suffered such intense and continuing distress. Some friends and even a few members of my family contributed to the

---

* The *Reader's Digest Great Encyclopedia Dictionary*, including *Funk and Wagnalls Standard College Dictionary* (Reader's Digest Association, Pleasantville, N.Y.).

strain of those days by a lack of understanding of the events and issues and the law applicable to them.

That this misunderstanding and confusion was widespread was evidenced by the many thousands of letters I received, as well as phone calls and telegrams. In my role as the Chairman of the Committee—judicial in nature—I felt it improper to read or otherwise take more than casual note of most of the approximately 30,000 missives received. I knew that in this objective hearing I ought to be persuaded by demonstrable facts, not the popularity or unpopularity of the debate or its principals. Even if I should not have had this conscientious reason for not reading them, there would not have been time to consider the mail and to take part in the proceedings.

That these communications would not have been conducive to a calm, judicial appraisal of the issues was clearly confirmed by my recent reading of them. A wide range of attitudes were expressed, with noticeable trends; I should have been most amazed at the time had I realized that in the minds of many Americans it was *I* who was on trial; not Senator McCarthy.

And in this trial there appeared to be little understanding of the purpose, procedures, and authority of the Committee I was chosen to head, or of the fact that its consideration of censure was in no way connected with the fight on communism. This apparent ignorance encompassed the press, other public media, and members of the Senate as well.

The McCarthy controversy began with wholesale charges by Senator McCarthy that communist traitors and their sympathizers were numerous and deeply entrenched in places of responsibility and authority in the United States government. At the end, McCarthy had not named or presented sufficiently credible evidence against a single one of the 205, 81, or 57 "communists" he at various times declared himself ready to name.

Certainly much of the Nation, already converted to anticommunism by world events, and excited by the many spokesmen of special interest, rallied to the support of McCarthy. My present opinion, greatly reinforced by time, experience, and reflection, is that the apprehensions raised by Senator McCarthy were largely destructive and in only a small way useful.

Paramount to my personal point of view and reactions to the entire McCarthy episode—and very possibly of relevance to my appointment to the censure Committee—is my strong belief that the Constitution of the United States is an inspired document. This point is basic to my Mormon faith and heritage and has always been a tenet of the Church of Jesus Christ of Latter-day Saints, popularly called the Mormon Church.

Those institutions which derive from the Constitution (and this includes specifically the Senate of the United States, in the present context) are entitled to the respect and honor of every citizen. It was and is my stand that a Senator, above all, should in his speech and actions demonstrate this same conviction to contribute to and uphold the dignity of the Senate. The implications of this are compounded when we remember that a Senator is not required to answer in any other place for his conduct on the floor of the Senate or in its committees. Unless the Senate itself protects this unique privilege, any individual Senator with less regard for his obligations and his honor can greatly misuse his prerogatives.

While it is not the province of this book to research the personal peculiarities and political motivations of Senator McCarthy in the working out of what has since become known as McCarthyism, I will advance my personal opinions. These matters have been thoroughly explored and documented by others. But my own evaluations and judgments of the man during our coinciding two terms of office— and most definitely as a result of the hearings which I chaired—are, I am still convinced, well-founded and substantiated.

My role in the censure of McCarthy, and indirectly in the repudiation of Mc- Carthyism by the American people, I believe, deserves telling. The passage of years has long since tempered any feelings of hurt and indignation over the im- moderate attacks on me by McCarthy and his supporters. In addition, I believe, I can be reasonably objective in my analysis of my defeat in my bid for re-election to the Senate following the censure proceedings, in which the bitterness of the pro-McCarthy faction was a direct factor.

I have been hesitant to write about some matters: details of my personal history, my indignations, my desire (perhaps) to justify certain positions and some of my judgments at the time, and to provide the answers to some of the hundreds of questions thrown at me by outraged citizens. But it is as a window on the times, perhaps even as a source book for future political scientists, and certainly a con- tribution to the continuing analysis of McCarthy and his "ism," that I write this book.

Even today, how many can answer these questions: What authority does the Senate have to discipline its members or expel them? How is that power executed? What, if any, Senate rules apply to censure or condemnation resolutions? Can any Senator be prohibited from voting on such a resolution by reason of prejudice or personal interest? What were the charges against Senator McCarthy? Did the Select Committee have the authority, without further action by the Senate, to consider additional charges against McCarthy? Could and did the Senate itself consider additional charges and evidence? Did the Select Committee hold hearings on all the charges against McCarthy? Why didn't the Committee recommend censure of Senators Flanders, Fulbright, and Morse?

Why did the Committee refuse to let Senator McCarthy put in the record all material that he offered? Did the Committee have the authority to really "try" Senator McCarthy? What was the principal function of the Committee? To what extent, if any, was McCarthy's fight against communism involved in the Committee's recommendations? Which body really had the right, the Senate or the Committee, to "try" McCarthy? Why weren't the Committee's proceedings televised or open to direct reporting by radio?

These questions, and more, will be answered for those who read the following pages.

CONTENTS

ENOUGH ROPE

1 *Commitment to the Ordeal*

THE HEAT AND HUMIDITY OF WASHINGTON'S EARLY AUGUST CANNOT EXPLAIN the feeling of uneasiness, even dismay, which I felt upon receiving word in my office early one morning in 1954 that Senate Republican Leader William Knowland was on the line. I reached for the telephone, expecting to be confronted with an invitation that I could not relish. Several appropriate reasons for declining it tumbled to the fore in my mind.

Following the usual courtesies, Senator Knowland merely asked me to drop by his office later in the morning. It was not with relief, however, that I replaced the phone in its cradle, for while Knowland had not stated his business I still felt that I knew what was to come.

Only a few nights before, I had had a dream in which I had been named to serve on the Select Committee to consider the charges against Senator Joseph R. McCarthy of Wisconsin—charges that ". . . the conduct of the Senator from Wisconsin is unbecoming a member of the United States Senate, is contrary to Senatorial traditions and tends to bring the Senate into disrepute and such conduct is hereby condemned." In my dream—still worse—I had been made Chairman of the Committee. So realistic was the nightmare that I had awakened, struggling to free myself from its unpleasant implications.

Now, alone in my office and musing over the happenings which were apparently coming to a head, I tried to recall how much I actually knew of McCarthy. I had not formed a personal judgment of any consequence, principally because I was deeply involved in my own work in the Senate. I was sponsoring the highly controversial refugee bill, to redeem President Eisenhower's campaign pledge to help individuals displaced by the war in Europe. I was Chairman of the Indian Subcommittee and deeply interested in Indian legislation. At the same time, I was co-sponsor of the mammoth Upper Colorado River Storage Project —which also brought bitter opposition.

As for McCarthy's general objective, to expose communists and communist fellow-travelers in Government, I was certainly sympathetic. I had served on the Senate's Internal Security Subcommittee, under the chairmanship of Senator Pat McCarran of Nevada, from the first meeting of that Committee in 1951. McCarran kept us busy trying to stop infiltration of communists into Federal offices and positions of trust, as had Senator Bill Jenner of Indiana since he took over after the Republican election victory of 1952.

Of course, I was aware that it was not McCarthy's vigorous anti-communist activities but his behavior in the Senate that had brought about a move to censure him. As I have mentioned, Senator Flanders had initiated a censure move with the

1

introduction of Senate Resolution 301, and Senators Fulbright and Morse had offered amendments setting specific charges against Senator McCarthy. Curiously, McCarthy had welcomed the move to set up a committee, probably because another effort was on foot to secure an immediate vote for censure in the Senate, and—it was said by some—Joe McCarthy could fare far better if his case were to be heard by a small committee where the power of his personality could more easily be felt. Only a dozen Senators, all of them McCarthy opponents who favored immediate censure, voted against the referral of the Flanders resolution to a Select Committee for the holding of hearings and the making of a report.

Specifically, the action of the Senate called for the formation of a Select Committee, composed of three Republicans and three Democrats, to hold hearings and to make a report before the close of the Second Session of the 83rd Congress. The members of the Committee were to be appointed by the Vice President, upon recommendation of the Majority Leader (Senator William Knowland of California) and the Minority Leader (Senator Lyndon B. Johnson of Texas). Hearings were to begin immediately upon recess of the Senate in August of 1954.

Cloakroom gossip had it that the leaders were hoping to persuade senior Senators with a great deal of prestige to serve. Senator Knowland, it was reported, had asked veteran Senator Gene Millikin of Colorado, while Senator Johnson was urging Senator Walter George of Georgia to serve. Senator George, it was said, would serve only if Senator Millikin would accept, but Millikin declined because of ill health. It was admittedly difficult to find the right men for the assignment.

It was thought that only Senators not up for reelection that year should be considered, and because of the factfinding and judicial nature of the forthcoming hearings, that lawyers or former judges would be preferable. In addition, they should be men with whom almost any Senator could comfortably identify—Senators ordinarily busy with their committee jobs, representing their State's interest and that of their Country, eschewing publicity for its own sake and therefore not frequently in the national press. As it has since been amply developed by commentators, most of the qualifications sought for by the Senate leaders were sufficiently general for me to fit into quite readily.

Nevertheless, I walked down the corridor to Senator Knowland's office preparing my excuses. It would be nice to look back and report that "my pace quickened with confidence and purpose"—particularly in view of my prophetic dream, and the workings of destiny. My assignment may well have been inevitable, but it did not seem so to me until Senator Knowland spoke.

In an almost matter-of-fact way Knowland said: "Arthur, you have been selected as a member of the Select Committee." I observed at once that he had not asked me, but told me. Under the circumstances, it seemed cowardly to offer any excuse. After all, no one is forced to become a Senator. One must be prepared to accept the responsibilities, even if it means sitting in judgment on a fellow Senator, rare and unforeseen as such an event must certainly be.

As senior Senator among the three lawyers named to the Select Committee, and as a Republican in a Republican-controlled Senate, it appeared that I would be made Chairman. This was another post I would have preferred to dodge, but once again the assignment seemed to be inevitable, and it was.

In Knowland's office there was little to say and I soon left—committed to an ordeal.

NOT FOR A MOMENT DID I REALIZE THE MAGNITUDE OF WHAT WAS IN STORE for me as a member of the Select Committee. Apprehensive as I was about the assignment, and even more concerned that the role of Chairman might fall to me, I never suspected that this matter would upset my life for months to come and color it for my remaining years. Within 24 hours of the public announcement that I had been named to the Committee, I received the first blow from my family.

In some respects my background may have prepared me well for the things to come. My Welsh-English and Swiss ancestry and my Mormon background gave me determination, the ability to face misunderstanding without bitterness, and the strength to survive persecution. In other respects, nothing in my entire life prepared me for some things that were soon to happen.

The newspapers hit the streets that afternoon with the announcement by Richard Nixon (as President of the Senate) of the six who were to serve on the Select Committee. Fortunately, I felt, my name was not featured beyond the others. There was the expected inquiry from the press, and excitement among some of my office staff. I rode to my home in the Virginia suburbs with my head in a whirl, and there was some banter around the dinner table as to my readiness to tackle Senator McCarthy. There was not a word or thought to prepare me for the telephone call from my sister in Los Angeles.

That call came the next morning at the office, and my sister was in tears and suffering great distress.

"Arthur," she said, "you should not . . . you must not . . . serve on the Committee. You shouldn't be a party to this anti-McCarthy effort."

Then, ominously, she added: "They will ruin you. They told me to warn you. They are powerful, and you won't have a chance! They will destroy you!"

"Who are 'they'?" I asked, and persisted in asking. "Who told you to warn me? Who will destroy me?"

She would not tell me specifics. It seemed so mysterious, so weird. It was hard to believe that it was my own sister talking to me. She continued in the same vein for 20 minutes, warning me and urging me to keep out of the McCarthy censure matter.

"McCarthy has the evidence," she said. "I have seen it. He is right, and there is no stopping him!"

The mysterious organizers of the "support McCarthy" group that she was talking about—the powerful ones who would destroy me—were, it seems, local

right-wing extremists. Their exact identity I have never learned, out of deference
to my sister and her fears.

I hung up the phone with a great feeling of distress, not because of the
threat or the existence of extremists who might destroy me but because they had
reached my sister. They had not only frightened her, they were so "convincing"
that she was willing to believe them rather than trust me and my competency to
handle the situation in Washington.*

She had seen the evidence, she said. She had seen the documents! The statement called to mind an earlier experience I had with Senator McCarthy, whose
seat in the Senate was next to mine. One day upon entering the Chamber when
the Senate was in session, I had found McCarthy in his seat. He had placed
upon my chair a large traveling bag, which was open and closely packed with
large numbers of sheets of paper, standing on edge. Casually, I asked Senator
McCarthy what he was carrying around with him. He readily explained that the
briefcase contained the "ammunition" used in his anti-communist speeches around
the country.

"Depending on the size of the audience," said Joe, "I pass around these mime-
ographed sheets. My assistants take a handful each and go around the group. We
let the folks see the sheets and then gather them up and move to the next row.
We gather them up and save them for the next meeting."

This seemed a sensible arrangement, I said, but my curiosity was not yet satisfied. Asking permission to see some of the papers, which he readily gave, I
plucked out a handful and read them. They were affidavits from Government
employees (in the State Department and other agencies) stating that they had
been ordered by their superiors to burn papers which had been handed to them.
The individuals making the affidavits said they had carried out the orders. As I
recalled, none of the statements said the affiants had noted or remembered any
information from the documents.

"As evidence," I said to the Senator, "they aren't worth anything, are they?
They merely say that documents were destroyed, and that isn't uncommon in
Executive departments. How are you proving anything with these?"

Senator McCarthy had laughed at this. "Of course," he said, "this wouldn't
stand up, but the people I show these to don't know that. For them, this is
evidence . . . these are the real thing." He appeared greatly amused at my
expression of surprise.

Somewhat perplexed, I sat down. Then, turning, I was about to add that if
Government officials should be working for the enemy and wished to protect

*Later my sister had her eyes and ears opened to the truth and became one of
my strongest supporters.

themselves— in the event their loyalty was being questioned—they would hardly turn over incriminating documents and evidence to a group of subordinates to destroy. McCarthy was already pre-occupied in something else, and it didn't seem appropriate for me to chide another Senator on his procedures.

Now, thinking back on this event, I couldn't help but wonder if my sister and her friends in the anti-communism group in California had not seen these very papers.

As for possible misunderstanding of my own position, I had no real fear. Anyone who was truly interested could refer to my own anti-communist work on the McCarran Committee. In any event, I had experienced considerable prejudice and misunderstanding when I was in the mission field in the Eastern States for the Mormon Church. A faithful Mormon should scarcely shy from persecution, for there had certainly been enough of that for over one hundred years, and our people had survived.

This thought gave me pause, and I thought back over my life, as if to derive some support or remember some prior experience which would prepare me for what was to come.

I was born in December, 1886, in the little settlement of Midway, located in the Utah "Alps." My grandfather Watkins was yet living and my grandmother Gerber also. As a young boy, I heard from grandfather's lips the story of his migration from England in 1856, by way of a sailing vessel to America and then by handcart from Iowa City, Iowa, to Salt Lake City.

Grandfather John Watkins, of Welsh and English descent, had been a contractor, architect, and builder in London. There he heard the Mormon missionaries, and becoming converted, moved to America. With his wife and two small children he joined the Martin Handcart Company of pioneers to walk 1,200 miles across the plains to the new settlement in Utah. The party left rather late in the year and got caught in Wyoming in early winter. Many of the members lost their lives and the remainder were rescued by a party sent out from Salt Lake City with clothing and food. Grandfather and family finally settled in the village of Midway, in the central part of the state.

The Gerbers brought similar strength and determination to my mother's line. My mother's father, Dr. John Gerber, ordained minister of the Lutheran faith and a doctor of medicine, was a Swiss from Bern. With his first wife (who was soon to die in childbirth) he went to Africa as a missionary, a kind of pioneer Albert Schweitzer. He obtained a new bride from England, but she too soon died in childbirth. Finally, after ten years in Africa, his church sent him to America and he preached and worked in Ohio. There his third wife died. Securing an immigrant Swiss girl to care for his surviving children, he soon married her. She was much younger and became his nurse in his practice. Anna Maria Ackeret was her name, and she was my grandmother.

They moved to St. Louis, Missouri, where grandfather was a highly esteemed physician and minister. They met the Mormon missionaries, however, and were converted to Mormonism. Grandfather's friends and patients immediately turned against him, refusing to pay their bills and even burning the fine Gerber home. Outcasts, they trekked to Utah. Dr. Gerber's aged father, who had been living with the family, had also joined the church and longed to see Zion. The old gentleman died within hours after the family arrived in Salt Lake City in 1854.

Needless to say, having reached Utah, neither the Watkins or Gerber families escaped further trials. As pioneer families, they suffered the usual privations of hunger, storm, and constant work. Sometimes huddled in their cabins, drenched with driving rains through every crack, and sometimes facing icy winds and wading miles through snow to help stricken friends, they survived every hardship. Knowing hard work and enjoying few material gifts, they were nevertheless blessed with many children and wonderful community fellowship. I marvel as I read their stories, and particularly note the large number of those first generation children who became very substantial citizens.

Yes, I concluded, my heritage was good. My grandparents and parents had set remarkable examples of determination and loyalty to principle. Their ability to withstand stress, trial, and deprivation had made a profound impression on me.

I must admit that in my earlier years none of this seemed so remarkable. I accepted the characteristics of my progenitors and the stories of their trials as commonplace things. Indeed, they were common to most of my friends and relatives. As time passed and my acquaintances became more diverse, I gave more thought to my particular inheritance. Whether or not my origins determined in any way my conduct in the Senate and in the McCarthy censure hearings I cannot say, but it is a background developed by most reporters who have written about me.

Reflecting further, I recalled how when I was ten my family moved to Vernal, a little-settled area in northeastern Utah. We had a small farm where my brother Frank and I worked alongside our father. We had time to work for others, too. From this latter employment, Father earned $1.50 a day and my brother and I received 75 cents a day. We had a local church school, which gave us two years of high school, after which I went to Brigham Young University in Provo.

My college training was interrupted by a call from the Presidency of the Mormon Church to accept a two-year mission in the Eastern States. In keeping with usual practice, my family and I met all the cost of this missionary effort. I ran into a good deal of prejudice and misunderstanding, eye-opening for a country boy.

Finishing my mission, I enrolled at New York University Law School. The summer following my first year I took a course at Columbia University, where I did well. Dean Gifford of Fordham University was my summer instructor and he suggested that I apply for admission to Columbia, promising a letter of introduction to Dean Stone. With this encouragement and considerable application on my part, I entered Columbia and graduated two years later.

I began the practice of law at Vernal, and about a year later married Andrea Rich (daughter of Ben E. Rich, who had been President of the Eastern States Mission of the Church). After two years, we moved to Salt Lake City, where I wanted to practice law. There I served as assistant county attorney for two years and then continued in general practice. I became seriously ill with a duodenal ulcer and barely survived a massive hemorrhage. This necessitated time out from the high-pressure life of law, and I took over the management of a 600-acre irrigated ranch near Lehi, Utah. Recovering my health, I moved to Orem. I also started a weekly, the *Voice of Sharon* (later I named it the *Orem-Geneva Times*) and enjoyed being its editor. In the meantime I was back in law and also elected judge of the Fourth District Court, in which office I served four years. I was defeated for a second term in the Franklin Roosevelt landslide of 1932.

This was a critical time—not just for me, out of a job, but for the Nation— as the Great Depression of the 1930's reached its most dismal low. Attempting to return to the private practice of law and with my farm to support me, I threw myself into a public-service activity which was to have tremendous implications for the people of Utah and which would ultimately pave the way to the Senate for me (although, at that time, I did not aspire to the office). This "new" career" on which I launched myself was water resource development and it began in 1933, immediately after my defeat as district judge.

Westerners know the value of water to an area's economy, and the Mormon pioneers had been famous for their diversion of streams for irrigation. Indeed, many of the substantial families of Utah had founded their modest fortunes on the beneficial use of such water. But since many old-timers thus had all the water they needed, except in times of drouth, there was no particular effort to build storage facilities which would hold spare water and utilize it for growth and expansion of the economy.

The truth is that many were content to see the area stand still, thereby avoiding many of the problems of expansion. Some stalwarts in the Church, as well as our conservative political leaders, were agreed that these major construction programs would "saddle the people with debt" which would take generations to get out from under. Thus, mine was initially a selling job.

Secondly, we had to be assured of certain financial mechanisms for such water development, for Federal reclamation projects call for repayment of construction costs by the water users and other beneficiaries. To enter into valid repayment contracts, we had to deal with legal entities such as municipalities and water districts. Sometimes their charters had to be tested in the courts to see if they were legally competent to make contracts. This all meant a great deal of work, forthright and sincere educational efforts, and much dedication to purpose.

Looking back on the success of the Provo River Project* and what the availability of water has meant to the state in increased population, jobs (such as bringing in the Geneva Steel Plant), income, and tax revenues, I have found much satisfaction. The work not only was preparation for a successful election campaign to the Senate, it also served me well within that body and helped earn me the friendship and respect of President Eisenhower.

Also, it was during this period that I was appointed President of the Sharon Stake of the Mormon Church, a position of considerable importance and responsibility, all the more so because of the Great Depression. The area of the Sharon Stake was mostly small fruit farms together with some dairy farms. In the early days of the Depression, there were no government units at the local level in Utah qualified to distribute state or Federal assistance, so the Mormon Church, and its subdivisions called Stakes (made up of smaller units or congregations, called Wards), took on this chore until the proper governmental units were organized to take on the task.

There was considerable labor turmoil among coal miners, whose work was necessary to fuel the steel mill and other industries and homes. Strikes were frequent and brought distress to the Utah County area. I became irked with New Deal policies and thought about running for the Senate. The idea of winning seemed utterly impossible, for the Democrats had been in power in Utah for a long time; the New Deal was in full flower.

Campaigning almost on my own resources alone, I won two primaries and the general election of 1946. I had little money and virtually no organization in this election, and though county committees were very active, the Republican State Committee was moribund. So I went to Washington as a Senator indebted to no contributors, entirely a free agent. I recall meeting former President Herbert Hoover, who still enjoyed Washington social and political life, at a Washington, D.C. party function. He said to me: "My, I am glad to see you! You are a gift of God. Nobody ever expected you."

My constituents had contributed less than $300 to my campaign, and the

---

*The project was constructed under the Federal Reclamation Act of 1902, enacted during President Theodore Roosevelt's administration. This act provided Federal help in Western arid areas where landowners did not have the resources to build costly water storage projects which were necessary before the lands could be brought under cultivation. Towns and cities where the landowners could live had to be established as an essential part of the projects.

My work was the organization of Water Users Associations and Metropolitan Water Districts which could contract with the Federal Government for the construction of the projects and repayment of the costs of construction. Also the people of the area had to be convinced that the project was feasible and necessary to the growth of their several communities. From January, 1933, until I was elected to Congress in 1946, my services on this project were continuous.

state committee nothing. I did get a contribution through former Senator John Townsend of Delaware, Chairman of the Republican National Senatorial Campaign Committee, who advised me that the Committee had decided not to send me any money, but he would get some of his friends to help. Many years later I learned that the committee had not provided me any money—although I had sent the message that I thought I could win with a little help—because local party leaders had told the Committee that I didn't stand a chance to win and the money would be wasted. Altogether, from all sources, I had about $8,000 to carry me through two primaries and an election.

Having been an "old man" since my mid-thirties (as I used to say, because I had acquired a shock of white hair) and with conservative Republican principles and traditional Mormon ideas about hard work and integrity, I was considered serious and not at all a headline getter. I pursued my assignments in the Senate without fanfare, and liked to consider myself something of an authority on Indian matters and reclamation. I have considerable satisfaction in having been able to get the abandoned Bushnell Military Hospital at Brigham City, Utah, turned into a highly successful school for Navajo Indian children.

Soon after Dwight D. Eisenhower was nominated for his first term and before the presidential campaign really got underway, I was invited by the then General Eisenhower to a conference with him at his Denver headquarters. At a meeting which followed I pointed out to him that one of the most important programs for the four upper basin states (Colorado, New Mexico, Wyoming, and Utah) would be a vast reclamation project which would enable these states to put to use their respective shares of the Colorado River.*

I reminded the General that the Federal Reclamation program had its beginning during the administration of President Theodore Roosevelt. He immediately made it clear that he knew the necessity for such programs and that he would never rest until—so far as it could be done by one administration—all the unused waters in the arid states had been put to work.

During the first year of Eisenhower's administration, I sponsored the Refugee

---

*The Colorado River is both an interstate and an international stream. Ninety percent of its waters rise in the states of Colorado, Wyoming, Utah, and New Mexico and flow southwest through parts of Arizona and Nevada, thence along the state line between Arizona and California to the Mexican border and on to the Gulf of California.

The four states first named comprise the Upper Basin. The other states make up the Lower Basin. In 1922 a compact was entered into between the two groups and the Federal Government for the division of this water resource between the two Basins and also between them as a unit and with Mexico. The competition between these three entities was keen until agreements dividing the waters of the river had been adopted. In spite of the Colorado River Compact, some powerful interests in Southern California vigorously opposed the Upper Colorado River Storage Project.

Act of 1953 for the President. Among other things this act passed after a bitter fight, made provision for the immigration of 214,000 homeless war refugees to the United States.

Rather servere restrictions were set for the eligibility of refugees. This displeased most of the nations with eligible refugees. I was urged to visit these countries to "sell" the Act to them.

Mid-East nations had refugee problems. Up to 2,000 Palestinian Arab refugees, living along the borders of Israel, were eligible for visas to the U.S. They refused the opportunity to come to this country, but we were contributing most of the cost of keeping them alive. It seemed to me that since they would not come to the U.S. they would be a perpetual burden to us.

As one who had specialized in reclamation projects before coming to Washington, I took a good look at the possibilities for reclamation in the Mid-East, as a very practical way of solving the refugee problem and hopefully of helping to bring peace to that troubled area. I reported my trip to the President in late December, 1953, and it was during a discussion of that report that the Upper Colorado River Storage Project was used as an illustration of what could be done in the Mid-East.

The same day I was reporting to the President, he was scheduled to leave for Bermuda for a meeting with Churchill and Joseph Laniel, the French Premier. So we did not finish the discussion, but a date was set early in March to further consider the proposed reclamation programs. In March, 1954, the discussions were resumed. Then on March 20, 1954, the President shocked the opponents of the Colorado River Storage Project by issuing a press release announcing that he had approved recommendations for the development "of the Upper Colorado Basin including the controversial Echo Park Dam."

On that date and for at least three months thereafter, there was not the slightest prospect that a censure proceeding against Senator McCarthy would be under way in August of that same year, or at any other time for that matter.

Ordinarily, it would not seem necessary to recall my relationship with the President or rehearse what occurred at the meeting with him in Denver before the election and after my trip to the Mid-East.

But I have in mind the eventual charges from some McCarthy supporters that I had made a "deal" with the President . . . a deal whereby the President would promise me his full support on the Upper Colorado River Storage Project if I would go along with the "get McCarthy" conspiracy . . . and also the Robert Welch (founder of the John Birch Society) tirade against President Eisenhower, charging him in effect with betraying his country.

And I cannot forget the incredibly heavy flood of mail which I ultimately received during the McCarthy censure hearings. Tens of thousands of letters, some apparently from substantial professional and business people, revealed an amazing willingness to believe the wildest and most fanciful accusations against me and the President.

I can report as authoritatively as anyone that President Eisenhower, as many then and since have commented, did indeed remain aloof from the McCarthy fracas. He did not discuss the matter with me, encourage me, or in any way indicate his ideas or preferences, before or during the censure proceedings. Only when the Senate vote had been registered did he invite me to the White House and thank me for conducting a fair and dignified hearing.

This comment must be particularly significant in view of current implications by Senator Joseph McCarthy's former assistant, Roy Cohn, to the effect that the entire McCarthy censure proceedings were the product of an Eisenhower plan and conspiracy. This is simply not true.

IMMEDIATELY FOLLOWING THE FRENCH REVOLUTION WITH ITS EXCESSES, there was fear in the newly united American states that the common people of this country might entertain ideas similar to those of the French Communes. It seemed reasonable enough to some few privileged Americans that the people—heady with the wine of their own revolution—might demand more "liberty, equality and fraternity." All this, of course, would be at the expense of the landed gentry, the rich merchants, and the established authorities.

The fear was really groundless, for in America the frontier offered sufficient opportunities for those harrassed by debt and boredom to change their way of life without a Reign of Terror. But reason has little force or weight with the fearful, as has been amply demonstrated before in history, and some politicians injected the frightful spectacle of French mob rule into their own efforts to perpetuate their terms of office.

This first American venture in fear-mongering has sometimes been cited as the precedent for other arousals of excitement between the haves and have-nots, the Godfearing and the Godless, those who are "right" and those who are benighted. Speculation on this score can't help but be interesting.

With the opening of the Twentieth Century, however, there was to be a new economic interpretation of history by Karl Marx and Nikolai Lenin. As their turn came upon the world stage and communism in its modern context was born as a word of hope or fear—depending on those who judged it—a new uneasiness spread across our Nation. Then came the excesses of Bolshevism in Russia, and once again there was the reaction of the fearful, in the arrests and deportations which came with the Mitchell Palmer period of the early 1920's.*

The specter of communism, rising as it did in the bloody aftermath of the establishment of the Soviet State in Russia and Asia, was not to lose its fearful aspect. Although there were apologists for Soviet extremism and the communist ideology in the 1930's—and many of these were to be found in the Executive Departments of the United States Government—it was not until the U.S. and the U.S.S.R. coincidentally found themselves fighting against Nazi Germany that the image of the Red menace began to fade for many.

Then, in the years following World War II, the expansion of Soviet influence in the war-devastated states of Europe and Asia was seen as Soviet imperialism

* It was under Mitchell Palmer, Attorney General in the administration of Woodrow Wilson, that aliens suspected of sympathy with the new and frightening Bolshevik revolution in Russia were rounded up and deported.

and recognized as a physical threat to the security of the United States and the whole allied world.

Some analysts stop here and are content. Others say that internal political stresses of the mid-century in the United States were not eased by the normal cycle of change of political parties, and that when Franklin D. Roosevelt successfully sought a third term and still a fourth term there was no natural release for the tensions of the party out of power. Searching for issues to sway the voters, the Republicans are said to have exploited "The Communist Threat to the American Way of Life."

There are, of course, other speculations about the heightened concern in America during these years. Regardless of this, the discussion at hand is about that concern as it was manifested in the McCarthy era, as the early 1950's have been called.

Part of this story must be the documentation of my own efforts as a Senator to expose communists in American society, if my role as Chairman of the Select Committee is to be seen as an objective one. I see myself in this objective role and believe that my efforts in this writing can have real value when seen in this perspective.

Scholars today are wont to credit the so-called McCarran Committee—the Internal Security Subcommittee of the Senate's Judiciary Committee—as the principal investigatory committee of the Senate and probably of the whole Congress, in laying bare the communist conspiracy, and this with a minimum of pain and embarrassment to innocent victims and bystanders (although there was, admittedly, some anguish among those whose careless actions and muddy thinking were so resolutely probed).

The Senate Internal Security Subcommittee, with Senator Pat McCarran of Nevada as its Chairman, came into being in December, 1950. From the first meeting of the McCarran Committee, as it was soon called, I took an active part and participated in or conducted a number of hearings involving subversive or communist influence in educational institutions, labor unions, and Government agencies.

Pat McCarran and I became friends. We were in opposite parties, of course, but in many ways alike. He was a devout Catholic and I am, I hope, a conscientious Mormon. From our respective religious faiths, we shared a deep distrust of communism and were both dedicated to the exposure of communists in places of influence and their removal from places of trust. McCarran and I had also been judges—he was formerly a judge of the Nevada State Supreme Court, and I of the 4th District Court in Utah. We agreed that investigations should be conducted fairly, guided by the evidence and the dictates of judicial practice.

In company with other Senators, I participated in hearings inquiring into communist influence in labor unions. In association with Pat McCarran, we held hearings in Salt Lake City on the International Mine, Mill, and Smelters Workers Union. There seemed to be infiltration by communists into the copper mining industry through that union.

I held hearings alone in Cleveland, Ohio, on alleged infiltration by communists in labor unions, and on their activities within the unions. On one occasion, I held hearings alone in New York City, to take the testimony of a witness just arriving from the Orient. I did this on a Sunday, and I was ill at the time. As a result of this concern for duty, beyond what the Committee Chairman expected of me, I was rewarded with a thank-you letter from Senator McCarran. Subsequently, this letter got into the closing days of the debate on the McCarthy censure—as evidence of my own study, investigation, and knowledge of communism and my active participation in efforts to end its inroads in our society.

The letter reads as follows:

June 23, 1952

Honorable Arthur V. Watkins
United States Senate
Washington, D.C.

My dear Senator:

Your willingness to upset your own schedule, on a Sunday, and to disregard your own personal convenience, in order to make a hasty flight to New York to facilitate the business of the Internal Security Subcommittee seems to me worthy of special commendation, and I want to thank you on behalf of the subcommittee. You have been most assiduous throughout the session in aiding the work of the Internal Security Subcommittee, so that your action in accepting a special and unusual burden on Sunday was completely in character; yet I think it does deserve special mention.

Without such assistance as you have given, from yourself and from other members of the subcommittee, it would have been impossible to have carried on the work as it has been carried on.

I have been informed that after you had agreed to go to New York on Sunday on the subcommittee's business, you became indisposed; notwithstanding which, you sought no change in the schedule and made no effort to get out from under the responsibility you had accepted. This also was in keeping with your character as I have come to know it.

Thanks, again, both for the Internal Security Subcommittee and for myself as Chairman; and kindest personal regards.

Sincerely,
s/d
PAT McCARRAN
Chairman

The Senate Internal Security Subcommittee, among other investigations of note, inquired into the Institute of Pacific Relations. The IPR, as it was abbreviated, was a world-wide organization of travelers and scholars who hoped to promote international understanding. They were particularly concerned with the lessening of tensions between the United States and China.

One of the Far Eastern experts, Owen Lattimore, called the "top Russian espionage agent" by McCarthy, was thoroughly investigated by the McCarran Committee.* The Committee inquired into the charge that Lattimore, along with others of the IPR, had been a useful instrument of the communist party in promoting communist objectives and influencing the State Department. Lattimore, of course, was not a regular employee of the State Department, but he was— as he said—an "advisor" to important officials in the State Department, and performed certain missions for that agency.

Senator McCarthy entered the anti-communist arena in January, 1950, we have been told, after lunching with Father Edmund Walsh of Georgetown University and accepting the latter's suggestion that he take up anti-communism as a political technique.

McCarthy apparently needed little urging, and in a series of speeches starting on Lincoln Day in West Virginia, he began the sensational charges which appeared on the front pages of most of the newspapers in the country.

The charges were directed primarily at the State Department, and McCarthy promised to reveal the names of 205, 81, or 57 (he was never consistent in his account) of card-carrying Communists in the Department. He dramatized the charges with such statements as "I hold in my hand. . . ."

Goaded by the charges, and convinced that they would be disproved, the Democratic leadership of the Senate ordered an investigation, and assigned the task to a subcommittee of the Senate Foreign Relations Committee headed by the late Senator Millard Tydings of Maryland.

Called by the Tydings Committee,** and pressed to reveal his names, McCarthy appeared reluctant to be specific. Finally, McCarthy selected the name of Owen Lattimore as one of half a dozen employees of the State Department supposedly involved in communism and called him "an extremely bad security risk." A little later McCarthy changed this to "the top Russian espionage agent" in the U.S., and finally he modified this charge to say that Lattimore was a "policy risk" and the "architect" of the State Department's Far Eastern policy.

McCarthy selected his charge against Lattimore as the one he was "willing to

*Lattimore was a witness before the Internal Security Subcommittee when it investigated the Institute of Pacific Relations during 1951 and 1952. Lattimore was investigated during that time. Senator McCarthy had criticized him just prior to these investigations.

**A subcommittee of the Senate Committee on Foreign Relations, investigating communist efforts to subvert employees in the State Department.

stand or fall on" in his testimony and added, ". . . the Subcommittee would be justified in not taking my other cases too seriously" should this charge fail to have substance.

Although the Tydings Committee cleared Lattimore of the espionage charges in its final report, the Senate Internal Security Subcommittee pursued the matter further. The final judgment of the McCarran Committee was that Lattimore was an able spokesman for conciliation with the Chinese Reds, and even "a conscious articulate instrument of the Soviet conspiracy," but we could not prove that he had participated in any kind of espionage activity. Lattimore, it must now be concluded, had exercised his rights as a private citizen to express his opinion and to campaign for acceptance of his own ideas, right or wrong, as his ideas may be determined by history (and we thought them wrong). He may well have had some influence on the thinking of some friends in the State Department, but this scarcely makes him an "architect" of our foreign policy.

As mentioned, I was a diligent anti-communist, but not one to seek newspaper publicity. Perhaps I was naive to believe that doing my job on the McCarran Committee was all that was necessary to establish my credentials, but I was more than a little surprised to find during the McCarthy censure proceedings that Joe McCarthy could call me a "dupe" of the communists.

Prior to McCarthy's "discovery" of communism, he had been regarded in his own state and in the Senate as a rather ordinary politician, with very little to say about communism. Indeed, it has been suggested* that he won his party's nomination to the Senate in 1946 (when he ran against the vigorous and careful anti-communist, Senator Robert LaFollette, Jr.), with the tacit support of allegedly communist-dominated labor unions in Wisconsin. Some preferred the amiable, earthy Joe McCarthy (who said: "Communists have the same right to vote as anyone else, don't they?") to the effective LaFollette. McCarthy may well have won the election without communist help, but two facts remain: he won by a small margin, and the numerous union members in Milwaukee and other industrial centers were violently anti-LaFollette. (In Wisconsin's "cross-over" primary, even Democrats could vote in the Republican primary to eliminate an enemy).

In the Senate, McCarthy first occupied himself with the interests of soft drink and home construction companies, and other small matters. He didn't make a big splash in the newspapers until he espoused the cause of the German war criminals sentenced to death for shooting American prisoners of war and Belgian civilians in the Malmedy Massacre.** This apparent catering to German-American con-

*Jack Anderson and Ronald W. May, *McCarthy: The Man, The Senator, The Ism* (Boston, Beacon Press, 1952).

**The Allies under General Eisenhower as Chief Commander were driving the German forces out of France as World War II neared its end and were approaching the German border. The German forces made a major counterattack and succeeded

stituents, with relatives in Germany, is of special interest because of his alleged use of material provided him by Rudolf Aschenauer, later to be identified as a communist agitator and organizer in Germany.

Of greater significance to the account of McCarthy's censure by the Senate—for activities unbecoming a Senator and for abuse of his fellow Senators—is the way Joe McCarthy acted in the Senate investigation of alleged torture in this trial of the German war criminals. McCarthy, who was not even on the Subcommittee of the Senate Armed Services Committee which inquired into the matter, nevertheless claimed a seat as an observer and from that vantage point dominated the hearings and roundly denounced its chairman, Senator Raymond Baldwin of Connecticut.

In April, 1949, a three-man Subcommittee was named to secure the facts in the case of the Malmedy killers. The Germans—members of the notorious "Blowtorch Battalion" of the First SS Panzer Regiment—had appealed their death sentences on the grounds that they had been tortured into making confessions. The German press, including communist publications, made a great issue of this charge. Senators Baldwin, Estes Kefauver of Tennessee, and Lester Hunt of Wyoming were given the job of investigating the charge.

Sitting in on the Subcommittee, McCarthy challenged a survivor of the Malmedy shooting, and the American officers and judges in charge of the prosecution

in forcing the Americans to retreat. This attack came to be known as the "Battle of the Bulge."

The Germans captured several hundred American troops in this battle, and retired with their prisoners under Allied pressure to a point near the Belgian village of Malmedy. The Germans were found guilty by a United States Army Court of killing some of these prisoners during December 1944 and January 1945. The culprits were sentenced to be executed. Appeals were taken to the War Crimes Commission which was created to try German war criminals. This matter swung back and forth as various legal moves, including an appeal to the Supreme Court of the United States, were made in behalf of the convicted Germans. The net result was that the number of Germans originally found guilty was greatly reduced, and the sentence were commuted to reduced terms of imprisonment.

Public indignation caused the Senate Committee on Armed Services to authorize a subcommittee, chaired by Senator Raymond E. Baldwin, of Connecticut, to hold hearings and investigate the Malmedy Massacre and all matters connected with it. The investigation and committee hearings took place during the months of April, May, and June of 1949. Over a thousand pages of testimony and reports were accumulated by the subcommittee.

The entire matter was so complicated that a short general statement in a note is extremely difficult to achieve. It is suggested that those interested should read the hearings record and Committee reports. See S. Res. 42, *Investigation of Actions of Army with Respect to Trial of Persons Responsible for the Massacre of American Soldiers, Battle of the Bulge, near Malmedy, Belgium, December 1944.*

of the Germans, and accused them of lying. Very shortly, he charged the Sub-committee with the "deliberate and clever attempt to whitewash the American military," and finally he denounced Chairman Baldwin as "criminally respon-sible." I remember rising on the floor of the Senate when this matter was being discussed to caution Senator McCarthy and Senator Baldwin to be careful in their statements and to avoid misstatements of fact. I urged them to refer to the record with respect to questions which the two were disputing.

Faced with what he considered to be McCarthy's overbearing and offensive tactics, the gentlemanly Senator Baldwin was thoroughly convinced that politics was not for him and he retired from the Senate in midterm. Many a Senator shook his head sadly at the spectacle.

It was when McCarthy appeared before the Tydings Subcommittee inquiring into communist subversion in the State Department, that the junior Senator from Wisconsin had his first real bloody fight with a fellow Senator. In January and February, 1950, McCarthy began his now famous numbers game involving how many communists there might be in the Department of State. In March of that same year, Senator Millard Tydings, Democrat from Maryland, began hearings on the relevance of these charges. McCarthy was Tydings' first witness.

The Democratic Administration was sensitive to McCarthy's charges and counted on Tydings to show him up. The hearings were acrimonious, and Tydings attempted to limit McCarthy's telling of his story on communist sub-version by throwing procedural blocks in his way. A very bitter spirit was demon-strated by the two, and it was fixed into apparent hatred on Joe's part when the Tydings Committee finally issued its report in mid-summer, calling Mc-Carthy's charges a "fraud and a hoax" and making bold allegations on McCarthy's truthfulness.

Presumably, this accounted for McCarthy sending his aides into the Maryland election race to campaign for Joe's new friend, John Butler, who was running against Tydings. It was in Maryland, it may be recalled, that McCarthy's aides and friends came up with the tabloid featuring a composite photo of Tydings and communist leader Earl Browder.

Whether Senator McCarthy may logically be given major credit for defeat-ing Tydings, he claimed it. The implication of this campaign was plain to some Senators—"cross McCarthy and be destroyed." In his jokes in the Senate Cloak-room and his remarks to the press, McCarthy was willing to leave the impression that bucking him in his anti-communism drive was an unhealthy thing to try. Mail from constitutents back home, whipped up by some elements in the press, tended to support this idea.

Senator McCarthy had other scrapes with his fellow Senators both on and off the floor of the Senate. In October, 1951, during his hotly-waged battle before a subcommittee of the Senate Foreign Affairs Committee to prevent Senate confirmation of Phillip Jessup to a new term as a U.S. delegate to the United Nations, witness Joe McCarthy locked horns with Senator J. William Fulbright of Arkansas. The latter had questioned McCarthy's "flimsy" charges. McCarthy angrily reminded Fulbright and his colleagues on the committee of other Senators who had opposed him (Baldwin and Tydings) and who were no longer in the Senate. The session went on with McCarthy making an oblique reference to Jessup as a "slimy creature" and then, upon McCarthy leaving the stand, Fulbright said: "I want to say for the record, in all my experiences in the Senate, never have I seen a more arrogant or rude witness . . . ."

As pro-American and highly regarded as Jessup was—and in spite of his good references, including one from General Dwight D. Eisenhower—the subcommittee voted three to two to report unfavorably on the nomination. This was another victory for McCarthy, resulting from great publicity given his charges and the timorous reaction of some Senators (but not Senator Fulbright) to the flood of mail from McCarthy fans.

A little earlier, in August, 1951, another free-for-all had begun in the Senate which was ultimately to figure large in Senator Flander's resolution to censure McCarthy and the hearings thereon before the Select Committee. This was the move by Senator William Benton—freshman Senator from Connecticut and a liberal Democrat—to have McCarthy expelled from the Senate for his role in the Tydings-Butler election campaign in Maryland. This was, of course, a partisan move, but it was soon to have bipartisan support. McCarthy's response was to pass off as if insignificant "the tripe put out by Connecticut's odd little mental midget."

Benton's resolution, referred to Senator Guy Gillette's Subcommittee on Privileges and Elections, was followed by months of acrimony. One of the questions arising was the propriety of the Subcommittee making an investigation of McCarthy's activities, and Chairman Gillette (who had not been too eager to have the hot potato dumped in his lap, but was manfully seeing the matter through) was sustained by a Senate vote of 60 to 0 in his handling of the investigation.

Charges other than McCarthy's unorthodox interference in Tydings' election campaign had also arisen. Most significant among these were questions as to Joe McCarthy's integrity and fitness to sit in the Senate because of alleged conflict of interest. Inquiries into sources of McCarthy's income were made, and particular attention was paid to a $10,000 fee which the Senator had received from the Lustron Corporation.

Joe McCarthy refused to appear before the Gillette Subcommittee, however, and it was this attitude of brushing aside the "invitation" to appear before the Subcommittee and his disrespectful attitude toward "proper Senate business" which became a principal point of issue in the ultimate censure move.

The months rolled on and no action was taken against Senator McCarthy for what many were now calling his contempt for the Senate and its procedures, and of contempt for an increasing number of Senators. McCarthy, himself, seemed to feel immune not only to criticism but to restraint. He believed and stated that anyone who criticized his methods was automatically against his objectives, and that anyone who opposed his brand of anti-communism was for communism.

Finally, McCarthy reached the zenith of his publicity and his anti-communism hunt—as well as opposition for his roughshod methods—in what was soon to be known as the Army-McCarthy hearings.

As will be recalled, Senator McCarthy used as the instrument of these investigations into alleged communist infiltration into the Army (and Army installations) his Senate Permanent Subcommittee on Investigations. This was a Subcommittee of the Committee on Government Operations.* The use of the Subcommittee for this purpose—as well as his earlier inquiry into subversion in the Voice of America and other overseas agencies—was something of a surprise. After all, the Senate had always construed the purposes of the Government Operations Committee as one of overseeing the fiscal and administrative efficiency of Federal agencies.

During the latter part of 1953 and in early 1954, McCarthy probed the Army for any signs of communism or weakness in the area of security. For its part, the Army initially showed few signs of worry. The capacity of this farflung and giant organization to absorb or thwart, and therefore to survive, investigative excursions of this type had long been demonstrated. Robert Stevens, Secretary of the Army, made every effort, however, to placate and appease McCarthy in the latter's probings (without, however, turning the military organization and its files completely over to the Senator). It has often been said that Joe bore a grudge against the Army, but in any event McCarthy became more and more frustrated over his inability to come up with anything of substance to prove his increasingly broad charges of subversion.

One promising lead was the discovery of an obscure Army dentist, Captain Irving Peress (soon to be promoted to Major) who was said to be a communist. After thus being identified by McCarthy and called to appear at a hearing, Peress declined to testify under the protection offered by the Fifth Amendment. The inexplicable then happened. Major Peress received an honorable discharge from the Army. The affront to Senator McCarthy, as he saw it—the promotion and then discharge of Peress under honorable conditions, in seeming reward for the latter's arrogance in taking the Fifth Amendment—became the issue of the hearings. This, too, is a story told in this book.

The story of the well-publicized Army-McCarthy hearings, under the hot lights of TV, scarcely needs to be retold here. Most of the hearings were taken up

---

*McCarthy had become Chairman of the Committee and its Investigations Subcommittee after the Republicans won control of the Senate in the 1952 elections.

by the Army and its counsel exchanging recriminations with McCarthy and his aides. In the process, however, Senator McCarthy settled upon General Ralph Zwicker as his scapegoat.

Curiously, and ironically, as it turned out, Zwicker had originally put McCarthy staffers onto the trail of Peress and had supplied such information as McCarthy was to obtain on the dentist. Then, Captain Peress's name came up routinely on a roster for promotion and passed without question as to his alleged communist leanings (the incriminating dossier became "separated" from Peress's military record). Finally, after his name had come to public attention, Peress was discharged to get rid of him, but in the absence of proof as to any wrong doing, and conviction therefor, Peress was given an honorable discharge.

Zwicker couldn't or wouldn't pin-point any official responsible for this chain of circumstances (and, in any event, refused to admit that someone might have acted improperly). On the basis of this, Senator McCarthy charged General Zwicker with evading the truth and then said, in effect, that he was not fit to wear the uniform.

There was a feeling among many members of the Senate that McCarthy had abused General Zwicker and others, and this became one of the points in the censure charges.

In this brief sketch, I have attempted to provide some historical perspective for the main body of my discussion on the charges of contempt and the hearings which were to result in the censure of Senator McCarthy. There might well have been considerable elaboration here, but I have purposefully left these details for other writers.

DURING THE MONTHS OF THE ARMY-MC CARTHY HEARINGS, I WAS DEEPLY involved in my various Senate assignments, and like a majority of my Senate colleagues, did not preoccupy myself with the doings of the junior Senator from Wisconsin.

Of course, I had seen the smoke and confusion of the Army-McCarthy hearings and knew that McCarthy and representatives of the Army had many bitter exchanges. That the hearings had come to an end in mid-June without any substantive findings was no surprise, and I shared the confusion of many of my colleagues as to what should be done (if anything at all) about Joe McCarthy's unorthodox investigative techniques.

While I was not particularly concerned with Joe's "McCarthyism," there were a number of Senators who had been offended aesthetically, professionally, and personally by the Wisconsin Senator's roughshod methods and sometimes abrasive personality. The Republicans among this group were also concerned with the effect that McCarthy was having on party image and effectiveness.

The Republican Policy Committee voted to study rules for the conduct of investigations, but the rank and file did not support this recommendation as it would limit the role of the chairman.

It was at this time that I heard direct from a member of the Republican Policy Committee an interesting sidelight on this Committee's concern for McCarthy's methods. The Committee's Chairman and one other member called in Senator McCarthy to counsel with him on his methods used in his fight against communism. They were apparently of the opinion that Joe would inspire more confidence in his activities if he were more conservative in his public statements.

Senator McCarthy's reply was characteristic: "When you fellows, or anyone else, find a communist the press gives the story about an inch of space with a headline to match. On the other hand, when I give out a statement I announce that I have the proof which shows that I have discovered hundreds of communists in some government agency, then the press puts my statement on page one with banner headlines. The magazines, radio, and television give me the same kind of coverage." Whereupon, after giving this rationale for his methods, Joe walked out of the meeting and promptly made good on his statement by securing more front page headlines.

Some Republicans on Joe's Subcommittee had fallen in the habit of absenting themselves from hearings so as not to be identified with him. McCarthy frequently found himself the sole signer of Subcommittee reports. With this, the White House was reported to have urged Senate leadership to get Republicans to attend hearings in order to tone down the ebullient McCarthy and otherwise have a restraining effect. There was some effort on the part of Subcommittee members to have the Chairmanship taken from McCarthy. This half-hearted effort, however, gave way to the indignation of Senator Ralph Flanders of Vermont.

As Flanders introduced his initial resolution, which merely called for stripping the Chairmanship from McCarthy, the latter sought to divert publicity by announcing that his Subcommittee was moving to Boston to hold hearings into communist infiltration of defense plants there. Senate leaders, however, persuaded the Senator to hold his hearings in Washington. Then, on Friday, July 16, Flanders announced that he was substituting a new resolution which called for the censure of McCarthy. Flanders—because of his great courage, his age, his independent financial position, and the solid support within his own state—could well afford to tangle with McCarthy without fear of reprisals.

Describing his resolution to newsmen, Flanders said: "By every standard this new resolution is in keeping with the procedures by which the Senate historically has disciplined one of its members when he has violated basic codes of ethics." He added that he believed that because of McCarthyism, the Republican Party was facing a crisis in unity and leadership.

The charges which Flanders made against Senator McCarthy were essentially that the Senator had contempt for the Senate and for his fellow Senators, contempt for the truth, and habitual contempt for people. Speaking to this last item, Flanders said: "The astonishing thing is that the Senator does not know that he is insulting . . . which makes plain the impossibility of controlling exhibitions of innate character by any change in the rules. The Senator can break rules faster than we can make them."

He went on to say: "When it comes to ridding the country of communism, the really serious and effective work has been done by others without the blowing of trumpets or the beating of drums." This remark stemmed from Joe's countercharge that his fellow Senators were only sore because he was getting all the publicity and, furthermore, they weren't keen on fighting communism.

With respect to the debate on the Flanders resolution, the Washington *Post* said editorially: "The question is not whether the Senate approves the fight against communism but whether it wants an effective fight or the kind of whirling dervish diversion from the real issues that Senator McCarthy conducts."*

By the end of July, with debate welling up on the floor of the Senate over the Flanders resolution, it appeared at first that the Senator from Vermont would get nowhere. *The New York Times,* on August 1, reported that ". . . Republicans presented an almost solid front in seven hours of debate in its drive to defeat the punitive action" against McCarthy.

*Washington *Post*, July 30, 1954, Editorial: "Up to the Senate."

Senator Knowland, as Majority Leader, told reporters that debate on the resolution would not be allowed to drag on. He opposed the censure resolution, he said as "unfair and unprecedented" and predicted that it could not win. Vice-President Nixon said that he did not believe the resolution would pass "in its present form" and possibly not in any form.

When questioned about President Eisenhower's attitude toward McCarthy and censure, Knowland said, "It is the position, I understand, of the President that this is a problem for the Senate of the United States and that it would be improper for him to inject himself into it."

Meanwhile, Senator Flanders was joined in his efforts to secure a censure resolution by Senators Fulbright, Morse, and others. Fulbright and Morse believed a "bill of particulars"—specific charges of wrongdoing—would strengthen the resolution, and offered amendments accordingly. Fulbright, in effect, became floor manager of the censure movement and its most articulate spokesman. Fulbright argued for the censure of McCarthy as a defense of the Senate, its powers, and its reputation. Reminding the members of the Senate that a Senator may not be held accountable "in any other place" for anything he might say in the Senate, Fulbright added, "When members have violated the canons of good conduct, have been contemptuous of the traditions of the Senate, the only place they can be held accountable is in the Senate itself."

By providing a bill of particulars and hoping for useful debate on the floor of the Senate, Fulbright and a number of other Senators attempted to settle the McCarthy matter promptly and avoid sending the issue to a committee for study. (Senator Morse, interestingly enough, was for further study of the censure charges.)

To many Senators—and to others outside the Senate—it appeared obvious that sufficient evidence already existed and was known to every Senator that a censure charge could be supported against McCarthy. They felt and said forcefully, that failure to censure McCarthy forthwith on the floor of the Senate was to let McCarthy escape censure.

On this wise, the Washington *Post* was for immediate censuring of McCarthy and said editorially that the effort to send the resolution to a committee for study was a "spurious move" and added ". . . there have been committee studies already. Now it is time to act, for, as Senator Bush said, 'the Senate itself has a real responsibility here . . .'" The *Post* went on to say: ". . . additional investigation now simply would postpone the inescapable day of reckoning for the Senate, which already has been brought into disrepute by Senator McCarthy's refusal to respect the Senate's own rules and traditions." *

The entire debate on the floor of the Senate, immediately prior to the vote which created a Select Committee to investigate the McCarthy censure matter,

---

*Washington *Post,* August 2, 1954, Editorial: "The Senate's Good Name."

is extremely interesting. Selections from the *Congressional Record* for August 2, 1954 yield some of the flavor of this debate:

MR. MONRONEY: Those who think we shall be able to finish with this case in a week, or two weeks, or two months, or six months, are the world's greatest optimists. Speaking of a man who has had two years of this experience, I can only say that if we intend to conduct the kind of investigation that will be satisfactory to the junior Senator from Wisconsin—and make no mistake about it, we shall be absolutely unable to make it satisfactory to him unless he runs the committee—we shall find that the committee members, no matter who is chosen to serve, no matter how much dignity, or how much prestige they have will be suddenly found to be coddling communists, soft on communism, attempting to destroy the valued work of the great junior Senator from Wisconsin.

Senator Mike Monroney, earlier, as a member of the House of Representatives served and won fame as vice-chairman of the Joint Committee on the Reorganization of Congress during the 79th Congress. Senator Monroney who had a record as a brilliant reporter and political writer before his election to Congress won further distinction in the Senate. He led off the final debate against the motion to refer the proposed McCarthy censure resolution to a Select Committee of three Republicans and three Democrats for hearing and report. Again from Senator Monroney:

The only time he will find no further complaint is when we make him the great McCarthy who runs all our great campaigns to eradicate internal subversion and communism, even though the FBI, the world's greatest internal security organization, has spent $540 million, more than a half billion, since 1947, more than $400 million of which was given by that party of treason, those 21 years or 20 years of treason—the junior Senator from Wisconsin made it 21 the other day to make it bi-partisan—that party of treason had started out to give $400 million—and I will say the distinguished President [Eisenhower] has added enough money to make it $548 million—and yet the distinguished junior Senator from Wisconsin will not be satisfied unless we say, "You are the champion of all communist hunters in the wide, wide world, Senator McCarthy. You can find the communists and you can protect and save this nation with $225,000." J. Edgar Hoover must be a sap. He requires $548 million to protect this country. . . .

No one denies the speech he [McCarthy] made on the floor of the Senate about General George C. Marshall accusing him of subversive infamy so black that when the truth is finally known it will dwarf all previous conspiracies, or words to that effect. Those are the words in the record. . . .

My own principal objection is that the Senator is my agent as an official of the United States Government. I think that is the reason why we have a right to criticize, why we have a right to say to an employee, "we do not like the kind of work you are doing; we do not like the kind of job you are doing; we think you have flopped and fizzled in every way possible, brought the Senate into disrespect and disrepute, destroyed our standing around the world with our friendly allies, and destroyed the very agency that this nation must depend on to win the cold war against communism."

We have seen a shambles made of that great organization, the State Department, the Voice of America, when it should have been strong, determined and factual at the time of the death of Premier Stalin, was suffering from a case of shell shock from Cohn and Schine as they marched ruthlessly across the friendly nations of Europe, enjoying and demanding more attention, more consideration and greater prerogatives than the majority leader or the minority leader of this great body would ever have thought of demanding. . . .

The Army has just come back with bloody wounds and one hundred thousand—some-odd casualties from fighting the red communists in the hills of Korea. It is being pilloried for being soft on communism and coddling communists. It is sought to discredit great generals. Great secretaries of the Army have been forced to knuckle under to the strange power that has grown up in the United States Senate, and forced, because of fear of destroying the great reputation of the wonderful body of men who wear the uniform of the United States, to take orders from the clerks of a committee of the United States Senate. I say to you that this is on the conscience of the United States Senate, it cannot be passed on no matter how we wish it to six men, no matter who they are.

Senator J. W. Fulbright of Arkansas has won so much distinction and fame as a scholar-legislator, and as a member and Chairman of the Foreign Relations Committee of the Senate, that his name has become a household word in the United States, if not in most of the English speaking world.

In approving the position of Senator Monroney, Mr. Fulbright commented:

MR. FULBRIGHT. Mr. President, I appreciate very much the contribution of the Senator from Oklahoma (Mr. Monroney) and I wish to associate myself with his statements. Mr. President, that is about all I have to say. I think the Senate is making one of the greatest mistakes it will ever have made in assigning this to a committee without the slightest hope, I think, of resolving this question.

As I said a moment ago, I cannot believe that it can be any more successful in reaching a conclusion which can be passed upon here than those which have already handled these matters.

Therefore, I shall feel constrained to vote against the motion to refer to a special committee, and I regret very much that the leadership has seen fit to prevent a straight vote upon the amendment to the resolution offered by the Senator from Arkansas.

Senator Capehart, the concluding speaker before the vote on the resolution, had served in the Senate since 1944 and also enjoyed a reputation as an able businessman. (He was a very successful manufacturer of radio, phonograph, and television products.) He was also a veteran of World War II. In his speech closing the debate, the Senator among other things elaborated the doubts and the bewilderment he had with respect to the "McCarthy issue."

Mr. Capehart of Indiana then addressed the President and obtained the floor.

MR. CAPEHART. We in the United States Senate tonight have the American people very much confused. When I came to the United States Senate on January 3, 1945, if anyone had stood upon the floor of the United States Senate at that time and said an unkind word about the Communist Russia he would have almost been tried for treason. The Russians were our allies. We were talking about them as being great, brave people. We were spending billions of dollars helping them.

At that time we were discussing and 'cussing' the Nazis, the Germans. They were terrible people. When the War ended we tried the German leaders for the war crimes and we put many of them to death.

Then in 1947, or perhaps 1948, when the President of the United States, Mr. Truman, sent a message to the United States Congress in which he asked for $500 million to stop communism in Greece and Turkey, the Congress of the United States voted him the money.

From that time on in the United States and in the Congress we have been spending billions of dollars to stop communism. In practically every bill we have passed since that day we have said we were doing so in order to stop communism. We went to war in Korea to stop communism. We suffered about 150 thousand casualties to stop communism.

There is not a Senator on this floor who has not made a speech against communism, stating how terrible it is and how it will destroy the world.

Yet we have one man in the United States Senate by the name of McCarthy, from Wisconsin, who has tried to do something about communism. I will admit that his methods have not always been the methods I would have used. I will admit I have blown hot and cold in my likes and dislikes with respect to this Senator. I think he has made many mistakes. He has said things and done things I would not have said or done.

I think that possibly is true of every one Senator, but I say to Senators that we have the American people confused, when we ask them to spend billions of dollars to stop communism, when we send an army into Korea and suffer 150 thousand casualties, and then talk about washing out—that is what we are talking about—the one man in the United States who has been fighting or trying to fight communism at home. . . .

We had better look to the American people, because they are not going to stand still for this washing out of one man who has tried to do something about communism without some sort of substitute being offered. Believe me when I say that. Believe me when I say the American people are divided over this issue. Any man can go anywhere in the United States—I care not where he goes—and if there are six people, moreorless, gathered together and the subject of McCarthy or McCarthyism is brought up, he will find these people, and before it is over the division will be very, very bitter.

I do not know what percentage of the people of the United States are for or against this Senator. But I do know this: the American people are confused, they cannot understand the President of the United States, they cannot understand individual Senators, and they cannot understand people who will say to them, 'we are going to take billions and billions of American dollars to fight communism.'

Then we stand on the floor of the United States Senate and make speeches and condemn the one man who the American people think is trying to do something about communism in the United States. Now the American people are not going to stand for that, whether they are dealing with Republicans or whether they are dealing with Democrats. Some substitute is necessary.

Perhaps this Senator should be washed out. Perhaps his efforts have been all wrong. But I say to Senators unless we are careful we shall prolong and prolong, and agitate and agitate, and split the American people right down the middle. . . .

I am not taking the side of the Senator from Wisconsin. On that subject I have blown both hot and cold. There have been times when if I could have gotten hold of him, I think I would have thrown him out. There have been other times when I thought, 'By golly, there is a great guy.' I think that has been the experience of most all of us.

I am pleading with Senators. It seems to me that the majority of us want to refer this problem to a committee. I shall vote to do so because I think the majority of us want it that way, but I am pleading with Senators that is not the way to do it. . . .

MR. ANDERSON. Mr. President, may the motion as modified be stated?

THE PRESIDING OFFICER. The clerk will state the motion as modified.

The chief clerk read as follows:

I move to refer the pending resolution (S. Res. 301) together with all the amendments proposed thereto, to a Select Committee to be composed of three Republicans and three Democrats, who shall be named by the Vice-President; and ordered further, that the committee shall be authorized to hold hearings, to sit and to act at such times and places during the sessions, recesses, and adjourned places during the sessions, to require by subpoena or otherwise the attendance of such witnesses and the production of such correspondence, books, papers, documents, and to take such testimonies as it deems advisable, and the committee be instructed to act and make a report to this body prior to the adjournment sine die of the Senate in the second session of the 83rd Congress.

THE PRESIDING OFFICER. On this question the ayes and nays have been ordered. The clerk will call the roll.

The legislative clerk called the roll.

MR. MC CARTHY. (when his name was called), I vote 'present.'

The result was announced—ayes, 75; nays, 12; voting 'present' 1, not voting 8.*

Thus the Select Committee was created and the matter of the censure of Joseph McCarthy was submitted to it for consideration and report.

The Washington *Post* of August 3, in an editorial entitled "Pettifoggery," was irked by the action of the Senate and said that the vote to send the matter of censure to a Select Committee was a "shelving maneuver" and "a mere camouflage for inaction."

While some papers said that the Senate wanted to dodge its responsibility by referring the censure matter to an investigative committee, others took a different line. In an editorial on August 3, The Washington *Star* said it was "the proper thing to do," and added: "Whether Senator McCarthy deserves censure for his conduct remains, after all, a matter of sharply divided opinion. The *Star* is of the opinion that he does. But the accusations against him must be sustained by evidence, he must be given formal opportunity to refute the charges, and the traditional method . . . is to follow the procedure of committee investigation and report. Any other course would establish a dubious precedent, and probably give McCarthy a clean bill of health to boot."

---

* The Senators voted as follows:
Ayes—75. Aiken, Anderson, Barrett, Beall, Bennett, Bricker, Bridges, Burke, Bush, Butler, Byrd, Capehart, Carlson, Case, Clement, Cordon, Crippa, Daniel, Dirksen, Dworshak, Ellender, Ervin, Ferguson, Frear, George, Gillette, Goldwater, Gore, Green, Hayden, Hendrickson, Hickenlooper, Holland, Ives, Jackson, Jenner, Johnson, (Colo.), Johnson, (Tex.), Johnson, (S.C.), Kennedy, Kerr, Kilgore, Knowland, Kuchel, Langer, Lennon, Long, Malone, Mansfield, Markin, Maybank, McCarran, McClellan, Millikin, Morse, Mundt, Murray, Pastore, Payne, Potter, Purtell, Robertson, Russell, Saltonstall, Smathers, Smith, (Me.), Stennis, Symington, Thye, Upton, Watkins, Welker, Wylie, Williams and Young.
Nays—12. Chavez, Cooper, Douglas, Duff, Flanders, Fulbright, Hennings, Hill, Humphrey, Lehman, Magnuson, Monroney.
Voting 'present'—1. McCarthy.
Not voting—8. Bowring, Eastland, Kefauver, Neely, Reynolds, Schoeppel, Smith, (N.J.), Sparkman.

The following day, Roscoe Drummond, a columnist appearing in the *Christian Science Monitor* and other papers, wrote that ". . . the way the debate has now shaped up nothing which the Senate does on censure will significantly affect the role or influence of Senator Joseph R. McCarthy." He added: "Three conditions would have to be met if the censure resolution were to have an important effect: It would have to have the active support of the leadership of the Republican Party. It would require the visible backing of President Eisenhower. It would need to be accompanied by (McCarthy's) removal as Chairman or the enactment of an enforceable code of fair procedure for Congressional investigation." Since these were all absent, said Drummond, the Senate's action "exercised minimal weight."

It appeared to many that the move against McCarthy was headed for compromise or even outright defeat. Senator Fulbright was reported to have said gloomily that: "Joe can buffalo any committee on earth."

McCarthy's private opinion as to what might be best for him, given the alternatives of investigation by a committee or an immediate vote on the floor of the Senate to censure him, may be surmised by his public statements. When asked about the vote to refer the matter to a committee, McCarthy said (according to the Washington *Star*), "I'm very happy. This is good."

Senator McCarthy, indeed, was not worried. Before a cheering crowd of 2000 American Legionnaires in Washington, D.C. he said of those who had wanted to censure him that they were "nice little boys" who lacked "guts" to help him expose communists. Some papers put the story on the front page.

THE SEVERE CRITICS OF JOE MC CARTHY CALLED THE SENATE'S REFERRAL OF the charges to a Select Committee a "vote to duck the issue." *The New York Times* said that such a move could "hardly be conclusive," and the Washington *Post* called it, as we have noted, a "shelving maneuver . . . a mere camouflage for inaction."

It seems clear that the Republican leadership did hope to see a compromise. This might have been accomplished, according to the belief of some at the time, by "a word of apology" from McCarthy (which, of course, would have been completely out of character for him), or a moderate "slap on the wrist" by the Senate.

As for the Democratic leadership, the spectacle of a Republican Senator feuding with a Republican Administration was a delight. Arthur Krock, in commenting in *The New York Times* of August 6 on Democratic unwillingness "to set a dangerous precedent" in any possible removal of McCarthy from his chairmanship of his committee, said that any "victory" for the junior Senator from Wisconsin in surviving a censure attempt would have "blunted" the edge of the partisan issue which Democrats intended to raise in the November elections. This was the supposed reason, he said, for Democratic Minority Leader Lyndon B. Johnson's "coolness" toward the Flanders resolution.

As to Lyndon Johnson's role in the censure of McCarthy, Evans and Novack have written* that the naming of the Select Committee came about "just as Johnson had planned it" . . . that is, none of the six were controversial, none were on record for or against McCarthy. These authors, who got their story direct from the horse's mouth, indicated that Johnson was instrumental in the censure move.

It is true, of course, that when it came to the final vote, the Minority Leader engaged in his usual effort to achieve unanimity through compromise—a traditional Johnson role—but at the expense of an important issue. In this instance, Johnson appeased certain southern Senators and held them in line at the expense of the Zwicker matter (which, as we shall see, involved the alleged right of Senators to abuse witnesses). In addition, Johnson preserved a potent political issue, the supposed failure of the Eisenhower Administration to manage the affairs of the Army efficiently.

On August 5, Vice President Richard M. Nixon announced on the floor of

---

*Rowland Evans and Robert Novak, *Lyndon B. Johnson, The Exercise of Power* (New York, The New American Library, 1966), p. 84.

the Senate the names of the Select Committee. In addition to myself, there were two other Republicans. Francis Case, of South Dakota, was born in 1896 and served as an Army officer in World War I. Case had been a newspaper editor before serving five terms in the House of Representatives, and then became Senator in 1951. Frank Carlson, of Kansas, was born in that state in 1893 and lived there as a farmer and stockman. He served six terms in the House, returned to Kansas as Governor, and then came to Washington as Senator in 1951.

The Democrats on the Committee were: Edwin Johnson, of Colorado, who was born in Kansas in 1884, became a railroader and then homesteaded in Colorado, served in the legislature, became Lt. Governor and then Governor, and was elected to the Senate in 1936. John Stennis, of Mississippi, born in 1901, was a lawyer and judge, served in the state legislature, and was elected to the Senate in 1947; and Sam J. Ervin, Jr., of North Carolina, born in 1896, was a lawyer and judge of a trial court and of the Supreme Court of his state, served in the House of Representatives and was elected to the Senate in 1954.

I was the senior Republican, with a legal and judicial background, and as such I was named Chairman by vote of the Committee.

Senator Knowland, in asking me to serve on the Select Committee, did not in any way indicate his personal preferences. He did not instruct me, even to the slightest degree, to go easy on McCarthy. (As is clear from subsequent events, Knowland was opposed to the censure of McCarthy, as indicated in his statements in the Senate and to the press.) Presumably the other Republicans on the newly appointed Select Committee were treated as respectfully by Senator Knowland.

While I cannot speak authoritatively for the Democrats on the Select Committee, I have no reason whatsoever to think that Senator Lyndon Johnson had indicated his personal preferences to them. At all times, each and every Senator on the Select Committee acted as a free agent and as representative Senators.

Of course, the theory of a "Select" Committee is that it is representative of the Senate, empowered to speak and act in the name of the entire Senate in the area and matters designated. A Select Committee, for example, may be named to represent the Senate at ceremonial functions.

In establishing the Select Committee for the purpose of inquiring whether or not Senator McCarthy should be censured, the Senate made a broad grant of power. This power included the right to subpoena witnesses, to call for records and information from any source, and to otherwise establish its own procedures. It was further instructed "to act and make a report" before the adjournment of the Senate that year.

More specifically, the Committee interpreted its duties, functions and responsibilities under the Senate order: (1) to analyze the charges against Senator McCarthy, determine which were sufficiently substantive and which were to be eliminated as duplications or not of sufficient merit or relevance (even if true) to warrant censure, (2) to thoroughly investigate those charges which appeared to be substantive, (3) to prepare a record for use by the body of the Senate in its final consideration and vote on censure, including a written report to the Senate. We decided to accept for our rules of procedures those rules which applied to the conduct of Senators on the floor of the Senate.

Having known and observed Senator McCarthy (even though none of us had paid special attention to him), we recognized that we may have had opinions with respect to his conduct as Chairman of his Committee. I reminded the group—speaking from my days as a judge—that we were human and subject to the usual weaknesses, but that we could and should recognize any preconceptions that we might have, and would have to examine the facts and the law applicable with complete objectivity and fairness. All agreed that we could do this.

Senators Stennis and Ervin jokingly spoke of an old Southern legal saying appropriate to the occasion: "Salt down the facts. The law can wait!" In view of the short time in which we had to work, and the necessity of getting the facts before the body of the Senate, we agreed that this advice was sound and helpful.

We agreed that we were not sitting to determine whether Senator McCarthy's allegations of communist influence in Government were true or false. Communism was not the issue. At issue was the Senator's alleged misbehavior on the floor of the Senate and outside the Senate, in committee, his lack of respect toward his fellow Senators and the Senate itself, and his treatment of witnesses.

What we had to determine, for example, was how McCarthy had behaved toward the Gillette Committee and that Committee's responsibilities. We did not have the authority to take up again the charges which had already been examined by the Gillette Committee (particularly since the conduct of the Gillette Committee had been sustained on the floor of the Senate by a vote of 60 to 0).

After completing all the initial arrangements for the hearing and setting the date to begin, August 31, we prepared for what was to be in several senses of the word the "trial."

The pro-McCarthy press had not yet taken our measure, and was not yet critical. The McCarthy critics were still doubtful that any effective censure of the Senator would come from our work. The Senate is a club, they said, and "the spirit of the club will prevail." The nature of the Senate, they said, is to tolerate free expression, even extreme expression, and many expected that the Select Committee would react *against* the critics of the Senator.

Senator McCarthy, himself, seemed completely at ease and without apprehension. He, too, seemed to feel that the spirit of the Senate club would preclude any real censure.

The day after my name had been announced as Chairman of the Select Committee, McCarthy came up to my seat on the floor of the Senate and genially stuck out his hand to me. "I want to congratulate you on being named Chairman of the Committee, Arthur," he said. "I hope you will conduct a fair and orderly hearing and will enforce all the rules."

"Thank you, Senator," I replied. "You can be sure that is precisely what I intend to do."

Joe's smile faded. As he moved into his seat he looked back toward me as if seeing a person completely unknown to him.

Stewart Alsop was soon to say in his column that the "man-eating tiger" was about to face an "elderly mouse." Other wits quickly refined this to the most popular joke in Washington at the time: "The lion has been thrown into a den of lambs!"

THE DAY BEFORE THE SELECT COMMITTEE'S PUBLIC HEARINGS WERE scheduled to begin, Senator McCarthy and his counsel—the very able and well-known teacher and practitioner of law, Edward Bennett Williams—came to an executive session of the Select Committee to hear the rules we had laid down for the hearing.

So that we might have a more orderly hearing, one which could not degenerate into a shouting contest, and deal only with such evidence as would be germane to the hearings, we adopted a rule requiring that all evidence offered and received should be material, relevant, and competent to the issues. Further, we provided that if Senator McCarthy started to speak or to question a witness or make an objection on any subject, his counsel could not be heard on the same items. Conversely, if the counsel raised a question, made an objection, or began an examination of a witness, then the Senator would be barred from direct participation in that discussion or questioning.

Frankly, the Committee had taken notice of McCarthy's propensity to monopolize any proceeding in which he was a participant. His aggressive conduct at hearings was well known. We felt unless we enforced a rule of this kind the hearings would be unnecessarily extended, and it would be difficult to conduct a dignified and meaningful hearing befitting the importance of the occasion.*

The Senator and his counsel, Mr. Williams, had already made an agreement that McCarthy would not do any talking except when he was testifying, and Mr. Williams would have complete charge of the case, so they readily accepted the Committee's rule.

When this item had been taken care of, Senator McCarthy and his counsel left the meeting but returned a few minutes later. The Senator appeared to be greatly agitated. He exhibited a news clipping from the Denver, Colorado, *Post* and wanted to know what we were going to do about it. Those of us who were members of the Committee hastily examined the clipping.

The story purported to be an interview with Senator Johnson of Colorado. It

---

*We of the Select Committee were very much aware of what had happened at the recent Army-McCarthy hearings. I had attended but one session, and that for not more than ten minutes. On that occasion, there was comparative quiet. Later, of course, I became aware of the nature of the hearings as I saw television news and repeats in the evenings. These TV selections revealed an almost total lack of orderly procedure. The shouting and name calling were beyond belief. Senator McCarthy, it seemed to me, was the principal actor.

quoted him as saying that "there was not a Democrat in the Senate who didn't loathe Senator McCarthy."

The Committee was completely taken by surprise. We had insufficient time to make any extended consideration of the newspaper account. I indicated to my colleagues that it might be irrelevant and immaterial to the proceedings, but that we would study the matter and meet the issue if and when it arose.

The hearings had been set by the Committee to begin Tuesday, August 31, 1954, in the famous Caucus Room of the Old Senate Office Building. As I entered the Caucus Room that morning, I glanced about and noted that it was packed. We six Senators of the Select Committee sat at a long table at the head of the room, and Senator McCarthy and Mr. Williams sat at a small table facing us. In a solid block in front of us sat hosts of reporters at their tables, but none of them were smoking. No one smoked, of course, because we had determined that the rules for the hearing would be the rules of the Senate floor sessions (and it was not without some personal appreciation that I observed that this included no smoking).

The Committee initiated the hearings with a careful deliniation of the charges, and gave Senator McCarthy and his counsel an opportunity to be heard.

Joe McCarthy was permitted to introduce into the record a statement of his own position. This was to the effect, I think it fairly may be stated, that he was fighting communist subversion and that this fight was being obstructed by: (1) communists and their sympathizers, (2) those who denied that this subversion was a threat, and (3) those who opposed the "vigorous measures" necessary to stamp it out. He then added that he hoped all the charges against him might be examined and disposed of so that he could get back to his work.

Mr. Williams, for his part, wished to discuss precedents in the censure of a Senator. We explained that this had been thoroughly explored by our Committee in advance, but assured him that his brief might be made part of the record.

These procedures were lengthy and fatiguing. We were approaching the time which I, as Chairman, had set for the recess at the day's end. It was at this time that a discussion of the newspaper clipping (with the Johnson story) was intro- duced by Senator Johnson.

Now the Committee faced its first test. This was an attempt by Senator Mc- Carthy to determine if he could (as virtually everyone had assumed he would) dominate this hearing by the force of his aggressive personality and his take-over tactics, as he had every other proceeding. As Chairman, I was determined that we would stick to the rules. In this I had the solid backing of my colleagues who had anticipated what the Senator might do.

The interesting dialogue, as it appears in the record of the hearings, follows:

SENATOR JOHNSON. Mr. Chairman, on yesterday evening Senator Mc-

Carthy and his attorney, Mr. Williams, called the attention of this committee to a published article in the Denver Post on March 12, 1954, in which an interview by telephone with me was stated or was used, and I desire to make a brief statement with respect to that publication.

The CHAIRMAN. You may proceed, Senator.

SENATOR JOHNSON. Mr. Chairman, I did not say on March 12, or at any other time, that I personally loathed Senator Joseph McCarthy. In response to a telephone call from Denver, I agreed that some of my Democratic colleagues did not like Senator McCarthy. My March 12 statement, as published, did not say that I personally loathed Senator McCarthy. The Flanders speech on the Senate floor, which was the forerunner of my March 12 statement, pertained to the question whether or not Senator McCarthy be removed from the chairmanship of the Senate committee.

My position then and now is that that matter should be decided by the majority party in charge of the organization of the Senate and that it was not the business of the Senate Democratic Party at all. I have full faith in my ability to weigh the charges which have been made against Senator McCarthy, together with whatever evidence may be presented without prejudice.

The CHAIRMAN. Thank you, Senator.

At this point Senator John Stennis discussed some points which do not contribute to my present telling of this story. Mr. Williams responded to them, and then referred back to the matter of the clipping and its purported quotations of Senator Johnson.

MR. WILLIAMS (continuing). I would like also to say at this time, if I may, sir, that the record might be straight in open hearings, I think it should be stated at this time that at no time has either Senator McCarthy or myself challenged Senator Johnson's qualifications to sit on this committee.

What we did was to call to the attention of the committee a matter that was called to our attention exactly 5 minutes before we brought it to the Committee. I felt that as counsel to Senator McCarthy, and as counsel serving before this committee, I should be derelict in my duty if I did not bring to the attention of the committee something upon which the committee might want to take action.

Now, I do not know whether the Chair desires to have read into the record what I called to the attention of the committee or not. It seems to me it would be appropriate to have it there so that Senator Johnson's remarks might be viewed in proper context.

What I did call—

The CHAIRMAN. I do not think it is necessary to this hearing. Nobody has challenged Senator Johnson. He was appointed by the Senate, and this committee has no authority to remove him or even to accept a resignation of his from the committee.

Since that is the record, why is it necessary to clutter it up with a lot of extraneous matter? I rule that we will not follow that suggestion.

MR. WILLIAMS. The only thing we had hoped for, Mr. Chairman, was this: At least—maybe I am in error—but I was led to believe as I left the executive session last night—I do not know whether Senator McCarthy shares my understanding or not—but I was led to believe that Senator Johnson was going to call the editor who bylined this story, and either confirm or deny the reported contents thereof.

The CHAIRMAN. If it is immaterial to this hearing, what difference does it make whether he called him or did not call him? I do not think it makes any difference whatsoever. We are not trying Senator Johnson; no accusations have been made against him, no challenge has been made as to him.

SENATOR MC CARTHY. Mr. Chairman, I have desisted from making any comments, so far, and I would like to ask a question, if I may.

The CHAIRMAN. Just a moment, Senator. Let us get this clear: I think the fair interpretation of the rule is that when your counsel speaks on a matter, that precludes you from addressing the Chair of the committee on the same matter. If you want to take it over yourself, why then, you start it, and then we will let you finish it. But we are not going to permit both of you to argue this matter.

SENATOR MC CARTHY. Just a minute, Mr. Chairman, just 1 minute.

MR. WILLIAMS. Senator McCarthy is really extending a thought that I had, and that I had suggested to the chair.

I had come away from the hearing yesterday, feeling that we were going to get a statement from Senator Johnson either affirming or denying the story which is reported in the March 12 Denver Post. Now, I was not idly curious on that subject, Senator. I felt that I needed that information in order to intelligently advise Senator McCarthy as to what position he should take with respect to this matter.

The CHAIRMAN. I would say to you, Mr. Williams, that Senator Johnson, if he was able to make that telephone communication, will tell you privately what was the result of the conversation. But I cannot see why it has anything to do with this matter. There is no challenge. We have not any authority over Senator Johnson.

MR. WILLIAMS. I do not have information enough at this time, Mr. Chairman, to make a challenge. I do not know whether I should advise Senator McCarthy to make a challenge or not, because I do not know yet whether or not the reported statements in the Denver Post are true or are untrue, and I have relied upon the representations made in executive session as to the source for my information on that subject today.

The CHAIRMAN. I would say that the Chair has already ruled on this matter that it has nothing to do with the committee. We have no authority to change the personnel. We could not—it is not material to our investigation.

The personnel have been selected; members of this committee have been selected by the Senate itself, and this committee certainly has no authority under the order set up under the Resolution 301 to remove any of its members, to consider any challenge to its membership.

MR. WILLIAMS. So that I might understand the ruling of the Chair, it is that we are not entitled to the information as to the truth or falsity of the statements of March 12?

The CHAIRMAN. I say you are entitled to it if you wish to get it from Senator Johnson, but I say that it is not material to this hearing and for that reason I am not going to permit, or should not permit colloquy to go on back and forth.

Senator Johnson has made his statement, and that is it, and you have made your statement.

SENATOR CASE. Mr. Chairman—

The CHAIRMAN. Senator Case.

SENATOR CASE. It occurs to me that all of this discussion is immaterial to the purposes of the inquiry, for the record of this inquiry.

SENATOR CARLSON. Mr. Chairman, I would like to be in a position—

The CHAIRMAN. Senator Carlson.

SENATOR CARLSON. I confirm Senator Case's remarks, so far as this particular record is concerned.

SENATOR MC CARTHY. Mr. Chairman, I would like to ask one question. Are we entitled to know whether or not the quotations of March 12 are correct or incorrect.

I would like to know whether the Denver Post—

The CHAIRMAN. You may get it, Senator, and I am going to rule on this, and I have already ruled, you may get that some other place. But this committee has no jurisdiction over those matters, whatsoever. This committee was appointed by the Senate; the only condition laid down was that there would be 3 Democrats and 3 Republicans and here we are, 3 Republicans and 3 Democrats, and this committee is not going to take on the job of the Senate and going to decide whether this committee is a proper committee or not. This committee is—

SENATOR MC CARTHY. Mr. Chairman—

The CHAIRMAN. Just a moment, Senator. You have filed no challenge, and, in the first place, I believe it is improper for you to do so, because we have not any jurisdiction.

SENATOR MC CARTHY. Mr. Chairman, I should be entitled to know whether or not—

The CHAIRMAN. The Senator is out of order.

SENATOR MC CARTHY. Can't I get Mr. Johnson to tell me . . .

The CHAIRMAN. The Senator is out of order.

SENATOR MC CARTHY. Whether it is true or false?

The CHAIRMAN. The Senator is out of order. You can go to the Senator and question and find out. That is not for this committee to consider. We are not going to be interrupted by these diversions and sidelines. We are going straight down the line.

The committee will be in recess.

I had announced previously that the committee would recess until 10 o'clock tomorrow morning and that is the order.

I pounded the gavel, and continued to pound the gavel as Senator McCarthy tried to speak. This has been described by the press as an exciting and colorful point in the hearings, but it might not appear so from the dry record here reproduced. Finally he gave up the attempt, (I believe) flabbergasted. After the recess, he was recorded as saying: "This is the most unheard of thing I ever heard of!"

Having silenced Senator McCarthy for speaking out of turn (since we had agreed in advance that he could not participate when his attorney was attempting to make a point and vice versa, a matter Mr. Williams had also considered of crucial importance to his handling of the case) and, ruling that material not pertinent to the inquiry could not be injected, we set the tone for the remainder of the hearings.

The importance of thus establishing a judicial tenor for this inquiry can hardly be overemphasized. Without it, we would very likely have had the "circus" that many writers predicted it would become. As exciting—and as headline filling—as this might have been, it would not have been conducive to a fair and expeditious weighing of the facts in the case. Nor would any definitive answer have been forthcoming from such an emotionally charged affair.

However, after gaveling down the hitherto irrepressible Joe McCarthy (who remained docile throughout the remainder of the proceedings), I was subjected to a torrent of abuse from the several radio and newspaper commentators who thrived on the near-hysteria which ran concurrently with McCarthyism. I was preventing McCarthy from presenting his side of the case, they said, and thereby demonstrating my own preconceptions in the matter.

As this theme—denying McCarthy his right to be heard—was drummed so mightily and endlessly by his friends and supporters after that first-day's session, I believe it important to insert at this point the authoritative comments of McCarthy's own attorney.

In his book, *One Man's Freedom,* Edward Bennett Williams tells about a number of famous trials in which he defended well-known persons.* In his chapter on McCarthy, Mr. Williams describes a meeting in his home in which he and the Senator agreed in advance how to conduct the defense. He wrote, speaking of McCarthy, that:

> He further agreed that he would say nothing throughout the hearing except when he was testifying. In short, I was given the power commensurate with the responsibility insofar as the hearing went. We shook hands on what I thought was a very carefully detailed understanding . . .
>
> But I soon discovered I had been guilty of a tremendous oversight. I had not foreseen that under the terms of our agreement he would be free to make whatever comments he chose outside of the hearing room either

*Edward Bennett Williams, *One Man's Freedom,* (New York, Atheneum, 1962), pp. 63–64.

about the hearing itself or about the committee members. He used that freedom to the fullest, from the opening gun he was holding press conferences and making statements over television networks. He attacked the committee members individually, and he attacked the manner in which they were conducting the inquiry. Day by day our relationship with the committee worsened, but I was unable to dissuade the Senator from continuing his verbal assaults on Senator Watkins and his associates.

Watkins and the committee had set out to establish rules which would make the hearing as fair as legislative trial could be.* McCarthy had been informed specifically of what the charges against him were. He was allowed to have counsel at every stage of the proceedings. His counsel was allowed to object to procedures and to specific questions and to cross-examine adverse witnesses, as well as to present evidence on McCarthy's behalf. There were no television cameras to distract the attention of witnesses and committee members. Although the press coverage was heavy and audiences were large, the publicity pressure which had surrounded the Army-McCarthy hearing was gone. Watkins kept the whole inquiry on such a dryly technical level that much of the excitement was drained out of the day-to-day proceedings. All in all, they were conducted with somewhat more decorum and calmness than usually surrounds a congressional hearing, although this one was as potentially explosive as any investigation had ever been.

*Williams' generally favorable comments on the procedures of our Committee are in contrast to his remarks about the Gillette Committee, against which he did level a number of criticisms.

7   Contempt for the Gillette Committee

ALTHOUGH SENATOR MC CARTHY HAD CLASHED WITH A GREAT MANY SENATORS before the Select Committee—it was not until he encountered Senator William Benton that the events were set in motion which ultimately resulted in his censure.

Benton said himself that he was going to go after McCarthy with "hammer and tongs." His resolution—calling for the expulsion of Senator McCarthy from the United States Senate, principally for his alleged behavior in the election campaign which unseated Senator Tydings of Maryland—was referred in August, 1951 to the Subcommittee on Privileges and Elections of the Committee on Rules and Administration, chaired by Senator Guy Gillette.

Senator Benton followed up his resolution with specific charges before the Gillette Subcommittee. These were serious allegations as to what use was made of money which the public sent to McCarthy for his "fight on communism," questions of conflict of interest, and instances of abuse of public figures such as General George Marshall, and other examples of "fraud and deceit," "libelous statements," and "deliberate deception."

On the face of it, Benton's charges were unusual and grave. If proved true, the alleged misbehavior of McCarthy might well have provided grounds for expulsion of the junior Senator from Wisconsin from the Senate. It is no wonder that Senator Gillette moved circumspectly.

After the Gillette subcommittee received and considered Benton's resolution, it moved to hear Senator Benton himself. Meanwhile, having received on September 17 a sharply worded letter from McCarthy asking permission to cross examine any witnesses (and speaking of Senator Benton as a "friend and sponsor" of those McCarthy had already named as members of a "communist front"), Gillette wrote McCarthy. Senator Gillette's "Dear Joe" letter was brief and friendly and said that Senator Benton was going to appear before the subcommittee, and—while Joe couldn't cross examine the witness, since this was the business of the subcommittee—he could be present as an observer. The hearing, to avoid publicity until the nature of the charges could be examined, was to be in executive session.

Senator McCarthy did not answer the letter. A few days later, Benton duly appeared before the subcommittee. A week later, still without fanfare, Gillette wrote to McCarthy—this time a "My dear Senator" letter—and told him of Benton's appearance and further offered McCarthy an opportunity to be heard "at an hour mutually convenient." This brought a prompt "Dear Guy" reply, saying: "Frankly, Guy, I have not and do not intend to even read, much less answer, Benton's smear attack. I am sure you realize that the Benton type of material can be found in the *Daily Worker* almost any day of the week and will continue to flow from the mouths and pens of the camp followers as long as I continue my fight against Communists in Government."

Unhappily, Senator Gillette had little alternative to act except to hire some investigators to check into the allegations of wrongdoing. As an attorney, McCarthy knew that (in the absence of his own cooperation with the Subcommittee) Gillette was required to take the initiative. It was the Subcommittee's responsibility, as called for by the Senate itself, to inquire into the facts of the case and to present the matter to the Senate for consideration in any manner that body wished. It was the Senate that would act, in fact, as the court. McCarthy's attitude of ignoring the charges against him, or of calling them "smears," did not make them disappear, but his failure to appear did have the effect of making it extremely difficult for the Committee to carry out its mission.

After two months of this, McCarthy wrote a "Dear Mr. Chairman" letter to Gillette in which he made some allegations of his own. The subcommittee, wrote McCarthy, had exceeded its authority by making an "unlimited investigation" into his private affairs (and not merely matters of irregular campaign practices) and was employing "a horde of investigators hired by (the subcommittee) at a cost of tens of thousands of dollars of taxpayers' money" . . . and this with the "obvious purpose to dig up campaign material for the Democrat Party."

In doing this, said McCarthy, the subcommittee was "guilty of stealing just as clearly as though the members engaged in picking the pockets of the taxpayers and turning the loot over to the Democrat National Committee."

Although Senator Gillette was hurt and disturbed (particularly because this strongly-worded attack against himself and his Subcommittee had been read to members of the press corps by McCarthy prior to delivering it to the Subcommittee), he responded on December 6 with a very civil statement that the "subcommittee certainly did not seek or welcome the unpleasant task of studying and reporting on a resolution involving charges looking to the ouster of one of our colleagues from the Senate. However, our duty was clear in the task assigned to us and we shall discharge that duty in a spirit of utmost fairness to all concerned . . ." As to the "expenditure of a large sum of money in investigations," said Gillette, that is "of course, erroneous." He also promised that no individual outside the subcommittee would have "any influence whatever in the work assigned to us to do."

In a subsequent exchange, Gillette gave McCarthy information on the number of investigators employed and their salary. This was followed with the names of the investigators which the subcommittee had employed, which turned out to be a very handy bit of information for McCarthy. He discovered that one of these individuals had subsequently had a mental breakdown and been placed in a mental institution. This opened wonderful opportunities for publicity, and within a few months he would exploit them to the fullest.

By the end of 1951, Gillette complained in a letter to McCarthy that matters which should not be discussed publicly were appearing in the press and that letters were appearing in the press before the subcommittee had received them.

McCarthy, not yet finding the mentally sick investigator and still reaching for an issue, then wrote Senator Carl Hayden (Chairman of the parent Committee on Rules and Administration) to question the jurisdiction and legality of the subcommittee in inquiring into every aspect of his life. In this letter (and referring to himself in the third person), McCarthy said:

> I felt that the Elections Subcommittee had no authority to go into matters other than elections unless the Senate instructed it to do so. However, it is obvious that insofar as McCarthy is concerned that is now a moot question, because the staff has already painstakingly and diligently investigated every nook and cranny of my life from birth to date. Every possible lead on McCarthy was investigated. Nothing that could be investigated was left uninvestigated. The staff's scurrilous report, which consisted of cleverly twisted and distorted facts, was then "leaked" to the leftwing elements of the press and blazoned across the Nation in an attempt to further smear McCarthy.

This question of jurisdiction of the Subcommittee—and, incidentally, confidence of the Senate in the handling of the investigation—was posed to the entire Senate by a resolution introduced by Senator Hayden. The Senate, upon consideration of the matter, voted 60 to 0 to support the subcommittee, while 36 Senators did not vote. This was on April 10, 1952.

In May, the Gillette subcommittee inquired into the matter of the $10,000 "fee" which McCarthy had received from the Lustron Corporation. At issue was whether McCarthy had accepted funds from this company interested in housing development and intervened with Federal housing agencies on behalf of it. Gillette told McCarthy of a public hearing to be held on this matter and extending to McCarthy "the opportunity to appear at the hearings for the purpose of presenting testimony relating to this charge."

McCarthy didn't choose to appear, but later he did offer his explanation on the floor of the Senate; the $10,000 was a fee for writing a booklet on Federal housing programs. In a letter to the subcommittee, McCarthy posed counter questions, such as: "I would like to know what you claim that improper conduct to be" with respect to the Lustron incident. He then pointed out that Benton had sold some of his own material (films) to the State Department. With respect to this, he said: "Do you plan on investigating this matter? Or, like Benton, do you consider it proper for a Senator to take money directly from a Government agency but improper to deal with a private firm which has a loan from a Government agency?"

Senator McCarthy used this opportunity to continue his attack against Benton. Describing how communist party organs attacked McCarthyism as "fascist poison," McCarthy went on to say:

All of the above objectives of the Communist Party have been adopted by William Benton as his objectives also. You must agree that the aims and objectives of both the Communist Party and Benton are identical insofar as McCarthy is concerned. The only question is whether it is knowingly or through stupidity that Benton is trying to perform what the Communist Party has officially and repeatedly proclaimed its No. 1 task.

In another paragraph of this letter, McCarthy said:

The Communists will have scored a great victory if they can convince any other Senator or Congressman that if he attempts to expose undercover Communists, he will be subjected to the same type of intense smear, even to the extent of using a Senate committee for the purpose. They will have frightened away from this fight a vast number of legislators who fear the political effect of being inundated by the Communist Party line sewage.

Gillette again wrote Senator McCarthy on May 12, 1952, to invite him to appear before his Subcommittee, saying it "seemed the courteous thing to do" to invite him to present any evidence he had to refute information dug up by the Subcommittee's investigations. Meanwhile, McCarthy had sprung publicly his new-found information about the Subcommittee's investigator—now in an institution—and wrote the sarcastic letter which follows:

May 11, 1952

Gentlemen:

I have learned with regret that your public hearings are to open tomorrow without the presence of your star witness. You have my deepest sympathy.

Some doubting Thomases might question the importance of this witness, except that after nearly a year of investigating, you and your staff decided that the public hearings must open with his intelligently presented, clear-cut expose of the dangers of McCarthyism. The Nation owes you a debt of gratitude for so carefully and honestly developing this witness who could have advised the Senate and the voters of Wisconsin to get rid of McCarthy. If only you had set the hearings 10 days earlier before the judge committed your star witness to an institution for the criminally insane, you would not have been deprived of this important link in the chain of evidence against McCarthy.

Some shallow thinkers may say that you gentlemen are dishonest to have planned to use your committee as a sounding board to headline the statements of a witness after your staff had reported he was mentally unbalanced. I beg you not to let this distract you from the honest, gentlemanly job you are doing. Those critics fail to realize that everything is ethical and honest if it is done to expose the awfulness of McCarthyism. After all, had not your staff reported that while this witness was mentally deranged, his mental condition would help to make him an excellent witness for you.

Certainly, you cannot be blamed for not knowing that some unthinking judge would do the country the great disservice of commiting him to a home for the insane before the committee had a chance to publicize and place its stamp of approval on his statements about McCarthy. Certainly, you cannot be blamed for being unable to distinguish between his testimony and the testimony of the other witness, Benton, who asked for and was given the right to appear before your committee and publicly "expose" McCarthy.

The Communist Party, which is also doing an excellent job of exposing the evils of McCarthyism, has repeatedly proclaimed that no stone be left unturned in the effort to remove McCarthy from public life. As Lenin said, "resort to lies, trickery, deceit, and dishonesty of any type necessary," in order to destroy those who stand in the way of the Communist movement.

I ask you gentlemen not to be disturbed by those who point out that your committee is trying to do what the Communist Party has officially proclaimed as its No. 1 task. You just keep right on in the same honest, painstaking way of developing the truth. The thinking people of this Nation will not be deceived by those who claim that what you are doing is dishonest. After all, you must serve the interests of the Democrat Party— there is always the chance that the country may be able to survive. What better way could you find to spend taxpayers' money? After all, isn't McCarthy doing the terribly unpatriotic and unethical thing of proving the extent to which the Democrat administration is Communist ridden? Unless he can be discredited, the Democrat Party may be removed from power.

Again may I offer my condolences upon your failure to have your star witness present as planned to open the testimony. Do you not think the judge who committed him should be investigated?

Sincerely yours,

(s/d) Joe McCarthy

In late fall, Senator Benton, campaigning for his first full term in the Senate, invited McCarthy to come into his home state and debate the issues (McCarthy had earlier filed a libel suit against Benton and then dropped it, saying he couldn't find anyone in the whole country who believed Benton's charges and it was no longer necessary to press the charge). Benton lost the election.

During the summer, Senator Herman Welker (McCarthy's friend) had resigned from the Gillette Subcommittee in protest over the continued pursuit of McCarthy. Then Gillette, himself, resigned. Senator Thomas C. Hennings, Jr., took over as Chairman. The latter had the Subcommittee's chief counsel write a stronger letter to McCarthy, "inviting" him to appear at the hearings and setting a deadline shortly after the middle of November.

Senator McCarthy was out of town and later said that he had not received the letter in time to respond, but his administrative assistant had implied to the Subcommittee that the desired information would be forthcoming. As a result, the Subcommittee sent another letter to McCarthy and listed the information it wished McCarthy to provide. This letter, delivered by hand to McCarthy's office on November 21, 1952, delineates the items which most concerned the Subcommittee. As a matter of interest, for this reason, the last few paragraphs of the letter follow:

> The subcommittee is grateful for your offer of assistance, and we want to afford you with every opportunity to offer your explanations with reference to the issues involved. Therefore, although the subcommittee did make itself available during the past week in order to afford you an opportunity to be heard, we shall be at your disposal commencing Saturday, November 22 through, but not later than, Tuesday, November 25, 1952.
>
> This subcommittee has but one object, and that is to reach an impartial and proper conclusion based upon the facts. Your appearance, in person, before the subcommittee will not only give you the opportunity to testify as to any issues of fact which may be in controversy, but will be of the greatest assistance to the subcommittee in its effort to arrive at a proper determination and to embody in its report an accurate representation of the facts.
>
> Pursuant to your request, as transmitted to us through Mr. Kiermas, we are advising you that the subcommittee desires to make inquiry with respect to the following matters:
>
> (1) Whether any funds collected or received by you and by others on your behalf to conduct certain of your activities, including those relating to communism, were ever diverted and used for other purposes inuring to your personal advantage.
>
> (2) Whether you, at any time, used your official position as a United States Senator and as a member of the Banking and Currency Committee, the Joint Housing Committee, and the Senate Investigations Committee to obtain a $10,000 fee from the Lustron Corp., which company was then

almost entirely subsidized by agencies under the jurisdiction of the very committees of which you were a member.

(3) Whether your activities on behalf of certain interest groups, such as housing, sugar, and China, were motivated by self-interest.

(4) Whether your activities with respect to your senatorial campaigns, particularly with respect to the reporting of your financing and your activities relating to the financial transactions with and subsequent employment of Ray Kiermas, involved violations of the Federal and State Corrupt Practices Acts.

(5) Whether loan or other transactions which you had with the Appleton State Bank, of Appleton, Wis., involved violations of tax and banking laws.

(6) Whether you used close associates and members of your family to secrete receipts, income, commodity and stock speculation, and other financial transactions for ulterior motives.

We again assure you of our desire to give you the opportunity to testify, in executive session of the subcommittee, as to the foregoing matters. The 82d Congress expires in the immediate future and the subcommittee must necessarily proceed with dispatch in making its report to this Congress. To that end, we respectfully urge you to arrange to come before us on or before November 25, and thus enable us to do our conscientious best in the interests of the Senate and our obligation to complete our work. We would thank you to advise us immediately, so that we may plan accordingly.

This letter is being transmitted at the direction and with the full concurrence of the membership of this subcommittee.

Sincerely yours,

(s/d)   Thomas C. Hennings, Jr., Chairman

Senator McCarthy was deer hunting in Wisconsin (so he claimed) and did not respond until December 1, at which time his reply—in the form of a brief letter—brushed off the "six insulting questions." To top off Senator McCarthy's cavalier attitude toward the Subcommittee, he said to the press (in a bitter statement about the Subcommittee) that one of its members, Senator Robert Hendrickson, Republican of New Jersey, was "a living miracle in that he is without question the only man who has lived so long with neither brains nor guts."

McCarthy, it seems apparent, was principally concerned with preventing the Gillette-Hennings Committee from taking action. Any delay in action, as a matter of fact, was greatly in his favor.

He accomplished this by attacking the Committee and its members, refusing to cooperate or to appear before the Committee, and—most significantly—by employing the advantage offered him by the press, radio, and TV.

Every blast, every challenge to the Committee, made by McCarthy was considered news. On the other hand, every decent effort on the part of the Committee to be fair and to give McCarthy a chance to be heard received no attention. Before the Committee's position could be made known on any aspect of its investigation, McCarthy had already seized the initiative (he had his friends within the Committee, both on the staff and among the Senators composing the Committee). One of the principal evidences of his taking the initiative—going on the attack—is in McCarthy's snide letters to the Committee chairmen, which he consistently released to the press before the Committee received them and before the Committee could counter the charges.

It should be noted that a characteristic of McCarthyism, as practiced by its author, was to be constantly on the attack. Repeated charges, given great publicity, may be believed by large numbers of people who—as the old adage has it—conclude that where there is smoke there must be fire.

If McCarthy's challenge to the Committee's integrity could have been supported—and if he, who claimed to have great courage, had appeared before the Committee and demonstrated the supposed prejudice of its members and had refuted the charges against himself—What a triumph that would have been!

Had this been possible (and McCarthy did try this on other occasions where he felt he could demonstrate his points, as in the Army-McCarthy hearings and where—as we shall see in a later chapter—he tried to outwit me in calling me before his Subcommittee on Investigations to prove his "Secret Master" theory) we can be certain that he would have attempted to do so.

The internal evidences of the case against McCarthy were certainly damaging. However, the Select Committee (as I must continue to emphasize) did not believe its function was to try McCarthy again for the alleged offenses for which he had been called before the Subcommittee on Privileges and Elections. We considered our responsibility as that of inquiring into McCarthy's alleged contempt for the Gillette Committee and therefore of the Senate, and that we were authorized to do so there was no question.

We determined that the Senate, as a continuing body * has the right to inquire into any matter pertaining to a Senator's fitness to hold his seat in the Senate, even though the matters of question occurred before his election. As

---

* The concept of the Senate as a continuing body is supported by history, precedent, and authority. Members of the Senate are elected for a term of six years, and are divided into classes in order that only one-third of the seats become vacant at the end of each Congress. Therefore, there are always two-thirds of the Senate in office so that the business of the committees of the Senate can be carried on irrespective of elections and even during times when the Congress is not in session.

See page 20 of the Report of the Select Committee, S. Res. 301, in Appendix for further discussion and citation of authorities.

for the Gillette-Hennings subcommittee, this was a lawfully constituted committee, and it had every authority to examine Senator McCarthy's past actions. McCarthy had been given every opportunity to appear before the Subcommittee to answer serious and grave charges but had declined. An invitation, as we will show, is—under the circumstances—as good as a subpoena, and McCarthy had a duty to respond.

The critical issue is that Senator McCarthy had been charged with such wrongdoing that, in the words of the Select Committee, "The mere reading of these matters without deciding or attempting to decide whether they are true or not, makes it clear that the honesty, sincerity, character, and conduct of Senator McCarthy were under inquiry." Thus:

> . . . when the personal honor and official conduct of a Senator of the United States are in question before a duly constituted committee of the Senate, the Senator involved owes a duty to himself, his State, and to the Senate, to appear promptly and cooperate fully when called by a Senate committee charged with the responsibility of inquiry. This must be the rule if the dignity, honor, authority, and powers of the Senate are to be respected and maintained. This duty could not and was not fulfilled by questioning the authority and jurisdiction of the subcommittee by accusing its members of the dishonest expenditure of public funds, or even by charging that the subcommittee was permitting itself to be used to serve the cause of communism. When persons in high places fail to set and meet high standards, the people lose faith. If our people lose faith, our form of Government cannot long endure.
>
> The appearance which we believe was necessary was before a subcommittee of the Senate itself, to which subcommittee the Senate, through its normal processes, had confided a matter affecting its own honor and integrity. In such case, legal process was not and should not be required.

The Select Committee carefully reviewed every exchange between Senator McCarthy and the Subcommittee. It determined that the members of the Subcommittee had been "uniformly courteous and cooperative" in their efforts to get Senator McCarthy to appear and to accommodate themselves to his convenience. Whereas, McCarthy's conduct was "contemptuous, independently of his failure to appear before the subcommittee."

Also, the conduct of Senator McCarthy toward the Senate as a whole was "contumacious" as determined by the Select Committee. The committee's report said:

> It is our opinion that the failure of Senator McCarthy to explain to the Senate these matters: (1) Whether funds collected to fight communism

were diverted to other purposes inuring to his personal advantage; (2) whether certain of his official activities were motivated by self-interest; and (3) whether certain of his activities in senatorial campaigns involved violations of the law; was conduct contumacious toward the Senate and injurious to its effectiveness, dignity, responsibilities, processes, and prestige.

The Select Committee's conclusion, which was to be the principal issue in the final resolution to censure McCarthy, was that "the conduct of the junior Senator from Wisconsin toward the Subcommittee on Privileges and Elections, toward its members, including the statement concerning Senator Hendrickson acting as a member of the subcommittee, and toward the Senate, was contemptuous, contumacious, and denunciatory, without reason or justification, and was obstructive to legislative processes. For this conduct, it is our recommendation that he be censured by the Senate."

Throughout his dealings with the Select Committee, McCarthy was relying upon his proven formula: attack the Committee and its members. On the other hand, he dared not treat the Select Committee with the same contempt shown the Gillette-Hennings Committee, so he did appear before us to answer to the charges. However, he made no effective defense, because his usual method of "defense" was to make a vicious counterattack and the Select Committee would not permit this at the hearings. Since his statements before the Select Committee were required to be pertinent to the issue under investigation, the hearings record on this most crucial issue shows few interesting McCarthy exchanges.

As with the Gillette-Hennings Committee, McCarthy made his main defense before the TV cameras in the hall outside the hearing room and through friendly political columnists in the press, making allegations of prejudice on the part of the Select Committee and its members and challenging the Committee's authority and procedures.

FEW INDIVIDUALS OUTSIDE OF WASHINGTON COULD HAVE AN IDEA OF THE trauma suffered by large numbers of Government employees and their superiors from Senator McCarthy's continuing and pressing encouragement—even demands—that his followers and believers in Government offices send him such information about wrongdoing (and wrong-thinking) in their agency and among their acquaintances as they could supply.

The nature of the appeal was such that perfectly innocent people could be (and, indeed, were) reported to McCarthy for investigation. This could happen to anyone, and many government employees soon got the idea that it was very possible and even likely that it would happen to them. As a result, the atmosphere in Washington was very unsettled.

I learned subsequent to the investigations by the Select Committee (and subsequent to the McCarthy era) some examples of the sickness that overcame many otherwise normal employees. Some employees were so distraught that they either left Government service or became physically ill. Others, caught up in the excitement of supplying information to McCarthy and his Subcommittee, went to excess and then suffered fits of depression as their office friends and acquaintances suffered suspicion and harrassment. Many individuals who felt basically insecure in their jobs or in their personalities undertook to demonstrate their own purity by denouncing or otherwise casting suspicion on others.

That these things were happening was evident to many on Capitol Hill and to many concerned commentators. For this reason, a principal charge made against Senator McCarthy by his colleagues was that he (in the words of Senator Morse's amendment to Senate Resolution 301):

> Openly invited and incited employees of the Government to violate the law and their oaths of office by urging them to make available information, including classified information, which in the opinion of the employees could be of assistance to the junior Senator from Wisconsin in conducting his investigations, even though the supplying of such information by the employee would be illegal and in violation of Presidential order and contrary to the constitutional rights of the Chief Executive under the separation-of-powers doctrine.*

Beyond any inconvenience and unpleasantness to individuals, of course, was the basic threat (as it was widely thought) to orderly administration and con-

*Hearings on S. Res. 301, Part 1, p. 3.

duct of Government. On the other hand, as the Select Committee saw it (and, of course, as Senator McCarthy argued it) was the right of Congress to secure information. The resolution of this perplexing question was difficult.

The following example, studied by the Select Committee, is illustrative of the problem and is certainly the most interesting and well-publicized incident of McCarthy's having obtained information from a Government employee.

During the Army-McCarthy hearings, Senator McCarthy had produced in a rather dramatic fashion a 2¼-page carbon copy of a letter allegedly from FBI Director J. Edgar Hoover to Major General A. R. Bolling of Army Intelligence. This letter, according to the Senator, listed "communists at Fort Monmouth." The question had immediately arisen as to how McCarthy could have obtained such a document and whether his possession of it was a breach of Federal espionage laws.

Not immediately recognizing the document McCarthy held in his hand, and apparently assuming that it was genuine, Army Secretary Robert T. Stevens and Army Counsel Joseph P. Welch* had asked for a ruling from the Chair (Senator Mundt) that the letter not be shown or discussed without obtaining permission from its presumed author, J. Edgar Hoover. Senator Mundt's discretion prevailed over Senator McCarthy's efforts to press the matter, and the FBI was asked to study the document and comment on it.

A legal aid of the Mundt Subcommittee then obtained the letter from McCarthy's assistant, Roy Cohn, and took it to Mr. Hoover. This man, Mr. Robert Collier, was subsequently questioned at length about the alleged letter by Mr. Welch. In the course of this questioning—all of which was ultimately read into the record of the Select Committee's hearings—Mr. Welch was able to demonstrate that the alleged letter was, in fact, a condensation of some information from a classified, 15-page official memorandum from the FBI to Army Intelligence. The original memorandum had listed names of a number of employees at Army installations and followed each name with such derogatory and other information as the FBI had in its possession. The alleged 2¼-page letter had given the names of individuals who were supposed to be part of an espionage ring but did not give any details as to informants or any factual, supporting documentation.

There were two possibilities as to the source of the 2¼-page letter—which, incidentally, McCarthy denied was "spurious" or that it contained "unlawful information"—and it was important to the Select Committee to know which possibility was in fact the truth of the matter. On the one hand, there was the possibility that McCarthy or members of his staff had somehow obtained the

---

*Welch, a Boston lawyer in private practice, had been employed as special counsel by the Army for the hearings.

15-page, original classified document of the FBI and prepared what Army Counsel Welch called a "phony." Or, someone in either the FBI or Army could have prepared the alleged 2¼-page letter from the original 15-page document and forwarded it to McCarthy or one of his aides as a bona fide document . . . and one which would have provided McCarthy with a list of names for his own investigations.

Each member of the Select Committee examined the alleged letter and the testimony taken with respect to it and found no overwhelming evidence to demonstrate either allegation. The Committee, however, considered that McCarthy could well have seen the original 15-page document. One of the reasons for this is to be found in the Senator's original testimony at the Army-McCarthy hearings when he said, with respect to the letter: "If he (Senator Jackson) will look at it, I believe he will find each and every word is identical to the original letter, with the exception of the fact that where there is listed the names of Fort Monmouth employees and the word 'derogatory' put after it in the FBI report, you will find the derogatory information and, perhaps, the names of the informants. If that were included in this letter, Mr. Chairman, then it would be objectionable. We would be violating the rules by submitting it to the Committee. That security information was not in the letter." *

McCarthy insisted that he did not get any of his material from J. Edgar Hoover, and attributed his information to a "young man" in the Army. While he said that the Army informant was "very careful not to include any security information" (which indicates that the Army man may have prepared it), it should be noted that in the statement quoted above, the Senator not only implies detailed knowledge of the original but also seems to take credit for "declassifying" some information (the names) and determining that other facts should not be divulged. Mr. Hoover, in his comments to Mr. Collier, had said that no part of the original memorandum should be revealed to the public.

Walter Winchell, the columnist, was called before the Select Committee to testify because in a syndicated column of his, published in May, 1954, he had said that he had a copy of the 2¼-page letter. Before our Committee he testified that he could not remember who had given him a carbon copy of the letter, but that it was his impression that other newspapermen had also been given copies.

While Mr. Winchell was further asked if he would recognize the person who had passed him the copy of the letter, while standing at the door of the Senate Caucus Room in early May, 1954, and Mr. Winchell said that he thought he would, we did not pursue the matter. It appeared unlikely that further investigation would prove productive.

*Hearings on S. Res. 301, Part 1, p. 104.

Winchell also described before the Select Committee* a conversation he subsequently had with J. Edgar Hoover in which he said: "I have a copy of that letter, John. I want to ask you something. Would you arrest me if I published it?" To this, Mr. Winchell said that Mr. Hoover replied: "Yes." "You're kidding, John," Winchell had responded. "No; I am not," Mr. Hoover is quoted as having answered.

In the hearings before the Select Committee, we established the fact that Senator McCarthy had on numerous occasions invited Government employees to send him information in his capacity as Chairman of the Permanent Subcommittee on Investigations for the Committee on Government Operations. At the time of the Army-McCarthy hearings, for example, the Senator had said: ". . . I would like to notify those 2 million Federal employees that I feel it is their duty to give us any information which they have about graft, corruption, communism, treason and that there is no loyalty to a superior officer which can tower above and beyond their loyalty to their country . . ." And, in addition, he had said: "I don't think that any Government employee can deny the people the right to know what the facts are by using a rubber stamp and stamping something 'secret.' " **

There was no problem here, for McCarthy not only admitted having said these things (or did not deny them), he went on before the Select Committee to add in his own behalf: ". . . I was not asking for general classified information. I was only asking for evidence of wrongdoing."

The Select Committee found that the statements of Senator McCarthy were subject to alternative constructions. On the one hand, the Senator may have—as Chairman of his Subcommittee—merely invited Government employees to supply him information on wrongdoing acquired in the ordinary course of their duties. The second construction was that the Senator's statements urged employees to ransack confidential files regardless of their lawful access to such material and to provide him with classified documents.

If the statements of McCarthy were subject to the second construction, he might well have merited censure on this charge (we concluded), but if the former, more charitable construction was accepted he was probably acting within the prerogatives of his responsibility.

Realizing, as we did, that Congress should not set any precedents which might limit its own access to information, and wishing to be objective and judicial in its ruling, the Select Committee ruled in favor of the first construction and stated that it was "convinced that the invitation so made, affirmed and reasserted by Senator McCarthy was motivated by a sense of official duty and not uttered as

*Hearings on S. Res. 301, Part 1, p. 153.
**Hearings on S. Res. 301, Part 1, pp. 87 and 89.

the fruit of evil design or wrongful intent." * The Committee added that the conduct of Senator McCarthy in inviting employees to supply him information ". . . without expressly excluding therefrom classified documents, tends to create a disruption of the orderly and constitutional functioning of the executive and legislative branches of the Government, which tends to bring both into disrepute. Such conduct cannot be condoned and is deemed improper." **

The Select Committee went on to conclude that it preferred to give Senator McCarthy the benefit of whatever doubts and uncertainties may have confused the issue in the past, and in recognition of his responsibilities as a Chairman of a Senate Committee, it did not feel justified in proposing his acts in this area as ground for censure.

However, the Select Committee moved to tighten up procedures in the Senate by recommending to the Senate leadership that it bring Senators with Committee responsibilities together with heads of executive agencies to "clarify the mechanisms" for obtaining restricted information.

As to the specific additional charge that Senator McCarthy had obtained a classified document, or one containing classified information (the 2¼-page letter) and had attempted to place this in the public record, the Select Committee used stronger language. It said: "This conduct on his part shows a disregard of the evident purpose to be served by such a document and overlooks the serious import which attaches to a document affecting the national defense, and the dangers flowing from causing such information to become public knowledge." Then again, the Select Committee said: "This disposition on the part of Senator McCarthy to determine for himself what is or is not security information regardless of the evident classified marking on a document, confirmed by the opinion of a duly constituted agency authorized to make such a ruling, evidences a lack of regard for responsibility to the laws and regulations providing for orderly determination of such matters." †

The Select Committee gave McCarthy credit, however, for acting in a "bona fide belief that the document was a valid rather than a spurious instrument and offered it in evidence as such." ‡

The formal conclusions of the Select Committee were that: ". . . in offering to make public the contents of this classified document Senator McCarthy committed a grave error. He manifested a high degree of irresponsibility toward the purposes, of the statutes and Executive directives prohibiting the disclosure to unauthorized persons of classified information . . ." But finally, that McCarthy

*Report of the Select Committee, p. 38.
**Ibid., p. 39.
†Ibid., p. 43.
‡Ibid., p. 44.

". . . was under stress and strain of being tried or investigated . . . He offered the document in this investigation, which was then being contested at every step by both sides. The contents of the document were relevant . . ." For these "mitigating circumstances" we did not recommend censure on this matter.*

Now, looking back upon what the Select Committee did when I was Chairman —and, make no mistake about it, there was always unanimity within the Committee—I can see no alternative to our conclusions. This is not to say, as some have so blithely been willing to charge, that I was blind to what McCarthy was doing in soliciting information from Government employees. There can be no question that he was searching for names of individuals to haul before his Subcommittee. From this he obtained headlines. This was his method.

With respect to the charges in this category of "encouragement to violate the law" we were required to stick to the issue. That human beings, many of them obviously innocent of wrongdoing, were dragged roughly through the dirt was another question. This was to be resolved—at least in part—by the Senate in its final action against Senator McCarthy.

*Ibid., pp. 44–45.

ANOTHER MAJOR CHARGE AGAINST SENATOR MC CARTHY REFERRED TO THE
Select Committee was that described by Senators Flanders and Morse in their
respective amendments: that McCarthy had "ridiculed his colleagues in the Senate,
defaming them publicly and in vulgar and base language" as Flanders put it;
and that McCarthy had "unfairly accused his fellow Senators Gillette, Monroney,
Hendrickson, Hayden and Hennings of improper conduct in carrying out their
duties as Senators" as Morse phrased it.

Much of this, of course, had been inquired into with respect to McCarthy's
attitude toward the Gillette Committee. However, we heard the testimony of
two Associated Press reporters that bore specifically upon two of McCarthy's
best-known remarks about his colleagues.

Bernard Livingstone, an AP reporter assigned to Capitol Hill, was called
before the Select Committee to tell about the story he filed in which Senator
McCarthy made his alleged remarks about Senator Flanders.

The time was during the Army-McCarthy hearings, and Senator Flanders
had prepared a speech to deliver on the floor of the Senate in which he spoke
about our civilization coming to an end and in which he drew a parallel between Hitler and McCarthy. Learning of this speech, Livingstone obtained a
copy—marking certain passages of interest, on which he hoped to get Mc-
Carthy's response—and during the hearings stepped over to McCarthy to show
him the speech.

Livingstone testified that McCarthy looked at the speech and smiled, and when
asked if he had anything to say replied (speaking of Flanders): "Senile! I think
they should get a man with a net and take him to a good, quiet place."

Joseph Hall, Jr., another AP reporter on the Hill, was similarly called before
the Committee to tell about a news story that he filed in which McCarthy (in
discussing what we have called the Gillette Committee's report) was quoted as
making unflattering remarks about Senator Hendrickson on the Subcommittee
on Privileges and Elections.

Mr. Hall was asked to read paragraphs from his news account. In his telephone
comment, McCarthy said:

> This report accused me either directly or indirectly or by innuendo and
> intimation of the most dishonest and improper conduct.
> If it is true, I am unfit to serve in the Senate. If it is false, then the
> three men who joined in it—namely, Hendrickson, Hennings, and Hayden
> —are dishonest beyond words.

If those three men honestly think that all of the four things of which they have accused me are true, they have a deep, moral obligation tomorrow [the opening of the 83d Congress] to move that the Senate does not seat me as a Senator.

If they think the report is true, they will do that. If they know the report is completely false and that it has been issued only for its smear value, then they will not dare to present this case to the Senate.

This Committee has been squandering taxpayers' money on this smear campaign for nearly 18 months. If they feel that they are honest and right, why do they fear presenting their case to the Senate?

I challenge them to do that. If they do not, they will have proved their complete dishonesty.

I can understand the actions of the leftwingers in the administration, like Hennings and Hayden. As far as Hendrickson is concerned, I frankly can bear him no ill will.

Suffice it to say that he is a living miracle in that he is without question the only man in the world who has lived so long with neither brains nor guts.

The Select Committee stated in its report: *

The remarks of Senator McCarthy concerning Senator Flanders were highly improper. The committee finds, however they were induced by Senator Flanders' conduct in respect to Senator McCarthy in the Senate caucus room, and in delivering provocative speeches concerning Senator McCarthy on the Senate floor. For these reasons, the committee concludes the remarks with reference to Senator Flanders do not constitute a basis for censure.

It will be noted here, in response to questions of a number of newspaper columnists and letter writers at the time, that the Select Committee did not excuse Senator Flanders for what might be considered his "highly improper remarks" about Senator McCarthy. The Select Committee could not recommend censure of Flanders for, even if we had desired to, that was not our assignment from the Senate. We were assigned to inquire only into charges against Senator McCarthy.

With respect to Senator McCarthy's remarks about Senator Hendrickson, the Select Committee made its judgment in connection with the entire matter of Senator McCarthy's attitude toward the Gillette Committee.

Referring to the comments by McCarthy, the Select Committee said: **

*Report of the Select Committee, page 46.
**Ibid., pp. 29–30.

It is the opinion of the select committee that these charges of political waste and dishonesty for improper motives were denunciatory and unjustified.

In this connection, attention is directed to the charges referred to this committee relating to words uttered by the junior Senator from Wisconsin about individual Senators.

It has been established, without denial and in fact with confirmation and reiteration, that Senator McCarthy, in reference to the official actions of the junior Senator from New Jersey, Mr. Hendrickson, as a member of the Subcommittee on Privileges and Elections, questioned both his moral courage and his mental ability.

His public statement with reference to Senator Hendrickson was vulgar and insulting. Any Senator has the right to question, criticize, differ from, or condemn an official action of the body of which he is a member, or of the constituent committees which are working arms of the Senate in proper language. But he has no right to impugn the motives of individual Senators responsible for official actions, nor to reflect upon their personal character for what official action they took.

With respect to what McCarthy said about his colleagues, it should be carefully noted that concern was not based on heated exchanges on the spur of the moment but stemmed from his attitude toward—that is, his contempt for —the Senate. The Committee said, in the same context as the above quotation: "If a Senator must first give consideration to whether an official action can be wantonly impugned by a colleague, as having been motivated by a lack of the very qualities and capacities every Senator is presumed to have, the processes of the Senate will be destroyed."

ONE OF THE LARGEST, MOST VOLUBLE PETITION CAMPAIGNS IN THE HISTORY of the United States involved the issue of "Who Promoted Peress?" Thousands upon thousands of postcards and letters poured into Washington from all over the country and piled up on the desks of every Senator and Congressman. Similar correspondence made its way into the "letters to the editors" columns of newspapers throughout the land. Almost all contained the simple query about Peress, and many contained diatribes about communism and the influence of communists in Government. Many were vicious, and used language as crude as any ever permitted to pass through the mails.

Printed stickers asking the same question were stuck on envelopes and letters of business and ordinary personal mail. Bumper stickers too posed the ubiquitous query, and certain radio and TV commentators played upon the listeners' confusions by inserting the perennial question: "Who Promoted Peress?" Nearly two million signatures, so it was reported, were collected on a petition backing McCarthy's insistence upon an answer and thousands rallied at mass meetings where placards paraded the slogan: "Who Promoted Peress?"

The point at issue may seem very small indeed and from the vantage point of many years away, it appears in fact to be petty. But to millions at the time, it was a *cause célèbre*.

A dentist from Queens, New York, Irving Peress was caught up in the doctor draft during the Korean War. Entering active duty at the rank of captain, he continued his filling of cavities in the service of his country. Several months after induction he requested and received transfer to a post close to home, in order to be near his ailing family. This brought him to Camp Kilmer, New Jersey (a staging area for personnel going to and from Europe and of little strategic importance) on March 14, 1953.

Shortly after his arrival the Army's red-tape slowed administrative apparatus discovered that Peress, when inducted, had completed and signed a personnel form, which said among other things that he was not and had not been a member of any subversive group. A month and a half later he failed to sign a loyalty certificate, which was not immediately noticed. When questioned about it later and asked through what is technically called an "interrogatory" about affiliations with subversive organizations, he refused to answer, claiming it an infringement on his privacy and upon his Constitutional rights under the Fifth Amendment.

The then Commanding General of Camp Kilmer ordered a "complaint type investigation" which turned up some allegedly derogatory material. This material, completed on April 15, 1953, was forwarded to headquarters of the 1st Army with recommendation for Peress's discharge (which action had to be taken at that level). On April 30, 1953, the Surgeon General recommended Peress's discharge, as did the Assistant Chief of Staff, G-2 (military intelligence), 1st Army, on July 7, 1953.

Meanwhile, on the 29th of June, 1953, a law was passed correcting or adjusting the rank of nearly 700 officers in the medical, dental, and veterinary corps who had been inducted as captains but were clearly qualified to be majors. Accordingly, an order was issued by the Surgeon General on October 14, 1953, calling for automatic adjustment of the rank of every officer on the list including Captain Peress, and a large number of others elsewhere. The file containing the derogatory information on Peress (having been forwarded to 1st Army headquarters) was no longer at Camp Kilmer. In the press of a great many personnel actions it did not come to the attention of anyone that Peress was being "promoted." This action, making Peress a Major, was completed on November 2.

Meanwhile General Ralph Zwicker, destined to be the real victim of the Peress furor,* assumed command of Camp Kilmer on July 15, 1953. Zwicker, a solid, old-line Army man, had received several awards (including the Silver Star, Bronze Star, and Legion of Merit) for bravery and gallantry in action in World War II. Managing such a large personnel operation was new to the former battlefield commander, and Zwicker went about learning his job methodically. On October 20, 1953, according to a schedule Zwicker had set up, his G-2 man came in to discuss security matters and said that the only pending case was that of Peress. Zwicker was outraged over the delay in securing the recommended discharge of Peress, and on the very next day (October 21) wrote his superiors urging the immediate separation of Peress from the service. As Zwicker tells it today: "I didn't want a man in the Army who had reservations about signing a loyalty certificate and who, in effect, had falsified his record."

Later, on November 3, 1953, Zwicker wrote a more sharply worded letter to his superiors stating that there was information in the files which ". . . determined that this officer (referred to by Zwicker as "Captain" Peress, and obviously not yet informed that Peress was now a Major) was a known and active communist in Queens, New York." There was other information, supposedly corroborating this judgment, which has never been made part of the public record. At any rate, as a result of Zwicker's urging and personal interest, the order to discharge Peress "within 90 days, or earlier if the officer so requests it" came down from 1st Army headquarters on December 30, 1953.

McCarthy, daily more anxious to produce a bona fide communist from the

---

*Peress himself is said to have benefitted from the publicity surrounding the affair; he set up a new office after his discharge from the Army.

vast numbers he was hinting at, is reported to have "discovered" the Peress
case (but, apparently, not the name of Irving Peress) in December 1953.
According to former McCarthy aide Roy Cohn,* a "high-ranking general" who
was becoming "increasingly alarmed at the inefficiency of the Army's Security
program" and who "had watched the Peress case develop" alerted McCarthy by
telephone to the possibilities of an investigation at Camp Kilmer. According to
the record, the first check at Camp Kilmer was made on January 22, 1954, by a
McCarthy investigator, C. George Anastos.

Anastos called General Zwicker and reported that he had heard of a "doctor"
at Camp Kilmer who was under investigation. Apparently, Anastos had no
other lead.** Zwicker replied that if Mr. Anastos was indeed from Senator
McCarthy's office he would be glad to give such cooperation as he could and
any information which might not be classified, but that he wished to verify
Anastos's claim and would like to call him back. With the Peress file in front of
him (for this was the only case that Zwicker could think of), the General called
McCarthy's office and verified the call from Anastos. With Anastos on the line,
Zwicker then said: "I think the case you are referring to is that of one Irving
Peress."

Later, in the harangue that continued for months and years through three
Senate investigative committees, Anastos was to "reconstruct" (from memory,
and also supposedly from notes—which were never produced—made by a stenog-
rapher in Anastos's office who claimed she had listened in on the conversation)
the telephone call in which he claimed that Zwicker provided the McCarthy
investigator with details of Peress' alleged communist background (including
the alleged communist activities of his wife, Elaine). Zwicker recalled for the
benefit of subsequent investigating committees that he had offered no confidential,
security information at all and had merely given Anastos the customary information on name, address, and the like.†

*Roy Cohn, *McCarthy* (New York City, The New American Library, 1968), pp.
96 and 99.
(Note: Senator McCarthy told the Select Committee in its hearings—page 182,
thereof—that it was his belief that he first learned of the Peress case in November
1954, after a conversation with Maj. Gen Kirke B. Lawton.)
**As Robert Kennedy pointed out in the hearings on the nomination of Brig.
Gen. Ralph W. Zwicker (page 8, Hearings before the Senate Committee on Armed
Services, February 20, March 21, and 22, 1957): "Mr. Anastos said, stated under
oath, at that time the committee did not have even Irving Peress' name, let alone
any of the other information." At the same hearing (page 18) McCarthy admitted
the same thing.
†As the several investigations contorted in upon themselves, Zwicker was ultimately investigated by the FBI (at McCarthy's insistence) for evidence of perjury,

Making the most of the possibilities for embarrassment created by a bureaucratic slip, and embarking upon a harrassment of Zwicker which would last until his own death in 1957, McCarthy pursued the "Peress issue" with his usual flair for publicity. He ordered Peress before the Permanent Subcommittee on Government Operations for questioning. Appearing, Peress took refuge in the Fifth Amendment, and requested and received discharge from the Army the following day.

Senator McCarthy and his staff then called a hearing in New York City on February 18, 1954, to inquire of General Zwicker how Major Peresss had received his promotion and why he had been honorably discharged from the Army the day after having refused to answer questions under the right offered by the Fifth Amendment.

Zwicker, with an aide, arrived at the courthouse on Foley Square in New York the morning of the day he was to appear in executive session. As there was a public hearing that morning, during which the Peress matter was being further examined through other witnesses, Zwicker and his aide went in as observers. As it happened, they sat immediately behind a New York salesman who was to report to McCarthy and bear witness against Zwicker to the effect that the General was disrespectful and uncooperative.*

McCarthy (or someone on the staff) recognized General Zwicker in the audience and asked him to stand in order to answer a question about Peress. This question was whether Peress had access to secret information after, as McCarthy put it, ". . . it was fully known that he was a communist."

General Zwicker replied that Peress did not have access to secret information. McCarthy contradicted him, saying that the dentist's Army file showed that he had been considered for sensitive work. Then the Senator instructed General Zwicker to have an aide call Camp Kilmer and obtain the information from the official Army confidential file before the General was to appear in executive session that afternoon.

General Zwicker responded: "Even if I did know, I would not be privileged

his promotion held up, and was finally cleared by the Justice Department. (His nomination to Major General was considered by the Senate Armed Services Committee, debated on the floor of the Senate on April 1, 1957, and finally confirmed by a vote of 70 to 2 . . . with only Senators Malone and McCarthy opposed.) The conclusion: Zwicker could not possibly have given the specific information Anastos has asserted he had obtained from Zwicker, because it had never been available to him to give. Anastos—perhaps through inadvertance—had combined information in his report about the Zwicker call with information he had obtained from his own investigative sources and suppliers of information.

*Testimony of William J. Harding, Jr., Hearings on S. Res. 301, part 1, pp. 175–181. Quotes from the hearings record.

to tell you, under the Executive Order which forbids us to discuss matters of that nature."

Senator McCarthy then said sharply: "I may say, General, you will be in difficulty if you refuse to tell us what sensitive work a communist was being considered for. There is no Executive Order for the purpose of protecting communists. I want to tell you right now, you will be asked that question this afternoon. You will be ordered to make available that information."

Upon sitting down, according to the testimony of the witness sitting in front of Zwicker, the General was supposed to have muttered: "You S.O.B.!" Then turning to his aide, the General was supposed to have said: "You see, I told you this is what we'd get!" This was not corroborated, and General Zwicker later said that he must have made another statement which was misinterpreted.* Nonetheless McCarthy seems to have given credence to the witness' uncorroborated story and his relations with General Zwicker quickly worsened. (Although during the noon intermission, as they met briefly in the men's room and certainly before McCarthy got the report on Zwicker's alleged remark the two talked about Wisconsin in a friendly manner.)

Although Zwicker had been helpful and cooperative with McCarthy's aides (Anastos and Juliana) from the beginning, supplying them such information as regulations permitted, and he had been sympathetic with McCarthy's avowed objectives of anti-communism, this first observation of McCarthy "at work" greatly cooled his enthusiasm.

As Zwicker now tells of the incident, not only had he seen McCarthy abuse witnesses, but for no apparent reason except to publicly humiliate him as an officer of the United States Army—and this at first sight, and without provocation—McCarthy had attacked him. It was this, he said, that put him on alert.

The General resolved to be circumspect in all his answers and, further, he felt required to rely on his interpretation of the Executive Order against release of information of a confidential, security nature. It was precisely this type of information that Senator McCarthy had demonstrated he was determined to obtain.

The record shows beyond question that Zwicker had made every effort on his own to have Peress removed from service, long before McCarthy got on to the case. In addition, after being contacted by McCarthy's office, Zwicker

*Senator Case reminds us (see Congressional Record, Vol. 100, Part 12, November 18, 1954, page 16123) that McCarthy had just asked Zwicker if Peress had ever served in a sensitive position such as Officer of the Day (or, in Army parlance, O.D.). The possibility that Zwicker may have muttered something like: "He never served as O.D."—plus Zwicker's insistence that he did not call the Senator an S.O.B.—is sufficient to give the General the benefit of the doubt.

provided such information as he could without violating security regulations. Further, on his own initiative, Zwicker called McCarthy's office to say that Peress was being discharged. Later Zwicker gave Mr. Juliana of McCarthy's office a copy of the instructions from the Adjutant General to discharge Peress.* It should be noted that this precise information was in McCarthy's hands five days before Zwicker was hailed before McCarthy and abused for his supposed hesitancy to name the superior who had signed this order.

At the time he reported to McCarthy the imminent discharge of Peress, Zwicker had also inquired carefully into legal possibilities of holding up Peress's discharge, and had learned that there were no legal grounds on which this could be done (Peress had committed no overt act).

On Saturday, January 30, Peress—before the Subcommittee on Investigations —had been asked by McCarthy if he had been asked to resign. "Yes," said Peress, he had been asked to resign (or, more accurately, he had been told he was to be discharged no later than March 31 but could elect to select an earlier date). Upon learning this, and apprehensive that Peress would get out of the Army before further inquiry could take place or before a court martial could be held, McCarthy hastened on Monday morning, February 1, to write Secretary of the Army Stevens a letter asking for both further investigation and a court martial of Peress. On the same morning, Peress asked Zwicker for an immediate discharge which he understood was his right. Zwicker said that it would take a day to process. At First Army headquarters, that afternoon of February 1 and the following morning, it was determined that Zwicker's discharge could not be held up as there were no legal grounds for doing so. In his own confrontation with McCarthy, Zwicker was careful to point out these facts and that he had no alternative but to give Peress his discharge.

McCarthy also knew, of course, that the "promotion" of Peress had been an automatic adjustment of rank required by law and that it affected several hundred officers. Zwicker had taken pains to point this out to Anastos and later to Juliana.

Finally, two days before the Zwicker questioning, McCarthy had received a long and detailed letter from Secretary of the Army Stevens fully explaining the handling of the Peress case. In the face of all these facts, in the questioning of General Zwicker before the Committee, it would appear that McCarthy and Roy Cohn were chiefly interested in leading General Zwicker into making statements which would contribute to the over-all objective of showing an Army "cover-up" for the promotion and honorable discharge of Irving Peress. General Zwicker resisted this effort, leading McCarthy to become frustrated and furious.

The questioning of General Zwicker was in executive session, with only

*Hearings on S. Res. 301, Part 1, Page 455.

Senator McCarthy—of the entire Subcommittee on Investigations—present, with some of his aides. Zwicker, who had a digestive upset that day, took with him Captain William J. Woodward, a medical officer, as his personal physician.

The record: *

MR. COHN. Now, General, would you like to be able to tell us exactly what happened in that case, and what steps you took and others took down at Kilmer to take action against Peress a long time before action was finally forced by the committee?

GENERAL ZWICKER. That is a toughie.

MR. COHN. All I am asking you now is if you could, if you were at liberty to do so, would you like to be in a position to tell us that story?

GENERAL ZWICKER. Well, may I say that if I were in a position to do so, I would be perfectly glad to give the committee any information that they desired.

MR. COHN. You certainly feel that that information would not reflect unfavorably on you; is that correct?

GENERAL ZWICKER. Definitely not.

MR. COHN. And would not reflect unfavorably on a number of other people at Kilmer and the First Army.

GENERAL ZWICKER. Definitely not.

The CHAIRMAN. It would reflect unfavorably upon some of them, of course?

GENERAL ZWICKER. That I can't answer, sir. I don't know.

The CHAIRMAN. Well, you know that somebody has kept this man on, knowing he was a Communist, do you not?

GENERAL ZWICKER. No, sir.

The CHAIRMAN. You know that somebody has kept him on knowing that he has refused to tell whether he was a Communist, do you not?

GENERAL ZWICKER. I am afraid that would come under the category of the Executive order, Mr. Chairman.

The CHAIRMAN. What?

GENERAL ZWICKER. I am afraid an answer to that question would come under the category of the Presidential Executive order.

The CHAIRMAN. You will be ordered to answer the question.

GENERAL ZWICKER. Would you repeat the question, please?

MR. COHN. Read it to the general.

(The question referred to was read by the reporter.)

GENERAL ZWICKER. I respectfully decline to answer, Mr. Chairman, on the grounds of the directive, Presidential directive, which, in my interpretation, will not permit me to answer that question.

The CHAIRMAN. You know that somebody signed or authorized an

* Hearings on S. Res., Part 1, page 237 and following.

honorable discharge for this man, knowing that he was a fifth amendment Communist, do you not?

GENERAL ZWICKER.   I know that an honorable discharge was signed for the man.

The CHAIRMAN.   The day the honorable discharge was signed, were you aware of the fact that he had appeared before our committee?

GENERAL ZWICKER.   I was

The CHAIRMAN.   And had refused to answer certain questions?

GENERAL ZWICKER.   No, sir, not specifically on answering any questions. I knew that he had appeared before your committee.

The CHAIRMAN.   Didn't you read the news?

GENERAL ZWICKER.   I read the news releases.

The CHAIRMAN.   And the news releases were to the effect that he had refused to tell whether he was a Communist, and that there was evidence that he had attended Communist leadership schools. It was on all the wire service stories, was it not? You knew generally what he was here for, did you not?

GENERAL ZWICKER.   Yes; indeed.

The CHAIRMAN.   And you knew generally that he had refused to tell whether he was a Communist, did you not?

GENERAL ZWICKER.   I don't recall whether he refused to tell whether he was a Communist.

The CHAIRMAN.   Are you the commanding officer there?

GENERAL ZWICKER.   I am the commanding general.

The CHAIRMAN.   Then, General, you knew, did you not, that he appeared before the committee and refused, on the grounds of the fifth amendment, to tell about all of his Communist activities? You knew that, did you not?

GENERAL ZWICKER.   I knew everything that was in the press.

The CHAIRMAN.   Don't be coy with me, General.

GENERAL ZWICKER.   I am not being coy, sir.

The CHAIRMAN.   Did you have that general picture?

GENERAL ZWICKER.   I believe I remember reading in the paper that he had taken refuge in the fifth amendment to avoid answering questions before the committee.

The CHAIRMAN.   About communism?

GENERAL ZWICKER.   I am not too certain about that.

The CHAIRMAN.   Do you mean that you did not have enough interest in the case, General, the case of this major who was in your command, to get some idea of what questions he had refused to answer. Is that correct?

GENERAL ZWICKER.   I think that is not putting it quite right, Mr. Chairman.

The CHAIRMAN.   You put it right, then.

GENERAL ZWICKER.   I have great interest in all of the officers of my command, with whatever they do.

The CHAIRMAN.   Let's stick to fifth-amendment Communists, now. Let's stick to him. You told us you read the press releases.

GENERAL ZWICKER.   I did.

The CHAIRMAN.   But now you indicate that you did not know that he refused to tell about his Communist activities. Is that correct?

GENERAL ZWICKER.   I know that he refused to answer questions for the committee.

The CHAIRMAN.   Did you know that he refused to answer questions about his Communist activities?

GENERAL ZWICKER.   Specifically, I don't believe so.

The CHAIRMAN.   Did you have any idea?

GENERAL ZWICKER.   Of course I had an idea.

The CHAIRMAN.   What do you think he was called down here for?

GENERAL ZWICKER.   For that specific purpose.

The CHAIRMAN.   Then you knew that those were the questions he was asked, did you not? General, let's try and be truthful. I am going to keep you here as long as you keep hedging and hemming.

GENERAL ZWICKER.   I am not hedging.

The CHAIRMAN.   Or hawing.

GENERAL ZWICKER.   I am not hawing, and I don't like to have anyone impugn my honesty, which you just about did.

The CHAIRMAN.   Either your honesty or your intelligence; I can't help impugning one or the other, when you tell us that a major in your command who was known to you to have been before a Senate committee, and of whom you read the press releases very carefully—to now have you sit here and tell us that you did not know whether he refused to answer questions about Communist activities. I had seen all the press releases, and they all dealt with that. So when you do that, General, if you will pardon me, I cannot help but question either your honesty or your intelligence, one or the other. I want to be frank with you on that.

The CHAIRMAN.   Let me ask this question: If this man, after the order came up, after the order of the 18th came up, prior to his getting an honorable discharge, were guilty of some crime—let us say that he held up a bank or stole an automobile—and you heard of that the day before—let us say you heard of it the same day that you heard of my letter—could you then have taken steps to prevent his discharge, or would he have automatically been discharged?

GENERAL ZWICKER.   I would have definitely taken steps to prevent discharge.

The CHAIRMAN.   In other words, if you found that he was guilty of improper conduct, conduct unbecoming an officer, we will say, then you would not have allowed the honorable discharge to go through, would you?

GENERAL ZWICKER.   If it were outside the directive of this order?

The CHAIRMAN.   Well, yes, let us say it were outside the directive.

GENERAL ZWICKER.   Then I certainly would never have discharged him until that part of the case—

The CHAIRMAN.   Let us say he went out and stole $50 the night before.

GENERAL ZWICKER.   He wouldn't have been discharged.

The CHAIRMAN.   Do you think stealing $50 is more serious than being a traitor to the country as part of the Communist conspiracy?

GENERAL ZWICKER.   That, sir, was not my decision.

The CHAIRMAN.   You said if you learned that he stole $50, you would have prevented his discharge. You did learn something much more serious than that. You learned that he had refused to tell whether he was a Communist. You learned that the chairman of a Senate committee suggested he be court-martialed. And you say if he had stolen $50 he would not have gotten the honorable discharge. But merely being a part of the Communist conspiracy, and the chairman of the committee asking that he be court-martialed, would not give you grounds for holding up his discharge. Is that correct?

GENERAL ZWICKER.   Under the terms of this letter, that is correct, Mr. Chairman.

The CHAIRMAN.   That letter says nothing about stealing $50, and it does not say anything about being a Communist. It does not say anything about his appearance before our committee. He appeared before our committee after that order was made out.

Do you think you sound a bit ridiculous, General, when you say that for $50, you would prevent his being discharged, but for being a part of the conspiracy to destroy this country you could not prevent his discharge?

GENERAL ZWICKER.   I did not say that, sir.

The CHAIRMAN.   Let's go over that. You did say if you found out he stole $50 the night before, he would not have gotten an honorable discharge the next morning?

GENERAL ZWICKER.   That is correct.

The CHAIRMAN.   You did learn, did you not, from the newspaper reports, that this man was part of the Communist conspiracy, or at least that there was strong evidence that he was. Did you not think that was more serious than the theft of $50?

GENERAL ZWICKER.   He has never been tried for that, sir, and there was evidence, Mr. Chairman—

The CHAIRMAN.   Don't you give me doubletalk. The $50 case, that he had stolen the night before, he has not been tried for that.

GENERAL ZWICKER.   That is correct. He didn't steal it yet.

The CHAIRMAN. Would you wait until he was tried for stealing the $50 before you prevented his honorable discharge?

GENERAL ZWICKER. Either tried or exonerated.

The CHAIRMAN. You would hold up the discharge until he was tried or exonerated?

GENERAL ZWICKER. For stealing the $50; yes.

The CHAIRMAN. But if you heard that this man was a traitor—in other words, instead of hearing that he had stolen $50 from the corner store, let us say you heard that he was a traitor, he belonged to the Communist conspiracy; that a Senate committee had the sworn testimony to that effect. Then would you hold up his discharge until he was either exonerated or tried?

GENERAL ZWICKER. I am not going to answer that question, I don't believe, the way you want it, sir.

The CHAIRMAN. I just want you to tell me the truth.

GENERAL ZWICKER. On all of the evidence or anything that had been presented to me as Commanding General of Camp Kilmer, I had no authority to retain him in the service.

The CHAIRMAN. Would you tell us, General, why $50 is so much more important to you than being part of the conspiracy to destroy a nation which you are sworn to defend?

GENERAL ZWICKER. Mr. Chairman, it is not, and you know that as well as I do.

The CHAIRMAN. I certainly do. That is why I cannot understand you sitting, there, General, a General in the Army, and telling me that you could not, would not, hold up his discharge having received information—

GENERAL ZWICKER. I could not hold up his discharge.

The CHAIRMAN. Why could you not do it in the case of an allegation of membership in a Communist conspiracy, where you could if you merely heard some private's word that he had stolen $50?

GENERAL ZWICKER. Because, Mr. Senator, any information that appeared in the press or any releases was well known to me and well known to plenty of other people long prior to the time that you ever called this man for investigation, and there were no facts or no allegations, nothing presented from the time that he appeared before your first investigation that was not apparent prior to that time.

The CHAIRMAN. In other words, as you sat here this morning and listened to the testimony you heard nothing new?

MR. COHN. Nothing substantially new?

GENERAL ZWICKER. I don't believe so.

The CHAIRMAN. So that all of these facts were known at the time he was ordered to receive an honorable discharge?

GENERAL ZWICKER. I believe they are all on record; yes, sir.

The CHAIRMAN. Do you think, General, that anyone who is responsible for giving an honorable discharge to a man who has been named under oath as a member of the Communist conspiracy should himself be removed from the military?

GENERAL ZWICKER. You are speaking of generalities now, and not on specifics—is that right, sir, not mentioning about any one particular person?

The CHAIRMAN. That is right.

GENERAL ZWICKER. I have no belief for that kind of person, and if there exists or has existed something in the system that permits that, I say that that is wrong.

The CHAIRMAN. You have a rather important job. I want to know how you feel about getting rid of Communists.

GENERAL ZWICKER. I am all for it.

The CHAIRMAN. All right. You will answer that question, unless you take the fifth amendment. I do not care how long we stay here, you are going to answer it.

GENERAL ZWICKER. Do you mean how I feel toward Communists?

The CHAIRMAN. I mean exactly what I asked you General: nothing else. And anyone with the brains of a 5-year-old child can understand that question.

The reporter will read it to you as often as you need to hear it so you can answer it, and then you will answer it.

GENERAL ZWICKER. Start it over, please.

(The question was reread by the reporter.)

GENERAL ZWICKER. I do not think he should be removed from the military.

The CHAIRMAN. Then, General, you should be removed from any command. Any man who has been given the honor of being promoted to general and who says, 'I will protect another general who protected Communists,' is not fit to wear that uniform, General. I think it is a tremendous disgrace to the Army to have this sort of thing given to the public. I intend to give it to them. I have a duty to do that. I intend to repeat to the press exactly what you said. So you know that. You will be back here, General.

Upon conclusion of the executive session, and prior to excusing General Zwicker, Senator McCarthy shook his finger at Zwicker and said: "General, you will be back on Tuesday, and at that time I am going to put you on display and let the American public see what kind of officers we have."

Then, contrary to the rules of his own Committee which provided: "All testimony taken in executive session shall be kept secret and will not be released or used in public sessions without the approval of a majority of the subcommittee," McCarthy immediately called reporters into the hearing room and gave them a résumé of Zwicker's testimony. This, of course, was McCarthy's unflattering interpretation of it.

McCarthy said that Zwicker had testified he could do nothing to hold up the discharge of Peress. He added that he would ask Secretary of the Army Stevens to "have a 'new look' at the top echelon of the Army or whether those who have coddled communists, a practice which has been going on for 20 years, are to continue in command." *

He added that Zwicker's appearance before the committee was "a disgraceful performance."

The next day, Zwicker countered with his own version of what happened (at the request of Army Secretary Stevens) and added that McCarthy's statements were distorted. As a result of the charges and countercharges, the Subcommittee on Investigations ordered released the transcript of the hearing.

Zwicker never appeared before the McCarthy committee again (although summoned) because of the intervention of Stevens. The Army Secretary referred to McCarthy's treatment of Zwicker and the language he used as "shocking" and "humiliating." ** He said that these "unfair attacks" on officers would destroy Army morale if permitted to continue, and ordered all Army personnel to ignore summons to the McCarthy committee, saying that he would appear to testify if McCarthy wanted to know more. The sparks flew for several days over this affair between McCarthy and Stevens, but McCarthy did not press the matter and chose to confine his comments to charges of Army cover-up of personnel in high places.

McCarthy's release of his version of the Zwicker hearing to the press, without appropriate approval, was one of the points of censure recommended by the Select Committee. In developing the facts of the case, the Select Committee noted that McCarthy had first denied that he had given material to the press † and then admitted that he had given a "résumé," which he lamely excused as the usual practice of his committee.

There were several legal questions considered by the Select Committee with respect to Senator McCarthy's conduct toward General Zwicker. In the first place, the Select Committee resolved the question of whether Zwicker was telling the truth or was in any way intentionally irritating or evasive or arrogant (as McCarthy had charged). The Select Committee concluded that Zwicker was "a truthful witness" and that "his examination was unfair" and that "General Zwicker testified as fully and frankly as he could."

*Washington *Post,* February 19, 1954, page 12.
***Ibid.,* February 22, 1954, p. 1.
†Hearings on S. Res. 301, Part 1, pages 349–350.

Further, the Select Committee concluded that the "source of any resulting irritation on the part of the examiner (McCarthy)" was his own conduct in asking "long and hypothetical questions and questions that are not clear even upon careful inspection and reflection." Zwicker, on the other hand, was "cooperative and helpful" and there was "in the record no single instance which supports the conclusion that he (Zwicker) was intentionally irritating."

As to the law governing the treatment of witnesses before Congressional committees, there "are no statutes and few court decisions bearing on the subject," which in the last analysis "entrusted to those who conduct such investigations . . . the responsibility of upholding the honor of the Senate."

The Select Committee then said:

> Under the circumstances, the conduct of Senator McCarthy toward General Zwicker in reprimanding and ridiculing him, in holding him up to public scorn and contumely, and in disclosing the proceedings of the executive session in violation of the rules of his own committee, was inexcusable. Senator McCarthy acted as a critic and judge, upon preconceived and prejudicial notions. He did much to destroy the effectiveness and reputation of a witness who was not in any way responsible for the Peress situation, a situation which we do not in any way condone. The blame should have been placed on the shoulders of those culpable and not attributed publicly to one who had no share in the responsibility.

THE SELECT COMMITTEE HAD BEEN INSTRUCTED BY THE SENATE TO investigate the charges against Senator McCarthy and to report to the Senate in time for that body to consider and act upon the matter before the end of the second session of the 83rd Congress on December 31, 1954.

While the Senate had not specifically asked for our recommendations, we felt that this was a reasonable and expected part of our assignment. We knew that the report was to be debated on the floor of the Senate, and our reasoning and our recommendations would be asked. If we included our recommendations from the outset, all would have time to consider them.

Each of the six on the Select Committee had his own Senatorial aides available to be of assistance. In addition, we had the very able witness of Select Committee Counsel, E. Wallace Chadwick, and his assistant, Guy DeFuria. Each Senator took the responsibility of preparing a portion of the report in draft form. Thus we divided our labors, and we who were best informed made our own conclusions and phrased them. Not all committees take this personal and serious concern for their responsibilities.*

Since, from the outset, the Committee recognized that it could explore only a certain number of charges with any degree of thoroughness, it first examined them all from the points of view of legal sufficiency and the evidence available as suggested in the charges themselves. The Committee construed its responsibilities as those which were to determine the substance of charges which tended to support a motion to censure a Senator. We recognized that while some conduct might be "distasteful" and "less than proper," it might not constitute censurable behavior.

While choosing to drop some of the charges from the list we were to investigate, we wanted to make it clearly understood that by doing so we were not condoning any specific behavior. Further, we did not want to establish a code of "noncensurable" behavior.

Applying ourselves to the problem, and conscious of the time factors involved, we established 12 considerations for judging whether any given action should be investigated or not. One or more of the reasons might apply to any specific accusation.

---

*An example of a committee charged by some with neglect of personal attention of its members to the investigation at hand and suffering from an over-dose of staff-written conclusions is the Warren Commission which inquired into the death of President John F. Kennedy.

For example, and by way of illustration, we determined that charges should be dropped which, even if substantiated, would not in our judgment be censurable conduct. In this category, we chose to eliminate such interesting but legally insufficient allegations as McCarthy's personal claims as to his war record, wounds received, and the fact that he referred to himself as savior of the country from communism, and the fact that he had never turned up (or turned over to the Justice Department evidence against) a single alleged communist of the numbers he claimed to have knowledge.

Another basis for dropping a charge was the doubtful validity of the matter referred to as a reason for censure, such as the instances where he held "executive session" but permitted outsiders to attend, according to his own whim (as one time where a group of school girls and on other occasions his friend, Gerald L. K. Smith, were invited in).

Other charges were dropped because of the apparent difficulty in finding substantiating evidences or because other Senate committees had already inquired into the matter as thoroughly as seemed warranted.

In summary, we selected a few major charges which on the face of them indicated that they might be productive of logical inquiry and which appeared to be legally sufficient for recommendation of censure. It should be noted, as McCarthy himself said, that if only one charge proved to be censurable he could and should be censured by his colleagues. Therefore, it appeared unnecessary and unproductive to inquire into all of them. Thirty-three charges were dropped (some of them, notably, containing serious allegations), and 13 within five categories were looked into.

Regrettable enough were those situations in which, as the charge by Senator Flanders put it, McCarthy had used distortion and innuendo to attack the reputations of citizens of substance and renown (former President Truman, General Marshall, columnist Marquis Childs, etc.). Equally regrettable was his alleged abuse of little-known citizens.

With respect to allegations of financial irresponsibility, some Senators were to be critical of the Select Committee for passing over these matters. Senator Allen J. Ellender from Louisiana was one of these. He said to reporters, as reported in the November 15 Washington *Post* with respect to the Select Committee: "I would have been more satisfied if the Committee had been able to delve into the many contributions made to him by people who contributed toward his fight on communism. They made huge contributions. What he did with it, nobody knows except himself. If the censure committee had gone into that and reported, I'd feel better. If he came before the Senate and convinced me he has not used these collections, that would satisfy me. He has ample opportunity to clear his skirts. If I were he, I wouldn't have that question dangling over my head five minutes."

The substance of this charge, of course, was part of the basis for the investigation of the Gillette Committee. We determined that we were not going to re-open this matter in which jurisdiction had been given to the Gillette Committee. As we have noted, when this jurisdiction was challenged by McCarthy it was sustained by a unanimous vote of the Senate. As suspicious as Ellender found the facts to be—and they still seem to be today, particularly looking back on McCarthy's refusal to face up to the charges and appear before the Subcommittee—we concluded that this was not our domain. It was, on the other hand, entirely germane to consider McCarthy's attitude toward the Gillette Committee and his remarks about his Senatorial colleagues discharging their duties as assigned by the Senate.

The basic categories, consideration of which did require our attention, have already been discussed individually in preceeding chapters.

> Our final recommendations on these categories, to which all of our activities and inquiries from the moment of our appointment had been steadily directed:
>
> 1. That on the charges in the category of "Incidents of Contempt of the Senate or a Senatorial Committee," the Senator from Wisconsin, Mr. McCarthy, should be condemned.
> 2. That the charges in the category of "Incidents of Encouragement of United States Employees To Violate the Law and Their Oaths of Office or Executive Orders," do not, under all the evidence, justify a resolution of censure.
> 3. That the charges in the category of "Incidents Involving Receipt or Use of Confidential or Classified or Other Confidential Information from Executive Files," do not, under all the evidence, justify a resolution of censure.
> 4. That the charges in the category of "Incidents Involving Abuse of Colleagues in the Senate," except as to those dealt with in the first category, do not, under all the evidence, justify a resolution of censure.
> 5. That on the charges in the category of "Incident Relating to Ralph W. Zwicker, a general officer of the Army of the United States," the Senator from Wisconsin, Mr. McCarthy, should be censured.

A more detailed analysis may be found in the Select Committee's Report, which is included in this volume as Appendix B. We concluded that there was ample evidence to support a resolution to censure the Senator from Wisconsin and there was no need to inquire further.

Speaking for myself, I did not relish the thought of censuring any Senator. I believe the others felt the same way. We did not want to see the dignity and sobriety of the Senate suffer further recriminations. Each of us believed, I am sure, that if McCarthy (faced by the evidence and unswerving purpose of the Senate) would choose to purge himself from his contempt of the Senate his act would be accepted. I would have been the first to have accepted any bona fide evidence of regret and repentance on the part of McCarthy. (Many times as a judge, I had permitted an individual to purge himself from contempt by admission of error and through repentance.) Given McCarthy's pledge of good conduct, so to speak, I believe that far fewer would have voted for censure.

This is a matter of deep personal conviction with me and stems directly from my ethical and religious beliefs. Man, we are taught, is on this earth to learn from personal experience and to be perfected throughout the ages and beyond the grave. Regrettably, some can learn only from sad personal experience but when we clearly see that this has been the case we must—no less than God our Heavenly Father has Himself promised—forgive and forget those indiscretions of which our brother has repented and concerning which he has reformed.

This is by way of preface to my shameless admission that during the entire time of the investigation and especially during the time of the preparation of the report, I prayed earnestly (not only for myself, but for the Committee and the Senate) that we might be entirely fair and completely free from prejudice as far as is humanly possible. As for justice, this I knew was to be left in the hands of the Senate and with God.

Had I not so prepared myself, and had there been any wavering, doubt, or trepidation of spirit, I could not have survived the exhausting physical and psychological ordeal I was to be called upon to face. I hope there was no malice in my heart for Joe McCarthy, as we prepared the document which recommended his censure—there seemed only a great depression that this conclusion was inevitable. Matters of the greatest moral significance, affecting the integrity of the United States Senate and of the very future of our Nation, had too long gone unattended to and the day of reckoning was before us.

Needless to say, the Select Committee's recommendations, as announced to the press the last part of September, were not enthusiastically received by all. An increased flurry of mail came immediately from McCarthy fans. While more restrained than many, the following letter is typical of those received:

Bronx, New York
October 6, 1954

Dear Senator:

Please permit me to express my indignation at the biased, unfair and dishonest report which your committee has submitted to the U.S. Senate, recommending censure of Senator McCarthy.

It is my opinion that your committee has given aid and comfort to the communists and their friends in bringing in such a report.

God bless Senator McCarthy! We need more men in the U.S. Senate with the courage and honesty of McCarthy.

I hope Senator McCarthy's name and religion did not influence your committee in bringing in such a biased report.

> Very truly yours,
> (Signed by a man)

An undated and unidentified clipping was mailed to me from someone who read it in a California newspaper. By a pro-McCarthy columnist, George Rothwell Brown, it said: "Getting as far away as it could from the deadly communist political issue involved in the left-wing conspiracy to destroy Sen. Joe McCarthy, the Watkins Committee has groaned like a mountain and produced a mouse."

Going on to cite alleged Democratic smears which our Committee supposedly used in compiling its report, Brown then concluded: "The Watkins Committee ignores all these smears and insinuations and bases its censure recommendation on the ground of contempt on Joe's part for not knuckling down to New Deal partisans out to get him. Only Senate rules, not moral law, allegedly have been violated."

In a more refined manner was David Lawrence's expanded "editorial analysis." Usually found on a single back page of the *U.S. News and World Report*, his piece ran six pages in the October 29, 1954, issue. In his concluding paragraph, Lawrence, too, argued that McCarthy should not be censured for his methods (although he does not condone them). Lawrence's conclusion:

Fundamental Issue of Free Speech

A courageous Senate, free from passion and the proddings of pressure groups, true to the historic principles of liberalism which have governed the American people from the foundation of the Republic, will seek to uphold the highest principles of American jurisprudence.

The Senate, therefore, should table the "censure" resolution and promulgate a rule in an orderly manner prescribing the standards for future conduct of its members. But such rules must be written so as not to prejudice the right of free speech guaranteed by the Constitution of the United States to everybody—including members of the United States Senate itself.

Where are the true liberals in America? Let them stand up and be counted on this fundamental issue of free speech.

Typical of David Lawrence's many newspaper columns* which attacked the "Watkins Committee," and in which he frequently presumed to correct the

---

*Lawrence's specious arguments on the "legality" of the Select Committee, matters of precedence and other items of concern to the more moderate critics—who attempted to present logical cases for their positions—will be answered in Appendix A, on "Questions."

Select Committee in its interpretations of "Constitutional Law," this long analysis also falls far from the mark. It was not for McCarthy's "free speech" but for his studied and contumacious attacks on Senators for conducting their business as assigned to them by the Senate itself, that we recommended his censure. This was also an issue in the Zwicker case, where McCarthy was contemptuous of the rules and responsibilities of a Senate Committee and his own chairmanship in abusing a witness (not in an effort to get the facts, for he already knew them, but because of personal spleen and for publicity).

Far more understanding of the Committee's work was the editorial for September 28, 1954, which appeared in the Winston-Salem *Journal*. It reads, in part:

> The report of the Watkins Committee on the motion to censure Senator McCarthy is in keeping with the committee's conduct from the beginning. It looked at the charges against the Wisconsin Senator dispassionately and without partisanship, followed the rules of judicial procedure, and reached a unanimous verdict accordingly . . . .
>
> Whatever (the Senate does) about the report, the Senators ought to commend the members of the committee for conducting a hearing free of the sound and fury that McCarthy has always generated in the past. Senator Watkins silenced him—kept him from raising divisive and irrelevant issues —and for that the chairman ought to get a medal of some sort.

Most complimentary of numerous comments which did reflect favorably upon the Select Committee was this one from *Time* magazine for October 4, 1954:

> *Documented & Direct.* The Committee's recommendations were, perhaps, not as important as its manner. Its report, like its hearings, was a product worthy of an unusually able appellate court. It was direct, documented and unequivocal. Its impact was far broader than the two censure recommendations. In sum it was a scathing indictment of McCarthyism, condemning the Wisconsin Senator for disregarding the principles of democracy, good government, fair play and decency.

While I had avoided reading either the favorable or unfavorable letters and newspaper comments until long after the censure, I could not be completely isolated from public opinion. This October 4 issue of *Time* was one publication which came immediately to my attention. It carried my portrait on its cover, and several individuals brought copies to me for my autograph. I thought *Time*'s coverage was thorough, objective, and well-presented.

The censure debate was well along on its way on the floor of the Senate before I took notice of my other mail. Even then I did not have the opportunity to read it all, but my staff pointed out a new trend in the mail and described it to me. I received a number of "Thanksgiving Day" letters, which by their tone contributed to my humility. It was reassuring to learn that I had the support of so many fine people in my very earnest efforts to perform my duty.

It is possible that the inspiration given me by this new knowledge helped to sustain me in the debate to come. Without it, I might well have collapsed prematurely under Joe McCarthy's toe-to-toe challenge to defend my personal integrity and honor. As it was, I did debate him to exhaustion (which I am sure that Joe was bidding for) and had to leave the floor for a short time.

IMMEDIATELY AFTER THE NOVEMBER ELECTIONS IN 1954, AND A FEW DAYS before the Senate was to return to Washington to consider the report of the Select Committee, I received a request from Senator McCarthy to return to Washington immediately to appear before his Subcommittee on Investigations' hearings on the Army's handling of the promotion of Dr. Peress.

The so-called Peress case had been before the country for several months, and "Who promoted Dr. Peress to be a major," and later, "Who gave him an honorable discharge?" were questions headlined in the national news media.

This was one big case in which the Senator and his voluble supporters were certain they had struck pay dirt in digging out communists in Government. "Who protected Peress?" became their battle cry.

McCarthy had charged that a "Secret Master," a "protector of a 5th-amendment communist," a "cover up" for traitors operated within the Department of the Army, and was responsible for the protection of Dr. Peress, who was designated by the Senator as a 5th-amendment communist.

The heavy publicity buildup on this "Secret Master" or master spy was so widespread and intense that literally thousands of citizens took part in a nation-wide crusade to help McCarthy find this dangerous character. Apparently it was taken for granted that Dr. Peress had already been convicted of being a communist, and with that matter out of the way, the big crusade was on to find out what traitor in the Army was protecting communist Peress.

That there was such a traitor Senator McCarthy's followers seemed not to have the slightest doubt. The Army had released an official statement on the facts of the case but this was lost in the election news of November 3. So Senator McCarthy came up with the idea that I should be required, as Chairman of the Select Committee, to give his Investigation's Subcommittee the answers to their big problem, who was this "Secret Master" or spy? He claimed the Select Committee (Watkins Committee) had indicated in its report that I knew who, in the Department of the Army, was protecting Dr. Peress.

Shortly after McCarthy had by letter requested me to appear, I received this telegram:

> This is to confirm our request that you appear Monday (November 15) at 9 o'clock a.m. in room 357 to give evidence in the case of Major Peress.
>
> (signed)   Joe McCarthy, Chairman
> of Subcommittee on
> Investigations.

Accordingly, on the date set I became a witness before the McCarthy Subcommittee at an unprecedented hearing, as far as I can ascertain, in the history of the Senate and especially in censure proceedings.

I should also note that, as usual, McCarthy released to the press and all other media his request that I appear before his committee to give evidence in the Peress case and to tell him who the secret traitor was who protected Peress.

To fully appreciate this hearing it should be considered in its entirety. For this reason I secured unanimous consent in the Senate to have the hearing record printed in the Congressional Record for November 18, 1954, pages 16112 through 16116. I felt that the Senate and the American people should know what transpired.

MR. WATKINS.   Mr. President, on November 15, 1954, at the hour of 9 a.m., I appeared in room 357, and later, at 10 o'clock, a hearing was held before the Subcommittee on Investigations.

Various excerpts from statements made at the hearing have been published in the press, many of them lifted out of context. So that the public may know exactly what happened, I ask unanimous consent that the entire transcript be printed in the body of the Record at this point in my remarks.

(There being no objection, the transcript was ordered to be printed in the Records, as follows:)

UNITED STATES SENATE,
SENATE PERMANENT SUBCOMMITTEE
ON INVESTIGATIONS OF THE COMMIT-
TEE ON GOVERNMENT OPERATIONS,
Washington, D.C., November 15, 1954

The subcommittee met, pursuant to notice, 10 a.m., in room 357, Senate Office Building, Senator Joseph R. McCarthy, chairman, presiding.

Present: Senator Joseph R. McCarthy, Republican, Wisconsin; Senator Everett McKinley Dirksen, Republican, Illinois; Senator John L. McClellan, Democrat, Arkansas; Senator Henry M. Jackson, Democrat, Washington; Senator Stuart Symington, Democrat, Missouri.

Present also: James Juliana, acting director; Bob Kennedy, chief counsel to the minority; Ruth Young Watt, chief clerk.

The CHAIRMAN.   The committee will come to order.

May I say we have a rule that the flash photographers will not take pictures during the hearings. So if you men will desist taking pictures of the witness and the members of the committee during the hearing, it will be appreciated.

Senator Watkins, you are called here this morning not to in any way answer for your activities as chairman of the Watkins committee. To ask you to answer about your activities on that committee would be, in my opinion, improper and beyond the jurisdiction of this committee.

However, in your report, you indicate that you have information in regard to a fifth-amendment Communist, Major Peress. I have been trying to find out for months who was responsible for the special treatment that this man got by those who knew that he was a fifth-amendment Communist.

If I may recite the facts of the case for the record briefly, Peress was identified as a Communist by an undercover agent—will you desist in taking flash pictures of the witness—Peress was identified under oath by a member of the New York Police Department as a Communist. He was identified as having attended a Communist leadership school. We had before us, and you had before you, the affidavit which he signed first saying he was not a Communist when he joined the military, which would make him, of course, subject to court martial, up to 5 years, and then later the statement which he signed refusing to answer whether he was a Communist or not.

The reason you are here, Senator, as I say, has nothing whatsoever to do with your activities as chairman of the Watkins committee. But in view of the fact that you have indicated that you have information about who promoted him, I felt that I would be derelict in my duty if I did not call you here to give you an opportunity to tell us what information you have. I will be very much surprised if you have that information, but we will get down to that shortly.

You say, for example, that Peress was in no way responsible for the Zwicker matter—strike that—that Zwicker was in no way responsible.

Despite Senator McCarthy's disclaimer, I believe that any fair minded reader will agree with me that the Senator's undeclared purpose was to carry on an attack against me and my fellow committee members.

I think that it would be fair to conclude Senator McCarthy's counsel, Bennett Williams, could have had this special hearing in mind among other activities of McCarthy when he declared in his book *One Man's Freedom* (p. 63) that McCarthy "from the opening gun . . . was holding press conferences and making statements over television networks. He attacked the committee members individually, and he attacked the manner in which they were conducting the inquiry. Needless to say, this did not make my role any easier. Day by day our relationship with the committee worsened, but I was unable to dissuade the Senator from continuing his verbal assaults on Senator Watkins and his associates."

The tone of McCarthy's questions and comments was sarcastic throughout, namely, that I was wasting the time of the committee if my "answers" and "advice" were all the information I could give the committee. I believe students of McCarthy's crusade will agree with me that this "special hearing" was a typical McCarthy performance. He insisted that at all times the Select Committee should conduct hearings in a fair judicial manner, reserving to himself the "right" as he claimed it, to attack and berate continuously the Chairman and the Committee generally over radio and television and through the press. This "right" he used to the limit of its possibilities. Neither McCarthy nor his voluble supporters seemed to realize that they were under the same obligations, in this quasi-judicial hearing, to treat respectfully the Select Committee as they would have been required to do had this committee been a court instead of a Senate committee. How long would a court tolerate a party to a proceeding before it to publicly denounce and ridicule the court, while the trial was under way? And suppose one of the judges trying the case was hailed before another court to answer charges of misconduct while the case was on trial or under advisement or further consideration? The answers should be self evident.

The record continues:

STATEMENT OF THE HONORABLE ARTHUR V. WATKINS, A UNITED STATES SENATOR FROM THE STATE OF UTAH

SENATOR WATKINS.   Will you call my attention to the place in the report where that appears?

The CHAIRMAN.   I will be glad to. Page 60 of the report.

If you will refer to the bottom of the page, the last paragraph, I will quote: "He" (meaning McCarthy) "did much to destroy the effectiveness and reputation of a witness who was not in any way responsible for the Peress situation, a situation which we do not in any way condone. The blame should have been placed on the shoulders of those culpable and not attributed publicily to one who had no share in the responsibility."

We will not get into an argument, Senator, as to whether or not I blamed Zwicker for the situation, but you say here that he was in no way responsible. You say I should have put the blame on the shoulders of those who were culpable. I find that you and I do agree that someone was culpable, that someone was at fault for keeping a Communist in the military while we are spending billions of dollars trying to fight communism.

Therefore, I will ask you, question No. 1: Do you know who was, as you say, culpable?

SENATOR WATKINS.   No, I do not.

The CHAIRMAN.   You do not?

SENATOR WATKINS.   But I think I can help you find the information that will show who had the responsibility for the promotion of Peress and who also had the responsibility for directing his honorable discharge.

The CHAIRMAN.   If you do that, you will be of great value to this committee, Senator.

We have asked Secretary Stevens for that information time after time. He has refused to give it to us. We do know who signed the order. We know the Adjutant General signs the order, but we are looking for the man, the secret master, if you could call him that, who is being protected.

If you can give us the name of the person who has been responsible, No. 1, for the promotion, knowing he was a communist; No. 2, the change in duty orders and No. 3, the honorable discharge—if you can, as you say, help us get that information, then you would be of great value to this committee.

SENATOR WATKINS.   With all the qualifications you put in, descriptions you put in, I, of course, may not be able to qualify the answer to comply strictly with that. But I can give you the source of information where you can get the names of the people who were responsible for his promotion and for his discharge, honorable discharge.

So I will proceed, if you will let me.

The CHAIRMAN.   I will be delighted to.

SENATOR WATKINS.   The statement you read from the report, of course, does not indicate that we know who the culpable people were. We said that Zwicker was not the person. I can call your attention to the testimony in the hearing record, if you wish, to substantiate just what I am saying about that. Zwicker himself was not the responsible person.

The CHAIRMAN.   Would you call my attention to that point?

SENATOR WATKINS.   I will read it, if you don't mind. On page 505—

The CHAIRMAN.   Just 1 minute until I get it—you may proceed.

SENATOR WATKINS.   It is the first volume of the hearing record. Mr. Williams had been examining General Zwicker.

The CHAIRMAN.   Just so the record is straight. Senator Watkins is now referring not to testimony taken before the investigating committee, but testimony taken before the Watkins committee.

Is that correct?

SENATOR WATKINS.   That is right. Otherwise known as the Select Committee.

The CHAIRMAN.   So when you say I knew what he was testifying to, you refer to what I knew after he appeared before your committee; is that right?

SENATOR WATKINS.   That is right; yes. I will read the testimony. Mr. Williams had been cross examining General Zwicker, and then he said:

"I have no further questions.
"The Chairman.   Mr. DeFuria,* do you have further questions?
"Mr. DeFuria. Yes, sir.
"General, did you promote Peress?
"General Zwicker. I definitely did not.
"Mr. DeFuria. Did you discharge him with an honorable discharge?
"General Zwicker. I did, sir.

*Mr. DeFuria was one of the attorneys for the Select Committee and an able examiner.

"Mr. DeFuria. Was that on your own initiative or under orders, sir?
"General Zwicker. It was under orders."

Now we can go on and get some additional testimony.

The CHAIRMAN. Senator, I wonder if you would do this for me. In your report—

SENATOR WATKINS.   May I say that was not contradicted before us.

The CHAIRMAN.   I don't want to use the gavel on you.

SENATOR WATKINS.   You don't need to. I am willing to cooperate with you a hundred percent.

The CHAIRMAN.   May I ask you to do this. Obviously, if there is anything in your record which shows who was responsible for covering up for this Communist, I will want you to point that out. However, at the present time, I am referring to your report which says that, in effect, I knew that Zwicker was not responsible. So this had to be some thing antedating the testimony taken before your committee.*

Could you show us any information which you have to show that Zwicker was not responsible, prior to what he said before your committee?

SENATOR WATKINS.   I was not acquainted with the matter prior to that time. My information, of course, is based on what he said in the committee, on the uncontradicted evidence. No one contradicted him. That was his statement, and I assume it is true, and I think other information I have discovered since, which I think will answer the question that we were talking about, that is to help you find the information as to who handled the Peress matter—I can give that to you, because I have—

The CHAIRMAN.   I wish you would, Senator. I wish you would have all the facts in mind. I refer you to the testimony taken before the investigating committee:

"Question. You know that somebody has kept him on knowing that he has refused to tell whether he was a communist, do you not?
"Zwicker. I am afraid that would come under the category of the Executive order, Mr. Chairman.
"The Chairman. What?
"Zwicker. I am afraid that an answer to that question would come under the category of the Presidential order."

So you know that prior to his appearance before our committee he did not deny that he personally as commanding officer was responsible. Do you know that?

---

* I also knew that Zwicker had told McCarthy's staff that Peress was suspected of being a Communist, etc. In fact, as we have seen, Zwicker had advised McCarthy's staff early in the McCarthy investigation in some detail on the Peress case.

SENATOR WATKINS.   I am not sure about that, because all I would have is the record, and I have read so many records that I couldn't be sure as to that positive statement. But I do have some additional information in this record which indicates very clearly that he was not the person responsible.

May I read it?

The CHAIRMAN.   You certainly may, but I want to get this in chronological order, if I may. You know, do you not—you knew when you signed the report, did you not—that Zwicker had refused to tell us who had ordered the promotion of Peress? Did you know that?

SENATOR WATKINS.   I think I had the evidence. I had the full record of the hearing you held in New York City, at which General Zwicker appeared. As I recall, in that he wasn't in a position, and so told you, to give all the information that he would probably like to have given, because of orders.*

The CHAIRMAN.   Do you think today—and time is running out, and we have a session starting at 11 o'clock—do you think today you can give us information which will help us to nail down the man responsible for the protection of this Communist in the military, do you?

SENATOR WATKINS.   I can give you information as to the men who had something to do with it, and probably all to do with it. If you will let me, I will proceed.

The CHAIRMAN.   Would you do that, please.

SENATOR WATKINS.   Yes; I did want to read that other, but since you say time is running out—

The CHAIRMAN.   Read whatever you care to.

SENATOR WATKINS.   All right.

After I got your telegram in Salt Lake City, or letter, and after I got back here, as soon as I could get to it, I called on Secretary Stevens to see what information I could get, and he did furnish me some information.

I will read now a letter which I think will tell where the material is:

"DEPARTMENT OF THE ARMY,
Washington, June 23, 1954.

"Dear Senator Mundt:"

This was addressed, so he advised me, to Senator Mundt, the acting Chairman of the committee which is now in session here—

"I refer to the case of Maj. Irving Peress, with which I am sure you are familiar. I have recently studied the thorough investigation made by

---

*That is, orders of Zwicker's superiors including the Presidential directive that names of those furnishing confidential information on personnel could not be revealed because sources of information would dry up.

the Inspector General of the Army of all the circumstances pertaining to this advancement in grade and separation from the service.

"This investigation disclosed no evidence of any subversive conduct with respect to personnel actions involving Peress. Furthermore, there is no evidence of disloyalty, pro-communist influence, or any other type of misconduct reflecting on the loyalty, integrity, or patriotism of the officers or civilians who processed the case.

"The investigation, however, did reveal that in several instances improper administrative handling of papers resulted in unwarranted delays in processing actions concerning Major Peress.

"On the basis of the facts now known and limitations imposed by outmoded regulations, and legislation pertaining to doctors and dentists, my original conclusion that the Peress case was not handled as it should have been has been substantiated. As will be remembered, when I returned from the Far East, February 3, 1954, and in my letter to Senator McCarthy dated February 16, 1954, I readily admitted that this case could have been handled better.

"The Inspector General's findings disclosed inordinate time was consumed in the processing of this case. Major commanders have been directed to take the appropriate steps against the individuals involved and at all levels of command administrative reforms consistent with existing law have been made, which I fervently hope will make it impossible for such errors to be made in the future.

"Further reference is made to the sealed envelope marked 'Confidential,' containing the names of Army personnel who in the course of their duties took some type of administrative action with respect to the disposition of Major Peress.

"As you will recall, on February 24, 1954, I agreed to submit to your subcommitee the names of these individuals as soon as they had been determined. In the course of the hearings, pages 1420 and 2253, I reiterated this promise, and by covering letter of May 13, 1954, I submitted to Mr. Jenkins in an envelope marked 'Confidential' the names of the individuals who had something to do with the Peress personnel actions. The covering letter, copy inclosed, was read into the transcript of the hearings at page 3761.

"Subsequently, on June 18, 1954, Lieutenant Murray, of my office, delivered to you an additional envelope marked 'Confidential' to replace the first one. This was necessary because a name had been erroneously included in the first compilation. On this occasion you inquired about the confidential character of this list. In answer to your question, I can only reemphasize my original request—that the names of these individuals not be made public under any circumstances.

"As you know, these names were obtained after a thorough investigation by the Inspector General of the Army. I wish to emphasize that the mere fact that the individuals are named as having some administrative respondibility or knowledge of the subject should in no way be construed to indicate culpability on their part. Should these names be made public, it would unnecessarily subject them and their families to unwarranted publicity completely out of proportion to the facts.

"I, therefore, request again that you do not publicize this list. To publicize these names without a full explanation of the circumstances surrounding their participation in the case could well cast public discredit upon the individuals concerned.

"In addition, such publication would go far to diminish the future effectiveness of the Inspector General Corps because, historically, investigations of this character have been successful information-gathering devices for commanders because of a strict adherence to the maintenance of a confidential relationship between the interrogator and the person interrogated. This is another reason for my definite desire not to have their names publicized.

"Also in the transcript, on page 2266, Mr. Jenkins stated: 'And then the names, as I understand it, the chairman ruled are to be submitted to this committee or to me as its counsel, privately and without exposing these names.' On page 2268 you stated: 'The other names requested should be submitted confidentially and to counsel for our committee.' See enclosure for full quote.

"Accordingly, it is my opinion that the confidential character of the list of names should be maintained and revealed only on a need-to-know basis to those who have a confidential clearance."

The Secretary advised me as a result of my inquiry that a list of 30 names, beginning with a general, had been given to Senator Mundt, the acting chairman of this committee. Those were the names that were to be kept confidential. As I understood it from him, they contained all the names of those who had anything to do—any of the responsibility for the promotion and the honorable discharge of Major Peress. That information, I understand, came into the hands of Senator Mundt, was delivered by a messenger—I mean the envelope that was marked confidential containing the names—and is now in the files of this committee and has been since June 23, 1954.

Now, I was further advised by Secretary Stevens that I could have a copy of that list, he exhibited an envelope which was marked confidential and sealed, that I could have a copy of those names. But he would expect me to keep them confidential. I said if your committee, if the McCarthy committee, has those names now, it is not necessary for me to have them, because that is their job. They can immediately go into executive session and call in these various persons to determine their share of the responsibility, whatever they did about it. I said, "Would you be willing to furnish these officers, to see that they get here, this personnel?" And he said, "We would do our level best to get them there upon the demand of this Permanent Committee on Investigations," the committee over which you preside, Senator.

To properly understand what is being discussed because of so many different committees and various chairman and rather complex situations which, of course, were understood (but none too clearly) by the participants, I shall attempt to clarify the situation for readers of this book and students of the McCarthy era, including the censure proceedings.

Three different committees are mentioned in this present proceeding. They are the McCarthy Committee, Select Committee to study censure charges (Watkins Committee), and Internal Security Committee (McCarran Committee).

The preceding letter of Secretary Stevens which I had just read, was addressed to Senator Karl Mundt, a member of the so-called McCarthy Senate Permanent Subcommittee on Investigations of the Committee on Government Operations, who was acting as temporary chairman of this committee which was investigating charges and countercharges between the U.S. Army and Senator McCarthy, who was the regular chairman of this subcommittee. He had stepped aside from his role of chairman because he was a party to the dispute with the Army.

And now back to the letter to Senator Mundt. Secretary Stevens had given me a copy of it which I read to McCarthy and his committee, and then followed my statement about the letter.

> The CHAIRMAN. I do not want to waste my time and the time of the Senators here, unless you have some information as to who is culpable. You say in the report "Zwicker was in no way responsible." I do not know what you know about the military. You should know, you made the statement, that a man is not promoted, he is not honorably discharged, unless his commanding officer makes the recommendation. If you read the record, you know that Secretary Stevens promised to have an investigation made that he would tell us who was, as you say, culpable—he did not use that word; he said at fault; you need the word culpable—in this case. That has never been done.
>
> Now if you merely intend to read from the transcript of the Mundt hearings, which you have been doing so far—*
>
> SENATOR WATKINS. I have been reading a copy of the letter from the Secretary to Senator Mundt.
>
> The CHAIRMAN. That is in the Mundt hearings, and has been in there for months.
>
> SENATOR WATKINS. He told me this had not been made public before.

*This refers to the Army-McCarthy hearings, of which Senator Mundt was the temporary chairman.

The CHAIRMAN. That is part of the Mundt hearings. Do you have any information today? Do you have any information today as to who was, as you say, culpable in this case?

SENATOR WATKINS. I have exactly what I have told you. I had no personal knowledge. I came to the conclusion, based on the uncontradicted testimony in our hearings, before the Watkins committee, that General Zwicker was not responsible. Then, in order to help this committee, because I am a member of the Internal Security Committee, which is charged with the responsibility of ferreting out these matters just as much as your committee —as a member of it I was personally very much interested in finding out, and I would like to find out.

But I do say now, in view of what has been said to me by the Secretary, as I have related it, that you do now have in your files the names of all the people who were responsible for the promotion and the discharge, of Peress. All you need to do is to call those men in an executive session, if you want to abide by the confidential request of the Secretary, and you can find out from them the part that each one had in that affair. That has been in your files since June 23.

The CHAIRMAN. I am afraid we are wasting the time of the Senate, if that is all the information you have.

So it appears that the Department of the Army was doing its best to satisfy McCarthy's demands. What was the Senator's attitude when I called this to his attention? His statement makes it clear that he was not really acting in good faith when he called me before his committee to give him information on who was culpable.

In his original questioning of Irving Peress, the Senator and his counsel professed to be interested in how Peress had come to be promoted after being identified as a "known communist," but the line of questioning ran on and on about the Major's alleged communist affiliations, to which Peress consistently replied by claiming his right to refuse to answer under the Fifth Amendment. Finally, after McCarthy asked: "Did any communists aid you in getting this promotion?" Peress answered by saying, "I again claim the privilege, but I will tell you how the promotion was effected if you want to know." * McCarthy completely ignored this offere and went on with his questioning about communists, for he did not want to develop this information but merely wished to continue his show.

Thus McCarthy already had available enough information to have begun the questioning of personnel who had acted in any way in proceessing Peress's "promotion" and honorable discharge. He also knew that Secretary Stevens was

*Hearings on S. Res. 301, Part 1, page 213.

prepared to have the 30 men named brought from wherever they were stationed to Washington so they could testify before the McCarthy committee.

The Secretary's letter also made a clearcut statement of the Army's proceedings in the Peress matter which were not flattering to the Army. The letter admitted that the Army made mistakes and that this case could have been handled better. He also disclosed what had been done "to make it impossible for such errors to be made in the future."

He also emphasized that there was "no evidence of disloyalty, pro-communist influence—or any other type of misconduct reflecting on the loyalty, integrity or patriotism of the officers or civilians who processed the case."

What more did McCarthy want? Well, it should be clear by now. For one thing, he wanted to embarrass me and the Select Committee I represented.

I am convinced that most of all, he didn't really want to question any one connected with the Army about the Peress case. He seemed to be afraid to push the search any further to find the great "Secret Master" or spy who he claimed was protecting Peress. The master protector or spy was already disappearing. McCarthy's charges were on the verge of a complete collapse.

SENATOR WATKINS. You invited me here. I did not—

The CHAIRMAN. Just a minute. Please, Senator. I will give you a gavel. General Zwicker when called said he could not tell who was responsible. We have a list of 30 names, an unusual list. It lists the people in head-quarters of the First Army, the Office of the Surgeon General, all the doctors in the Surgeon General's office who might have given this man a physical examination when he was promoted, the officers in the Adjutant General's office, again when he was appointed to the grade of major all of the doctors who were in the Surgeon General's office, and on down the line. You and I know that—you and I know that nothing will be gained by calling four or eight doctors from the Surgeon General's office and finding out whether or not they examined this man. I thought when you made this statement, Senator, this very serious statement made in your report—you state that I should blame the person who is culpable—I thought maybe you had some information. Let us see if I have your testimony clear today. It is that you have nothing except what was presented to the Mundt committee, including this list of 30 people. You know now as you knew at the time you signed this report, that when we had one of the individuals before us, he said, "I can't answer because of the Presidential order." You are aware of the Presidential order when you invoked before your committee in which you said that General Lawton could not even tell about the conversation now that that is all you have? You have nothing in addition except this conversation you had with Stevens in which he said "Here is a list of 30 names. If you want to take a look at them, if you think there is some way that

I can find out who was the secret master by looking at these names, I will give it to you."*

Keep in mind the ruling that you made—hand this down to the Senator, will you?

(Document handed.)

Keep in mind the ruling you made that one Army officer would not have to testify as to conversations he had with another.

SENATOR WATKINS.   I take it you are asking for my advice. That is what it sounded like. I would advise you—

The CHAIRMAN.   Not your advice, Senator. You have signed a formal report saying that I should blame the person who is culpable. That means that you should know.

SENATOR WATKINS.   Do you disagree with that?

The CHAIRMAN.   That means you should know. I have been trying to find out. I wired you and told you that unless you have some information I did not want you to waste my time and your time. You did not answer that wire. I gather today that you have nothing except what was before the Mundt committee and that the Secretary of the Army did not give you the result of the Inspector General's report. You knew, of course, Senator, you know now, that the Secretary of the Army promised that he would have the Inspector General make an investigation and that he would try and tell us then who was at fault or, using your word, culpable. You know that he has refused to do that. I thought maybe when you were. . . .

In the letter from Secretary Stevens to Senator Mundt, which summarized the Inspector General's report to the Secretary of the Army, the Secretary named all of those civilians and officers, in a separate envelope, who had something to do with the Major Peress case, but he did not point to anyone of this list as the guilty part, or the "culpable" person.

On November 3, 1954, the Department of the Army issued a comprehensive statement on the Peress case as a result of "exhaustive" investigations. For the benefit of students of the Peress episode and the McCarthy censure proceedings this statement is reproduced in full in Appendix C of this book.

*McCarthy's comment on the 30 individuals listed by Secretary Stevens' for questioning reveals a strange inconsistency in the Senator's thinking and conduct. He said, "You and I know that nothing will be gained by calling four or eight doctors from the Surgeon General's Office and finding out whether or not they examined this man." McCarthy claims he found a traitor—a fifth-amendment communist, in the person of Dr. Peress, whose only task in the Army was to care for the teeth of Army personnel. Why couldn't one of the "four or eight doctors" have been his "Secret Master?" If not among the doctors, he may have been one of the other personnel named. Why not? Whoever McCarthy's master spy was, he certainly wouldn't have been an obvious spy, or traitor.

SENATOR WATKINS. Just a moment. I do not know any of those things you are saying. Those are your statements, not mine. I am not agreeing with them just because I sit here. I am not agreeing with what you are saying because I have to sit silently.

The CHAIRMAN. You do not have to sit silently. You can talk all you like. I am not going to use a gavel.

SENATOR WATKINS. You ask me, in effect, as I get the purport of your question, how I would go about it to get this information. I would tell you exactly how I would go about it. I would serve on the Secretary of the Army a request for each one of those officers and I would have them brought before the committee in executive session so that I could protect the families of these people in the event there was nothing against them any more than administrative work. I am advised that this contains the list of the people who had all to do with this promotion and with this discharge.

I would go right down through that list. And then I would say to you, in answer to what you said about not being able to get the information out of them because of the orders—I would do exactly what I did in the Select Committee case. I called on the Secretary of Defense, Mr. Wilson, and I got him to give me a letter which permitted General Lawton to testify, which permitted General Zwicker to testify on the things that he* could not say before.

The CHAIRMAN. Let's keep the record straight. You did not get permission for Lawton to testify. Lawton refused to testify. So let's keep the record straight.

SENATOR WATKINS. Lawton came on the second time and testified when he was given the opportunity to recount and to give the statements that General Zwicker had made to him at a conversation with respect to Senator McCarthy and how he felt about it. When we gave him the opportunity—

The CHAIRMAN. Senator Watkins, let's keep the record straight.

SENATOR WATKINS. I am testifying. If you find it is wrong—you said I could talk all I wanted. Now let me go.

The CHAIRMAN. You can talk all you like.

SENATOR WATKINS. Let me go, then, and I can finish my statement. With your permission, I am doing this.

The CHAIRMAN. Okay. Proceed.

SENATOR WATKINS. All right.

I have forgotten where I was. Will you give me the last statement?

(The record was read by the reporter.)

SENATOR WATKINS. When we gave him** the opportunity to testify he could not recount or recall a single statement made by Zwicker. Then we

[* It should have been "they" instead of "he."]
[** General Lawton]

stretched the rule on giving evidence of that sort and said, "Ordinarily we would like to form our own conclusions from what was said, but you can go ahead and give your impressions." Then he did; that General Zwicker was antagonistic to you. Then when we go to Zwicker, he was permitted to say that he had been opposed to the promotion of Peress, he had been opposed to his honorable discharge, he had been against generals or any officials in the Army claiming the protection of the fifth amendment.

But he was not permitted to say to whom he objected. He had to stop there. But we got that through the letter Mr. Wilson and the counsel sent over from the War Department.

Senator, as a part of my advice from an older man, just a little older in years, I would say to you I think if you will follow on that procedure, if you will cooperate with the Secretary of the Army and the Defense Department, they will be able to help you a lot in actually pinpointing who, if anybody, is culpable; that is, any evil culpability, for the promotion of Peress and for his discharge honorably.

Now, I do not know whether this is going to be of any help to you or not. You have to decide that matter. But since you asked for it, that is the story. You have it in your files, and I think there is a reasonable procedure to follow. I recommend it strongly to your committee. And if you do not want to do it, give us the names in the Internal Security Committee and I will ask our chairman to proceed on that.

The CHAIRMAN. Then I understand that the only help you can give us is that we call additional Army witnesses and hope that they will not invoke any secrecy rule and try and get them not to invoke the secrecy rule. Beyond that, you can give no information, is that it?

SENATOR WATKINS. I would like to say that the report that you called my attention to does not profess to know the name of the person culpable. It merely says whoever they are, in effect, they ought to be held responsible. It does say positively that Zwicker was not culpable. That is all I have to say, Senator.

The CHAIRMAN. Where does it say positively that Zwicker was not culpable.

SENATOR. Well, I think, in what we read.

The CHAIRMAN. Where does it say that? I would like to read that into the record. You said the report that you got from the Army. I handed it to you. I am not asking about your report, Senator Watkins.

SENATOR WATKINS. That is what I thought you said. I am only responsible for my own report, nobody else's.

The CHAIRMAN. In other words, you were not referring to the Army report? I handed you a report. I thought you were referring to that.

There was some confusion at this point in the record. In the beginning of this hearing Senator McCarthy read a paragraph (or more) from the Select

Committee's report (the censure committee) which in effect said that Zwicker was not responsible (or culpable) for the promotion of Dr. Peress and for his honorable discharge. The Senator said that if Zwicker was not responsible then I must know who was responsible and he requested me to appear before his committee to advise it who was responsible or culpable for Peress' promotion and his honorable separation from the Army. It appears from the record I must have misunderstood the question and began to talk about the list of names that Senator McCarthy handed me which were given him by Secretary Stevens. The Secretary also gave me a sealed envelope containing this list of names which I could have retained but didn't—so I went on stating: "I could have had this identical list," and then proceeded to discuss why I did not keep it. The reason was the Select Committee did not have jurisdiction over this matter. It also had closed its hearings and had prepared its report which had been made public. And the discussion went on from there.

SENATOR WATKINS. I have the list, yes, the confidential list that you just handed me.

The CHAIRMAN. There is nothing on that?

SENATOR WATKINS. That is to be taken in connection with the letter which he gave you.* That is to be taken in connection with what he told me. I could have had this identical list, and if the Select committee had any job in connection with it, I would be only too glad to proceed and follow it. But that is within the jurisdiction of your committee and the Internal Security Committee as I see it. I cannot do anything about it. I said, "There is no use in giving that to me, Mr. Secretary, and have me hold it in a confidential capacity, even though it might satisfy some of my curiosity." But he said, "Positively that contains the list from the top down in grade, the people who were responsible for the handling of the Peress matter." That has been in your files since June 23, 1954.

The CHAIRMAN. You are aware, of course, of the fact that Zwicker said that he could have held up an honorable discharge if a man had stolen $50.

SENATOR WATKINS. I understand all of that, but you said you were not going into that. You were going to ask me what I knew about Peress.

The CHAIRMAN. I think you should have told me that you knew nothing about this before we wasted this time this morning. You came this morning and read a letter which is the Mundt testimony. You refer to a list of 30 people. The man who signed the honorable discharge—his name is not here. The commanding officer's name is not here. There are many names missing, although the letter says that all those administratively responsible. Your advice is, all you know is that we should call these men

[* Secretary Stevens]

and hope they would not do—would the young man desist while I am talking to the witness?

SENATOR WATKINS. Is it out of line for my administrative assistant to hand me some papers?

The CHAIRMAN. Let me finish my question. The only thing you have to give us, then, is the advice that we call all of the thirty-odd officers from the Surgeon General on down and hope that they will not invoke the privilege which Zwicker invoked. We asked Zwicker, you understand, who was responsible, and he said he could not answer. The only thing you can tell us now is, when you say I should have blamed the person culpable, is that we should call those 30 people?

SENATOR WATKINS. I called your attention—

The CHAIRMAN. Is that roughly it?

SENATOR WATKINS. Not exactly it, no. I call your attention to a letter of November 3, 1954, addressed to you by Mr. Stevens, in which he expressly, as I recall, leaves out two officers here. I think McManus and General Bergin, and it already appeared—"No action was taken against Maj. Gen. William E. Bergin, the Adjutant General, Brig. Gen. Ralph Zwicker or Maj. John M. McManus, because in the opinion of the Army no acts performed by them manifested the slightest indication of Communist sympathy nor any other dereliction of duty. These officers hold the same rank," et cetera. That was in the letter to you. The letter you wrote me had a paragraph in it like this:

"This indicates that you must have some information as to who was culpable and some information to the effect that Zwicker was not, the sworn testimony, uncontradicted testimony of Zwicker himself.

"This is information for which our investigating committee has been searching. You are therefore invited to appear before the investigating committee to give the information upon which you base the above statement."

I have now given it. That is the best I can do and I stand on my statement.

The CHAIRMAN. In other words, you and I will agree that somebody was culpable?

SENATOR WATKINS. Somebody actually promoted Peress, yes. In the same letter that Mr. Stevens sent you under date of November 3, it quotes the law with respect to the promotion of these people. It seems to me, as a reasonable human being, knowing how these things operate, that that probably was largely responsible for almost the automatic advancement of this man Peress. I would like to offer that for your record.

The CHAIRMAN. Seeing you bring that up, Senator, we will call your attention to the fact that a Dr. Belsky was before the committee also. He had the qualifications, apparently as great as Peress. He was not given a commission; he was not promoted; he was not honorably discharged. I merely call that to your attention so that you will know that when you cite a law there was no law that forced the promotion. I will ask you one final question.

You and I agree that somebody who covered up for this Major Peress is at fault?

SENATOR WATKINS. I do not think anybody covered up, as far as I can get it from the statements made by Mr. Stevens. I am relying largely on what he said. He has given you the names of the people who—all the people—had anything to do with that. You already knew about Zwicker and you already knew about Bergin and McManus. So you have had all of that list. I cannot go beyond that. And when you say "culpable" I do not know whether you mean criminally culpable or whether they actually did the work.

The CHAIRMAN. I am using your word.

SENATOR WATKINS. Culpable as far as we were concerned meant the people who did whatever was done. We do not prejudge people and say they are guilty of something simply because they may have recommended promotion of a man or his honorable discharge. That would be determined by a proper trial, whether they were criminally cuplable or not.

The CHAIRMAN. You said the blame should have been placed on the shoulders of those culpable. By the term "culpable" you meant nothing wrong?

SENATOR WATKINS. I did not necessarily mean criminally culpable. They were responsible. Responsible would probably have been a better word. But you cannot hang a man for writing a report with as many words in it as that if you get one word slightly off key. There was no intention to say that anybody had committed a crime, because we did not know that, and we do not step out and judge them in advance.*

The CHAIRMAN. I am not asking you about a claim. You say there was a wrong done, is that right?

SENATOR WATKINS. It stands for what it says, and I do not care to explain it further.

The CHAIRMAN. Senator, I am trying to find out. You say I should have put the blame on the shoulders of those culpable. I am trying to find out whether you think there was somebody to blame.

SENATOR WATKINS. Somebody was responsible for his promotion and discharge, that is what I meant.

The CHAIRMAN. There was nothing wrong with that?

SENATOR WATKINS. I do not know whether it was wrong or not. That would depend on the facts.

The CHAIRMAN. Senator, I perhaps should be censured for what I am about to say if I am to be censured for what I said to Zwicker. I might

[* CULPABLE—adjective from the noun *culpa*—a fault, especially of negligence; deserving of blame or censure. *Reader's Digest Great Encyclopedia Dictionary*, including *Funk & Wagnall's Standard College Dictionary*.]

say that a Senator who represents the great state of Utah, who comes here and says he does not know whether someone should be blamed for promoting, honorably discharging, a man who has graduated from a Communist leadership school, a Communist leader, a man who owes his duty to a foreign country, a man that was a traitor to this country; a Senator who says, "I don't know whether he is at fault, I don't know whether those who protected him are at fault or not—I would say, "but who says and argues on the Senate floor that the man who tried to find out who has been the secret master covering up for this man, that such a Senator certainly is derelict in his duty. And that is putting it very, very mildly.

Senator, you should be just as concerned as I am about finding out who is protecting the traitors in this man's Army. We know that somebody protected Peress. You know as well as I do that while I have been begging and coaxing the Secretary of the Army to give us the name of the man responsible, you know as well as I do that the Secretary promised that he would have an investigation, that he would give us that information. You have indicated in your report that you know who was at fault.

You say that the commanding officer was not at fault, although the commanding officer refused to answer whether he was at fault or not. I may say I wish you had not wasted our time this morning. I wish you had told me you knew nothing about this situation before I took this hour's time this morning.

If the other Senators have any questions to ask, they may proceed.

The Senator gave me no opportunity to reply to this tirade, but I suppose it was just as well he didn't because we were getting nowhere. He seemed to be completely opposed to my suggestion that he call in the list of officers and civilians furnished him by Secretary Stevens and at a hearing determine what happened, how it happened, and who, if anyone, was criminally or otherwise responsible in the Peress case. It should be remembered that in my conversation with Secretary Stevens when he gave me a copy of his letter to Senator Mundt (which had been read here) that he assured me (as I have already testified) that he would bring all of those named on his list to Washington to appear before Senator McCarthy's committee where he could question them on the Peress case.

SENATOR MC CLELLAN. Are you willing to make a motion in the Internal Security Committee to call these officers named in that letter and make inquiry of them with regard to their responsibility?

SENATOR WATKINS. I certainly am, if Senator McCarthy does not move rather promptly in that field.

SENATOR MC CLELLAN. If this committee does not proceed to do so, I will be glad to second your motion in the Internal Security Committee.

SENATOR WATKINS. That is right. You are a member of that committee with me.

SENATOR MC CLELLAN. Yes, sir; I am.

The CHAIRMAN. If they refuse to testify as Zwicker refused, will you find them in contempt or what will you do?

SENATOR WATKINS. I think I will get the answers with a little cooperation of the Army and Secretary Stevens. I think I will get the answers if I am permitted to proceed with it.

The CHAIRMAN. In other words, you think you can find out who has been covering up for Peress?

SENATOR WATKINS. I never could find out that which would satisfy you. I will say that very frankly. I do not believe you could ever be satisfied unless you can find somebody that ought to be shot or hung.

The CHAIRMAN. Do you think you could—I may say that I think a man who covers up for a traitor under our law should be shot or hung.

SENATOR WATKINS. Right; I will agree with you.

My answer to Senator McCarthy's question: "In other words you think you can find out who has been covering up for Peress?" brought outraged protests from many of McCarthy's supporters: "He is not that kind of a man. He is kindly." "No one should charge him with being a bloodthirsty man." This was the general trend of the protests, mostly from women. I took another look at my answer: "I never could find out that which would satisfy you . . . I do not believe you could ever be satisfied unless you can find somebody that ought to be shot or hung." And then the Senator's response: ". . . I may say that I think a man who covers up for a traitor under our law should be shot or hung." The Senator and I seemed to be in agreement, because I answered: "Right. I agree with you." It then occurred to me that my correspondents had only seen my answer in the press dispatches, but not the Senator's immediate comment (which was in agreement with my stand).

The exchange made certain another point—the reason McCarthy was dead set against following my advice to accept the offer of Secretary Stevens to have all the officers and civilians who had anything to do with the Peress case appear before the McCarthy committee for questioning. No doubt McCarthy had seen the summary of the Inspector General's report in the Stevens letter to Senator Mundt. He also must have seen President Eisenhower's statement that it was the fault of the procedures and errors in handling of the case; and also the Army statement of November 3, 1954, that there was no evidence that the promotion of Dr. Peress and his separation from the Army by an honorable discharge was the work of a communist or a communist sympathizer within the Army.

As a matter of fact, the availability of this information to the general public (as well as to McCarthy and all his staff) may be demonstrated by reference to a book published and released on August 13, 1954, entitled *McCarthy and the Communists,* by James Rorty and Moshe Decter, The Beacon Press, Boston, Massachusetts. This book, which ought to be read in any event by every student of McCarthy and his times, relates the story beginning on page 48, "The Case of the Pink Dentist; Targets: The Army, Zwicker, Stevens, Eisenhower." In this chapter, the authors set forth a complete and accurate summary of the Peress matter based on material made available by the Army to the Congress (including Senator McCarthy) and to the public. McCarthy had no need to pretend that he didn't know "Who Promoted Peress."

There need be no conjecture about the availability of the full facts of the Peress case to Senator McCarthy, however. The Army issued a 2,000-word statement on the entire history of the Peress matter. It was prepared in October, and marked for release on November 3, 1954, fully 12 days before McCarthy had me before his Committee to give window dressing to his charges that there was a "Secret Master" in the Army who protected communists. This report (already before the Committee) said: "The evidence shows clearly that it was the system which was at fault. Accordingly, the inference which has been made repeatedly during the past several months that these actions provide tangible evidence of 'coddling of Communists' by the Army is completely false."

In the face of this report—which, unfortunately, got only a line or two in most of the Nation's newspapers, if at all—McCarthy was able to put on his show and get columns of space in the press. It is even possible to speculate, and I do, that McCarthy seized the initiative and called me before his Committee precisely for the purpose of overwhelming with his peculiar kind of publicity any possible dampening effects the true facts of the Peress case might have on his own deteriorating situation and the support of his followers.

The support of his followers was now, more than ever before, very important to him. He was waging a very desperate campaign outside the Senate hearings to bring the people of the country to his support. He must have concluded that public demonstrations such as the Madison Square Garden mass meeting, petitions signed by millions of Americans, and the support of a portion of the press and other public media just *might* sway the Senate in his favor so that there would be no censure. The hysteria thus formented is the subject of another chapter.

Now, we look at my final exchange with McCarthy for the day:

The CHAIRMAN. Unless the Senators have some questions, I think we have wasted one morning. I had hoped that you could tell us ahead of time you knew nothing about this situation, Senator.

SENATOR WATKINS. It was my purpose to come before your committee and make such answers as I could make in response to your invitation.

The CHAIRMAN. You are asking that I be censured for not placing the blame on the shoulders of those culpable. You say now that you think by some mysterious process your committee might be able to get the witnesses to disregard the Presidential directives. If you have such a way of getting that information, you are welcome to proceed. I would like to see you try and get it.

The committee will be adjourned unless there are any questions to be asked.

(Whereupon, at 10:45 a.m., the committee recessed, subject to call.)

It appears to me beyond all doubt that Senator McCarthy had taken such a strong position that there was a "Secret Master," a "protector of the 5th Amendment Communist," a "cover-up" for traitors, a traitor "who should be shot or hung," in the Army that he could not now back down without losing face. He had thoroughly sold his followers that there was such a traitor; he could not dare to take a chance by following my suggestion of questioning the Army personnel whose names had been submitted to his committee by Secretary Stevens.

In the case of the Wheeling, West Va. speech, in which he charged that there were a large number of card carrying communists in the State Department, he had failed to prove his charge—in fact he couldn't name one communist—when put to the test. At that time he had but few followers—but now there were millions. They were deeply moved, as I and my fellow members of the Select Committee came to know through the violent, abusive communications we received. The Senator's newspaper supporters also joined in the din.

Included in the Chairman's final comments on my appearance before his committee at this special hearing two statements were made:

(1) "Unless the Senators have some questions, I think we have wasted one morning."

I do not wholly agree with the Senator. It was emphasized time and time again during this hearing he now had an opportunity to question the Army officers who had a responsibility in connection with the Peress case with a good prospect that his two questions: "Who promoted Peress, and who gave him an honorable discharge?" would be cleared up.

(2) "I had hoped that you would tell us ahead of time you knew nothing about this situation, Senator."

This suggests that he really didn't think I knew anything about "this situation" so he hoped that I would say so, and thus no hearing would then be necessary.

This raises an obvious question: why then did he communicate with me at all if he hoped I would say I knew nothing about the matter? The answer should be obvious: He was playing the publicity gambit to the limit. He got wide press, radio and television coverage on his plan to bring me before his committee just ahead of the Senate's consideration of the Select Committee report to the Senate recommending censure of the Senator for his mistreatment of General Zwicker. So far his strategy was succeeding.

I am convinced he was sure I would not agree to appear before his committee. He was bluffing as he was reputed to do in his poker games where he made big winnings on this strategy. His statement in this current hearing, I believe, was an inadvertent confession that he never expected that I would accept his request.

Personally, I believed at the time he was bluffing, but I also felt it would be an opportunity to face him publicly on the Peress matter, even if it (the hearing) was the unethical thing for him to plan under the circumstances.

In closing this hearing, Senator McCarthy challenged the Internal Security Committee of which I was a member, to get the information with respect to the Peress case which he had failed to get: "I would like to see you try and get it," he concluded. The censure proceedings of the Senate took a short vacation in the press and other public media from December 2, 1954, the day the McCarthy Censure Resolution 301, was adopted until a new Congress convened in January, 1955.

Shortly thereafter the McCarthy Committee was reorganized as the McClellan Committee. One of its first tasks was a further investigation of the Peress case under its new chairman by following the advice I had given Senator McCarthy. The story of this continued investigation and its results will appear in the next chapter.

13 *Who Promoted Peress?*

Despite recommendations of the Watkins Committee that the Senate should censure Joseph McCarthy on two counts, public opinion still wants to know who ordered the promotion and honorable discharge from the Army of Major Peress, who refused to answer whether he was a communist. The Watkins Committee hearing failed to bring out the answer to that so-embarrassing question.

Lead for an editorial in the Hearst
chain of newspapers during the McCarthy
censure proceedings in 1954.

TO KEEP THE RECORD STRAIGHT, IT SHOULD BE RECALLED THAT I RESPONDED to a request from Senator McCarthy to appear before his Senate Investigations Committee for questioning on November 15, 1954.

The congressional elections of 1954 resulted in the defeat of a number of Republican Senators, enough in fact to turn the control of the Senate over to the Democrats. Thus Senator John McClellan, ranking Democrat on the Senate Permanent Investigating Subcommittee (which McCarthy had chaired so long) succeeded to the post of chairman.

The new chairman lost no time in scheduling a continuation of the Major Peress investigation. The committee staff was headed by the late Robert F. Kennedy (who had earlier been a McCarthy aide). Kennedy was appointed by Senator McClellan to the position of chief counsel, and was directed to conduct a preliminary investigation by interviewing all Army officers and civilians who had anything to do with the Peress affair. Also, the staff reviewed many hundreds of official documents which were pertinent to the investigation. This preliminary staff work took six weeks to finish. Then followed the additional hearings which began on March 1st and ended on March 31, 1955.*

It is not my purpose to go into the details found by the Subcommittee on Investigations in its special investigation of Army personnel actions relating to the Major Irving Peress case. But I shall report and discuss the effect of the committee's report on McCarthy's highly publicized claim that there was a "Secret Master," who was protecting communists within the Army.

Among the Subcommittee's many findings were these: By letter dated Febru-

*Hearings before the Senate Permanent Subcommittee on Investigations of the Committee on Government Operations, 84th Congress, 1st Session, March 1955, on "Army Personnel Actions Relating to Irving Peress." See also Senate Report No. 856, on this subject.

107

ary 16, 1954, to Senator Joseph McCarthy, Secretary of the Army, Robert T. Stevens, admitted the Peress case revealed "defects in the Army procedure for handling of the Doctor's Draft Act," and that he had directed The Inspector General of the Army to initiate an "exhaustive investigation."

Later, Secretary of Defense Charles E. Wilson stated: "that the Army had committed administrative errors in handling the Peress case."

On March 4, 1954, President Dwight D. Eisenhower stated that the Department of the Army made serious errors in handling the Peress case and that it was correcting its procedures to avoid such mistakes in the future.

Among the Committee's conclusions were the following: *

> Irving Peress' promotion, change of orders, and honorable discharge were the result of a combination of factors: individual errors in judgment, lack of proper coordination, ineffective administrative procedures, inconsistent application of existing regulations, and excessive delays.
>
> During the period of time Peress was in the service, there was no well defined policy or prescribed procedures in the Army which would insure the effective handling of security risks.

The Committee also listed 48 errors in the handling of the Peress case.** There was not one word in the report that indicated that Major Peress' promotion or honorable discharge, was brought about in any other way than set forth in that document. Also there was nothing in the report that indicated, or even hinted, that Major Peress while he was in the service had committed any overt act as an alleged communist.

But the committee said nothing about the phase of the case in which the public was so deeply interested, whether there might be a "Secret Master" in the Army who protected Fifth Amendment Communists.

With this situation in mind it seemed to me that the late Senator George H. Bender, Republican of Ohio, a member of the McClellan Committee, was fully justified and rendered a great service to his country, when he submitted his individual views in which he pointed out: ". . . that not one iota of evidence was revealed to indicate any subversion, collusion or communist conspiracy concerned with the handling by the military of the Peress matter."

I noted also that there was very limited coverage in the news media on the report and the statement of Senator Bender. This may be accounted for by the fact that the committee report was issued on July 14, 1955. By this time interest in McCarthy's Peress charges had waned and the censure proceedings were no longer page one news. Nonetheless, this was a milestone in the McCarthy

*Committee Report, pp. 32 and 35.
**Committee Report, pp. 36–40.

period, and I reproduce the major portion of Senator Bender's statement which has important information on the Peress case, which the American people are entitled to have brought to their attention.

The Bender statement:

Sen. George H. Bender, a member of the Senate Permanent Subcommittee on Investigations, submitted the following as his individual views:

I am compelled to state additional views to this report of the subcommittee. It is my purpose in so doing to present pertinent facts not included in the report as well as to set the record straight on certain aspects of the report which are not stated clearly.

The purpose of the investigation into the Peress matter, as I understood, was to determine principally whether there existed any subversive collusion or Communist conspiracy in the Army that caused the induction, promotion, and reassignment from duty overseas of this dentist. A great hue and cry continued for nearly a year for the identity of the Communist conspirators and the "silent Communist master of the Pentagon" who "protected" and "covered up" the affairs of this "fifth-amendment Communist." This campaign produced a byproduct in the form of the question that became known nationally, "Who Promoted Peress?"

The subcommittee staff investigated this matter thoroughly. The Department of Defense furnished the greatest cooperation and assistance to this subcommittee by supplying personnel and records unstintingly.

Yet, there is not one word in this subcommittee report to inform the American public that not one iota of evidence was revealed to indicate any subversion, collusion, or Communist conspiracy concerned with the handling by the military of the Peress matter. It seems to me that this was the important question the American people and the Congress desired answered. Assurance had been given publicly and to the chairman of this subcommittee in February and November of 1954 by the Secretary of the Army that this case was the result of "mistakes" and "errors" but not due to Communist influence. Nevertheless the campaign continued until this subcommittee took up the investigation and hearings on the Peress case.

I think it is of paramount importance that this subcommittee should assure the people of this country that no Communist influence was found in the Army.

I cannot agree with the conclusion of the subcommittee that the Secretary of the Army, or "his superiors in the Department of Defense under whose direction he was acting," performed a disservice to the American people, the Congress, and the subcommittee by not revealing for nearly 1 year the facts of Peress' military career.

The record shows that by letter of February 16, 1954, from the Secretary of the Army to the then chairman of this subcommittee the Secretary said that the Peress matter indicated many "mistakes." The Secretary of Defense in testimony before the Senate Armed Services Committee on April 1, 1954, made a similar statement. The President of the United States in response to questions of the press on March 4, 1954, said that the Army made serious errors in the case and was correcting its procedures.

In an effort to quash the persistent rumors that the Peress matter might be tinged with collusion the Secretary of the Army in November 1954 replied to a letter from Senator McCarthy and stated categorically that investigations by his Department and the Defense Department revealed no Communist influence or collusion in this case. He reiterated that many errors had been made and corrective action had been taken. He did not reveal the names of Army personnel involved. The Secretary of the Army had an abiding interest in protecting his personnel, as he testified. Nevertheless, the campaign of doubt continued and in so doing promoted the Communist cause. As a last resort the Army released a detailed chronology on January 7, 1955, in further effort to quell the furor. Even this action was labeled as not giving the complete story.

The report of the subcommittee details these efforts of the Secretary of the Army and high Government officers to acquaint the public and the Congress with the fact that this case was due to errors. The subcommittee report confirms these statements in its findings and presents a detailed list containing many minor personnel failures in support of the finding.

These efforts do not amount in my estimation to a "disservice" in any degree.

One of the proposed conclusions is that the Department of the Army's list of 28 names was deceptive. Another is that the IG investigation* in this case was inefficient. The testimony shows that the list was prepared by the IG; in fact, it was almost wholly on the inadequacy of the list that the IG investigation was evaluated by this committee. The two conclusions are thus exaggerating one failure, that of the IG. While the inaccuracy of the list thus prepared was misleading, it was not shown to be deceptive, which to me connotes misleading plus intent to mislead.

A majority of the list of "major errors" in the last conclusion concern personal failures of various individuals who handled this case. (This serves well to pad our conclusions but does nothing to enhance the quality of the report.) As long as actions are taken by human beings, there will be personal failures. If the purpose is to state that in this case there was an inordinate amount of human error, that could have been stated in one sentence, as were the possible inferences of this fact, such as the policy of assigning inexperienced officers to the intelligence field.

The recommendations contained in the report could be strengthened considerably. As an example, recommendation No. 1 is concerned with cor-

*The investigation by the Inspector General of the Army.

rections of office administration in the Army Personnel Board. It is of greater significance to me that the Army take corrective action in the quality of the decisions of the Board and the number and kind of officer personnel assigned as members.

It is not conceivable that three officers can, with justice and equity, decide more than 700 cases on personnel and security actions in one month. It would seem appropriate to recommend that a greater number of officers be assigned to handle cases of this important nature.

I think that the testimony of the Board personnel gives ample ground to recommend that individuals experienced and trained in personnel and security matters should be assigned to duty thereon.

Senator McCarthy, as the ranking Republican on the committee, took an active part in its deliberations and the preparation of the report. He meekly signed it (although this didn't end his pursuit of General Zwicker). It was, however, with some personal satisfaction that I ultimately saw—through the efforts and the report of the McClellan Committee—that my position was sound and that the advice I gave McCarthy (when acted upon by McClellan) was vindicated.

Given the abundance of factual information available and from the vantage point of maturity, the objective student today may see as never before, in the handling of the Peress case and in the harassment of General Zwicker, the true nature of McCarthy and of McCarthyism. Even as McCarthy's attitude toward the Gillette Committee (as clearly documented as it was) exposed his contempt for the Senate of the United States, so the Peress case (which swung off course in a vicious and vindictive attack on General Zwicker) exposed McCarthy's contempt for the truth and for the rights and dignity of human beings.

Of course, there were many byproducts of McCarthyism, and perhaps the worst of these was the contagion of hysteria which resulted in individuals being fired forthwith from their jobs in private corporations merely for being called before the McCarthy committee and availing themselves of their right under the Fifth Amendment, when no overt act in violation of any law was either charged or sustained.

Students of American government and politics may some day assess the damage done by McCarthyism, and, too, they may inquire as to the good faith of McCarthy aides in supporting his objectives. To what extent were they aware, for example, that McCarthy had fabricated his entire presentation of the Peress matter purely for public show?

These are all questions which not only students but the American public have a moral obligation to inquire into and to answer.

"*. . . a moment of farce, of hysteria edging on madness.*"

—Emmet John Hughes

LONG BEFORE THE HEARINGS OF THE SELECT COMMITTEE HAD RUN THEIR course—and, to my way of thinking, even before they began—Senator McCarthy had concluded that he could not win his case. From his first rebuff in the hearings, he talked of the Select Committee as a "kangaroo court" and a "packed jury."

It was his decision, as we have seen (and not his attorney's), to make his defense in the form of attack. He maligned individual members of the Select Committee, spoke disparagingly of the Committee as a whole, and was contemptuous of the Senate itself. When he found that we would not permit him to make his attacks within the forum of the hearings—as had been his custom— he made his attacks upon leaving the hearing room.

In front of the TV cameras in the hall, the Senator made the comments which were considered news and so carried by this media. It was the nature and advantage of TV to feature such on the spot reporting. To millions of listeners and viewers, it was what McCarthy had to say in person and on TV that was the real story and the most interesting news. Delayed reporting in the press, even with the balance of editorials and the interpretive commentary boxed next to summaries of hearings in adjacent columns, as could be found in the more responsible newspapers, never quite caught up with the "reality" of television.

This active campaign by McCarthy—at a time his censure was being considered by the committee is in sharp contrast with what would have been permitted by any judicial body in the land. As will be remembered, McCarthy and his followers had insisted that the Select Committee follow strictly judicial procedures in examining him (which, also, had been our intention from the first), but the Senator felt free to disregard the most elemental procedures of a fair hearing. It seems probable that had his case been heard in any high court he would have been cited for contempt or enjoined from attacking the court.

The phenomena did not go unnoticed at the time, either by his colleagues or by alert commentators. Arthur Krock, wrote in *The New York Times* on September 5: "McCarthy risks much in 'trying' his case on TV."

Describing how the Select Committee had proceeded in a "calm, judicial atmosphere" and "followed the orderly methods of a law court to the extent that a political group can follow them," Krock then related how "chance came to McCarthy's aid" when I (as chairman) "made the mistake of giving an impromptu interview to television reporters whom, in the name of orderly procedure," I had barred from the public hearing.*

Krock said: "In answer to McCarthy's complaint [about Senator Ed Johnson's supposed comments in Denver about McCarthy] "Watkins courageously made the sound point that all members of the Senate, which is the court that will finally pass on the censure proposal . . . have acquired some opinion in the matter. If this were to be the test, said Watkins, the Senate could never render judgment on a colleague.

"But in the television interview, Watkins condensed his statement on this point into words McCarthy could cite as Watkins' view that previous bias was not stigma on the (Committee) which proclaimed, when formed, and since proclaimed itself, as a model of judicial fairness. The Wisconsin Senator pounced on the opportunity this gave him to try to discredit the group . . .

"He started a rival show in the corridor outside the 'courtroom,' where the banished television reporters and their cameras were happily and understandably available. The result was that they were getting a far better performance, from the standpoint of the viewers . . ."

Krock then pointed out that if the Select Committee had, indeed, been a court it "could require McCarthy to confine his defense to its courtroom."

Then, he added: "On the other hand, McCarthy could be on his way to a risk which could damage him beyond his calculations. If he becomes definitely embroiled with his judges, through conduct which will impress them as bearing out the general accusation that his behavior casts discredit on the Senate and calls for censure, this could contribute heavily to a final adverse judgment by the entire body."

Probably without forethought, McCarthy had developed an issue in the Army-McCarthy hearings of communist infiltration and subversion in the most vital structures of the Nation's defense. It was the slow-reacting bureaucracy of the military establishment's handling of personnel matters in the Peress case itself that contributed to the confusion and doubt, and which made McCarthy's forays into this area productive. Very likely, he succeeded beyond his greatest hopes.

*In keeping with judicial practice, and to further our intention of keeping the hearings objective and to the point of issue (that is, to prevent grandstanding, which is afforded by being "on camera"), the Committee had kept TV and other cameramen out of the hearings room. TV commentators, of course, were permitted to sit in as were other reporters. The evening of the first day of the hearings, I was set upon at the door by one of these TV reporters as I was trying to leave. He challenged me with his interpretation of what I had said in the hearing, and I curtly corrected his statement. While in the doorway, I was also on camera and did not realize it. This may be remembered while reading further in Krock's remarks.

As McCarthy made his attacks, the slow processes of truth never caught up with him. So it was in his "defense" of the censure charges. A highly charged, emotional and inflammable personal following resulted.

In the first round of McCarthy's free-wheeling investigations, the State Department and other Executive agencies had been intimidated with some success. Then followed the Army and some of its contracting private companies, such as General Electric. The formula was proven, the results (from McCarthy's point of view) were satisfactory. Now, it was the turn of the United States Senate.

In choosing to go over the head of the Select Committee, McCarthy was also going over the head of the Senate itself, in taking his case to the people. He presented himself as the anti-communist hunter who would not weaken, who would not be deterred, who would fight to the death to preserve the country in the fact of the unjust, evilly-conceived plans of his detractors.

What was happening was certainly not fully apparent to me at the time, although it may be clearly seen in retrospect. I defer to the commentators of the time for having an early insight into what was happening. Looking back over the "hot summer" of hysteria about which I am now writing, Arthur Krock wrote in *The New York Times* on December 2, 1954: "Therefore it must be assumed that (McCarthy's) aggravation of (the situation) since (the censure hearings)—by the nature of his attacks on Watkins and other committeemen —was deliberately designed to put the situation beyond substantive change in his own favor." Which is saying that McCarthy deliberately began to seek censure!

What in the name of sanity was the rationale for this action? It was, as we now see, in the remarkable numbers of McCarthy supporters who rallied to the Senator's support. It was in the possibility of becoming the political leader—the nationalist hero—of a cross-party-lines faction or even a third party.

There must have been some coordinating leadership to the support-McCarthy effort, but I do not have available sufficient information to demonstrate this. As in so many other instances, this lends itself to future research.

Fairness requires me to report, also, that some forums were made available to those critical of McCarthy. At a nationwide meeting of psychologists in New York City, on September 5, 1954, Dr. G. M. Gilbert made some sharp remarks about the Senator from Wisconsin.

Gilbert, Associate Professor of Psychology at Michigan State College and a former prison psychologist at the Nuremberg War Crimes trials, said * that the country's freedoms were being menaced increasingly by anti-intellectual forces. He cited "the sense of suspicion and intimidation with which McCarthy has poisoned the atmosphere of free inquiry in the intellectual world of America."

*The New York Times, September 6, 1954.

Gilbert said that the Senator was among the most dangerous of these forces and accused him of "compulsive or systematic distortion of the truth" and urged him to submit to psychological examination "in his own interest as well as that of the country he professes to defend."

While the feeling described by Gilbert—that there were anti-intellectual forces at work in America—was shared by some letter writers to both legislators and editors, it was restrained. As for myself, I saw virtually no evidence of anti-McCarthy organization. I am told today that there were some relatively small and insignificant efforts to mobilize public opinion against McCarthy. Almost all of this effort was oriented around college campuses. A group at Harvard University is said to have collected 2,000 signatures, but I have no idea who they attempted to petition.

On the other hand, the handiwork of pro-McCarthy factions was evident to me and to all other Congressmen and Senators in the tremendous flood of mail received from McCarthy's admirers. Because of my position as Chairman of the Select Committee, I felt I could not read or let myself be influenced by public opinion at the time. Even so, it could not escape my attention—as my aides pointed out the stacks of mail—that hundreds and thousands of postcards and other missives would arrive within days of each other, each using almost identical language and showing other signs of conforming to ideas of some director of opinion.

The uniformity of the vicious and inflammatory remarks which characterized the bulk of this mail so shocked my Senatorial colleagues and so impressed my assistants that one of them made the unfortunate remark to a reporter—which dogged me through the entire censure proceedings—that, compared to the pro-McCarthy mail which arrived in bulk, the letters which supported the work of the Committee and our efforts to be fair and objective ". . . came from a better class of people."

It was only toward the end of the summer, after the Select Committee had released its recommendations and the Senate had begun its debate, that letters favorable to our position and showing some recognition of our efforts to be judicial began to arrive in any number. During the summer, prior to this, one of my aides estimated that the pro-McCarthy mail was running 35 to 1.

With respect to the mail which flowed in to Capitol Hill, since I wish to describe my own mail in a separate part of this book, let me cite evidences as they were put in the record by Senator William J. Fulbright.

Fulbright, speaking on the floor of the Senate on November 30, just a day before the censure vote, and commenting on the mail which he and other Senators had been receiving, described the letters as vicious—often anti-Semitic —and frequently referring to Senator Fulbright himself as a "louse," "skunk," "coward," "dirty red," "jackass," and other epithets.

A few illustrative examples as inserted in the *Record* by Fulbright should suffice: *

> Sir: You ask for public support in this phony censure showdown. I am an ex-marine who fought in the South Pacific, to open the gates of this Nation for the commy Jews that Hitler did not kill?
>
> You are one of the phony pinko punks connected with Lehman, Morse, Flanders, and Bennett.

Another example from the same source:

> You English louse. Go back to England with your British wife and stay there . . . McCarthy has showed up you and your type of pinko Senators. Ship supplies to England, and England sells it to the Reds to kill our boys. Drop dead, you skunk.

And still another letter:

> Red skunk: I will not dignify you with the title of Senator. You are a disgrace to the United States Senate. A dirty Red rat like you should be kicked out. You are not fit to clean Senator McCarthy's shoes. Hope you are struck by God.

Further discussing the letters, Senator Fulbright went on to say that ". . . the junior Senator from Wisconsin, by his reckless charges has so preyed upon the fears and hatreds and prejudices of the American people that he has started a prairie fire which neither he nor anyone else may be able to control."

Another matter, which was pointed out to me, was the surprising number of letters containing identical reprints of pro-McCarthy literature printed by the usual "pro-America" and nationalist groups such as Gerald L. K. Smith's Christian Nationalist Crusade.

With respect to the rallies for McCarthy, the first evidences of what was happening could be seen in the neighborhood and city-wide pro-McCarthy meetings that were called by innumerable organizations, ranging from local American Legion Posts to "prayer" sessions led by local churchmen.

One of the first mass meetings to receive national publicity, as I have mentioned earlier, was the August 7 McCarthy appearance before 2,000 cheering American Legionnaires in Washington, D.C., where he spoke of Senate colleagues as "nice little boys" without the "guts" to fight communism.

Another group of veterans ** rallying to McCarthy's side met at the annual

---

Congressional Record, Vol. 100, Part 12, 83rd Congress, 2nd Session, November 30, 1954, p. 16197.

**While it may be demonstrated that the publications of veterans organizations published pro-McCarthy material, that the local chapters moved to sponsor and distribute pro-McCarthy petitions, and that the commanders and past commanders

communion breakfast of Catholic War Veterans in New York on November 7. Speaking to the 700 veterans was Msgr. Edward R. Martin, formerly an Army chaplain and then Pastor of St. Angela Merici Roman Catholic Church in the Bronx. Attending the breakfast as the personal representative of Cardinal Spellman, his remarks brought national attention and supplied "information" for hundreds of letter writers.

The Monsignor's remarks—from which Cardinal Spellman shortly disassociated himself—were to the effect that Senator McCarthy's ouster was being sought for his "Catholic ideals." He said: "I personally know that $5,000,000 has been pooled to kick McCarthy out of the Senate—only a small portion of what is pouring into Washington." *

As reporters of *The New York Times* bored in on the Monsignor for details (and pressed the Cardinal himself for comments), it developed that he could supply no supporting information. The impression was left that he had talked off the top of his head.**

On Veterans Day, November 11, a crowd of 3,000 gathered at Constitution Hall in Washington, D.C., to demonstrate their support of McCarthy. The rally was organized by Rabbi Benjamin Schultz of New York, National Director of the American Jewish League Against Communism.† Groups arrived from around

---

of veterans organizations lent their names to these efforts, I cannot believe that the majority of veterans (even of those veterans in such organizations) felt as their leadership evidently did with respect to the McCarthy censure.

The New York Times, November 8, 1954.

**The truth never caught up with the charge about the $5,000,000 slush fund, which of course did not exist. The following letter is an example of the reiteration of the charge:

Chicago, Illinois
December 5, 1954

> Senator Watkins
> Dear Sir:
>   How much money did you and your fellow senator, Mr. Bennett, receive from the special McCarthy fund? A telegram was published in our newspaper showing President Eisenhower's friends were major contributors.
>   Is that why you reported to the White House?
>   If you could visualize the rallies and closed meetings being held, you would *know* that the Republican Party is split beyond repair.
> Signed by a woman.

†McCarthy's supporters cited this group, along with the fact that the Senator had employed two Jewish young men—Cohn and Schine—as evidence that he was

the country by car, plane and bus. From New York City 873 came by train, marching in a group from Union Station to Capitol Hill to lobby with their home Senators.

As reported in the November 12 issue of the Washington *Post,* the meeting began emotionally: "On the stage were fathers, mothers, and wives of American fighting men missing and believed to be prisoners of the Chinese Reds.

"Some of these broke into tears when McCarthy cried out:

" 'You are the victims of a massive appeasement that has been going on for years. It knows no political bounds.'

"McCarthy's voice broke and he wiped away tears with a handkerchief as he went on:

" 'We don't know whether your sons or husbands are living in a bloodstained communist dungeon or are dead.' "

As the meeting progressed, (according to the *Post*) it took on the appearance of a political convention. It was reported that McCarthy waved his arms and shouted: "Regardless of what the Senate may do, this fight to expose those who would destroy this Nation will go on and on and on."

For two hours, as other speakers and guests made their appearance or were recognized (including Senators Goldwater, Welker, and Mundt, former Senator Burton K. Wheeler, and former Representative Hamilton Fish, Westbrook Pegler, and John Maragon), the audience applauded the name of McCarthy and hissed the names of his detractors. "Joe! Joe! Joe!" they screamed.

As an organist played, young people pranced up and down the aisles with placards, such as: "New York Firemen for McCarthy," "Moscow Hates McCarthy Too," and "Senator McCarthy Deserves a Citation Instead of Censure." *

The greatest mass meeting of them all was organized by a group of retired military men: Rear Admiral John C. Crommelin, Lieutenant General George E. Stratemeyer, and Admiral William H. Standley, at Madison Square Garden in New York on the night of November 29.

Pro-McCarthy groups across the Nation were pressed to send delegations, and organizational efforts were made in this regard by veterans groups and even religious organizations (with the Rt. Rev. Harry G. Graham, National Director of the Holy Name Society, mailing his personal invitations to attend).**

Madison Square Garden could hold up to 22,000 people but this was thought not enough, and plans were made for an overflow crowd outside to hear the

not anti-Semitic. The reader should know, however, that the most anti-Semitic agitator of them all, Gerald L. K. Smith, was a special McCarthy friend and attended many committee sessions on Capitol Hill as McCarthy's guest.

*See also *The New York Times,* November 12, 1959.

**See *The New York Times,* December 1, 1954.

talks by loudspeaker. As chance had it, 13,000 people (more men than women, according to the *Times*) showed up. A 45-piece high school band from Hortonsville, Wisconsin, was flown in for the occasion.

The Garden had the appearance of a political convention, with signs spotted for "state delegations." Another sign was prominent:

SENATOR JOE MC CARTHY FOR PRESIDENT
OF OUR GREAT CHRISTIAN NATION IN 1956
KEEP IT CHRISTIAN IN THE INTEREST OF
AMERICA FIRST

While McCarthy could not attend the rally (having injured his elbow, giving him a ten-day break in the hospital while the pro-McCarthy hysteria mounted), his wife, Jean, did make an appearance and was enthusiastically received. Other speakers, who could not be present (such as Alvin M. Owsley, former National Commander of the American Legion; Clyde A. Lewis, past Commander of Veterans of Foreign Wars; and Utah Governor J. Bracken Lee) were heard via telephone hook-up. As each speaker was heard, the crowd cheered the names of its heroes (General of the Army Douglas MacArthur, Senator Pat MacCarran, Senator John Bricker, and Senator William Knowland) and booed the villains (Senator Ralph Flanders, President Franklin D. Roosevelt, President Harry S. Truman, and General of the Army George C. Marshall).

As interpreted by Leo Egan in his November 30 story in *The New York Times,* what was really at stake in the McCarthy censure debate—according to the speakers—"is the right of Congress to investigate the conduct of the Executive Department."

Descriptive of the atmosphere of the meeting is Egan's portrayal of what happened to Lisa Larsen, staff photographer of *Time.* She had been "shooting" in the general direction of a couple who took exception to this and tried to force her to stop. As they struggled, the crowd began to shout: "Throw her out!" and this soon changed to an ugly "Hang the communist!" As a plainclothesman escorted her to safety, a singer was put on the microphone and continued until the crowd calmed down.

With reference, further, to this period of McCarthy's hospitalization with an injured elbow—which brought a recess in the censure debate on the Senate floor—*New York Times* columnist William S. White wrote on November 21:

"These coming ten days, therefore, will provide a remarkable test of the power or relative lack of it, the appeal or relative lack of it, of the organization called Ten Million Americans Mobilizing for Justice and of many others of like mind.

"The pro-censure forces, while beyond doubt formidable, have no such organization visibly active (in Washington). These people are large in number, but not organized as are the McCarthy supporters.

"But the anti-censure forces have drawn up a cadre that clearly represents the largest re-emergence and coming together of essentially Right-wing groups since before the United States entered the Second World War." *

What had been billed as a ten-day nationwide petition campaign was announced on November 14 from the Roosevelt Hotel in New York City by retired Lieutenant General George E. Stratemeyer, Korean War Air Force Commander. Called Ten Million Americans Mobilizing for Justice, it employed the services of "pro-America" and veterans groups to distribute petition forms and to solicit signatures on behalf of McCarthy. Also lending their names were retired Admiral John G. Crommelin, retired Admiral William H. Standley, retired General James A. Van Fleet, former Governor of New Jersey, Charles Edison, and Mrs. Grace L. H. Brosseau (head of the American Association of Patriotic Societies and former President-General of the Daughters of the American Revolution). The accounting firm of James W. Walsh & Company in New York was retained to certify the count. The group confidently expected to obtain 10,000,000 signatures.

Even with McCarthy's elbow injury, which delayed the necessity of delivering the petitions, the group was able to come up with only 1,000,816 signatures by the day of the censure vote.

On December 1, the petitions in grocery-store cartons were brought by armored truck from New York and unloaded outside the Capitol. Guards with drawn pistols stood over the boxes as photographers snapped pictures. One guard excused himself to go inside to the men's room and his holstered pistol caught the eye of the building guard. While the armored truck attendant surrendered the piece until he completed his business, someone brought news of the event to Senator William Fulbright, who in turn asked the Sergeant-at-Arms to inquire. Fulbright brought the matter to the attention of Senators on the floor.

A few minutes later, the guards lugged the heavy boxes into Vice President Nixon's office—right next to the Senate Chamber—where Rear Admiral John G. Crommelin had lined up the Vice President and Senators Knowland and Bridges for a presentation. Mr. Nixon accepted the petitions "on behalf of the Senate," whereupon they were carried out again to the waiting armored truck

---

*William S. White goes on to discuss the "interlocking structure" of the several pro-McCarthy groups, which especially featured former military men and veterans groups, and others who found common cause in McCarthy's anti-communism and opposition to the growing power of the Executive Department. White said they were pulled together by McCarthy as the "current catalyst."

and returned to New York. (After the censure, the counting of the petitions was stopped by Stratemeyer "because of the expense" with uncounted others "pouring" in. The count stopped at 2, 287,143.*)

In addition to organizational efforts, the various information media played a great role in focusing the hysteria of the time. I have described the natural effect of TV (probably inadvertent, as far as the TV people were concerned) in giving credibility to McCarthy's accusations. The printed word also made its contribution.

Louis F. Budenz, in a clipping I received from a letter-writer, from *The Catholic News* for November 6, 1954, developed at length a favorite theme. A Moscow-directed "communist conspiracy," he said, was aimed at the incoming Congress to force, through its actions, "national suicide." This would be brought about by a move to expel McCarthy from the Senate, the ending of all Congressional inquiry into communist subversion (". . . already so badly hampered by the 'battle against McCarthyism' "), and moves to prevent the FBI from functioning effectively.

"We can yet save America," wrote Budenz, and this could be accomplished only by writing every Congressman—and through letters to the press—to insist on an end to this ". . . communist created 'battle against McCarthyism.' "

Other writers, and radio and TV commentators, called for the same flood of mail. Newspaper clippings and reprints of articles and transcripts of broadcasts —ranging from the anti-Semitic smears of Gerald L. K. Smith to the American Legion magazine articles of the respected head of the FBI, J. Edgar Hoover— were copied by various processes (including hand presses) and at the expense of a large number of aroused local citizens and were mailed in every direction.

Most commonly, the clippings which came in my mail, and which I now have at hand to examine, were letters to the editor. The dates and names of papers were often indistinguishable, but I will cite three examples (most of the clippings mailed reflected the beliefs of the mailers and were not their own printed letters-to-the-editor).

Cambridge, Mass.

To the Editor:

Looking for a name for Hurricane F? How about Flanders from Vermont, the biased commie-dupe, a disgrace to the Green Mountain Boys who fought for freedom?

(Signed by a man)

The New York Times, December 2, 1954. See also the *Times for* December 6, and the Washington *Post* for December 2.

Queens, New York

To the Editor:

Will Maj. Peress be the next person to investigate Sen. McCarthy?—and by the way, WHO PROMOTED THE MAJOR ANYHOW?

(Signed by a man)

Unidentified locality

To the Editor:

I feel that United States Senator Joseph R. McCarthy should be extolled to the skies for his unrelenting fight against the Reds. I am concerned with the continuation of our America and I stand behind Senator McCarthy who so boldly and without flinching takes this true American stand.

(Signed by a man)

With each clipping from the Letters-to-the-Editor column there was usually a note, similar to the one which accompanied the last example above. This comment follows:

Dear Senator Watkins:

These clippings tell more than I can say. People everywhere are outraged at the tactics of your committee. Talk about McCarthy's methods. Don't worry time will tell.

(Signed by a man)

McCormick's Chicago *Tribune,* the Hearst papers, and Chandler's Los Angeles *Times,* as well as a variety of locally-owned Texas and other papers of reactionary bent, were continually critical of the Select Committee, of me, and of those Senators who pressed for the censure of McCarthy. The principal issue was the allegation that McCarthy had been recommended for censure because of his fight on communism. Second to this was the charge that the Select Committee (with me, its chairman) was prejudiced and had not been objective. Another great concern was the idea that the proposed censure of McCarthy was destroying the Republican Party (undermining its basic argument that only the Republicans were aware of the danger of communism and of the "twenty years of treason" perpetrated by the Democrats). More space than any, however, was given to the Peress matter.

William Randolph Hearst said in an editorial (in a clipping I have from the New York *Journal American,* for September 28, 1954): "After two investigations of Sen. McCarthy, the Peress question remains unanswered." In another editorial by Hearst (undated), he states again: "The Watkins Committee hearing failed to bring out the answer to that so-embarrassing question."

In the press handling of news on McCarthy and his charges, any student of this phase of the McCarthy story will observe that newspapers which traditionally "bend over backwards" to be objective (particularly *The New York Times*) gave careful attention to what was said by both sides. Other newspapers featured by headlines and placement of stories those events (particularly the pro-McCarthy newspapers) which reflected their publishers' predilections.

The columnists of the time were well-known for their particular interpretations. However, what is now known as interpretive news reporting was not extensively practiced. I have indicated that full information was available to McCarthy on what actually occurred in the Major Irving Peress case at the very time (the summer of 1954) that he made his allegations of cover-up, by the Executive Department and the Army, of a communist "Secret Master" in the United States Army. This was also the time that he attacked the Select Committee and me, its chairman, for being more concerned with "stopping McCarthy" than we were with finding the communists in the Army and other high places in Government. We must now conclude that these wild charges were deliberately fraudulant and calculatingly misleading.

A principal case in point was the official Army statement prepared in October and released for use on November 3, 1954, which was made available to McCarthy (by a covering letter from Secretary of the Army Stevens) but which McCarthy effectively "hid" from public attention by calling me before his committee for a highly-publicized search for a "Secret Master" in the Army. This play by McCarthy was made possible only because the original 2,000-word Army statement on Peress had received but a few lines in most papers and had been ignored by others. Admittedly, the press and public were preoccupied with news accounts of the Congressional and other elections of the day before. Yet, I submit, if the press had been doing its job, it would have made this Army statement available to the public in any balanced reporting of McCarthy's allegations with respect to the Army's performance in the Peress case.

With the next session of the Congress (and after McCarthy's censure)—and the Democrats now in a majority position, which put McCarthy out of his chairmanship of the Subcommittee on Investigations and McClellan into the job as chairman—the original Army statement was verified as a result of lengthy hearings, and through the availability of the ultimate report (signed, interestingly enough, by McCarthy, as the ranking Republican member of the Committee), the public did receive factual information on the Peress case. Even here, only a few newspapers pointed out the non-existence of a communist "Secret Master" in the Army.

A good example of the sober, interpretive analysis of the news which was so desperately needed at the time—and because of its validity is just as good today—follows.

Emmet John Hughes, *Time* and *Life* correspondent, cabled from London a dispatch printed in the October 4, 1954, issue of *Time,* which graphically described the fears of Europeans watching Senator Joe McCarthy and the growth of McCarthyism in America. He reported that to Europeans, McCarthy ". . . more than any other living American . . . has hurt his country's chances to rally the peoples of Europe against communism." He added, relative to his own experience in Europe as a correspondent: "A full year here produces evidence that is sickeningly sufficient. From Moscow to London, from Bremen to Bari, the disgust of Europe is as plain and great as the cost to America, although perhaps not matching the comfort to the Soviet Union."

Hughes explained that to Europeans, who do not fully understand the separation of powers principle in American political life, all U.S. leadership was ". . . confused and contaminated by the conduct of Senator McCarthy." He said: "The effect is that the President and the anti-McCarthy Republicans quite often seem to horrified European onlookers like rabbits transfixed by the headlights of an onrushing truck."

He finally came to that phrase in his dispatch which was so widely quoted at the time: "In the deadly struggle to turn back communist aggression (in Europe) . . . there suddenly seems to be injected a moment of farce, of hysteria edging on madness, when the news tickers of the world click out the report that Senator McCarthy is hot on the trail of a suspect typist trapped in the Pentagon labyrinth."

Describing how diplomatic success or failure in Europe so frequently hinged upon the little things—such as the aberrations of McCarthyism—which kept the U.S. from getting the "benefit of the doubt in the minds of so many," Hughes said: "On the basis of such facts, a case can be made that few men in American politics have so valuably served the forces they professed to be bent on destroying."

If the hysteria of McCarthy's supporters so influenced European politics—and other students have demonstrated a similar reaction elsewhere in the world—what was the effect at home? Political science students have yet to analyze fully and answer this question, but it appears that what has been described by commentators as the right-wing, know-nothing element of American politics came close to forming a third political party with McCarthy as its man on a white horse.

Except for the censure of McCarthy—with its preceding debate on the floor of the Senate, heavily weighted by bedrock sensibility on one side to offset the lack of sanity on the other—it appears to me that the Senator from Wisconsin could indeed have been carried to unbelievable (even unthinkable) power. It was the act of censure which marked the turning point, and it was McCarthy's own reaction to it that destroyed him!

ON MONDAY, NOVEMBER 8, 1954, THE REPORT OF THE SELECT COMMITTEE ON its study of the grounds for censure of the junior Senator from Wisconsin was presented to the Senate. It was my intention that the report be printed in the *Congressional Record* for the convenience of each Senator, as it was expected that discussion of the matter would begin the next day. Virtually the whole day's Senate activity was preoccupied with this procedural matter.

Draft copies of the report had been made available to certain key Senators so they could begin their study and preparations of arguments for or against censure. This included, of course, presentation of a copy of the draft report to Senator McCarthy.

In presenting the report to the Senate to be included in the record of the day's proceedings, I made the observation that some obvious errors in the draft copy had been corrected. These were almost all grammatical errors. Senator McCarthy wanted to know—through discussion in the Senate—what these errors were. Since the report had not yet been filed, neither it nor the changes could be discussed on the floor, as he knew. He seized upon this technicality to say that he could not prepare his defense without knowing the changes, and he said that he could not read the old and corrected drafts in one evening to see what had been changed. (I had offered to send for another copy of the corrected report, and I did send for it at once.)

"Why the secret?" said McCarthy.

"It is no secret," I replied.

Addressing himself to the Presiding Officer, Senator McCarthy then said of me, "He tells me he knows what these obvious errors are. I do not know how we can force him to tell us, but this gives my colleagues some idea of what I had to put up with for days, while this Senator who keeps secret obvious errors, sat as chairman of the committee."

After considerable back and forth about nothing in which Senators Chavez, Welker, and Knowland were involved with McCarthy, Majority Leader Knowland turned to me and asked if I couldn't possibly provide Senator McCarthy with the desired information as a courtesy.

"Nearly 30 minutes ago," I responded tartly, "I offered to send for the only other copy we have." With this I presented it to Senator McCarthy.

McCarthy said that this did not answer his question, that there were 72 pages in the report and he would have to go through each page comparing it with the original to see what changes were made. "Why does he not mark it for me?" he asked.

"They *are* marked in this copy," I said.

Thus the great debate on the censure of Senator McCarthy was set in motion by the most petty of exchanges.

On Wednesday, the 10th, the debate opened in earnest and proceeded for some time at a fairly rational level. As I began my presentation, there were many questions from Senator McCarthy which I endeavored to answer.

Initially, I took pains to tell my fellow Senators how we as as Select Committee had undertaken the assignment of inquiring into the actions of the Senator from Wisconsin. I paid a tribute to my colleagues on the committee: "None of them sought, nor did I, the appointment with which the Vice President honored us. However, I assure the Senate that everyone of us accepted the responsibility with the sincere determination to bring to it whatever wisdom, calmness, fairness, courage, and devotion, they—or shall I say we—might muster for so challenging and important a task."

I explained, further, that while we tried to conduct the hearings along semi-judicial lines, we were not the court. We set standards for the physical conditions of the hearing and for evidence. On the other hand, our findings were not—and should not be considered—an adversary's brief, and the Committee did not assume the position of a prosecutor. Although we had submitted our recommendations, I said, I hoped that the entire Senate would read and study the report carefully (and not be content with oral exchanges on the floor) and come to a decision on the basis of fact. Finally, I offered myself and my five colleagues to answer questions.

Whenever formal debates are held, whether in high school or on the floor of the Senate, each side is given time to make its presentation without interruptions. Rules are provided to insure that each side may be fairly heard.

Under Rule 19 of Senate Procedures,* a Senator must first address the Presiding Officer and obtain his consent to inquire of another Senator if he will yield

---

*In an official Senate handbook, "Senate Procedure—Precedents ˛and Practices," Rule XIX provides, among other things: ". . . no Senator shall interrupt another Senator in debate without his consent, and to obtain such consent he shall first address the Presiding Officer." The rule also provides that "A Senator may yield to another Senator for a question without losing the floor, but he may yield only for a question—and not for a statement, argument, or speech in the guise of a question." Further, "A Senator who yields for a question, or conditionally, has a right to withdraw his consent at any time or decline to yield further." Also, "A Senator desiring to interrupt another cannot read from a document under the guise of asking a question." See "Senate Procedure," pages 245–297.

It may be noted that I showed great patience with Senator McCarthy in his repeated violations of this rule. I didn't ask for enforcement of the rule because I did not wish to give him grounds for complaint that he had been unable to make

for a question. Should the Senator so making an inquiry and having been given permission to speak, take this opportunity to interrupt (as in attempting to read passages from a book) or to make assertions on his own he may be challenged by any Senator.

Further, under Rule 19, "No Senator in debate shall, directly or indirectly, by any form of words impute to another Senator or to other Senators any conduct or motive unworthy or unbecoming a Senator."

While, of course, I had the right and responsibility to make my presentation of the Select Committee's findings without interruptions and challenges, McCarthy deliberately and continually made them.

For some time, on that first full day of debate, I permitted Joe to interrupt for a question. Under the guise of asking a question, McCarthy would then go off on a tangent and make whatever declaration he chose. Readers of this account should know that I permitted McCarthy to ask "questions" as a privilege and not as a right. I did not wish to seem unwilling or afraid to face his challenges. Yet, this was not the usual or normal practice in a Senate debate, and McCarthy was permitted to do this as a special privilege only.

After some time of this, however, I tired physically and (as was well known by McCarthy and the other Senators) I had occasional gastro-intestinal distress from an earlier severe illness and operation.* This limited my talking and my standing for long periods.

I was not yet aware that McCarthy—whose technique of rebuttal had always been one of attack and challenge, as in the Army-McCarthy hearings, and although he had been denied this method of making his "defense" before the Select Committee—was now attempting to make his defense on the floor of the Senate, *not on his own time but through improper interruptions of me on my time!*

McCarthy was, in effect, grandstanding to the galleries and the press. Each point he raised had been thoroughly explored, disposed of, and explained by the Select Committee in its report. Further, as the debate progressed, each of the members of the Select Committee had an opportunity to contribute to this explanation. Even when answered, McCarthy's tactic was not to let go of what might seem to an uninformed public to be an issue of significance. Such a point was his reference to the witness who, it was later discovered, had a mental problem.

his "defense." Yet, of course, he did just this. In the Army-McCarthy hearings, Joe had conducted a show which became famous for its lack of order and decorum. Before the Select Committee, he attempted to do the same thing but was stopped. Now before the Senate, he attempted the same tactic.

* Some time before, during a lengthy floor session on the "Troops to Europe" debate, I buckled from exhaustion and collapsed across my desk.

A rather typical example of the difficulty I had in presenting the case for the Select Committee may be seen in the following exchange: *

> MR. MC CARTHY. I ask—
>
> MR. WATKINS. Just a moment. I have the floor. The important thing is these charges, not the sidelines and diversions which the Senator wants to keep us on. When a Senator makes certain charges and brings them before a body, they become his charges, and they are his sole responsibility, no matter who prepares the charges.
>
> MR. MC CARTHY. I think the Senator has made himself clear.
>
> MR. WATKINS. I hope so.
>
> MR. MC CARTHY. Then the Senate is to understand that the Senator from Utah believes, regardless of whether the Gillette Committee was performing its functions or not, and regardless of whether it may have called an insane witness, I—
>
> MR. WATKINS. The Senator is not asking a question. I insist on his asking questions.
>
> MR. MC CARTHY. I do not want to take the Senator's time indefinitely. I refer the Senator to pages 295 and 296 of the hearings. The Senator had in his hands by subpoena records which show that the Gillette staff had reported that not only was this man mentally incompetent, but that his testimony was valueless. I tried to show that I had asked the right to present this evidence. I wanted to show that the fact that he had been committed to a home for the criminal insane. I desire now to go to another point. On page 24 of the report—
>
> MR. WATKINS. Well—
>
> MR. MC CARTHY. Does the Senator wish to answer.
>
> MR. WATKINS. I do not know whether the Senator is asking a question or making a speech. I will say that it is repetitious. The Senator has been saying it for 20 minutes. I will not reply any further to it. I think that I have stated my position. All the Senator need do to get the answer is to read the report.

Senator McCarthy frequently read from the record, from newspaper clippings and otherwise engaged in diversions under the pretext of asking a question. The only question he would ask, sometimes, was: "Is that a correct quotation?" Exchanges of this nature and significance (or lack of significance) continued through much of the day.

After explaining that I was under "physical limitations" and wished, therefore, to deliver what I had prepared without interruption, McCarthy (although giving

*Congressional Record, Vol. 100, Part 12; November 10, 1954, pages 15927–15932.

some lip service to the state of my health) disregarded this plea and my lack of strength and began to berate and challenge me with increased intensity. On one occasion, because of a gastric upset, I left the floor and McCarthy accused me of running out on him.

I assured Joe that I would make myself available for questioning from him and from other Senators (Senator Welker was one who chipped in frequently on McCarthy's behalf) but I was forced to yield the floor.

McCarthy appealed to the Chair: "Mr. President, there is no way by which I can force the Senator from Utah to answer the very important questions which should be answered. I have no desire to try to compel him to answer those questions today. However, I think he should, as a courtesy, tell me when he feels he might be able to return and answer questions. Apparently he does not wish to answer questions————"

At this point, Senator Knowland (as Majority Leader) interrupted to say: "I am sure the Senator from Utah and the other members of the Select Committee would be glad to cooperate. Perhaps the questions could be asked in writing or orally. Rather than keep the Senator from Utah on his feet, perhaps my suggestion might furnish a satisfactory alternative to the junior Senator from Wisconsin."

From this moment, Senator McCarthy began to refer to me as a "coward" in comments to reporters and in his speeches and addresses he made before audiences during the time of the censure debate. Hastening to Milwaukee to make such a speech, McCarthy told reporters (according to an AP dispatch of November 13, which appeared in the daily press):

> Senator Joseph R. McCarthy today accused Senator Arthur Watkins, Republican of Utah, of the "most unusual, most cowardly thing I've heard of" in saying he would answer no future oral questions by McCarthy or any other Senator.
>
> "If a man is chairman of a committee, he should be willing to answer for errors in his report," Mr. McCarthy said. "Otherwise, he is miserably failing his duty as chairman."
>
> "It is the most cowardly, most unheard of thing I've heard of so far," Mr. McCarthy said.
>
> "I expected he would be afraid to answer the questions, but didn't think he'd be stupid enough to make a public statement," he asserted.

McCarthy's allegations in this statement, it may be seen, was a gross distortion of what actually occurred.

With respect to the same events, other writers interpreted the day's happenings quite differently. Speaking of Joe's "questioning," James Reston, in *The New York Times* for November 11, said:

These tactics did not win Mr. McCarthy any votes in the Senate; they merely aroused sympathy for Senator Watkins and gave point to the charge that Senator McCarthy has contempt for the manners and customs [rules] of the Senate.

Senator Watkins did not seek a place on the Select Committee to study the charges against Senator McCarthy. He did not want it; he took it only at the request of the Senate; and in so doing he relieved other Senators from an onerous and unpleasant duty. Many Senators were clearly conscious of this today, particularly as Mr. McCarthy stood in the next chair to Mr. Watkins and questioned him like a district attorney grilling a criminal.

What the Senators think now, however, is not Senator McCarthy's primary concern. He is not appealing to the Senate. He is aiming once more at the headlines; he is appealing to the people of the country over the heads of the Senate. And his theory is that, since violence and vituperation tend to make their way into the big type on the front pages, he will win a publicity if not a political victory.

Presumably to demonstrate "unanimity" of the Select Committee's study and recommendations for censure with the party line of the communist *Daily Worker,* Senator McCarthy asked to have inserted in the body of the *Record* (on the same day, the 8th, that the committee report was inserted) a compendium of articles and editorials from that journal. This compendium had been prepared by the House UnAmerican Activities Committee and showed that the *Daily Worker* had kept up a drumfire of anti-McCarthy statements during the spring and summer preceding the censure investigation.

During much of the debate on the floor of the Senate over the censure resolution, McCarthy's friends attempted to show that the alleged main issue of McCarthyism was being overlooked. This was, namely, the fact that McCarthy was the principal communist hunter and exposer of communist sympathizers in the country and for this reason should not be hindered. The argument was made, if the communists hate and fear McCarthy then he must be effective indeed. Let us not quibble about McCarthy's methods, said his friends, let's let him have his way.

This was the position, too, of the hundreds and thousands of pro-McCarthy fans who pressed into the visitor galleries to applaud their hero. While McCarthy, in making his defense professed to see empty chairs on the floor of the Senate, he saw no empty chairs on the floor of the Senate, he saw no empty chairs in the gallery. Saying that McCarthy's complaints about losing his senatorial audience were somewhat justified, Mary McGrory in her column for the 13th of November in the Washington *Star,* said: "Yesterday, while vacant chairs yawned all around him on the floor, the Senate hall was jammed to the rotunda with flag-waving legions who gladly went hungry and thirsty for the chance to hear [McCarthy]."

She went on to describe one lady from New York City with "frizzy hair" coming out of the gallery and remarking: "McCarthy's not *rough enough* for the women of this country."

It is true, of course, that the Select Committee never considered McCarthy's anti-communism as an issue. Everyone was anti-communist on the Select Committee, and I am sure the same could be said for the Senate. The issue was McCarthy's contempt for the Senate and his abuse of fellow Senators and witnesses. Admittedly this was not clear to the public then, and perhaps not even today.

As to McCarthy's opposition from the communists, as witnessed in their comments in the *Daily Worker,* it should be remembered that for most of the world and for a large segment in America, the fear of McCarthyism and of "American fascism" was very real. Taken right from the compendium which McCarthy put in the *Record,* the *Daily Worker* on April 4 said:

> Some people say they oppose McCarthyite methods but favor its goals.
> But this is absurd: McCarthyism's goal is police state and war.
> Can there be nice methods for getting fascism and war?
> McCarthyism's goal is fascism, and so are its methods.
> The two cannot be separated.
> If the Communists are robbed of their democratic right to advocate their opinions, no one else has any freedom left.
> All you have to do to kill an idea—like job protection, or peace—is brand it "Communist." That will finish it, as long as McCarthyite fascism is allowed to get away with its big lie.
> Communism is not the issue in the United States. The issue is jobs, peace, and democratic liberty.
> Don't be fooled any more by the fake of the Communist menace. The menace is McCarthyite police state and its war conspiracies.

Without attempting to comment on this quotation from a communist source, except to remind the reader that for decades the "big lie" technique has also been a tool of communist propaganda, I have used this insert, which McCarthy himself put in the *Record,* to demonstrate how the pro-McCarthy people attempted to equate censure efforts with communist "get McCarthy" objectives.

Various writers have said, and I concur, that the communists played their anti-McCarthyism to the hilt because of the similarity in McCarthy's appeal to his following and that of Hitler and his early rise to power, through the sowing of fear and suspicion. By this association, McCarthyism could be made to appear as fascism. Making this comparison as strong as possible, the communists could say that their own avowed goals and objectives looked pretty good. Certainly, in comparison with traditional American liberties and opportunities, communism could have no appeal! (The communists have been as quick to attack J. Edgar

Hoover, Dwight D. Eisenhower, and myself—as a member of the McCarran Committee—on other occasions.)

Much was made of this "don't stop McCarthy because he is hurting the Reds" philosophy by Joe's Senatorial friends.

McCarthy, himself, set the tone by his "handmaidens of communism" speech which he had inserted into the body of the *Congressional Record* on November 10.* McCarthy said in this prepared but never delivered speech that he wanted to discuss some of the implications of the censure matter. He went on:

> If I lose on the censure vote, it follows, of course, that someone else wins. Now, I ask the American people to consider carefully: Who is it that wins? And then, having answered this question, I ask them to contemplate the shocking truth revealed by the fact that the victors have been able to win.
> There is one group that is pretty sure about who has won.
> When the Watkins committee announced its recommendation of censure, the communists made no attempt to conceal their joy.

> The real strength of the Communist Party is measured by the extent to which communist objectives have been embraced by loyal Americans . . . I would have the American people recognize and contemplate in dread, the fact that the Communist Party—a relatively small group of deadly conspirators—has now extended its tentacles to that most respected of American bodies, the United States Senate; that it has made a committee of the Senate its unwitting handmaiden. . . .
> I regard as the most disturbing phenomenon in America today the fact that so many Americans still refuse to acknowledge the ability of communists to persuade loyal Americans to do their work for them. In the course of the Senate debate I shall demonstrate that the Watkins Committee has done the work of the Communist Party, that it not only cooperated in the achievement of communist goals, but that in writing its report it imitated

---

*McCarthy was expected to make his speech, but did not do so. Therefore, Knowland had difficulty in finding speakers to fill the time and keep the Senate busy. It is of interest to note that McCarthy waited until the end of the day to ask permission to have this material inserted in the body of the *Record* (not the Appendix). McCarthy said: "I should like to have the *Record* show that I had intended to give it as a speech, but time was used up, and I could not do so." Readers should know that McCarthy could never have given this material as a speech because it was a flagrant violation of Rule 19. He would have been instructed to take his seat and could not have spoken again without permission of the Senate.

McCarthy had released this material to the press the night before, saying that he was going to give it as a speech the next day. As the material was libelous, he was desperate to get the protection of having delivered it on the floor of the Senate. The speech may be found in the *Record* for November 10, 1954, pages 15951–15954.

communist methods—that it distorted, misrepresented, and omitted in its effort to manufacture a plausible rationalization for advising the Senate to accede to the clamor for my scalp.

But perhaps more important than explaining how the Watkins Committee did the work of the Communist Party is the job of alerting the American people to the fact that this vast conspiracy possesses the power to turn their most trusted servants into its attorneys-in-fact.

There are several notable examples of how Joe's friends in the Senate took up this line. During most of the censure debate on the floor of the Senate, the galleries were packed with observers. Many of these, it is true, were family and staff members of Democratic Senators, who were bitter about McCarthy's continued attacks against the "Party of Treason." Others were quite obviously McCarthy supporters, who occasionally broke out in applause and some cheering when one of the more flamboyant of the Senators supporting McCarthy made what was taken to be a telling point.

I remember one occasion when Senator William Jenner of Indiana, in a lengthy commentary and with obvious concern for the galleries, charged the Select Committee with "ignoring the activities of a conspiracy against the junior Senator from Wisconsin." When this brought loud applause from some of the spectators, the President pro tempore of the Senate threatened to have the galleries cleared if the demonstrations continued.* (Other Senators who were particularly conscious of the galleries while making speeches in defense of McCarthy were Senators Welker, Dirksen, and Goldwater.)

Of course, the "conspiracy" which Senator Jenner was speaking of with respect to the discrediting of Senator McCarthy was the communist conspiracy. Jenner performed a rather delicate balancing act in his allegation that the Select Committee, itself, served the interests of the communist conspiracy. He went on to say:

> I am not attempting to insinuate any charge of procommunism against any member of this body when I say the strategy of censure was initiated by the communist conspiracy.
>
> There is a long and secret trial from decisions of the top communist strategists, through many devious channels, before they appear well disguised in the words of loyal Americans.
>
> There are a thousand degrees of relationship between the communist high command and the many ranks which help it in its work.
>
> I do not need to define exactly the many ways in which the communist conspiracy has influenced, consciously or unconsciously, the members of Congress who have done its secret bidding.

*Congressional Record, Vol. 100, Part 12; November 15, 1954, page 16014.

Senator Jenner's innuendos continued a moment later with the remark that the "communists are attacking us here in this Chamber," and then he implied that the communists "plot to elect their own members of Congress," and finally said that there was not a member of the Senate "unless he is a secret communist" who was neutral in the McCarthy censure contest.*

Jenner, in this statement as in the others, "suggested" that some members of the Senate might be secret communists . . . or at least doing the bidding of the communist high command, either "consciously or unconsciously," as he put it.

The members of the Senate chose to let these matters pass to avoid complicating the issue at hand, but the gall of the remarks remained. Obviously, Jenner was not attempting to persuade his fellow Senators on any factual matter but made his remarks to the galleries.

Senator Bricker, a good lawyer and logician, echoed the general comment that the central issue in McCarthyism was an effort to shut him up for his anti-communism. It may be noted, however, that Bricker did not lend himself to the suggestion that members of the Select Committee were the communists' "attorneys-in-fact." Bricker said: **

> Today the hue and cry is on throughout the land. The pack which hunts the hunters of communists has caught the smell of blood. Without any implication of bad faith or lack of patriotism on the part of my colleagues, whom I respect, I shall not run with that pack.

In commenting about the "incredible orgy of political cannibalism" in which American anti-communists were engaged, Senator Goldwater was not as circumspect as Bricker and approached, indeed, the excesses of Jenner. Goldwater said: †

> We know that this censure move is not a disconnected happening either in the career of Senator McCarthy or in America's fight against communism. It is a part of a sequence of events. Actually, those unknown engineers of censure hope that this will be the culminating act in the merciless fight to destroy a United States Senator and the fight against communism. . . .
>
> The masterminds of this fight have said one thing and meant another. Their propaganda has dripped with idealism, high-mindedness, and lofty sentiments. Their deeds have come from the darkness. . . .
>
> The culmination of their efforts is now to be seen upon the Senate floor, where the Senate is being asked to censure a member of this body

*Ibid., p. 16017.
**Ibid., p. 16000.
†Ibid., p. 16001.

for reasons that are alien to the original issue, but which will serve the purposes of the masterminds who have thus far waged the war against those who fight communism. . . .

The deadliness of the communist way of operating is shown by the fact that they have skillfully shifted the leadership of the campaign into the hands of highly respected American anti-communists . . .*

Senator Case provided the logical answer. He said on the floor:

The Select Committee did not create this situation; the Senate of the United States created the situation in which the committee found itself. If the Senate of the United States said to the Select Committee, "Here is a job you have to do," are we to welsh on it because we fear that the Daily Worker will say, "That is a little water on our wheel?"

Neither McCarthy nor any of his Senatorial supporters attempted to answer Senator Case.

An early point raised by McCarthy and his friends was that the Select Committee had demonstrated prejudices.

With respect to the continuing allegations that three of us (myself, Johnson of Colorado, and Ervin) had made "prior judgments" and actually sought to serve on the Select Committee in order to recommend censure of the junior Senator from Wisconsin, Senator Ervin said in debate: **

Every Senator, except Senator McCarthy, knows full well that there was not a single member of the Senate who desired to have anything whatever to do with the unpleasant task assigned to this committee.

There is only one explanation as to how it was possible to obtain any Senators to serve on the Select Committee. The explanation is simply this. When all is said and done, Senators do accept as true Gen. Robert E. Lee's assertion that duty is the sublimest word in our language.

It was not a prerequisite to membership on the Select Committee that a Senator should have possessed a vacant mind, totally devoid of any opinion whatever in respect to Senator McCarthy. Had such a requirement existed, no member of the Senate would have been eligible to serve on the Select Committee. It is doubtful, indeed, that six mental adults could have been

---

*I recognize myself in this last line quoted, but who were those "unknown engineers of censure?" Was Goldwater speaking of President Eisenhower and White House aides, who—it was so frequently charged—were masterminding the censure, and whose agent (for ample reward) I was supposed to be? Why didn't he have the courage to name these masterminds?

**Ibid., p. 16019.

found anywhere in the United States who did not entertain some opinion concerning Senator McCarthy and his activities.

In commenting on this, I am also reminded of the frequent charges by some that the censure maneuver was somehow "engineered" by communist master-minds working through willing or unwitting agents ("attorneys-in-fact") in the White House or Senate. The obvious answer is that those who first raised charges against Senator McCarthy in the Senate pressed for an *immediate* vote for censure (and very likely would have found a majority at that time). It was the moderates—supported by McCarthy's friends and the Senator himself—who moved for a study by a special committee. Most of the objective and anti-Mc-Carthy press thought the move was one for compromise, and so criticized it.

It was only when the Select Committee recommended against McCarthy that the idea was advanced of communist "engineering" through a prejudiced Select Committee. If there were truth in these charges, it falls back on the heads of McCarthy and his friends—they favored a committee and so voted!

Senator Bricker, whose prestige was great among all Senators and in particular with those who opposed the censure of McCarthy, had rational arguments to present. With respect to the Select Committee, in particular, he tried to lay to rest the allegation that it was prejudiced. Bricker said: *

> I wish to make it perfectly clear that I have the highest admiration and respect for the honesty and integrity of the six Senators who served on the Select Committee to Study Censure Charges. They are all able. They would not wittingly set in motion, or condone, any action that is inherently unjust. Nevertheless, in my judgment, that is the effect of their recommendations.
>
> I cannot agree with the junior Senator from Wisconsin that one or more of the members of the Select Committee were so biased as to preclude their making a fair appraisal of his case.

The principal argument made by Senator Bricker was based on two presump-tions. One was that McCarthy had not been permitted to present his case before the Select Committee. As I have pointed out, McCarthy chose not to make his defense before the Select Committee but before the TV cameras and in the press, and through interruptions on the floor of the Senate. I believe personally that McCarthy did not choose the usual course of debate in the Senate because he was most successful in his publicity seeking and weakest in logical argument. Further, his arguments had been anticipated and answered (but he didn't like the answers).

My decision and that of the other members of the Select Committee to permit

*Ibid., p. 15999.

McCarthy to make his defense in the assertive manner he used in his investigative work was designed to be fair to McCarthy under the circumstances of his weakness.

Senator Bricker agreed on this, for he said:

> In my judgment, the junior Senator from Wisconsin should have been allowed to make his full defense before the committee. The committee denied him that right. But since the entire subject is going to be ventilated here on the Senate floor, the junior Senator from Wisconsin will have his day in court. Whatever the conclusion of the Senate, the junior Senator from Wisconsin will have had a full and fair hearing.

Senator Bricker's other presumption was that in the absence of a prior rule establishing what behavior was appropriate or not appropriate, Senator McCarthy should not be punished. "No punishment," he said, "can be just if it is not based on any law that is known, knowable, or predictable." He also said that application of the law should be "impartial" and applicable in all similar cases.*

My answer to this was that in drafting the Constitution it was not possible to spell out, anticipate, or name offenses that could come under the general heading of "disorderly behavior." The language had to be left general. No one could have been censured or otherwise punished if there had to be precedents before action could be taken. Precedents are valuable, of course, and it should be noted that the censure of McCarthy later served as a precedent for censure of Senator Thomas Dodd of Connecticut, with respect to the latter's actions outside the Senate but which reflected upon the honor of the Senate.

In the debate, Senator Ervin said: **

> The rule goes back to the beginning of our Government. The Constitution of the United States, in many of its provisions, is self-executing. It requires no act of Congress to give them validity.
>
> The suggestion is made that the Senate is impotent to act, because no precedent has been established for such action.
>
> We have here a provision of the Constitution which is not to be interpreted by the courts of this land, but is to be interpreted by the Senate.
>
> Mr. President, when the Founders of the Republic wrote the Constitution and gave to the Senate of the United States the power in express words to punish its members for disorderly behavior, they impliedly said that every

*Ibid., p. 15998.
**Ibid., pp. 16324–16325.

Senator must refrain from disorderly behavior. No one contradicts the findings of fact in (McCarthy's) case, and if they do not show disorderly behavior, I venture the assertion that there is no mind with a sufficiently vivid imagination to imagine what disorderly behavior might be.

During much of the debate McCarthy persisted in trying to show that he was being recommended for censure because he "criticized" the Gillette Committee, questioned its jurisdiction and authority, and challenged the honesty and objectivity of its members.

The matter of jurisdiction and authority had been resolved, said Senator Stennis, by the membership of the Senate. "In spite of all the junior Senator from Wisconsin had said about the matter, if the decision made on the floor of the Senate had been respected, I would have been in favor of forgetting what the junior Senator from Wisconsin had said. But, after the vote of 60 to 0 in the Senate, the pattern continued in the same way." *

Senator Stennis and other members of the Select Committee said, in effect, it was not McCarthy's attacks on individual Senators (as such) that deserved censure, but his arrogant and contemptuous refusal to appear before a duly-authorized Senate body to inquiry and answer allegations concerning conduct which reflected on his honor—and his attack on Senators attempting to pursue their Senatorial responsibilities in this matter—which deserved condemnation. Also, his communications to the Gillette Committee were insulting and contumacious in the extreme and showed a lack of courage on his part to face the Committee.

Speaking of McCarthy's refusal to answer the charges against him, I said on the floor of the Senate:

> Looking over this group, I do not think I can see any Senator present, and I do not believe there is another member of this body, who would have refused the invitation to go before the committee when his honor and his integrity were under serious charges and serious investigation.
>
> As a matter of fact, I think this court has a right to take into consideration the conduct and attitude of the junior Senator from Wisconsin with respect to that committee, and the question of his willingness or unwillingness to appear.

Then, after detailing at great length the charges against McCarthy and the "surface evidences" which deserved further looking into—including the large sums of money sent to McCarthy by citizens hoping to fight communism, which appeared to have been diverted into his own investments—I said that I was

*Ibid., p. 15993.

pointing out the situation, not to indicate that these charges were proven true but that he ignored both the charges and his opportunity to appear and disprove them, if he could.

Then, adding that every Senator has the duty to respect and maintain the dignity, honor, authority, and powers of the Senate, I concluded: *

> Let me add, Mr. President, that when a Senator takes the oath of office to defend and to support the Constitution of the United States, that pledge is not merely with reference to a document containing certain words. It goes to the living Constitution. That living Constitution consists not only of words but the Office of the President, the Supreme Court, the Senate, and the House of Representatives which those words create. When a Senator does or says things which injure those institutions, he is violating his oath to defend and uphold the living Constitution of the United States.

Perhaps the most involved discussion in the censure debate concerned the General Zwicker and Major Peress matters. The back and forth among the various Senators developed much of the story told elsewhere in this volume, and it would not be fruitful to repeat the various comments here.

It was, however, on the Select Committee's recommendation that McCarthy be censured for his abuse of Zwicker that Senator Case suddenly weakened. This happened right after I had inserted into the body of the *Record* the transcript of my encounter with Senator McCarthy before his Government Operations on Investigations Subcommittee concerning the Major Peress matter.

Senator Case discussed at length on the floor of the Senate ** how it had come to his attention through reading of the letters exchanged between Senator McCarthy and Army Secretary Stevens that the Army had received the letter in time to take action the request of McCarthy that Peress not be discharged. This was, as noted in an earlier chapter, on February 1. A decision was made by the Army, it will be remembered, that there were insufficient grounds to withhold discharge of Peress. Senator McCarthy's request was rejected, and Army Secetary Stevens wrote a letter explaining this. Case had assumed, however, that the Senator's letter had arrived too late for favorable action. This, Senator Case said, was not so. This "new evidence" served as the basis of his complaint, and he seemed to feel that McCarthy was under some provocation when he harassed Zwicker. Senator Case continued:

> I think the Senate will not say that an adequate basis for censure exists, when the chairman of the committee wrote, in time, and his letter was

Ibid., p. 16061.
**Ibid.,* p. 16116.

received in time by the head of that executive agency, asking that it file
charges and look into the matter, whereas, instead of acceding to that
request the next morning that agency took adverse action, and instead,
respected the request of Major Peress, an admitted communist, that he obtain
an immediate discharge, and thus escape from the jurisdiction of the
Army.

That is the issue involved here, and I think the Senate should know it.

It should be clear that Senator Case was not condoning McCarthy's actions or
speech with respect to the Zwicker matter . . . nor was Case blaming Zwicker
for being leery of McCarthy's questioning before the subcommittee . . . it was
the Army's brush-off of a Senator's request that irked Case.

Senator Case said:

However, General Zwicker did not give Peress a discharge immediately
when Peress asked for it.

The record is clear that General Zwicker had alerted the Pentagon
through the Chief of Staff of the First Army, in the line of command, that
Peress had come in and asked for exercise of the option under the discharge and wanted an immediate discharge.

Thereupon, the Army had two requests before it. One was from Peress
for his immediate discharge. The other was from the chairman of the
Senate committee, who had requested that charges be filed against Peress
and that the matter should be looked into and that the Pentagon should
keep its finger on Peress.

Later, in the debate, Case was more explicit. He said: *

Nothing I have said would indicate that I approve the language Senator
McCarthy used with respect to General Zwicker.

My feeling is that we could disavow that action, and could say we
disapprove of the use of intemperate language in all instances, whether
such language is addressed to a witness representing the Executive Branch
of the Government or whether it be addressed to other witnesses.

However, if we proceed to condemn the chairman of a Senate committee
under the circumstances existing in the case of General Zwicker, when both
the Secretary of the Army and the Secretary of Defense have said that case
was badly handled, and when the chairman was slighted by a responsible
Army staff, in favor of a request from a man such as Peress, we shall
be establishing a very poor precedent.

*Ibid., p. 16369.

At the very beginning of the debate, Senator Butler of Maryland was the first to raise a specter about the censure of McCarthy for his treatment of General Zwicker. To punish McCarthy for his actions as committee chairman might well "deter, or devitalize" committees in their investigative work in the future, he said.

Perhaps never openly stated, the inference was read by many Senators that their roles as committee chairmen could be limited by censure of McCarthy on the Zwicker matter. Ever conscious of the claimed prerogatives of a United States Senator, Senator Goldwater touched on this sensitive subject. Senator Goldwater said: * "Today we are attempting to glorify a member of the armed services who appeared before the subcommittee and abused a member of the Senate." This "abuse," we may note from Goldwater's comments in context, was the "defiance" which General Zwicker had shown McCarthy.

Goldwater went on:

> I suggest again that we are dealing here with a dangerous thing, with a matter which is completely upside down. We are out in a sea of human emotions. We are blinded to what we might do to the Senate by censuring the junior Senator from Wisconsin on this count.

The Zwicker matter was a crucial issue involving the honor of the United States Senate. If sustained, the censure of McCarthy for his abuse of General Zwicker would have had (as Butler and Goldwater saw rightly enough, not to mention—as we shall see—a group of southern Democrats with great seniority who were about to take their positions as committee chairmen as a result of the November elections) a restraining effect on future committee chairmen.

I do not charge Senator Case with these considerations of personal privilege, but he was sensitive to what he called an affront to the Senate. The softening of Senator Case on this matter—and largely because he was a member of the Select Committee—cost the censure forces any possibility of getting Senate action on the Zwicker matter. Stennis and Ervin stood steadfastly with me on the importance of the Zwicker matter, as did Carlson and Johnson of Colorado.

The mythology of the Zwicker-Peress case was not easily laid to rest. One must assume that many people today would prefer the more exciting and emotional answer which might be found in some kind of a conspiracy.

Senator Goldwater's comments on the Zwicker matter may be cited again as an example of this thought process. He said: **

> Let us admit that the language (of McCarthy) was extreme, but let us at the same time admit that the provocation was as extreme as well. Admit,

*Ibid., p. 16366.
**Ibid., p. 16003.

too, that it would have been more politic of Senator McCarthy to have talked guardedly to a general who, it was later revealed, had extremely powerful and vengeful friends at the Pentagon.

Were these "vengeful friends" Army Secretary Stevens and Secretary of Defense Wilson, and with, perhaps, President Eisenhower in the background? If so, these men may be congratulated for standing firm on principle and for the honor and integrity of a good man.

The disposition of the Zwicker matter—or rather lack of action—is described in the next chapter. Suffice it to say, it was the legal (not the emotional) implications which were paramount in my mind.

The contributions of the other members of the Select Committee to all aspects of the censure debate deserve more than passing recognition. I am personally greatly indebted to them—not only for the time and energy they saved me by speaking (often without preparation, as during the time Senator Case took over for me and carried on for a day, when McCarthy who had announced that he was going to make a speech, delayed until closing, and inserted his offensive "handmaidens" speech in the *Record*), but also for their knowledge and wisdom. Senators Stennis and Irvin, did a great deal to clear up the legal questions involved. Each of my five fellow members of the Select Committee showed great resolve and courage and they have my eternal thanks and gratitude.

In this account, I have attempted little more than to give the flavor of the debate and to cover topics not thoroughly explored elsewhere. Naturally, a large portion of the discussions on the part of members of the Select Committee contributed to other Senators' understanding of our position. As the committee's conclusions on the censure of Senator McCarthy are elaborated throughout this book, it would be tedious to give details of the debate on these findings as they were developed on the floor of the Senate. Students may refer to the *Congressional Record* for a full first-hand account.

AS AUTOBIOGRAPHICAL AS THIS ACCOUNT OF THE "BEFORES" AND "AFTERS" OF McCarthyism has become, and in view of the bitter attacks hurled at me, I believe that I may be justified in paying tribute to (and accepting commendations from) some of the great men in the United States Senate.

I recall the kind words of my fellow member of the Select Committee, Democrat from Mississippi, Senator Stennis. He said: *

> Mr. President, if I may, I should like to say a word about a Senator on the committee who in a way has been under attack. I refer to the Chairman, the distinguished Senator from Utah. In all my public career I have never seen a better job done in holding the scales of justice evenly balanced than has been done by the chairman of the Select Committee. In my estimation, I do not believe that I have ever seen the equal of the job he has done under the circumstances. He had the moral fiber, the legal training, and the sense of devotion to duty that made such a performance possible. More than that, he had a great spiritual reservoir that came to his rescue and served as a solid foundation for him all the way through. I commend him, not for his conclusions, not for any ruling he made, but for the way in which he approached this matter, for his consecrated devotion to duty, and for his attitude all the way through.

Then there are the remarks of the man who since has become a truly valued friend and a great man in the Senate in the defense of our Constitution and our liberties, Senator Fulbright. I use his words, rather than my own, to lead up to the climatic action of the censure debate (which as Senators and newsmen alike have indicated came when I hurried off the floor of the Senate in sickness and exhaustion after my final speech on the censure matter). Senator Fulbright said: **

> We owe a special debt to the distinguished chairman of the committee. We are indebted to him for the manner in which he retained control over the hearings. I confess that last August, when this question arose, I was very dubious about the ability of anyone to cope with the junior Senator from Wisconsin in a committee hearing. I do not think anyone had done so successfully before the Select Committee.

*Ibid., p. 15986.
**Ibid., p. 16195.

We are also indebted to the senior Senator from Utah for the magnificent way in which he presented this complex and difficult subject to the Senate. In all my experience in the Senate I have never heard a more moving speech, or one delivered with greater dignity and conviction.

Lastly, we are indebted to the chairman because, as the agent of this body, designated by the Senate to perform this onerous task he was personally subjected to the vilest kind of abuse. He took that abuse on our behalf, so he deserves not only our sympathy, but also vindication by the vote of the Senate, if the Senate has any honor and self-respect left.

If there were no other reason to vote for the resolution of censure, the attempted intimidation of the chairman—and, through him, of the Senate —by the junior Senator from Wisconsin would be ample reason for the censure.

I would not fail, except for limitations of space, to give similar credit and extend my thanks to other Senators who spoke to and about me. (A most outspoken Senator, not noted for his humility, said to me as he left the Senate floor—and later put it in writing: "Arthur, I am a better man for having heard you today!")

The incident about which all of these men were alluding, and was behind their manifest expressions of sympathy and identification with me, was my reply to McCarthy's "handmaiden" speech.

In this hour-and-a-half talk, I covered again the main points of the censure report—and referred Senators to it, if there was any question of fact or meaning —and set forth the reasons why the Senate could well consider the censure of Senator McCarthy. In addition, there were some references to McCarthy's attack on me.

I began my address in this manner: *

> Mr. President, I regret that I do not have a voice as heavy and as loud as have some of the speakers who have preceded me in this debate. If I attempted to make it possible for everyone present to hear me, I would have to shout, and then it might be thought that I was angry. I should like to be dispassionate in this discussion, even though it involves my own honor. I wish to speak in tones of moderation.

Then, with reference to Joe McCarthy's comments in Milwaukee which referred to me as a coward, I said:

> I suppose I should be very indignant over that statement, but in many respects I feel more sorrow than anger over it. It reveals an attitude which

*Ibid., p. 16053.

has characterized the junior Senator from Wisconsin for some time. To be called a coward, of course, involves a stigma which no man relishes.

Upon this thought, then, I discussed McCarthy's own failure to appear before the Gillette Committee and answer questions involving his own integrity. I told the Senators that I felt confident that there was not another member of that body who would have refused the invitation to go before the committee when his honor and his integrity were under serious investigation. I detailed the questions involved and said:

I am not saying that (McCarthy) was afraid; I am not saying he was a coward, but I am saying there are some very serious questions connected with his conduct in which any judge, and particularly a Senate committee sitting as we were, under our own rules and regulations, would be very much interested.

After further calling the attention of the Senate to these matters, I said:

Lastly, in our own presence, here in the Senate, we have seen another example of the Senator's hit-and-run attack. Senators have seen what I have called to their attention, an attack on their representative, their agent. They have seen an attack made on that agent's courage and intelligence. They have heard the junior Senator from Wisconsin say that I am both stupid and a coward.

I am asking all my colleagues in the Senate—and it must be remembered that the members of the Select Committee were practically drafted for the job, and, so far as I am concerned, it was the most unpleasant task I have ever had to perform in all my public life—I am asking all my colleagues: What are you going to do about it?

Then I concluded my remarks with the statement on the necessity of every Senator to uphold the Constitution, as required by his oath (which I quoted in the previous chapter). When a Senator does or says things which injure our Constitutionally ordained institutions, I said, he is violating his oath.

As I sank into my seat, there was a moment of profound silence. Then the Senate broke into applause. The galleries joined in the applause and the Chair withheld the gavel.

I rushed from the floor of the Senate and found a couch in the Cloakroom where I lay down to rest and seeked to regain my equilibrium. Aides put screens around me, but I heard my colleagues passing and speaking about their resolve to uphold the honor of the Senate.

Shortly, the junior Senator from Utah, Wallace Bennett, sought me out. Bend-ing over me, he said, "Arthur, I want you to give me the privilege of moving to amend the censure resolution to include McCarthy's treatment of you." It was with great weariness that I accepted: "Thank you, Senator," I said. "I would appreciate your doing it, for I have decided that someone must do it . . . even if I had to do it myself."

Immediately after Senator Bennett had introduced his motion to add the additional charge of abusing the Chairman of the Select Committee to the other recommendations of censure, Senator McCarthy demonstrated his first evidence of concern.

This concern, it should be noted, was about the continuation of the debate. During the entire censure debate on the floor of the Senate, McCarthy had interrupted from time to time to say that the sooner the Senate could get the censure vote over with the better he would like it. His concern with getting on to the next step in his publicity campaign—as he had put it himself, appealing "to the great American jury beyond this room"—required a wind-up of the interminable debate. (McCarthy might well have appealed to his friend, Senator Welker, to refrain from chipping in at every turn with questions and commentary, for the verbose Senator took up a disproportionate amount of the time in the entire proceedings.)

As the new amendment was concerned largely with language which McCarthy had used with respect to me and my colleagues on the committee, Joe began by regretting his choice of words. In this, he emphasized that he was not compromising his position in his fight against communism. For his actions, he said, he had "no apologies." Said McCarthy: *

> The efforts to expose communism have engendered deep bitterness and heat on both sides. I know—perhaps better than any other member of the Senate—what it is to suffer abuse, heaped upon me to the point of exhaustion. I would be the last, therefore, to deliberately administer abuse to anyone else.
>
> . . . I say to those who feel they have been offended, that I had no intention in the words that were used of hurting the feelings of anyone; but in the facts and opinions that I held, I am unchanged. Like my colleagues, I am not without weaknesses. Like them, I have mistakes; and however I may strive otherwise, I suppose I shall make others in the future.
>
> It has been stated that the dignity of the Senate is involved. My greatest wish is to help increase the dignity of the Senate, for the dignity of the Senate is of great importance.
>
> Of even greater importance, however, is the honor, the safety, and the welfare of the Nation, and the security of its citizens, wherever they may be.

*Ibid., p. 16150–16154.

And while the attention of the Senate has been largely concentrated on Mc-Carthy, the world communist conspiracy has made dangerous and costly gains.

Frankly, I feel that we have discussed this question to the limit. I think there is no further light to be shed upon it.

I may say . . . that one of the reasons why I should like to see an end to this debate over words is, first the seriousness of the world situation, as I have previously pointed out.

A second reason is that our investigating committee has a tremendous backlog of work.* There are approximately—and I hate to use figures—42 fifth amendment communists who are working in defense plants at this very moment . . . But once they have been called before our subcommittee, and if they plead the fifth amendment, I feel confident they will be immediately removed from any classified work on defense contracts.

After a rather lengthy exchange on how McCarthy's proposal to limit the debate could be accomplished—and everyone was in accord with this objective —Senator Mundt obtained the floor and seemingly attempted to steer the debate toward a compromise conclusion based on a so-called McCarthy apology (something which Joe McCarthy had adamantly refused to agree to when efforts to compromise were unofficially underway). Said Senator Mundt:

As the Senator from Wisconsin proceeded with his statement, I construed it to be in the nature of an apology to the members of this body because of his alleged use of offensive language concerning individuals—although not necessarily a retraction of his statements about certain committee reports or committee activities. However, I judge it was in the nature of an apology insofar as his remarks about other Senators personally were concerned, I wonder whether my interpretation of his statement is correct.

McCarthy replied:

I thought I had made myself as clear as I possibly could. Let me say, I am not wedded to any particular words; for example when I referred to the Watkins committee as the "handmaidens of the communist party" I should say now that "handmaidens" is not a proper word to use in that connection, because a handmaiden is a female servant, and certainly the members of the committee are not female servants. The thought I tried to express was that the Watkins committee unwittingly, and I stress the word "unwittingly," was doing exactly what the Communist Party was clamoring for.

*McCarthy was to lose his chairmanship, because the Democrats had become the majority party through the elections just held that November.

However, insofar as the words used are concerned, I am willing to strike out all the words that are considered objectionable. On the other hand, I still have the same strong feeling about the actions that were taken.

Senator Mundt said that since it had been stressed by Senator Case that a "retraction" was important, he was "gratified" that McCarthy was willing to strike out the offensive words.

McCarthy responded a third time that he had no objection to striking out the words, "but I would not strike out a presentation of any of the ideas I have had on the subject." He implied that it was only the end of the debate he was seeking, and to discuss further his words during the censure debate was useless. "I was of the opinion," he said, "that nothing which was not germane should be offered as an amendment."

As far as our Senate colleagues were concerned, and also in my own opinion, McCarthy's statement was not an apology but an admission of error in tactics. He was "sorry" for the delay that his words had created but there was not the slightest sign that he had genuinely repented with respect to the conduct which brought the censure proceedings.

Senator Herbert Lehman of New York, and others, pressed to answer McCarthy. Senator Lehman said, with respect to the "handmaiden" speech: "That speech impugns and reflects upon the integrity, the good faith, and the loyalty of every member of the Senate. The attack is not limited to the Select Committee. It is directed against the loyalty and patriotism of every member of this body."

As to whether a bona fide apology from McCarthy would have modified the censure resolution as it was ultimately acted upon by the Senate, I am sure that it would have had this effect if he had shown sincere repentance and declared that it was his intention to avoid such practices in the future. My record is clear with respect to my personal attitude, for (as I philosophized further in another chapter) I was willing to "extend the olive branch" to McCarthy and that I was "willing to forgive."

The various "compromises" which were offered by such Senators as Dirksen, Mundt, and Malone were based more on the need to establish rules of conduct and of censurable behavior for the future—since McCarthy had acted, so they said, in an ill-defined area of what could be said and done—and they were unwilling to "punish" McCarthy ever so slightly because of the precedent it would establish. The precedent, they said, would permit any Senator—at any time in the future—to be censured for conduct that might be displeasing to a majority. In the several times that substitute measures came to a vote, they were rejected by roughly the same margin and by the same individuals who ultimately voted for McCarthy's censure.

The issues remained the same, with the exception that the Bennett amendment broadened the original charge of censurable conduct (with respect to the Gillette

Committee and Senator Hendrickson) to include the offense against the Select Committee and its Chairman, and dropped the charge against McCarthy concerning his abuse of General Zwicker.

There were two ideas prevalent on the floor with respect to dropping—or rather, not pressing—the Zwicker matter. One, held by some, was that Zwicker had not been fully cooperative and that perhaps his attitude had goaded Mc-Carthy into making excessive statements. Further, it was said with respect to the Peress matter, the Army had respected the request of Major Peress for an immediate discharge and had not respected the request of a Senator to delay that action. This, said Senator Case, would be "establishing a very poor precedent." Perhaps of greater significance from the political point of view, however, was the belief that to censure McCarthy for his conduct as a committee chairman would set a precedent which would limit future committee chairmen in examining witnesses. Southern Democrats (whose tenure made them committee chairmen when their party was in the majority) were particularly hesitant to censure McCarthy on this charge.

As we neared the time of the censure vote, Minority Leader Lyndon Johnson stopped by my chair on the floor and said to me: "Arthur, you are going to have to drop the Zwicker matter. There are at least 15 Democratic Senators who will not vote for the censure resolution if the Zwicker charge is part of it."

Very quickly, and right on the floor of the Senate, I gathered members of the Select Committee together and we considered Senator Johnson's statement. At this point, we felt, we could not jeopardize the censure resolution (with respect to which events had made us in effect the "prosecuting attorneys" contrary to the original mission of the Select Committee, and because of McCarthy's attacks), and we felt forced to acquiesce.

It was not without a statement on the floor, however, that I let the matter pass. I explained that I was "not abandoning at all my ideas or principles with respect to the Zwicker incident." I explained that "in the interest of having a censure resolution adopted, in the interest of not having the supporters of the resolution divided, I would support and accept" the Bennett resolution which changed the language of the censure resolution and had the effect, thereby, of dropping the Zwicker matter.

Stennis made a similar statement and added that he was supporting the Bennett language. "That will be my position with reference to the pending vote," he said, "without abandoning one bit my firm conclusion with reference to the merits of the so-called Zwicker incident matter."

During the maneuvering on the floor with respect to the various compromise resolutions and the Bennett resolution many of the Senators became anxious for action and there were frequent cries from here and there around the floor: "Vote!" "Vote!"

The amended resolution (S. Res. 301) was finally read:

Resolved. That the Senator from Wisconsin, Mr. McCarthy, failed to cooperate with the Subcommittee on Privileges and Elections of the Senate Committee on Rules and Administration in clearing up matters referred to that subcommittee which concerned his conduct as a Senator and affected the honor of the Senate and, instead repeatedly abused the subcommittee and its members who were trying to carry out assigned duties, thereby obstructing the constitutional processes of the Senate, and that this conduct of the Senator from Wisconsin, Mr. McCarthy, is contrary to senatorial traditions and is hereby condemned.

Sec. 2. The Senator from Wisconsin, Mr. McCarthy, in writing to the chairman of the Select Committee to Study Censure Charges (Mr. Watkins) after the select committee had issued its report and before the report was presented to the Senate charging three members of the select committee with "deliberate deception" and "fraud" for failure to disquality themselves in stating to the press on November 4, 1954, that the special Senate session that was to begin November 8, 1954, was a "lynch party"; in repeatedly describing this special Senate session as a "lynch bee" in a nationwide television and radio show on November 7, 1954; in stating to the public press on November 13, 1954, that the chairman of the select committee (Mr. Watkins) was guilty of "the most unusual, most cowardly thing I've heard of" and stating further: "I expected he would be afraid to answer the questions, but didn't think he'd be stupid enough to make a public statement"; and in characterizing the said committee as the "unwitting handmaiden," "involuntary agent," and "attorneys in fact" of the Communist Party and in charging the said committee in writing its report "imitated Communist methods—that it distorted, misrepresented, and omitted in its effort to manufacture a plausible rationalization" in support of its recommendations to the Senate, which characterizations and charges were contained in a statement released to the press and inserted in the *Congressional Record* of November 10, 1954, acted contrary to senatorial ethics and tended to bring the Senate into dishonor and disrepute, to obstruct the constitutional processes of the Senate, and to impair its dignity; and such conduct is hereby condemned.

When the matter was put to the vote, there were 67 voting "yea" and 22 voting "nay." There was one (McCarthy) voting "present." There were six Senators absent and not voting.*

*Resolution of censure adopted. The vote was as follows:
YEAS—67. Abel, (Nebr.), Aiken, (Vt.), Anderson, (N. Mex.), Beall, (Md.), Bennett, (Utah), Burke, (Ohio), Bush, (Conn.), Byrd, (Va.), Carlson, (Kan.), Case, (S. Dak.), Chavez, (N. Mex.), Clements, (Ky.), Cooper, (Ky.), Cotton, (N. Hamp.), Daniel, (S.C.), Danial, (Tex.), Douglas, (Ill.), Duff, (Pa.), Eastland, (Miss.), Ellender, (La.), Ervin, (N.C.), Ferguson, (Mich.), Flanders, (Vt.), Frear,

Immediately there was some question as to which was the stronger word: "censure" or "condemn."

Senator Welker had said that "condemn" was the stronger word, as we often read that someone had been "condemned to death" but never read that he had been "censured to death." I told the Senator that I would accept that construction.*

(Del.), Fulbright, (Ark.), George, (Ga.), Gillette, (Iowa), Green, (R.I.), Hayden, (Ariz.), Hendrickson, (N.J.), Hennings, (Mo.), Hill, (Ala.), Holland, (Fla.), Humphrey, (Minn.), Ives, (N.Y.), Jackson, (Wash.), Johnson, (Colo.), Johnson, (Tex.), Johnston, (S.C.), Kefauver, (Tenn.), Kerr, (Okla.), Kilgore, (W.Va.), Lehman, (N.Y.), Long, (La.), Magnuson, (Wash.), Mansfield, (Mont.), McClellan, (Ark.), Monroney, (Okla.), Morse, (Ore.), Murray, (Mont.), Neely, (W.Va.), O'Mahoney, (Wyo.), Pastore, (R.I.), Payne, (Maine), Potter, (Mich.), Robertson, (Va.), Russell, (Ga.), Saltonstall, (Mass.), Scott, (Pa.), Smith, (Maine), Smith, (N.J.), Sparkman, (Ala.), Stennis, (Miss.), Symington, (Mo.), Thye, (Minn.), Watkins, (Utah), Williams, (Del.).

NAYS—22. Barrett, (Wyo.), Bridges, (N. Hamp.), Brown, (Nev.), Butler, (Md.), Cordon, (Ore.), Dirksen, (Ill.), Dworshak, (Idaho), Goldwater, (Ariz.), Hickenlooper, (Iowa), Hruska, (Nebr.), Jenner, (Ind.), Knowland, (Calif.), Kuchel, (Calif.), Langer, (N. Dak.), Malone, (Nev.), Martin, (Pa.), Millikin, (Colo.), Mundt, (S. Dak.), Purtell, (Conn.), Schoeppel, (Kan.), Welker, (Idaho), Young, (N.D.).

NOT VOTING—6. Bricker, (Ohio), Capehart, (Ind.), Gore, (Tenn.), Kennedy, (Mass.), Smathers, (Fla.), Wiley, (Wisc.).

ANSWERED "PRESENT"—1. McCarthy, (Wisc.).
Absent, but paired for censure: Gore, Smathers
Absent, but paired against censure: Bricker, Capehart
Absent by leave of the Senate on official business: Wiley, (no vote)
Congressional Record, December 2, 1954, page 16392.

*The use of the word condemn instead of censure follows the Senatorial custom in these cases. The dictionaries indicate that the words are practically interchangeable.

SATURDAY MORNING, THE DAY AFTER THE CENSURE VOTE AND THE SENATE recess until after the holidays, I received a call from the White House. It was shortly after 7 o'clock when the telephone rang and I was still in bed resting. By temperament I am a very early riser and ordinarily would have been up long before and working on some project, but I was exhausted from the weeks of tension and especially from the arduous days of debate on the floor of the Senate. I was not pleased to hear the phone ring.

I picked up the phone by my bed and learned that the President had asked to see me and wondered if I could be there at 8 o'clock. I caught my breath and said that I would be there as soon as possible but that I had yet to shave and dress.

It was about 8:30 when I drove alone into the White House grounds and was promptly shown to the President's office. There were no reporters evident in the lobby and I noted this with some relief.* The President rose from behind his desk to greet me cordially and extended his hand.

He said "Good morning," calling me "Arthur," and motioned me to take the chair by his desk.

The President said that he wanted to thank me for the fair and orderly hearing which I had conducted and for the way the censure resolution had been presented to the Senate.

I thanked the President for this expression. I then went on to say that the Select Committee had earlier authorized me to tell the President—if the opportunity came to me to do so—that, if he should agree, the Secretary of the Army ought to be instructed to give the proper Senate committee the names of all officers, or civilians, who had anything to do with the promotion of Dr. Peress to the rank of major, and also the names of all those who brought about his honorable discharge from the Army. When this had been done, then this per-

---

*I had been to the White House before on early Saturday mornings—a time the President usually kept free, except for occasional, unscheduled appointments— and didn't really expect to find any reporters. The idea that I might enter by the East Wing and walk through the basement of the White House to avoid reporters— as the story has been perpetuated—never occurred to me and I wouldn't have known how to attempt it if I had wanted to. The story that I had done so may have been started as a wry joke by a reporter who wished he had been on the spot to see me come in but wasn't there.

sonnel should be made available to the Committee for questioning at the pleasure of the Committee.

I told him also that the Select Committee—as well as other committees of the Senate, and the Senate itself—would never be satisfied until this matter was fully explored, in depth, to find what actually happened. I explained that I had called on Secretary of Defense Wilson to ask his help and that he did help, but until the Army personnel were released from their instructions—those instructions pertaining to Executive privilege—we would never get the full information.

The President listened to these remarks and his face began to flush in a way which I recognized from other meetings. He pushed back his chair and started across his office. I could see that he was indignant. Someone less familiar with the President might have assumed that it was time to get up and be prepared to leave. I remained in my chair. The President paced back toward his desk and then exclaimed, more to himself than to me, that there was no reason—no reason on earth—why the Army shouldn't have given those names and made those witnesses available.

I advised the President that after the Senate had created the Select Committee to hear the charges against McCarthy, a list of names had been sent to the McCarthy Investigations Subcommittee and that subsequently a second list was given out by the Secretary of the Army—so that there were two lists—but that I felt that these lists were still not complete. In any event, I added, we could not know the truth of the Peress matter until these men were free to talk. The President further pondered the matter but made no direct reply.

I felt reasonably sure, sitting there watching his expression, that the information would soon be available. (Parenthetically, I may add that with the new Congress and with Senator McClellan presiding over the Government Operations Committee that Joe McCarthy had headed, the information was indeed made available. All 26 of the men named by the Army to that Committee were brought to Washington and testified as to what they knew.)

Shortly, my visit with President Eisenhower was over and he accompanied me to the door with his usual gracious manner. Press Secretary James C. Haggarty met us at the door, and at this point it occurred to me that the President's annual budget message to Congress would be under preparation at the time and it might be my only opportunity to urge the President to do something special for the Upper Colorado River Storage Project at the beginning of the new Congress. It was December, and the President's message would come immediately after the first of the year. It probably would be in the hands of the printer within a few days.

I said, "Mr. President, would you be willing to mention the project in your message to the Congress." He said he would if the drafting of the message had not gone too far to permit the insert. He then motioned to another aide who said it could be done with a slight change in the wording at a point somewhere near the beginning. The President directed that appropriate mention be made of the Upper Colorado River Storage Project, and it was done.

After this exchange with President Eisenhower, I moved on into the lobby where a group of reporters—having been alerted that I was visiting the President at his invitation—were waiting.

As the reporters gathered around me, Mr. Haggarty came out of the President's office and joined us. He gave a general statement of what had occurred in my meeting with the President, but did not mention the subject of the Select Committee's request to the President about expediting an investigation into the Major Peress matter.

With Haggarty standing by, I then added—rather enthusiastically—that the commitment which I had long had from President Eisenhower for his support of the Colorado River Project had been reaffirmed.

It never occurred to me that anyone would be prompted to make anything evil out of my request to the President or of his favorable reaction to it. There were charges by some, however, that the President was carrying out his part of a "deal" which involved his support of the Colorado River Project if I would "take care" of McCarthy. I have already given the answer to this charge in my "backward glance" in this book, which I sincerely hope will lay this allegation to rest.

I could not possibly have foreseen that I had fed the flame of the abominable charge by McCarthy and his cohorts (one still perpetuated in the writings of Roy Cohn) that the President had been a party to (yes, even the architect of) a "conspiracy" to discredit McCarthy.

My own convictions that President Eisenhower had, indeed, remained aloof from the McCarthy censure matter until after the judgment of the Senate have recently been further strengthened by my research. In the interests of "Republican unity" vigorous efforts by some Senate leaders (and by McCarthy's counsel) to find a basis for compromise were explored. Even here, I have private assurance, that the President, himself, was never a party to any effort to remove from the Senate any of its prerogatives in inquiring into the charges against the Senator from Wisconsin and to censure or condemn him.

THE NAME OF DOUGLAS STRINGFELLOW WAS ONE OFTEN LINKED WITH McCarthy's in letters I received in October, just following the McCarthy censure hearing and before the national congressional elections of November, 1954. Stringfellow was a Utah congressman who came to be discovered in a false claim of World War II heroism. The three samples reproduced here reflect a problem which I am convinced bothered many citizens across the country.

The first letter was from a medical doctor of New York City. He wrote:

> Dear Senator Watkins:
>
> Isn't it strange that you show so much Christian charity toward String-fellow and so much un-Christian hatred toward McCarthy. You are acting the part of a hypocrite. Can't you reverse yourself and act like a Christian? After all, what has Joe done worthy of official censure? We all make some mistakes—even you probably do—but Joe has done nothing that was ever censured before in the history of the Senate. Can't you see that you are being used?

One woman, also a resident of New York City, penned this missive:

> To my estimation you are showing extreme partiality to Mr. Stringfellow because he is a Mormon—and you yourself are a member of that faith.
>
> Mr. Stringfellow's case is a very small and only of local interest whereas Senator Joseph McCarthy is a Roman Catholic, his entire career is a credit to his religion and his country. His case is international and worldwide interest because he is fighting communism. It shows how small a man you are. You insult the dignity of the position you hold. And insult the integrity of all Americans.
>
> I would appreciate an answer.

From a woman residing in Chicago came this comment on a news clipping she enclosed. First the clipping:

> Watkins told reporters at the studio:
> I am not disposed to desert him now, regardless of any decision made as to his future as a candidate.* When a man is willing to repent, and does repent, I consider it my duty as a Christian to extend forgiveness.

*Congressman Stringfellow

155

My correspondent's comment:

> As a Christian you no doubt are familiar with the Bible quotation 'a liar is worse than a thief.' How strange you can find so much compassion in your heart for this man when you were so prejudiced, unfair and bitter towards your colleague and brother Republican, Senator McCarthy.

The authors of these letters are strangers to me. I do not doubt their sincerity in expressing their views, even though they are stated in the bitterest of terms. This very fact helps me to realize that they did not have a knowledge of the truth in each of these cases. I am confident, if they had, their letters would be much different than they are.

In this book I am telling the story of a legislator's reaction to the possibility of public disapprobation. So why not compare the Stringfellow episode with the censure of McCarthy? I think it will appear that in a way the two episodes had much in common. Also, there should be a moral lesson in the way the two men reacted to the charges against them. To make the Stringfellow story understandable, I must necessarily review some of the highlights of Utah political background of that period.

My first contact with Douglas Stringfellow was not in person but by mail and was unpleasant. Someone from Ogden, Utah, sent me a clipped news story in which Stringfellow was quoted as being very critical of me as a Senator, particularly with reference to my labor views.

I made inquiry about him, but the only information I could get was that he was a crippled World War II veteran who had been attracting considerable public attention in Utah. I felt his criticism of me was unjust and decidedly unfriendly. So I wrote him stating that I felt he was unfair in his criticism and that I hoped in the future he would get my views from me before he criticized me. My memory is that he did not reply to my letter.

I recall meeting him for the first time during the 1952 presidential campaign in Utah. He was a candidate for the Republican nomination for Congressman from the 1st District. His home was in Ogden, located in north central Utah, and mine was in Orem, in the south central part of the state. Only political activities brought us together.

Another Ogden native son, Marriner S. Eccles, who had held important positions in the Franklin D. Roosevelt and Harry Truman administrations, was an unsuccessful competitor of mine for the Republican nomination for United States Senator in 1952. He and his brothers were the owners of an intermountain chain of banks, finance agencies, a large construction firm, a sugar company and other business institutions too numerous to mention here. Except for one thing, the odds were heavily against me in the primary. Multi-millionaire Eccles had a difficult time establishing his Republicanism after serving under two Democratic Presidents—Franklin D. Roosevelt and Harry S. Truman—as a financial and economic advisor and Assistant Secretary of the Treasury.

It was strongly argued that Eccles would greatly strengthen the ticket with his prestige, his money, and his financial empire. Under these circumstances, Stringfellow, admittedly a novice, was not one of my supporters. I found it difficult to get acquainted with him at such times as we were campaigning for about a week together in southern Utah. I did find out, however, that he had great respect for Eccles and was courting his support.

Thus it should be clear that at this stage of our acquaintance we were casual acquaintances only. I should record the fact that after I defeated Eccles for the nomination, I felt a slight thaw in my relationship with Stringfellow. I got the impression that he was very much aware of the fact that his popularity exceeded my own, a fact I freely admit.

During this busy period of the election campaign, I never heard Stringfellow even once refer to his war experiences, except in the most general terms; and it was usually a rather lurid, but brief general description of the horrors of warfare. Occasionally, I would hear some comments by local politicians that Stringfellow had a great war record and was very popular. He was generally regarded as a "comer" in politics. I made some inquiries about his war record but no one seemed to know the details, so I gave up trying to find out more about this phase of his life.

General Eisenhower and the Republican ticket won a smashing victory that year (1952) in Utah.* It was quite a change for me to have a solid Republican delegation to work with. (Senator Wallace F. Bennett had defeated Senator Elbert Thomas, Democrat, two years earlier. Congressman William A. Dawson of the 2nd District—who was originally elected in 1946—was elected again in 1952.) I had visions of a harmonious relationship with my Republican colleagues and was looking forward to that happy state with high hopes of more worthwhile legislation for Utah, and the West.

Senator Bennett had an outstanding national record as President of the National Association of Manufacturers and our legislative activities complimented each other's very well from the beginning. It was different, however, with my colleagues in the House. I had yet to learn that many House members from both parties consider the two Senatorships from each state fair prey.

My House colleagues in a not too subtle way began their campaigns. Stringfellow's popularity as a speaker began to zoom early in his House career. The explanation made to me was that he was not only a good speaker but he had

*Stringfellow carried the 1st Utah Congressional District with a larger vote than did General Eisenhower.

status as a very interesting war hero. His speeches were in demand at $500 to $2,000 per appearance.

Following the McCarthy censure hearings I took a short vacation before returning to Utah to participate in the final two weeks of the 1954 congressional campaign.

Before leaving for Utah, Congressman Stringfellow, who was unopposed to succeed himself, told me that a county clerk (a Democrat) in Ogden was threatening to cause him trouble over the Congressman's war record. He wondered if I would help him if the trouble became serious. I said I would, but first I wanted him to put in writing the essentials of his war record because I never had heard the story in full—only snatches of his claim—which apparently had made a war hero out of him. I advised him I must be fully informed if I was to be of any worthwhile assistance.

Since I was very busy getting my Washington affairs in shape so I could leave following the censure hearings, I couldn't take the time to listen to his story then, so I told him that he should mail a statement of his record to my Salt Lake city office. He agreed to do that. (If he did do that, the statement got lost somewhere along the line, because I never did get to see it.) He was to take a plane to Utah later on the day of our interview. I left for Utah a few days later.

A crowd including a band met my plane at the Salt Lake Airport. The placards, which some carried, welcomed me home. Others praised the censure hearings and the Committee's report. It was not a large crowd but it was something new for me, and I admit I was a bit moved.

Somewhat to my surprise the first person to meet me at the plane's landing ramp was Congressman Stringfellow. While the photographers were getting shots, Stringfellow hurriedly told me he was in deep trouble, and that he needed my help at once. He advised me that he had some speaking engagements for fellow Congressmen in Missouri and was leaving within a few minutes to fill them.

He said President Eisenhower, who was in Denver, had been urged to order the Central Intelligence Agency in Washington to release their records which would prove his war story true, but the President wouldn't act. I held up my friends in the reception committee and members of my family while I quickly advised him to go to Missouri, make his speeches, and return to Utah Saturday morning as planned. In the meantime he was to deny all interviews until I could make some investigations in Washington by telephone. I would confer with him Saturday morning upon his return from Missouri. He agreed to this program.

One of the first things I did was to inquire of newsmen and others in Salt Lake about essentials of the Stringfellow story concerning his war record which had brought him so much sudden fame, but which now threatened him with dire disaster. As a result of bringing things together which I had heard and read (and under the spur of necessity brought about by the Congressman's request to me for help), I came up with this summary:

The bare bones of the numerous versions of Stringfellow's "OSS Mission" put him and an uncertain number of Army personnel deep into enemy territory and beyond German lines. Here they took part in numerous hair-raising escapades, including the kidnapping of Otto Kahn, a famous German nuclear scientist, whom they delivered into Allied hands.

But that achievement was small compared to Stringfellow's claim that Hitler's time table for world conquest was completely upset and with it the course of the war. As a consequence, the direction of history was changed by him and his brave companions under his leadership.

During the course of these events, Stringfellow claimed the group was imprisoned in Germany's notorious Belsen Prison where they were severely beaten and otherwise tortured. In one situation where he was left for dead lying on the ground, he stated that he had a remarkable religious experience, in which he realized the power of prayer and the presence of God.

There was more in the rambling tales that made up his speeches, but this summary of the various versions should be enough for the limited purpose of comparison with the Senate's Select Committee findings and recommendations in the Senator McCarthy censure proceedings.

My first move had been to telephone the legislative relations officer of the CIA in Washington with whom I had become acquainted through my activities on the Senate Judiciary Committee and its subcommittee, the Internal Security Committee.

He advised me that the agency had for several days been engaged in a search of its records to check the claims of Congressman Stringfellow. This had been done at the request of several newspapers, the Associated Press, and the United Press and others. (I assumed "others" meant members of Congress, etc.)

But the agency had not found anything which even mentioned a special army group such as the Congressman had designated. He said he had also checked with General "Wild Bill" Donovan, former Director of the Office of Strategic Services. The General had not heard of any army, or special unit, such as had been described by the Congressman, or of the capture of Otto Kahn, the German Scientist. The General made it clear that the story never happened; if it had he would have known of it. Such an operation would have been a part of the OSS activities.

The CIA said the Pentagon had been queried and their Army records showed that Stringfellow had been with his Army unit all his time in the service except while he was being given some preliminary training until the time of his hospitalization. My informant said they were continuing the search until all possibilities had been eliminated. But he explained he couldn't hold off much longer the press and others who wanted to know what the CIA records disclosed.

I advised him that I was also making an investigation and I hoped that he would not make a news release until I had time to finish it and then put my findings squarely up to Mr. Stringfellow. I expressed the thought that action might make any further investigation unnecessary. The official agreed to hold his report as suggested.

I now had enough information to enable me to know in essence what the Stringfellow war story consisted of—enough to justify me in taking speedy and vigorous action which I was convinced the situation justified.

So early Saturday morning (the second day after my return to Utah) I called Senator Bennett and relayed to him the information I had received from the CIA—that there was no support for Douglas Stringfellow's war story. Also we discussed the rumors each of us had heard that the Democratic State Committee was preparing a broadside exposé of the Congressman to take place at an early date.

I told the Senator that I had planned to go to Ogden immediately to discuss the situation with Stringfellow, and demand of him the truth in light of the CIA statement. I urged the Senator to join me in this mission. He was somewhat reluctant but finally consented.

Some 20 minutes later we were on our way. First we decided to call on President David O. McKay of the Mormon Church at his office (in Salt Lake City) because we had heard that he and Ezra Taft Benson, Secretary of Agriculture, had had an unsatisfactory session with Stringfellow shortly before my return to Utah.

President McKay told us that the Congressman insisted that his war story was true and that he and the Secretary could not shake him. I informed the President that the Central Intelligence Agency could not find any support for Stringfellow's story and that I felt, as the senior member of the Utah delegation in Congress, that I had some moral responsibility in the situation which had developed. Also, I explained that Stringfellow had asked me to help him and that was one of the reasons why I had taken up the matter with the CIA in Washington; and now joined by Senator Bennett I was on my way to report to the Congressman the result of my investigation, which was that the evidence was all against his war story. I intended to confront him with the CIA report, my report, and give him an opportunity to either give satisfactory corroboration for his story or admit it was a fake. I had every confidence that he would tell us the truth.

President McKay urged me not to go. He said he didn't want me to get hurt. But I insisted I should, that I was too far into the matter now to back out. (I also felt that it was unfair to other Republican candidates to have a scandal break out in Stringfellow's case and have it revealed by the Democrats; that Republicans should do their own housecleaning. And I had a feeling if we did not act immediately we would face a broadside of exposure by our opponents.)

Senator Bennett and I had agreed that if the Congressman confessed his war hero story was a hoax, then he should go on television that evening and make his confession to the Nation. We advised President McKay of our plans and then asked him if the Congressman did confess, would he clear the way on the Church-owned television station so that the confession and plea for forgiveness could be broadcast that Saturday evening. The President agreed and our conference ended.

To many readers who are not members of the Mormon Church, it may seem strange or unusual for Senator Bennett and me to call on President McKay about the Stringfellow matter. To these readers, I offer my personal explanation.

Throughout the comparatively short history of the Mormon Church it became the custom of its critics and its enemies to blame the Church for the alleged misconduct of its members. Bad conduct of members and especially those holding high positions in the Church, or state, or both, might be very damaging to the Church before the peoples of the world, and would bring deep sorrow to its faithful members.

Congressman Stringfellow held a position of trust and honor, and the charges against him were of grave concern, not only to Republican members of the Church but to Democratic members as well. Some of the leaders brought evidence of these charges to President McKay, I believe, because they didn't want the Church to get hurt if it could be avoided. I think they were acting in good faith. When President McKay was advised of the situation he brought the matter to the attention of Secretary Benson, a member of President Eisenhower's cabinet, who was also an Apostle of the Church, but with a leave of absence from most of his apostolic duties during the time he was in the cabinet.

Stringfellow responded to an invitation to meet with these Church officials who confronted him with the charges that his war story was false. He denied the charge of fraud and insisted that he had been telling the truth.

I had found that there was no evidence in the files of the Federal Government, so I determined I should advise him of my findings, and if he confessed he was guilty of fraud, I would further advise him to confess publicly. The main purpose, then, of Senator Bennett and me in calling on President McKay was to get him to clear time that Saturday on the Church-owned TV, in anticipation that Stringfellow would confess that his story was fraudulent.

Senator Bennett and I proceeded on to Odgen, where we were received by Stringfellow, who was expecting us. We wasted no time in getting down to business.

I told him I had made the investigation I had agreed to, that the CIA had conducted an extensive search of its records, and that it could find nothing to support his war story. In addition, General "Wild Bill" Donovan, Director of OSS, had been emphatic in his statement that he had never heard of such an operation by any of our armed forces or in the special field covered by the Office of Strategic Services. He had also said that if such an operation had taken place it would have been by the OSS. He felt that the Stringfellow story was a fake. The CIA had also said that it had checked with the Army, which reported that so far as their records were concerned, Private First Class Stringfellow had been with his army unit at all times after he was assigned to it; that he had been severely injured in a mine field clearing operation in France, and finally had been sent to the Bushnell Army Hospital in Brigham City, Utah, for treatment and rehabilitation.

I concluded my statement by making an appeal to Congressman Stringfellow: "You are the one person who knows for a certainty whether your story is true or false. You have been a missionary for the Mormon church and you have preached repentance with all that doctrine implies to peoples you met in your missionary service. If your story is false, you know what your duty is. If you do not confess your sin in this mortal life and make whatever restitution within your power, you know you will have to face it in the life to come. Now, on the other hand, if you still insist, after all I have told you, that you have been telling the truth, that your story is true, I will stand by you.* But we do want the truth and we want it now."

There was a painful pause—the Congressman turned his back to us for a few moments, put his head in his hands and burst into tears. Sobs shook his body.

Facing us he said, "I never was behind the German lines. I never did help kidnap Otto Kahn. The whole story is false."

We told him that we had made conditional arrangements for a telecast that evening in which he should make his confession public and include a plea for forgiveness. We pointed out to him that there good men and women who were candidates on the Republican ticket with him, who would be hurt by his faked story of war heroism; especially if the Democrats were first to expose him. We explained that we had to move fast, that he and his administrative assistant should prepare his statement. We were willing to help if they needed help. Senator Bennett offered the use of his Salt Lake business offices where the Congressman could prepare his television script. President McKay would get time for his statement on KSL-TV. There would not be time to get other television stations to set aside their programs to carry his confession at the same time. He agreed to this program and said he would be ready.

Before leaving we asked him to call Mrs. Stringfellow in and advise her of

*Even some Army people were reluctant to say Stringfellow's story was false. If it were a deep secret operation there might be a good reason for the CIA to deny the story for reasons peculiar to the Agency's future operations under similar circumstances.

what had happened. She seemed to be stunned by his admission of fraud. In the midst of her tears she said it was fortunate that they had not used any of the $25,000 first installment a moving picture company had paid him on a contract to produce a story of his life highlighting his war heroism.* I learned later that this money had been promptly returned to the company.

Shortly after noon, Stringfellow and his assistant came to Senator Bennett's office with a draft of the confession. Here it was reviewed by Senator Bennett and me and possibly the Republican State Chairman, who had been alerted to the situation.

Immediately after the confession I communicated what happened to President McKay and said we wanted the television time that evening so the statement of the Congressman could be made to the people of the United States. He told me everything would be arranged for a telecast that evening (Saturday) as we had suggested.

Thus at 7:00 p.m. on Saturday, October 16, 1954, Congressman Douglas Stringfellow appeared before a television audience in Salt Lake City to make an unprecedented confession of guilt in one of the most fantastic war story hoaxes of our times. He appeared at the television studio accompanied by his wife and his administrative assistant. I was also there as a spectator and a witness. Only the Congressman was on stage before the TV cameras. "I am Congressman Douglas R. Stringfellow," the speaker began, "my purpose . . . is to make a statement; the most difficult speech I have ever made in my lifetime. Difficult as the occasion may be, the decision I have made gives me a great sense of personal relief and unburdens my soul from a load I have borne for more than ten years."

He said the story began ten years ago while he was a patient in Bushnell Military Hospital in Brigham City, Utah, undergoing treatment for wounds caused by an explosion of a land mine in France, where he was helping as a member of a U.S. Army unit to clear the area of mines following the German retreat in World War II.

"My condition was critical," he said. "I faced the bleak life of a paraplegic—a cripple with little likelihood of ever having a normal life . . ." (there was no doubt of the truthfulness of this statement with respect to his injuries.) Then the "confession" described in some detail the process Stringfellow went through to regain a hopeful outlook on his future—the meeting with Shirley Lemmon, a beautiful young dancer and singer who entertained at the Army hospital, who later became his wife. Other details of his comeback were related that he believed helped him get into a situation in which he began the fabrication of his war record, and which finally resulted in his downfall and brought him to the present crisis in his post-war career.

*I subsequently learned that under this contract Stringfellow stood to receive a total of $250,000 from the picture company, depending to some extent on the success of the picture.

And then came his confession:

> . . . . This morning I reached my decision, and I am in this studio tonight for the purpose of giving you the truth. Here are the facts:
>
> I never was an OSS agent.
>
> I never participated in any secret-behind-the-lines mission for our government.
>
> I never captured Otto Kahn or any other German physicist.
>
> . . . . I come before this radio and TV audience tonight a humble, contrite, and very repentant individual. I have made some grievous mistakes for which I am truly sorry . . . . I wish before my Heavenly Father that I might undo this wrong. I ask your forgiveness and assure you I shall spend a lifetime repenting and trying to make amends . . . . The Republican Party selected me as its candidate for Congress from the First District. I have already told the officers of the party, that if they wish, I will willingly step aside to permit them to certify another candidate. If another is chosen I will support him wholeheartedly. If they ask me to continue, I shall carry on my campaign on my record in the 83rd Congress. It will be up to the people of the First District . . . to decide whether I shall be returned to the Congress . . . . I shall humbly abide by the decision of my party and the people of the First District.

This unprecedented public confession of Douglas Stringfellow, including his plea for forgiveness, was a national sensation. Other television and radio stations were, of course, disappointed that they did not have the opportunity to broadcast the story. Stringfellow repeated his statement Sunday over these stations at their request. So there was full national coverage within a period of 24 hours.

Stringfellow's admission that his war "heroics" story was a fake, coming when it did, gave the Republicans an opportunity to show that they did not support that kind of conduct on the part of their candidates and had promptly taken steps to eliminate such a candidate from their ticket.

But the admission of guilt of one of its candidates did not end the troubles of the Republicans. Election day was only 16 days away. What should be done and how should it be put into action came into my thinking as I lay in bed Sunday morning following the Stringfellow broadcast. I had noted that he was ready to resign as nominee, but he left it up to the party to make the final decision. What should that decision be? It flashed into my mind that there could be no doubt about the answer; he should resign immediately and give the Republican State Committee an opportunity to accept the resignation and then in compliance with law, fill the vacancy.

There was no time to lose, so I stepped to the phone and was hunting for Stringfellow's number when the phone rang. It was the Congressman. He told me that he had decided he ought to resign from the ticket immediately so the

Committee would have time to get another candidate. We were in agreement on this important matter of what should be done. I told him that he was taking the right action and that he should give his written resignation to the State Chairman. I advised him that I would get in touch with party officials and suggest that the State Committee be called to a meeting to consider the resignation, or withdrawal, of Congressman Stringfellow from the ticket and to name a candidate to take his place.

I also suggested to the State Chairman that he should invite National Committeeman George Hanson, National Committeewoman LaRue Jex, Governor Lee, Senator Bennett, Congressman Dawson, and myself to an informal conference to see what we could do to help the party officials under the circumstances.

O. J. Wilkinson, the state chairman, issued his call for a State Committee meeting Monday evening, October 18, to act on the resignation of the Congressman from the Republican ticket and, if it was accepted by the Committee, to fill the vacancy thus created. This notice had to go out immediately in order to give Committee members, who were scattered over the state, time to be present at the meeting.

At the informal meeting of party leaders, I reviewed the events which had already taken place and discussed the law applicable to the situation. While the meeting was in session I received a telephone call from Secretary of Agriculture Benson, in Washington, who said we ought to get Stringfellow off the ticket at once. He said this was the view of President Eisenhower and the party leaders in Washington. I told the Secretary that the Utah leaders could not under Utah law do this. It had to be done by the Republican State Committee and that a meeting of the Committee made up of members from all over the state had been called for Monday evening, October 18 at Salt Lake City. The Secretary argued that it must be done immediately. At this point he asked me to have Senator Bennett come to the phone. I reported to the leaders what the Secretary had said and Governor Lee backed the Secretary. He said we should "kick Stringfellow off the ticket at once."

Again I had to point out that under the law we party leaders and officials had no authority whatever to do this, that only the State Committee had the authority to act in the situation that confronted the party. No one challenged my statement.

The conversation then turned to the matter of a new candidate for the First District Post. Several persons were mentioned including Dr. Henry Aldous Dixon, President of Utah State University and a teacher of and patron of Stringfellow—in fact Dr. Dixon himself being urged to be a candidate at that time, had recommended Stringfellow to the Republicans in 1952.

I was deeply interested in finding a candidate who could win. The Eisenhower administration was seriously handicapped in carrying out its programs by the closeness of the votes in Congress. Even one more vote was very important.

I was convinced that Dr. Dixon would be our best candidate, but I knew that one of the reasons he kept out of politics was a heart condition which his doctor son said might be aggravated by the excitement of politics. But at this time his health was much better, and I believed that he might possibly be willing under the circumstances to make the race. I and other members of the group got in touch with him, but he said he hadn't changed his mind, so the answer was still negative.

The Republican State Committee, consisting of 100 members, met Monday evening, October 18, at the New House Hotel. The resignation of Congressman Stringfellow was read to the committee and was accepted unanimously. He was given a standing ovation in absentia. This cleared the way for the naming of his successor. Questions were asked about the availability of Dr. Dixon. It appeared that the committee was unanimous in its desire to name Dr. Dixon. I explained that I had anticipated this feeling and that I had tried to get another request to him, but he couldn't be located. Reluctantly, the committee began the consideration of other candidates.

It was at this point in the meeting that George Hatch, a member of the Democratic State Committee organization who was also the manager of several television and radio stations and also connected with the Ogden Standard-Examiner, was in the Democratic quarters in the same hotel carrying on his news gathering chores at the Republican meeting. He wanted to talk to Dr. Dixon and had finally located him in Ogden and had him on the telephone. He sent word to the Republican meeting that the Doctor was on the line and that if we wanted to talk to him he would hold him until we could get there. After a very long telephone conversation involving a number of party leaders, Dixon told me he would accept if nominated by the committee.

I hurriedly thanked him and carried the news to the committee, which promptly made Henry Aldous Dixon's nomination official by a unanimous vote. And so it was that the dejected Republicans were in the race with a strong candidate, one who had prospects of winning despite the fact that he had some ten days in which to conduct his campaign.

The Republicans, with able and popular Dr. Dixon as their candidate, waged a vigorous campaign in the remaining days before the election. Dr. Dixon was elected by a substantial majority. The fates had been kind to the downhearted Republicans.*

Douglas Stringfellow, now a very humble man, again became a radio pro-

---

*After serving three successive terms in Congress, Dr. Dixon retired. During that time he was a hard working Congressman who helped win the fight for the Upper Colorado River project. He also took an active part in furthering other valuable legislation, and became, in his short service greatly beloved in the House. Under the circumstances, it was a fitting climax to an illustrious career.

gram director in Utah. He worked at this job for a number of years until his employer sold the station. The new owner had employees to fill all positions at the station so Douglas had to seek employment elsewhere. Mrs. Stringfellow, in the meantime, supplemented the family income with miscellaneous employment and attended the University of Utah until she received her teaching certificate and later became a school teacher.

There was no cure for the Congressman's paralyzed lower limbs. He managed with the help of braces and a cane to get around in his work. His left lung was also collapsed when he was injured. This caused him trouble from time to time.

His physician advised him that he would probably be better in a warmer climate. So with his family of four children and his wife, he went to Mexico City. Here he became interested again in landscape and portrait painting, a leisure time activity in which he showed much promise. His paintings sold readily and were the source of considerable revenue to the young family.

But Douglas Stringfellow's paralyzed legs and his injured lung were causing much distress, so the U. S. Air Force flew him to Long Beach, California, where he was hospitalized in a Veteran's hospital. In the meantime Mrs. String-fellow had received her teacher's certificate and was able to get a position in California public schools. Douglas' condition worsened. Now his injured lung developed a blood clot which went to his heart and caused his death on October 19, 1967. He was then 43 years old.

In concluding this chapter I return to the three letters quoted in its beginning.

Two of the writers have substantially the same theme: How strange it is that I could find so much Christian charity or compassion for Congressman Stringfellow, a Mormon, and so much un-Christian like hatred and prejudice against Senator McCarthy, who was a Catholic. The third letter leaves out the Catholic reference; otherwise the thought is the same. And so it is said I have charity and forgiveness for Stringfellow, but no forgiveness for McCarthy; for him only prejudice, bitterness, and hatred.

Anyone who has carefully perused this book probably will not need further explanation from me, but since I have made it one of my purposes to help thousands of insufficiently informed Americans to make a correct judgment on the charges against the late Senator McCarthy, I shall try to make clear why I could have "Christian charity" for Congressman Stringfellow but could not for-give Senator McCarthy.

Stringfellow confessed to the people of Utah and the people of the United States his story of war heroics was false, that it was a hoax, and he begged forgiveness of the people he had deceived and wronged. He also sought to make restitution for what he had done as far as he was able. He resigned from the Republican Congressional ticket; he asked that his name be withdrawn even though polls indicated that after his confession he could have been reelected, because the voters felt he was sincere in his confession. He also returned $25,000 to the moving picture company which had been sent him as a down payment on a contract for the picturization of his war story. No one could have forced his withdrawal from the Republican ticket in the short time remaining before election. He knew this but made his decision to retire notwithstanding. His life of devotion to his family subsequent to his resignation also proved his sincerity, and finally his early demise was largely a result of his war wounds. These last items couldn't have influenced my earlier decision, but they certainly are a strong confirmation that my decision was right.

Senator McCarthy never made any admissions of misconduct on his part. On the contrary he attacked individual members of the Select Committee, with special emphasis on the chairman. Most of these attacks were made outside the hearing room.

McCarthy's conduct was such that if the Committee had been a court with all the powers of a court to punish for contempt, he most certainly would have been penalized for contempt of court.

Finally, he wrote his "handmaiden" speech attacking the Committee, released it to the press, television, and radio the evening before he was to make it in the Senate. Then, the next day, he did not attempt to deliver the speech, but within a few minutes of recess for the day, requested and received permission to have it printed in the body of the *Congressional Record.* That "speech" charged that the Communist Party had extended its tentacles to the United States Senate and made the Select Committee its unwitting handmaiden.

He used the word "unwitting" as a subterfuge to make it possible to get his charges in the *Congressional Record.* He knew that I had been an active member of the McCarran Committee which had been investigating Communists for many years, and that I knew as much or more about Communism than he. Senator McCarthy was not repentant in any sense of the word. He did not "confess" that he had been wrong in any of his activities, and he did not want to be forgiven.

19 I Lose My Bid for Re-election

IT WAS LATE SUMMER IN 1958, AND MOST MEMBERS OF THE CONGRESS WHO
were up for re-election had long since departed Washington to campaign in
their home districts and States. Naturally, I had some concern about my own
campaign. At the same time, I realized that the Senate couldn't function without
Senators, and I felt an obligation to the Senate to stay in Washington as long as
possible to help maintain a quorum. Striking a happy balance in this matter, as
in all other matters of duty and responsibility, offered some difficulty.

A principal responsibility for determining when the Senate should adjourn—
and for maintaining a quorum until that time—was the concern of Democratic
Senator Lyndon B. Johnson, Senate Majority Leader.

Therefore, I approached Senator Johnson one forenoon and said: "Senator,
when do you think we will adjourn? I am up for re-election, you know, and I
think this will be a tough campaign. Ex-Governor J. Bracken Lee will be con-
testing me, running as an independent; in reality he is the candidate of die-hard
McCarthyites. He was against me in the McCarthy censure. I have to get back
to Utah as soon as I can leave Washington."

"Well," said Johnson, speaking very seriously, "that's something you don't
have to worry about, Arthur. With your record you shouldn't have any difficulty
at all in getting re-elected."

Frankly, I found Senator Johnson's solemn assessment reassuring. Under the
then current circumstances, the Democratic Party in Utah did not appear to
have great strength. And, since it was not uncommon for a Senate leader to stay
out of a campaign where an opposing party Senator had been cooperative and
had rendered some unique service to the country, I gained the impression that
Johnson had no thought of campaigning against me and was trying to get that
assurance across to me. Such matters are usually unspoken, but implied.

Having been given the responsibility of heading the Select Committee to hear
the censure charges against Senator McCarthy—a responsibility over and above
the usual call of duty and at great personal political risk, as everyone will recognize—and remembering that Senator Johnson claimed he had corralled some
wandering southern Senators to make a decisive vote for censure, I felt we had
something in common. (Later, Johnson took great personal credit for engineering the censure of Joe McCarthy.)

It should also be remembered that the Democrats had far more at stake in
the censure proceedings than did the Republicans—McCarthy had branded the
Democratic Party as a party of treason for 20 years. The Gillette Committee
was Democratic-controlled. I wouldn't claim for a moment that I was entitled to

help from Senator Johnson, but under all the circumstances involved in the Senate censure proceedings, I firmly believed that this was one time when the ethical considerations were such that the Majority Leader should have remained neutral, at least, in the Utah Senatorial contest.

Further, I remember Johnson's expression of trust and confidence in me when he echoed Senator William Knowland's statement on the floor of the Senate—after I had been under vicious personal attack by Senator McCarthy—that with me as Chairman and supported by our fellow Senators on the Select Committee he would have no hesitancy to trust his life in our hands.

I develop this in some detail, for some may think it was naive of me to believe that Senator Johnson would stay out of Utah and not lend himself to efforts of the Democratic national organization to increase their party's majority in the Senate. It was not too surprising for me to assume this, I believe, in the light of considerable precedents (and illustrated, as a well-known example, by Lyndon Johnson's "neglect" to campaign in Illinois whenever Senator Dirksen came up for re-election). I also recalled an exchange which occurred during the first year of Johnson's Senate leadership which gave me some encouragement. The incident was reported in the *Congressional Record* for August 29, 1957: *

> MR. JOHNSON of Texas.   Mr. President, I ask unanimous consent that when the Senate concludes its deliberations today it stand in adjournment until 9 o'clock tomorrow morning.
> MR. WATKINS.   Mr. President, reserving the right to object—
> MR. JOHNSON of Texas.   I am not making a motion. I am asking that the order be entered.
>
> MR. WATKINS.   There is certain proposed legislation in which I am interested, and which I should like to have taken care of.
> MR. JOHNSON of Texas.   The Senator from Utah always takes care of legislation he is interested in. I do not know of any Senator who does a better job in the Senate in doing that. . . ."

I first learned that former Governor Lee would oppose me from Congressman William A. Dawson of Utah's 2nd Congressional District. Dawson notified me that he had received a letter from Lee saying that he intended to be an independent candidate for the Senate in opposition to me. Dawson said that with Lee in the race he would not contest me for the nomination, but would be a candidate to succeed himself in the House of Representatives. This was interesting news because Dawson had been for two years actively conducting an unannounced campaign for the Republican Senatorial nomination. Accordingly, I fully expected Dawson to be my opponent and strongly believed that Lee would

*Page 1649 *Congressional Record*–1957.

support him, but now it seemed that this combination had changed its plans so that Lee would become in effect the candidate of the followers of the late Senator McCarthy. As their candidate, he would have the strong financial support of wealthy Republican and Democratic backers of McCarthy which would make him a formidable opponent in Utah.

As I had been warned that my activities as Chairman of the Censure Committee would destroy me politically, I was not surprised that the die-hard McCarthy supporters (of whom Lee had been one of the most active) would seize this, their first, opportunity to vent their spleen against me.

The pro-McCarthy groups were intent upon punishing me and this could be accomplished most dramatically through my defeat which would end my Senatorial career. Governor Lee who had endeared himself with the McCarthyites (his telephone message of encouragement to the "10,000,000 Americans" drive has been discussed in Chapter 14 and as president of a "Pro-America" group (made up of wealthy Texas and California conservatives) was almost the perfect challenger for my Senate seat.

Former Governor Lee had no just cause for his hostility toward me. In 1944 prior to his first race for Governor, I wrote and published a full-page illustrated article on him and his activities as Mayor of Price, Utah, in a weekly paper which I owned, the Utah Valley News, published at Provo, Utah. The article was complimentary to the Mayor and his family. He was so pleased with it that he ordered 50,000 reprints of the article for use in the gubernatorial campaign. Although he didn't win his showing was respectable and he told me that I had done more for him than any other person in the State.

I was first elected to the Senate in 1946, before Lee was elected Governor. During the campaign I visited Price, Utah, and asked Mayor Lee (whose candidacy for governor I had aided) to introduce me to some of his people. He refused. He told me I did not have one chance in a million to be elected. Of course, I was stunned by his refusal, but this did not cause any break in our relations. Immediately after my election, Mayor and Mrs. Lee came to me to get their son James named to the U.S. Military Academy at West Point. James was a fine scholar and a deserving young man, so I was glad to recommend his appointment. He made a brilliant record at the Academy. Eventually Mayor Lee was elected to a four-year term as Governor of Utah in 1948 and was re-elected in 1952. I supported him both times.

My break with Lee came when he made it clear he was not satisfied with two traditional four-year terms as Governor but was planning for a third term. Since statehood no Utah governor had been elected to a third term. Also at this time the Colorado River Storage Bill had just become law. With Utah's deep interest in that measure in mind, most Utah Republicans believed the time was ripe for a Governor who by training and experience could best integrate Utah into that program. George D. Clyde, a nationally known water conservationist and a powerful advocate of the Colorado River Storage project, defeated Lee for the nomination and was elected Governor. (He served two terms.)

I supported Clyde for Governor that year, and also for his second term. This, in the eyes of Lee, was my unpardonable sin. When he opposed me in 1958, Lee boasted that he told his supporters he wouldn't become a candidate unless they got together a campaign fund of at least one dollar for each vote that he would need to win the election.

The formal opening of his campaign was in the nature of an elaborate extravaganza, held in the largest combination dance hall-auditorium in Salt Lake City. McCarthy supporters, movie actors, and other entertainers from Southern California, and Las Vegas, Nevada, made the speeches and furnished the entertainment. Large quantities of food and other refreshments were provided and the general public was invited to join in the festivities. (The press reported that there was a capacity attendance.)

Out of state For-America leaders, all impassioned McCarthyites, planned and ran the show for Lee, their National President. This Salt Lake gala-extravaganza should have dispelled any doubts that Lee was the hero of McCarthy's followers. For at least one night, the For-America president was knee deep in glory. Following his gala opening, Lee's billboards blossomed over the state as wild flowers in the desert after a heavy rain. His campaign was off to a roaring start.

Before leaving Washington to begin my own campaign, I had a conversation with Vice President Nixon. I pointed out to him the situation in Utah as it appeared to me. I observed that this was not a normal political situation and that I would need some special help. "To put it another way," I said, "the candidacy of Lee, backed by forces throughout the United States who supported McCarthy, is really a by-product of the McCarthy censure proceedings and should be treated as such. Neither you, nor President Eisenhower took sides for, or against McCarthy. The President stood by his position that whether or not McCarthy was censured was the sole responsibility of the Senate, and you discharged your duties as Vice President, and took no part in the McCarthy controversy, except as you were required by law and the rules of the Senate."

I also told him that I had a legislative record, as a Senator, and as a member of the Republican administration—which, entirely independent of my services as chairman of the Select Committee, I believed warranted his support and that of the President. I also advised him that I had to leave for Utah immediately to be present at the Utah Republican State Convention and therefore would not have the time to meet with the President before my departure.

The Vice President listened sympathetically to my appraisal and volunteered to talk to the President about my campaign in Utah and my need for help. A few days later I received a letter from the President:

THE WHITE HOUSE
WASHINGTON

September 11, 1958

Dear Arthur:

Your reelection campaign is very much in my mind, and I most earnestly wish you success.

No doubt many citizens, far from the activities of Washington, must find it difficult to keep abreast of excellent service such as you have been faithfully giving, day after day, month after month, during all your years in the United States Senate. I hope you can yourself make this known to all the people of Utah, and by all means I hope you will make clear how deeply I and many others in responsible places, both in the Congress and in the Administration, value your service and how constructive and useful it always has been.

Instances of your important contributions are many—to cite a few, our Middle Eastern policies, in respect to which I received your helpful report in December 1954 and had the benefit of your recent effective speech to the Senate—the giant Colorado River Storage Project and many reclamation projects—the Emergency Refugee Act of 1953 (fittingly known as the Watkins Act)—plus a host of other measures important to all our people. In respect to all of these, your leadership and thoughtful advice contributed much to administrative and legislative actions needed by our country.

It is because of this, and because yours is the kind of dedicated service needed in the Senate, that I gratefully send you this message. I feel sure you will find that the people of Utah value your experience, judgment and effective service as highly as I do. I anticipate that they will prove this by overwhelmingly supporting your candidacy on election day.

With warm regard,

Sincerely,

(Dwight Eisenhower)

The Honorable Arthur V. Watkins
United States Senator
1233 Newhouse Hotel
Salt Lake City, Utah

The President's letter greatly encouraged me and the loyal Republicans of Utah as well as a sizable number of Democrats who appreciated my services to the state and nation. I confess, I was pleased by the President's frank recital of some of my activities, reports and advice which he had found helpful in shaping the policies of his administration. Over the years I have seen some of the letters the President has sent to other members of Congress who were Republican candidates for re-election, but can't remember any which were as specific as his letter to me.

It may be helpful to the reader if I comment on some of the items mentioned in President Eisenhower's letter:

MIDDLE EAST

The waters of the Nile, Tigris, and Euphrates rivers which had sustained millions of people in ancient times, were now largely flowing into the oceans unused. I had suggested that if the unused land and water in the Middle East were made available through reclamation, the desert would bloom and the people of the area would then be so busy building homes and planting crops, that they would not have time to fight each other. Even hatreds might in time disappear. Nuclear power could also be used to make ocean water usable.

SOUTH EAST ASIA: VIETNAM, FORMOSA

I had urged that we stay out of wars in this area unless other allied nations would join us in intervening and that such action should be authorized by a Resolution of Congress. Such a resolution should also be obtained if armed force is needed to put down a hostile action which represented a threat to our security as a nation. The Formosa and Mid-East Resolutions, implement that suggestion.

RECLAMATION IN THE U.S.

The Colorado River Storage project, largest ever authorized by the Congress, was created at the President's request. I convinced the President of the project's worth and I was one of those who championed the passage in the Congress of the essential legislation.

The letter was, of course, a highly valued campaign document.

The incident of Senator Johnson's praise of me as an able legislator, recorded earlier in this chapter, seemed to be a break for me of some importance, even though it occurred in 1957, one year before the present Senatorial race in Utah. So, too, was Senator Johnson's encomium on the Senate floor. Sensing its political value, my campaign staff lifted it from the *Congressional Record* and used it as part of a large political advertisement in the Salt Lake Tribune on Sunday, October 26, 1958. The ad was headed, *"He gets things done—Watkins of Utah."* And endorsements by public officials headed by one from President Eisenhower, were quoted below a sub-head: *"Just a few things others say about Utah's Senior Senator*:

PRESIDENT DWIGHT D. EISENHOWER:

". . . I most earnestly wish you success . . . and I hope you will make clear how deeply I and many others in responsible places, both in the Congress and in the Administration, value your service and how constructive and useful it has always been."

VICE PRESIDENT RICHARD M. NIXON:

"He is more than just a sectional Senator, he is a Senator for all the people of the United States. He made a particularly significant contribution to the development of the strong, firm foreign policy of the Eisenhower Administration which has ended one war, kept us out of others and kept the peace without surrender of principle or territory."

SECRETARY OF AGRICULTURE EZRA TAFT BENSON:

"Senator Arthur Watkins has evidenced real leadership . . . He has exerted particular leadership in our successful efforts to pass major portions of the Administration's legislative policies."

SECRETARY OF THE INTERIOR FRED A. SEATON:

"Senator Arthur V. Watkins is one of the top six men in the Senate. Any impartial survey of the Senators as to effectiveness will bear this out completely."

SENATOR LYNDON JOHNSON OF TEXAS, DEMOCRATIC MAJORITY LEADER:

"The Senator from Utah always takes care of legislation he is interested in. I do not know of any Senator who does a better job in the Senate in doing that . . ."

SENATOR CLINTON P. ANDERSON OF NEW MEXICO, FORMER SECRETARY OF AGRICULTURE:

". . . A tower of strength on the Subcommittee on Irrigation and Reclamation . . . and one of the great reclamation lawyers of the Senate."

I was considerably heartened when, shortly after the appearance of the ad, a highly respected polling organization showed me leading my opponents for the Senate.

With this situation having developed, Bobby Baker (Lyndon Johnson's right-hand man in the Senate's Democratic organization) came to Utah. A cry had gone out from local Democrats backing Frank Moss that they needed help. The latest professional poll in the Senate—for late October—showed sentiment as follows: Watkins 37.7 per cent; Moss 31.3 per cent; and Lee 22.8 per cent. It appeared that only an unusual or dramatic event could change the situation in favor of one of the opposition candidates.

Parenthetically, a rather revealing conversation took place between Bobby Baker and one of the members of my staff after the election. Following is a verbatim quotation from a letter I subsequently received from the latter:

After returning to Washington following our '58 defeat, I ran into Bobby Baker in the Hall outside the chamber in the Senate wing of the Capitol. We exchanged the usual hellos that had been our custom from the early days of our friendship which began in '53. He expressed his regrets at your defeat since it meant my unemployment and I reassured him that that was all in the game of politics and that I knew the Senator-elect well. He then volunteered that he had been in Salt Lake City during the campaign. He explained that he had made an overnight stop in Salt Lake, talked with some Democratic party people and others, and concluded that Lee would pull enough votes to make the election of Moss a possibility. He said that he reported this to Earle Clements and suggested that this seat could be won if they put some money in the Moss campaign. He indicated that they did just that.

Senator Earle Clements was the nominal head of the Democratic Senatorial Campaign Committee, but Lyndon B. Johnson was the real director of those Senatorial campaigns where the result was in doubt. I feel free to assume that Bobby Baker reported the possibility of unseating me because of the Republican party split, which Lee's candidacy represented to his boss, Lyndon Johnson. Bobby's analysis probably included the need for Johnson to come into Utah and give his support to the Democratic candidate. At any rate, Senator Johnson did come to Utah with major funds for a last minute, crash drive.

I had always campaigned with very little money available and had won through a direct appeal to the people to support me on the basis of my record and by my generally acknowledged leadership in the reclamation and other programs of vital interest to Utah and the three other upper-basin states: Colorado, New Mexico, and Wyoming. I simply did not have the resources to counter the massive organizational efforts mounted by Bobby Baker and Lyndon Johnson in the last three days of the campaign. Also, my own party's Senatorial Campaign Committee in Washington was controlled by strong McCarthy supporters. The Committee contributed only a nominal sum, and when I called for additional help they said they were out of money. I learned later that money was available, but the Committee didn't make any efforts to get it.

Now I call attention to his one day appearance in the Utah campaign which was on Saturday, November 1, 1958, only two days from election day. The *Salt Lake Tribune,* in its Sunday edition, reported that Johnson severely criticized the Eisenhower administration for its record, and then he gave an all out endorsement to the Democratic Senate and Congressional candidates in Utah. He stated that the Democratic Senatorial candidate, Frank E. Moss, would, if elected, be given a major committee assignment as "soon as he reached Washington." He described me as a fine, kindly man; but said, "the G.O.P. candidate must be desperate to use a letter of commendation from the Majority Senate Leader as a reason why he should be elected. I am sure," he said, "that voters will not get the impression that a Majority Democratic Senate Leader wants a Republican returned." His accusation is completely untrue for I did not use a "letter" of commendation from Senator Johnson at all.

The only statement of Senator Johnson's that was used in my campaign was his comment, quoted earlier, during an exchange between us in the Senate. The comment had appeared in *Congressional Record* and was certainly not privileged in any way—anyone could use it. It appeared in my advertisement because it documented the way leaders in government appraised my work in the Senate. The statement was not featured by itself or given special emphasis. It was used because I felt it truly reflected Senator Johnson's feelings towards me. If I were untrue surely the Senator would have disavowed the remark immediately upon publication of the advertisement.

Nonetheless, with the limited time available for campaigning, with practically no funds at hand—but with willing and loyal supporters, and the determination to look ahead and not justify the past—I made a good run. The final count showed a close race. I lost by some 11,000 votes out of some 350,000 votes cast.

I am convinced the combination of Majority Leader Johnson and former Governor J. Bracken Lee, with the financial support of his millionaire friends from Texas, Southern California and elsewhere, were the determining factors in my defeat. Johnson's intervention was particularly effective because of its timing, just three days before election when there was not time to counter the move.

One important consequence of my defeat was the loss from Utah of virtually certain membership on the all-important Senate Appropriations Committee. A short time before my term expired there occurred a Republican vacancy on this committee. Senator Ives of New York and I had equal seniority for this post. We drew lots for the appointment with Senator Ives the winner. When the Senator later decided to retire from the Senate in 1958, that left me with a certain appointment to the Appropriations Committee at the opening of the new Congress had I been re-elected. Moreover Senator Knowland of California, a member of Appropriations, also was defeated. This opened up a second opportunity to have been named on this committee.

I, or any other Utahn for that matter with sufficient seniority to get on the Appropriations Committee, could have in the succeeding years helped greatly to accelerate reclamation and other public works projects vital to Western growth.*

*Saying this does not reflect on the dedication or ability of the present delegation from Utah, including my successor. The simple facts are, however, that following the elections of 1958 these resource development projects in Utah did not receive appropriations sufficient for their acceleration and completion. Some of the blame lies with a later Democratic Administration oriented to problems of the more populous East, and some to the drain of the undeclared (and unconstitutional) war in Vietnam. Today, in the Western States, there are huge projects such as the Upper Colorado River Storage Project authorized but not fully funded. Within the Upper Colorado River Storage Project is the participating Central Utah Project, estimated at the time of its over all authorization to cost $384 million. This project will cost the water and power users of Utah (since they pay for it directly, under the repayment principles of reclamation) a great deal more because of inflation and delays. This project—the Central Utah Project—is not yet where it should be: in its final stages. I mention this so that the voters of Utah, conscious of their pocketbooks as much as anyone, can "thank" their McCarthyite friends for this additional cost of the 1958 election.

Further attention must also be given to J. Bracken Lee. While to all appearances Ex-Governor Lee was campaigning vigorously, to the very end, to secure the Senate seat for himself (and there were still ads running in the papers the weekend before election that said: "A Vote for Moss is a vote for Watkins, Vote for Lee") there was an important change in the political situation that weekend. I was told by highly reliable sources that with Lyndon Johnson in Salt Lake City on the weekend before the election, and with the crash Democratic telephone campaign, Lee came to the realization that he had no hope of winning the election for himself.* He was determined, however, to keep me from being re-elected.

It is my own belief, based on information supplied to me by people in whom I have every confidence, that Lee's lieutenants met with the strategists for Johnson to work out plans to insure my defeat. We know of a certainty is that there was still a hard-core of McCarthyites in Utah who were marshalled by J. Bracken Lee. The arithmetic also shows that even with the intensive telephone campaign which was put in effort for Moss, I would never have been defeated except for the bitter, McCarthyite, anti-Watkins votes which went to Lee. This combination of Lyndon Johnson and J. Bracken Lee, not only denied me the election, but very likely also cost the people of Utah earlier development of reclamation and other Federal programs of great value to the State.

While I wasn't counting the cost in personal terms in my run-in with Mc-Carthy, and it was with some surprise that I actually lost the election, it all turned out to have been best for me. Upon being named Chief Commissioner of the Indian Claims Committee, by President Eisenhower in 1959, I found a quieter, more healthful life, and greater net income.** My life has undoubtedly been lengthened, and today I must honestly admit that I was and am better off.

Would I have been a vigorous fighter for the interests of Utah in these matters if I had wound up on the Appropriations Committee? The answer may be seen in my record (described earlier in this book) which first earned me the election to the Senate, and more significantly in the unprecedented speed with which I worked with President Eisenhower and others to initiate the Upper Colorado River Storage Project (signed by the President in April, 1956 and with construction underway on Glen Canyon Dam and Flaming Gorge Dam in October of that same year).

*The latest poll showed that Lee had dropped from second place to third and that Moss had gained votes from him.

**I can't help noting the treatment accorded me by Senator Mansfield, Democrat of Montana, who succeeded Senator Johnson as majority leader. When my name was before the Senate as President Eisenhower's nominee to the office of Chief Commissioner of the Indian Claims Commission, Senator Mansfield called up the appointment without reference to a committee and added a complimentary remark. I was confirmed unanimously within a few minutes after the appointment was received by the Senate.

MANY OBSERVERS AND COLUMNISTS HAVE COMMENTED ON MC CARTHY'S tactics and attitudes during the period of the censure proceedings. His deliberate rejection of what might be thought of as the usual ways a man might attempt to avoid censure have often been noted.

Just prior to the censure, we may remember, there was an attempt by members of the Republican Policy Committee to tone down McCarthy in his statements and methods, and thereby to reduce criticism. As the Flanders resolution was being debated, Senate friends urged Joe to make some kind of apology for his excesses and thereby to blunt or turn aside efforts in the Senate to censure him. During the hearings of the Select Committee, he made little effort to justify himself through the application of fact or law. On the contrary, he chose to make his "defense" in an emotional appeal before the TV cameras in the hall outside the hearing room and with the aid of friendly columnists. He supported his friends in their mass-meetings and petition drives to rally widespread public support. And, finally, as reported by Senate friends and his counsel, Edward Bennett Williams,* he refused any compromise which might have been obtained.

Parenthetically, I reject the notion that any compromise was possible short of an apology and reform on his part. It appears that he had gone too far for that in his appeal to public opinion, and, in addition, such a move was foreign to his nature.

My own feeling with respect to various compromise moves is indicated in my response to Senator Dirksen—who during the censure debate asked fellow Senators to approve a greatly modified resolution—when I stated on the floor of the Senate Chamber: **

. . . We tried to extend the olive branch to our young friend from Wisconsin.

It was indicated to him† that he might possibly have done wrong, that he might have said some things he should not have said, and the opportunity was given him to say whether he was willing to retract some of the words he had said and some of the things he had done. But there was no indication that he wanted any sympathy or a helping hand extended to him.

*Edward Bennett Williams, *op. cit.,* p. 68.
**Congressional Record,* Vol. 100, Part 12, December 1, 1954, p. 16325.
†The time referred to here was during the hearings of the Select Committee.

(Senator Case), a member of the Select Committee, during the debate also extended his hand and indicated that the door was still open for the prodigal to come in and make some amends, but the junior Senator from Wisconsin never made any effort to do that at all.

I am personally willing to forgive, that is a commandment which has been given us. But forgiveness is based on repentance, some works meet for repentance, and I have failed to see such works up to this hour.

My subsequent opinion (apparently confirmed by one of McCarthy's final acts in the Senate, as we shall see in this chapter) is that his contempt for the Senate—and for its procedures and traditions—was determining all his actions from the beginning.

From the first, McCarthy seemed to have the feeling that he would be censured. He seemed, in fact, determined to bring about his censure. A favorite remark during the entire period was that he was being taken to a "lynching."

I have earlier quoted Arthur Krock (writing on December 2 in *The New York Times*) as saying that McCarthy's conduct during the censure hearing was deliberately designed to seek censure.

William S. White—also writing in *The New York Times,* but after the censure, on December 5—said that it was clear that whatever happened to McCarthy, his future clearly would "lie outside the Senate." Explaining that the Senator still had all the privileges and prerogatives of the Senate, White observed that while "the doors of the Senate remain unquestionably open to him . . . the walls will in a very apparent degree now close in upon him." For," White went on, "the Senate did not lightly enter into this affair of disciplining Senator McCarthy" in its "final and decisive vote" of 67 to 22. Then columnist White said: ". . . McCarthy has been subtly but unalterably transformed into what the diplomats call persona non grata." This analysis, as it turned out, was amazingly accurate.

Some writers foresaw the possibility that McCarthy would take his case to the people, over the heads of the Senate, rallying millions of supporters (as, of course, he attempted to do during and immediately after the hearings), and possibly becoming the champion of a far-right wing, third party political movement. These crystal ball readers were far from the mark.

McCarthy's last days were a great departure from his heyday in the Senate. The contrast of before and after the censure is so great that it cannot be readily explained—as is so frequently attempted—by his poor health, his heavy drinking, his losses in the market, or even by his "broken heart, caused by a turncoat press." In my considered judgment, as of now, the answer lies deeply within the character of the man.

For those who saw the man in action—particularly after he "found himself," so to speak, in anti-communism—Senator McCarthy, it would be seen, was a person delighted with himself. He relished the spotlight and savored personal power, but no pleasure (it seems to me) was greater than the recounting of his exploits.

By virtue of his position and his anti-communism campaign, he enjoyed a following. I remember seeing and hearing small groups of women—visitors to the Capitol—meeting him in the corridor during the time of the censure debate and squealing with excitement at their nearness to him. "I touched him!" they would call out to each other. There were also reporers (some permanently assigned to follow him around), scurrying aides at his side, and the curious. He was a great showman and never failed an opportunity to make use of any forum for offhand and flip remarks.

I remember an occasion in the Senate Republican dining room, some time prior to the censure proceedings, as a number of us lunched leisurely and enjoyed each other's company. Joe had just recently run into Drew Pearson at a party, and walking up to Pearson in the washroom, had struck him to the floor for uncomplimentary remarks in the latter's column.

Now, retelling the event with gusto and encouraged by the chuckles and appreciative remarks of some colleagues, he said that each time he saw Drew Pearson he was going to knock him down. After this imaginative exercise had drawn its calculated response, I spoke up with a word of admonition.

"Since I am your elder by many years, and having served on the bench—as, of course, you have," I told Joe, "I would like to urge some prudence on your part. From a legal point of view, if Drew ever got word of what you just said, he might very well be within his legal rights—expecting an attack from you—to shoot a hole right through you the next time you walk up to him. I think any judge, or jury, would exonerate him under the circumstances."

The smile faded from Joe's face and he looked at me with some surprise, but otherwise no show of emotion. He said nothing. Our colleagues said nothing. After a few moments of silence, the conversation began to pick up on other subjects.

McCarthy, it seemed to me at the time, carried his liquor well and some (including myself) did not recognize that he was influenced by it. Senator Barry Goldwater of Arizona, discussing with me the subject of Senator McCarthy's censure after the event (and it will be remembered that Goldwater supported McCarthy in that vote), said that Joe's drinking during the debate on the floor of the Senate caused his associates some distress. He explained that McCarthy would order his staff to prepare remarks in a certain vein for him to give on the floor, and although the staff would do as they were told his Senatorial friends would manage to hide, or lose, the material just as McCarthy was to go into the Senate Chamber, to prevent him from further discrediting himself.

Senator Everett Dirksen, who had also voted for McCarthy "in the interests of

Republican unity" as he put it, said to me on the same subject of keeping Mc-Carthy from excesses: "I'd go crazy if I had another like him to defend."

A curiosity with respect to McCarthy was the difference between the man "loaded" and sober. It was a frontier saying that the "real man" is the one you see under the influence of alcohol and released from his inhibitions. Many a man, it used to be said, was the model of propriety sober but mean while drinking. In his later years subsequent to the censure, Joe McCarthy was frequently seen in circumstances which implied that he was drinking.

The early McCarthy seemed to enjoy his role. In the Senate Chamber, Joe might belabor a colleague for his lack of wit or consistency—perhaps doing this chiefly for the benefit of an audience—and then moving off the floor and meeting his supposed enemy standing in the Senate Chamber would put his arm around the latter's shoulders and utter pleasantries.

Sometimes McCarthy's assumed camaraderie would prove embarrassing. In such a situation, Senator Flanders was once described by reporters as "giggling." I believe from observations that McCarthy immensely enjoyed those playful incidents for the way they threw off his opponents.

Illustrative of Senator McCarthy's unpredictable manner is this story, in the period immediately after the censure.

McCarthy had been seated next to me on the floor of the Senate. Immediately after the censure, however, he requested a change of seats and this was accomplished, bringing him nearer the President's podium.

As McCarthy would leave the Chamber to go to the Republican Senator's cloakroom, he would pass my seat. Slowing down, as he neared me on the aisle, he would lean slightly toward me and hiss: "How is the little coward from Utah?"

The first few times this happened, I reacted good-naturedly with a "Hi, Joe." Soon, I chose to ignore him completely when these occasions brought him near me, and this was much easier for me. Joe, however, was puzzled by this behavior and seemed to be thrown off stride. He finally desisted from this childish insult.

Then, months later, we met face to face as we approached the Senate's marble washroom simultaneously. He stopped and in a very respectful and friendly voice said: "How are you, Arthur?" I returned his greeting in kind, and for a few minutes we exchanged pleasantries. I wondered what change had occurred in the man.

Right after this interlude, Senator McCarthy recommenced his insolent "greeting" as he passed my seat on the aisle.

From these admittedly limited observations, I finally drew the conclusion that the Senator's alcoholic content determined his actions in his last days as much as anything else.

I also saw that McCarthy suffered when he was ignored, and his inability to re-assert his position as a headline-grabber and leader of public opinion stemmed from a new attitude toward him which became evident on the part of the press, his Senate colleagues, and the general public.

McCarthy, who had been the subject of many headlines, did not disappear from the front pages immediately nor willingly. Shortly after the censure vote, he made an effort to find a new issue and a new campaign. He made a show of "breaking with Eisenhower," even though he had never had a good relationship (and there is evidence to indicate that his anti-Eisenhower feeling stemmed from his anti-Army hang-up).

On December 7, Joe attacked the President for being "weak on China" and with this charge he made some front pages. This flurry didn't catch on and McCarthy was not pressed for elaboration. The show fizzled.

There was no concerted effort at all on the part of his Senate colleagues to give him the icy treatment, but increasingly as McCarthy got up on the floor of the Senate to make remarks the other Senators would drift off the floor and find other interests in the cloakroom, or go to the washroom. If a group of Senators stood in the cloakroom enjoying a story and Joe joined them, the laughter quickly faded and the various Senators went on their way.

At lunch, Joe might sit at a table with former intimates and soon these would finish their bean soup and sandwich and murmur an excuse about the need to return to their offices. The merriment had long since disappeared from McCarthy's eyes, and he could be seen watching after his departing colleagues with a look of real puzzlement on his face.

As a result, McCarthy's interests were turned from the political arena, from communist hunting, and from badgering the Army. When his former Senate Government Operations Committee thoroughly explored the Major Peress matter, its Chairman, Senator McClellan reported that the Army had blundered in its handling of the case, and . . . said nothing about communist influence. Newspaper accounts of this report added the observation that there was no "Secret Master." McCarthy, as a Committee member, meekly signed the report. Joe, instead of pursuing communists, began talking about a little ranch in Arizona.

Further, it was reported, Joe began to plunge more erratically in the stock market. It is said that he was trying for a killing to finance a longed-for livestock venture in the Southwest. Possibly because of a decline in his ability to figure things carefully, he suffered severe losses.

Finally, Joe made a political testament in the form of reports to his constituents—a statement which was the denouement of a rather poorly conceived, although occasionally brilliantly acted, performance. Late Friday afternoon on January 4, 1957, the day after the opening of the First Session of the 85th Congress, Senator McCarthy came onto the floor of the Senate and sat down. It had been a particularly fatiguing day, filled with Senate organizational matters. There were few Senators in the Chamber. McCarthy rose and asked unanimous consent to have inserted in the *Record* a series of newsletter-type reports he had sent constituents. There being no objection, the Chair ordered the matter printed into the *Record*.

I did not see the material, and it was not until some time later that the senior Senator from Wisconsin, Senator Alexander Wiley, called it to my attention. In the body of this report there was an item called: "Some Facts on the 'Censure' Vote." Senator Wiley thought that I might wish to comment—indeed, ought to comment—on the floor of the Senate about this latest McCarthy statement on the censure vote.

Among other things, McCarthy had written:

> In talking to some of my Wisconsin friends I got the impression that they may not have had a complete report on what happened before and subsequent to the so-called censure vote. At that time I was condemned because I would not reveal all of my finances to the Gillette Committee, although I had told that committee that I would appear if they decided to subpoena me, but I would not dignify their kangaroo court by a voluntary appearance . . . .
>
> Actually rather than to have voted to condemn McCarthy they should have made it stronger and voted to hold me in contempt of the two committees which I have mentioned, and in contempt of the Senators who voted to approve the report to the effect that it was improper to criticize any Senator. The reason I say they should have made the resolution stronger and voted in contempt is because I had and have the utmost contempt for the Gillette Committee and also for the Watkins Committee, as well as the Senators who tried to establish the rule that no Senator could be criticized for his activities.

He then added:

> The greatest example of cowardice that the Senate has witnessed in its long history was when Senator Watkins, after having taken the chairmanship of this so-called censure committee, refused to answer my questions or debate the ridiculous provisions of the report they had issued. For example, when I started to question him about the provision of the report that said it was improper to criticize a Senator, he dashed from the floor and said he would not answer any questions by me unless they were submitted in writing a day ahead of time—an unheard of thing—a disgrace to the State of Utah and a disgrace to the United States Senate.*

***Congressional Record,* Volume 103, Part 1, January 4, 1957, page 222.

Thus, as we see, Senator McCarthy not only publicly affirmed his contempt for those Senators of the two committees who were performing their assignments by the Senate as a whole in inquiring into questionable attitudes and actions of the junior Senator from Wisconsin, but he also held in contempt the two-thirds of the membership of the Senate who voted for the censure.

There would have been some merit in my speaking on the floor of the Senate, to point out the arrogance of McCarthy's remarks. However, some time had elapsed since they had been inserted in the *Record,* and Joe's excessive drinking was now obvious to us all, as was his poor health. Further, I bore no ill will toward Joe and it was easy to forebear.

Joe McCarthy, as it turned out, was close to death. On the evening of May 2, 1957, Senator McCarthy died in Bethesda Naval Hospital after a long illness, which was diagnosed as hepatitis. His wife asked that his funeral be held in the Senate Chamber, as was permitted. In the customary eulogies on the floor of the Senate, many of the Senators who had fought his methods spoke kindly of his person.*

Columnist George Sokolsky wrote of McCarthy: "He was hounded to death by those who could not forget and could not forgive." Not so. McCarthy was not hounded at all, but died—as he faded away—largely because of physical deterioration and also because he had alienated his audience. McCarthy, it now seems apparent, could not stand being ignored, and without an appreciative audience he had no spirit.

As for my personal thoughts, I could not help but feel it was a pity that this man—with his evident ability to reach into and touch the emotions of hundreds of thousands of people—could not have applied his talents more constructively, but he chose otherwise. I am reminded of Whittier's words: "Of all sad words of tongue or pen, the saddest of all are 'It might have been.' "

---

*The Reverend Frederick Brown Harris, pastor of Foundry Methodist Church in Washington and Chaplain of the Senate, had earlier written me, saying: "After faithful and able service in the U.S. Senate you were suddenly called by your colleagues to step into a position of great—yea, vital—importance, frought with unusual delicacy and difficulty. You have performed that duty which you did not seek superbly well. With the eyes of the nation focused upon you you have displayed elements of real greatness. You have been judicial, firm, fair and utterly without bias. You have shown the qualifications of judge. In spite of provocation, you have kept your patience . . ." In his opening prayer at McCarthy's funeral in the Senate Chamber, Dr. Harris spoke with almost equal grace of the late Senator's virtues. Later, in the usual Senate eulogies, many Senators followed suit, hoping to help the living and ignoring the past.

FROM THE TIME MY NAME WAS FIRST PUBLICIZED IN CONNECTION WITH being named to the Select Committee, I began to receive letters, telegrams, and even telephone calls. When the Committee chose me to be its Chairman, and the Committee began to be referred to as the "Watkins Committee," the sprinkle of comments from citizens across the country became a flood.

I saw some of the first letters and helped my staff develop some standard replies, but almost immediately it became impossible to read the daily mail (let alone analyze or reply to it). I also had a strong feeling that it would become improper for me to read this mail when it began to discuss the merits of the charges, as I was about to preside over a quasi-judicial proceeding.

During this early period, it appears that very few letters attacked me personally. There were few, indeed, which spoke well of me or of my new assignment. Some, however, were kindly but pointedly directed to telling me how to do my job. Only a few of these first letters were nasty: referring to me as a "dupe of communism," a traitor, a tool of Zionists, calling me a senile old man, or sneered at me for wearing religion on my sleeve as a member of the "Moron" Church. The flood of "anti-Watkins" letters was to come later.

While some of the early mail was not retained after processing (my staff estimated the mail during and immediately after the censure proceedings at over 30,000) a large percentage of it was kept in file boxes for the possible benefit of students or historians. It was with no difficulty at all that I refrained from reading this mail for 14 years. With my retirement in the fall of 1967 as Chief Commissioner of the Indian Claims Commission, and with the intent to write about my experiences, came the opportunity for the first time to read through some of this mail. Handily, it had been sorted to a degree by students at the Brigham Young University in Utah where my "censure" mail had been deposited for future use by students of political science.

The surprise at stumbling right off into the following letter prompted me to continue my research:

Los Angeles, California
October 4, 1954

Senator Arthur Watkins:

I feel you should know how very *heartstick the Christians of the United States* are that you received our support *at election,* that defeated *a known left-wing man* and put you—a me too stooge devoid *of all Christian prin-*

cipals in: *who gladly persecute God's Anointed* to *cleanse His Kingdom* of His Enemies *Zionists & Communists.* They killed our Lord Jesus Christs, and now would kill and *Mongrolize* His people.

Please read the inclosed literature, then *honestly repent,* that your *name* not be placed with Benedict Arnolds for Posterity.

In Christs Service,
Mayflower Puritan,

(Signed by a married woman)

Reading many hundreds of letters, as I did, revealed the possibility of defining certain patterns in the mail and in categorizing the writers according to personal charcteristics. That this could probably be done, with some benefit and interest, must be admitted. For myself, I have been content to take some notes and to separate out some letters, to pass on in this book as the results of my own generalized survey.

The great majority of letters were extreme in their pro-McCarthy views, but it would be unfair not to admit that I found several "rational" pro-McCarthy letters which demonstrated that not all his supporters were primarily swayed by emotion. For example, this letter from San Antonio, Texas, is moderate in its approach:

I am sure you will do the right thing for Senator McCarthy. . . . I think, or believe, Senator McCarthy is a great American . . . .

Also, from Auburn, California, is this one:

Please vote in the affirmative for Senator McCarthy. Suppose he has made mistakes, we all do! If all the employees in the Government were as *pro-American* as *he* we would have a better country today!

Some of the pro-McCarthy letters were simple statements of support for his "rooting out" of communists in the Government. A number of the letters, however, were many-paged and laboriously handwritten. While some of these letters attempted point-by-point documentation of facts and legal precedents, a few were rambling diatribes.* The intemperate language in the vast majority of these letters, however, is what stamps them as peculiar in the normal course of communication.

Apparently, some of those writing in support of McCarthy were prompted by a belief (stated by a few) that the Committee had received a great quantity of

---

* One letter ran to 17 single-spaced typewritten pages.

mail calling for censure of McCarthy and that it was necessary for them to write to offset or balance this flood. This was not the case, for there is little evidence of any organized popular effort to censure McCarthy. Nor can I identify the source of this particular idea, altough I don't doubt that most of the pro-McCarthy mail was actually prompted by the reading of opinion makers like Westbrook Pegler, Fulton Lewis, Jr., George Sokolsky, David Lawrence, and others of similar persuasion who were frequently quoted, as well as radio commentators. Amusingly enough, incidentally, were those individuals who wished to "file evidence" by enclosing clippings from these newspaper writers and quotations from radio and TV personalities, as well as from other sources.

The first "issue" taken up by the letter writers in August was the belief that the wrong Senator was being investigated. "You should censure some of those pink boys such as Cellar, Lehman (that is Russia Firsters) and that Vial Mouthed Flanders," wrote a man from Elmira, New York.

On the other hand, the fear expressed by a few writers was that McCarthy was going to "get away with another circus" in the investigation by the Select Committee. "Please—*you preside* at the meetings of which *you* are *Chairman!* Don't let Joe!" wrote one lady. She added: "Show Joe in your quiet dignified manner that a calm gentlemanly chairman *can* and *will* preside!"

The decision to conduct the hearings under the rules and procedures applicable on the floor of the Senate itself excluded radio and TV live coverage. This upset representatives of the industry, as I have said, and their comments called the attention of citizens to this matter. As the written word must necessarily depend upon interpretation, and many ordinary people were skeptical of the objectivity of reporters and commentators, there was a natural desire to see and hear the accusers of Senator McCarthy—and to see the Senator—in the hearings and to judge for themselves. Many writers directed themselves toward the topic: "Let the people see the show!"

Some people were convinced that objectivity could only be served by prohibiting live coverage of the hearings, and thereby avoiding many of the abuses and excesses of the Army-McCarthy hearings. It was my own belief that a judicial atmosphere was desired and, indeed, essential. Examples of this more thoughtful approach in letters arriving on my desk during the middle of August—and while I was still looking at the mail—are these from, respectively, Davis, California, and Berea, Kentucky. The letters:

Davis, California

Dear Senator Watkins:

We hear by the radio that pressure is being brought to bear on you by the broadcasting networks to televize the McCarthy hearings. We respectfully urge you not to allow television during this new Senate hearing on McCarthy. It seems to us that one reason for the failure of Army-McCarthy hearings was the fact that all people concerned with the hearings played to the gallery rather than trying to establish the justice of the claims and counter claims. If your committee is to do the best possible work for the country and for the Senate we feel that it should operate without television, though reporters should not be barred.

Very sincerely yours,

(Signed by a married woman)

Berea, Kentucky

Dear Senator Watkins:

I am unalterably opposed to televising or radio casting hearings to be conducted by the special committee set up to investigate the manifold charges against McCarthy.

Another ludicrous "circus" as was the Army's McCarthy hearings, would cause the American public (except the lunatic fringe) to lose confidence in and respect for the United States Senate.

Sincerely,

(Signed by a man)

It should be remembered that television crews were permitted to set up their cameras in the hall outside the Committee room. And McCarthy, as I have described, conducted his "defense" before the TV cameras and not before the Select Committee, as part of his attempt to "go over the heads" of the Senate and appeal to the American people. That his own side of the story, as contrasted to an objective report of the procedures as it appeared in many responsible newspapers, did reach the people via TV is certainly an interesting commentary and one still deserving further analysis.

A widely-expressed fear of "flagrant slanting, pro and con" in news reporting prompted at least one writer to suggest new information techniques. This woman, from Palo Alto, California, suggested staff-written "official" news releases, similar to those issued by the Government in wartime. "During a war," she wrote, "intelligent people skip the rumors and guesses and rely only on official news for their information . . . All I yearn for is news releases that cannot be tampered with by prejudiced reporters or editors on one side or the other."

This expression of doubt as to the fairness or adequacy of reporting and commentary seemed to be particularly distressing, although I do not personally feel that most reporters—especially those of the wire services—were at fault in their writing. Editorial selection and use of their material, and editorial commentary is something else and it has not been possible for me to research this matter.

Many columnists, on the other hand, were certainly off in their analysis of fact and in their "legal" interpretations of the Constitution and the hearings.

There were a number of themes that could be found in the letters, such as a marked anti-Zionist and anti-Semitic link with anti-communism, which I have already illustrated in part. Another example of this, from Eagle Rock, California is this:

> If Congress would investigate the Anti-Defamation League—the spawning ground for Zionist Internationalism, they would find the kernel of the world's troubles. . . .

While "Internationalism" was a favorite word, I was very surprised to find very little comment at all in these letters on our then current problems in Korea and with the Red Chinese.

One eyebrow lifter that never failed to surprise me was the willingness of individuals to brag about friends and co-workers that they had "turned in" as communists. Just what agency received this information was never clear to me. One example, from a woman in Long, Beach, California, will suffice.

> If perchance, it is now a crime in these United States to give information concerning suspected communists, please advise me so that I can turn myself in before they come and get me. I have ten to my credit, or disgrace, as the case may be.

There were, of course, flocks of cards and notes at intervals from people who merely asked: "Who promoted Peress?"

A curious refrain was one from individuals who professed to be "ex-Republicans," who because of what the Republican Party and Republican Administration were doing to a "great American" would never vote Republican again, and would in fact vote Democratic. These writers inevitably foresaw the death of the Republican Party, a prophecy which—it need scarcely be noted—was premature, especially in light of President Eisenhower's sweeping victory in 1956 (which greatly exceeded the vote which he received in 1952).

The letters from "ex-Republicans" were nearly always followed in the file by letters from critics of "fuzzy-minded Democrats" and "socialist Democrat traitors" who had hired all the communists said to be still in hiding in Government offices.

The repetition of certain words or phrases in many different letters arriving at approximately the same time strongly implies a common source of inspiration. Hundreds of postcards and letters—as well as some telegrams—used the expressions "stacked deck" and "kangaroo court" for the Select Committee which inquired into the charges against Senator McCarthy. Many others chose to sign their letters with the signature: "A Taft Republican." I have not determined the precise origin of these expressions, but they were almost certainly sparked by McCarthy himself in frequent TV interviews or by columnists and radio personalities who were addicted to flamboyant language.

The so-called "Taft Republicans" had another curious thing in common. This was the tendency to scorn Vice President Nixon for "abandoning" McCarthy. Apart from the fact that it was Richard Nixon who, in his official capacity as President of the Senate, had named me and the other members of the Select Committee to our assignment, it wasn't what Nixon had done but what he *hadn't* done to support McCarthy that drew the ire of these individuals.

A fairly reasonable and lengthy letter from a trial judge in Nebaska is an example of this anti-Nixon bias, in the final paragraph, which reads:

> The only conclusion that a Republican can reach is that your role in this matter has been dictated from the White House by Sherman Adams, supported by the anxious sycophancy of Richard Nixon. The latter is now going around the Country preaching "unity" in the Party on behalf of an Administration whose own acts are the sole cause of the disunity which now splits the Republican party until Mr. Adams leaves the White House and Mr. Nixon retires from his role of Republican spokesman.

Of course, as I hope I have adequately explained elsewhere, neither Sherman Adams nor anyone else in the White House—and this includes the President specifically—ever counseled with me or indicated to me in any way in advance of McCarthy's censure any feeling that I should prejudge Senator McCarthy. I played no "role" in this matter "dictated" by the White House (or by anyone else for that matter). As to Richard Nixon, my personal opinion is that his conduct justifies the conclusion that he wished to keep completely away from the issue.

Another type of letter, containing a favorite bit of humor, was for a pro-McCarthy writer to pretend to be a communist or fellow traveler and to send me his "encouragement." Here is a sample:

Dear Senator:

> I hope you will find McCarthy guilty of improper conduct as it will be a great boost to our moral if you do so. Thanks. Joe must go.

Yours truly,

(s/d) A Communist Sympathiser

Beginning the middle of November, I began to receive more complimentary letters and messages than at any time in the past. The Committee's report had begun to have its effect. A gentleman, writing from Arlington, Massachusetts, is as typical of these writers as any:

> I cannot pretend to speak for anyone but myself and my wife, but we are two who admire your strong efforts to restore sanity, probity, and law to the Congress and to the task of internal defense. Please do not compromise this issue.

A rather touching note was the number of letters written on Thanksgiving Day, many upon returning from church service. Three typical samples:

> This is Thanksgiving and we have so much to be thankful for. We thank you for preserving our constitution and the Bill of Rights in the face of McCarthy's fascism.

> You are handling the McCarthy censure matter so very well that my family and I hope you will continue your splendid efforts and send you our best wishes.

> We have just returned from giving thanks and our hearts are filled this Thanksgiving that the Senate of the United States has men of your stature.

None of the above were from Mormons, apparently, or from Utah. Immediately after this, however, there was a flood of bitter letters from across the country. One of these called me a "moral bastard." And one was from Odgen, Utah, but hopefully not from a fellow churchman. He wrote:

> Senator Watkins:
>
> You are unfit to sit in the U.S. Senate. You are a rotten liar and disgusting Russian jerk.

No doubt there are readers of these pages who are reading ahead with racing eyes and fingers to find what prejudice I may demonstrate—what bias. I now have in my selections of material, and had during the period of McCarthy's censure—with respect to McCarthy's religion and his support from Catholics.

It will take a better student than I to show that any percentage of pro-McCarthy letters, either small or large, came from fellow Catholics. How many millions of Catholics never wrote me at all? Should I speculate on which names are of Italian or Irish origins—or which addresses, reflecting ethnic or Catholic concentration—give evidence of this type of support? It would be as "logical" and as fruitless to try to pinpoint Jewish or Mormon support for me and for my role on the Select Committee. Some Mormons wrote me with expressions of pro-McCarthyism as bitter as any.

To be sure, there are many letters with expressions such as this one from Oakland, California:

> It all commences to look like it is persecution of McCarthy for no other reason than his religion; I think that is the rub.

The same idea is expressed by someone from Hackensack, New Jersey, who wrote:

> The principle "charge" against McCarthy is that he is a Catholic. Nothing else has been proven.

Several Catholics wrote to say—with only limited documentation—that the Catholic press and spokesmen were the most vigorous of McCarthy's supporters. I am also aware that many Catholics opposed McCarthy. I received a brief letter from a man in Flushing, New York, who stated:

> As a Catholic, who knows Christ as Savior, I say speak the truth as He directs you. God bless you.

I know not what religion the writers of these following excerpts belong to, but they are typical of many who invoked the name of God. This one was written by someone from New York without signing a name:

> God has picked you to see to it that Senator McCarthy is not taken from the head of his committee or censured for anything.

A woman from New York also wrote:

> As for my part I say God bless Senator McCarthy, may God protect him from the strange enemies he has in our Country.

That I should be sent to the wall for my part in the McCarthy censure is the theme of several who wrote such remarks as:

> God has judged you. McCarthy will be avenged, if not by the courts then by God's own people.

A woman from Los Angeles, whose printed letterhead containing a quotation from the King James Version of the Bible might indicate that she is a Protestant, is an example of a very large number of people whose anti-communism led to certain irrational and even hysterical conclusions. The letter:

Dear Senator Watkins:

We loyal—true—Christian Americans have looked upon your Committee's catering to the left-wing *'pinkos'* in our land with *sorrow* and *disgust*. It seems our Country is lost to the Communists and we are helpless except for God.

We crucify a Senator who tries honestly and concernedly to ferret the *reds* out of our State Department, Pentagon and defense establishments to save us and you Congressmen who should help him do all you can to hinder him.

If, and it surely will, our Country goes under Communist dictatorship we will blame you in part and you can blame yourselves because we only have the Congress left to save us. The rest of our Gov't, Supreme Court and State Department are already in *red* grip. God help us!

Yours in Christ,

I would not imply that religion and anti-communism cannot be combined on a rational and effective basis. Two letters from great religious leaders within the spectrum of American Christianity are of such interest and significance that they deserve to be read in their entirety. The first is from the well-known pastor of Riverside Baptist Church in New York City. It follows:

Dear Senator Watkins:

I am one of the silent millions who have taken it for granted that the report of the Committee under your leadership would be adopted, and that Senator McCarthy would be censured. Because many of us have taken this for granted, we have not flooded Washington with letters and telegrams. Now, however, we are shocked at what is happening, and we hope that our silence will not be misunderstood.

That Senator McCarthy should be censured for his outrageous conduct, mercifully dealt with in your report, and for his later accusations that his Senatorial opponents are evidence of communist infiltration of the Senate, and that they are "handmaidens of communism," seems to be obvious. During a long lifetime I have seen nothing much more abominable in this nation's public life than Senator McCarthy's behavior. It has brought the Senate to an all-time low in the estimation of the free world in general and of millions of our own citizens.

I am convinced that the total effect of his abusive and insulting conduct, directed as it commonly has been not against communists but against our own army and our senators, had done the communist cause far more good than harm. The evidence repeatedly presented in the editorials of the New York Times, for example, seems to me conclusive that no well informed anti-communist can possibly be pro-McCarthy.

As a militant anti-communist myself I am writing warmly to commend your admirable stand, and to hope that no flabby compromise may be permitted to block your recommendation of censure.

Sincerely yours,

(s/d) Harry Emerson Fosdick

For me, and for all Mormons, the second letter has particular significance. It comes from the man whom Mormons believe to be "prophet, seer and revelator." The letter from the President of the Church of Jesus Christ of Latter-day Saints follows:

December 11, 1954

Dear Senator Watkins:

Before I left last week for the Solemn Assembly in the St. George Temple and for subsequent duties in Los Angeles, it was my intention to write and tell you how happy I have been as I have noted your outstanding leadership and tact in handling the McCarthy case, but one thing and another, particularly procrastination, prevented my doing so.

Now that your victory is won, permit me to extend to you many hearty congratulations and high commendation for your clarity, sound judgement, and true dignity manifested throughout the entire hearing and the final disposition of this most difficult case.

You have won merited honor to yourself, retained the prestige of the Senate, and brought credit to your State and to the Nation.

May health and the blessings of the Lord continue to attend you.

Sister McKay joins me in sending kindest personal regards and best wishes to you and to Sister Watkins.

Cordially and sincerely your friend and brother,
(s/d) David O. McKay

The great bulk of the pro-McCarthy letters which I received was certainly intemperate, but the evidence which I see in the printed letterheads and the carefully typed and handwritten messages is that most of them did not come from poorly educated and culturally deprived individuals. Many of these writers, in fact, took great pains to declare their importance as prominent people in their communities: lawyers, judges, physicians, businessmen or (more frequently) their wives. Yet the strange thing—after these declarations of good character and standing—is the almost universal tendency to slip in highly ungenerous and even vicious remarks of a personal nature which are so surprisingly characteristic of this correspondence.

What manner of communication is it that purports to be an effort to persuade or influence a Senator and then, in the middle of what is presented as logical reasoning, call the recipient of that letter a "doddering old fool," or "one of the passle of communist stooges" in the Senate of the United States?

These lapses reflect a highly emotional state in the letter writer. They are an upwelling of fear, insecurity, and even hatred which demands expression in more forceful and colorful words than we usually condone in polite society.

It can hardly be doubted that it is to the thousands of people with these psychological inadequacies and emotional disturbances that some radio and newspaper commentators appeal.

Students of the phenomena should realize that letter writing may be the easiest and safest way for an individual to exhaust from his system the pent up poisons of his own brewing, but there are other expressions much more frightening. It may be that a man who "prays" for the murder of the President is not one to attempt it, I do not know, but it is a shock to come across a letter (although there were but a few) like the following:

Gary, Indiana
September 16, 1954

Dear Senator Watkins:

I can understand now why only old men were picked to serve on your maleficient Committee—being blind, deaf, puerile, and half dead, they are ideal figureheads for a Bolshevik President. I can understand now why you demanded a closed door session—the Roosevelt and Truman guttertrash officials demanded closed doors, too. They are now in prison for their secret work. All gangster officials prefer to work in secrecy; they do not prefer to talk before the American public.

I see no difference between the Communists in Moscow and the Communists in the White House. Both depend on lies and secrecy, gangster henchmen, gags, directives, and censure.

Are the White House Communists writing the McCarthy Censure for you? I can't imagine that they would risk a Senate Committee to do something on its own; some shred of truth might leak out.

For the good of the country my only prayer is that Communist Eisenhower will soon be impeached or assassinated.

Sincerely,

(Signed by a man)

Thus I have run through most of the thousands of letters, giving a sampling—as unscientific and perhaps unsatisfactory as it may well be—but hoping to reflect a cross section of American feeling during a period of political crisis.

To correct any possible lack of courtesy in not answering these letters at the time, I wish to acknowledge now an appreciation for receiving them. How wise it was, in retrospect that I waited so long to read them—how calmly and with so little distress did I see my name spoken of in scorn and with hatred—and with what feelings of humility did I read those which were friendly. After pulling out several dozen Thanksgiving Day letters and reading them, I continued my exercise in humility by reading or scanning through several hundred vitriolic postcards.

However, there was an additional letter which gave me comfort as well as amusement. Earlier, when I had been appointed chairman of the committee, a well-known writer interviewed me about my plans for running the hearings. I told him, "I intend to run an orderly hearing on McCarthy and permit no diversions."

The reporter was amused—I really couldn't blame him (I know I didn't present a formidable appearance). Later he told his friend, "It was funny in a sad sort of way, like an elderly mouse telling how he would keep the man-eating tiger under control."

With the hearings ended and the Senate debate on McCarthy under way, I heard from my reporter friend again. He sent me a note:

November 17, 1954

Dear Senator:

This is a note to congratulate you most sincerely for the magnificent courage you displayed on the Senate floor yesterday, and indeed throughout this affair of the censure of McCarthy. It is always a moving thing to see real courage displayed, but perhaps especially so in the circumstances in which you found yourself.

If you remember that piece I wrote about you some weeks ago, it appears abundantly clear that the "man-eating tiger" has met his match, and more than his match, in the "elderly mouse."

Sincerely,
Stewart Alsop

For those who never received a "card of thanks" or note from me at the time, this must be my answer to some 30,000 or more Americans who took the time to write.

Conclusion

DURING THE MC CARTHY PERIOD—AND CERTAINLY NOW—MORE THAN A decade away from the political commotion about which I am writing—no rational or informed person could entertain any question as to my own attitude toward communism, which I have explained at several points in this book. My personal philosophy (and the clearcut position of my religion and my allegiance to my Mormon faith) precluded any possibility of pro-communism. Even McCarthy, with his characteristic looseness of expression and exaggeration, seemed to question only my faculties and not my loyalty when he called me a "dupe" and an "unwitting" handmaiden of communism.

It would be unseemly for me further to labor the point, but my own anti-communism (as sober and objective as it may or may not be) should be accepted if my interpretations of McCarthy and McCarthyism are to be given much weight.

During the entire time of the censure proceedings, I gave McCarthy his devil's due for sincerity in his anti-communism crusade. Today, while I can see the point argued by some that he actually contributed to the growth and strength of communism around the world, I cannot agree that he consciously pursued this end.

The judgment of the years, however, is that McCarthy exploited McCarthyism as an instrument to power and personal glory. As a skilled bellringer, he played all the changes and excited his numerous followers with variations of alarm and patriotism with a skill that has seldom been equalled by any demagogue. Yet, I cannot believe that he was a true "prophet," for it was not the cause of anti-communism which inflamed him but the "show" itself and wielding the instruments of power.

When he lost his credibility and standing, and when his showmanship techniques of derring-do (which included terror and abuse) no longer served him but actually turned increasing numbers of people from him, he collapsed like a pricked balloon. No one primarily dedicated to a cause increases his drinking and gambling when faced with a setback, as Joe McCarthy did so noticeably. McCarthy's censure caused him no loss of Senatorial privilege and could have been but a temporary check to his progress if he had retained his venom and had chosen to renew his attack. Many interpreters of the time fully expected McCarthy to lead a massive right-wing movement.

The evidence strongly implies, however, that McCarthy knew that he had been exposed. He had made McCarthyism an instrument to power and not merely a manifestation of it, and it appears that he no longer enjoyed the role he had taken. Worst of all, he was out of the news and being ignored.

Anti-communism no longer served McCarthy's purpose. It appears to me that McCarthy hunted "communists" solely for the attention, publicity and tumult it earned him—and for the headlines. When he lost these, he lost everything that counted.

If McCarthyism had not served its creator well, in the long run, it certainly did not contribute to the political health of the Nation. Many people observed (and I noticed it myself) that insecure and frightened people had frequently demonstrated their "patriotism" and "loyalty" by raising questions concerning the patriotism and loyalty of their fellow workers and sometime-friends. This was one of the ugliest symptoms of the period. No Nation can long prosper in an atmosphere of suspicion and distrust.

We know that many Federal workers, convinced that it was their duty to report their suspicions direct to Senator McCarthy and to his Subcommittee, made allegations that frequently were not supported by even the most elemental statements of fact or proof. Oftimes, self-appointed "agents" wrote anonymously. Seldom, if ever, did a suspected person have the opportunity of facing his accusers or of testing the evidence, or indeed of even knowing that charges had been made against him.

It has been amply documented by others and, in fact, almost universally observed that the McCarthy period was noted chiefly for character assassination, slur, and suspicion.

Elements in the Executive branch of Government—down through the agencies and departments which comprise it—were frightened by the prospect of coming to the attention of anti-communism hunters ("don't stick up your head or you may get it lopped off") and removed numbers of employees for no reason except the possibility that their presence on the payroll could attract an investigation. The Department of the Interior, for example, in a single night, combed its files and suspended six employees only hours before having to report on its internal security.

Some reporters have stated that the Senate panicked before the onslaught of McCarthyism. I doubt this. All I know is that I didn't panic. Many Senators, it is true, would rather not have concerned themselves with Joe McCarthy and his tactics. These Senators had their business to attend to and Joe could tend to his. It was a natural enough reaction, considering the nature of the Senate "club" and the mutual extension of courtesies. The issue, when it came to a head, was— and let history not be confused on this—McCarthy got his comeuppance not for his abuse of individual witnesses or his fight against communism but for his contempt of the Senate.

It was not McCarthy's insufficiencies of character, as appalling as they may well have been, but scorn for Senatorial courtesies and procedures, for his actions and words on the floor of the Senate of the United States, and for his abuse of his fellow Senators—who were discharging their committee responsibilities—which were condemned by his fellow Senators.

It has been said by others that McCarthy's political tactics of allegations, exaggerations, misrepresentations, and falsehoods were not devices turned up or contrived in the heyday of his Senate career but were products of his entire background and a revelation of his personal character. Whatever truth there may be in this, and there is logic here, the fact remains that before McCarthy's discovery of McCarthyism—and subsequent to his censure—very little was seen or heard of him and very little to mark to his credit.

There is no question that McCarthyism had a profound effect on America and upon the world. In some other nations, people who had suffered intensely under a variety of demagogues were alarmed at the possible rise of such a figure in this country. The blurring of objectives on the part of communist-hunters in America, resulting in inquiries into the politics and ideas of native American radicals (of which we have always had an abundance) led some of these investigators to abuse their authority. There was great uneasiness on the part of all thinking people as the spectacle of McCarthyism ran on.

On the other hand, I feel that some good resulted from the national obsession about communists and their infiltration into positions of responsibility. The war had conditioned most Americans to think of the Soviet Union as an ally, and that nation's post-war imperialism and resulting threat to the security of the United States had not yet been fully recognized. In the jargon of McCarthy, "fuzzy-minded liberals and communist dupes" could and did represent a danger. Treason, while not rampant, was incipient. The excitement which was christened with McCarthy's name ended the false broadmindedness which had tolerated this hanky-panky with the communist siren.

Many Americans sensed danger in communism, and in their inability to discriminate they lashed out wildly at anything and everyone they could not understand. Motivated by fear and other primitive emotions, they dashed madly wherever the finger of their particular hero pointed. As far as the public was concerned, it was the methods of McCarthyism and not its announced objectives which rang down the curtain upon its author, Senator McCarthy, in the middle of his act.

An unexpected and wholesome byproduct of McCarthyism—or at least of the Nation's reaction to it—was the effective "defusing" of communism as a political issue. After the demise of McCarthy, the American people became increasingly sophisticated in this matter and soon were able to distinguish between valid issues and purely emotional or "panic" alarums. It appeared that the injection of communism into any or all political issues was no longer a sure-fire, vote-getting gimmick. This had the admirable effect of raising the level of political debate.

It should not be overlooked, either, that the end of the McCarthy era did not mean that communist conspirators had a free field in which to promote their traitorous schemes, without hindrance or effective opposition. There yet remained the several powerful and accomplished agencies which had effectively and without fanfare protected our country and its institutions from communist conspiracy and attack.

There were the FBI and the CIA, the military intelligence agencies, the departments of Justice and State, and lesser organizations which had as their concern the protection of our Nation from conspiracy within and from without by attack. In the Senate of the United States, there was the Internal Security Subcommittee of the Judiciary Committee. In the House, there was the Un-American Activities Committee.

In addition to these various agencies mentioned, there are stronger institutions in which we may justly place our confidence: namely, the free press—including radio and television—and other means of expression, our schools and churches and associations, and the family. If this were not true, sorry indeed would be our situation.

After many decades of public service, I have set myself to telling the story of my role in facing up to the challenge of Senator McCarthy. Out of the bitterness of that prolonged episode and from the vantage point of many years' distance (and the mellowness of age), I express my conviction that it is both possible and absolutely necessary for sincere men to face their critics (sometimes when those critics are armed with truth and striking in good faith, and sometimes not) and answer them with facts, directness, and sobriety.

Love of truth, tolerance, and understanding must be brought to any question and to any contest from a lifetime of preparation.

In devoting a section of this book to answering questions which probably have not been answered sufficiently, if at all, I want to make it clear that I am not attempting a technical brief, but rendering my personal opinions as to what the answers should be. My opinions are, I believe, based on sound principles and rules and precedents adopted by the Senate during a period approximately of 178 years.

One of the questions of particular importance in the Censure proceedings is related to the Fifth Amendment to the Constitution.

QUESTION NO. 1: When Major Irving Peress took the Fifth Amendment with respect to charges of Communist activity, wasn't he, in effect, admitting his guilt? Wasn't Senator McCarthy justified in calling Peress a "Fifth Amendment Communist"?

ANSWER: "No" to both questions. There are many reasons which may prompt a person to take the Fifth Amendment, and these may have nothing to do with any overt, criminal act which the person may or may not have committed or be in any other way concerned with the purposes of the investigation.

Congressional investigations are, theoretically, concerned with gathering information for the formulation of legislative policy. They are not, obviously, branches of the Justice Department or the courts of the land.

Nevertheless, there have been instances where a legislator seems to have a preconception of an individual's guilt. Even though he may be trained as a lawyer (and sometimes even when he has served as a judge), he may disregard our judicial traditions which call for an impartial weighing of the facts and thus provide for the one charged to make his reply, summon his own witnesses, and otherwise "have his day in court" with all that implies.

In addition, under our system of law, a person must be proved guilty beyond a reasonable doubt, if at all, by the prosecution, and there is no requirement that a person must prove himself innocent. For this reason, among others, the Constitution provides, as a right, that an individual cannot be required to testify against himself.

Possibly, having preconceptions of an individual's guilt—or even, perchance, having what he regards as absolute and convincing evidence—a few Congressional investigators may be inclined to try to trap and expose an individual for the publicity which may be obtained—that is, for the political coup. However, I believe these instances are rare when all legislative business is considered as a whole.

In the event a witness senses the danger of entrapment, the luckless individual has only one recourse to protect his constitutional rights against self-incrimination, and that is to refuse to answer—under the right protected by the Fifth Amendment —any question which by answering at all, may open up a line of investigation in which he may be required to furnish evidence against himself. Now, some investigators—as in the example of Senator McCarthy questioning Major Peress—would like the public to believe that taking the Fifth Amendment is in itself evidence of something to hide—that it is prima facia evidence of guilt.

In courts of review, a case may be thrown out merely because of such allegation.* For instance, the matter the individual may wish to avoid having exposed may be something seemingly unrelated to the investigation at hand. Here, again, it is unjust to make any such assumption. As a matter of fact, in Congressional investigations of the type we have been discussing, the individual may take the Fifth Amendment solely for the purpose of preventing the investigator (who, as we say, may have a preconception of the individual's guilt) from going off on a long "fishing expedition" for the purpose of seeing what possibly might be dragged up, or for the purpose of trapping the individual in a field, or incident, which might be the basis for a criminal prosecution, or in some contradiction, and for which he can be tried for perjury and be imprisoned (perhaps irrespective of the legislative purposes of the investigation).

If abuses of Congressional investigations can be shown—and of course they can—then we can understand, if not condone why an individual may refuse to answer any or all questions under the Constitutional right. In any event, we are permitted only to speculate in private as to a person's reasons for taking the Fifth Amendment and we cannot leap to conclusions as McCarthy did so frequently when he called such a witness a "Fifth Amendment Communist", as if the individual's guilt of some overt, criminal or treasonable act had already been established.

As Senator Prescott Bush, Republican of Connecticut, said on the floor of the Senate during the censure debate with respect to the harassment of General Zwicker: "For, if a witness—particularly one of undoubted loyalty and honor— cannot feel secure in cooperating with his Government by testifying before Congressional committees—then such committees may find themselves hamstrung, indeed, because . . . even honorable patriots may be driven to shield themselves behind the Fifth Amendment when they may not, in fact need it. They might well be frightened into taking its shelter."

* Following are cases which make clear the principles involved and support my answer to this question:

In the case of Grunewald v. United States, 353 US 391, 1 L Ed 2d 931, 2 ALR 2nd 1344, 77 S Ct. 963 (1957) the Supreme Court Stated in part:

It should be noted that in the Peress case, in hearings,* Senator McCarthy and his aide Roy Cohn asked Major Peress a number of provocative questions to which he responded in each case by taking the Fifth Amendment. Such questions were asked as: "Are you a member of the Communist Party today?" "Is your wife a member of the Communist Party?" "Did any Communists intervene to have your orders changed so you would not have to leave the country?" "You are a graduate of the leadership training course of the Inwood Victory Club of the Communist, are you not?" "Did you deliver talks at Communist discussion groups . . . urging the overthrow of the Government of the United States by force and violence "Did you attempt to recruit any of the military personnel (at Camp Kilmer) into the Communist party?"

While it might well be possible that the investigators had information which indicated that these things could be true, it is obvious that the questioning also implies (especially to the unsophisticated listener without legal training) that the allegations were indeed true.

The important thing to remember is that even if the investigators had asked such questions as: "Did you yourself steal secrets pertaining to the construction of the atomic bomb and personnally deliver them to agents of the Soviet Union?" (which if true, would be an act punishable by death), Major Peress could not possibly have answered "No" even if innocent, without opening himself to a whole series of other questions which under the law, as it is interpreted by the courts, he would have to answer. Having answered one question, he would have waived his right to the protection of the Fifth Amendment, and would have been forced to reply to all questions or go to jail for contempt.

---

* Hearings of Senate Permanent Subcommittee on Investigations, January 30, 1954.

". . . It was prejudicial error for the trial judge to permit cross-examination of defendant as to whether he had invoked his constitutional privilege against self-incrimination before a grand jury in response to same or similar questions in response to which he had testified fully on the question.

". . . . These conclusions are fortified by a number of other considerations surrounding Halperin's claim of privilege:

"First, Halperin repeatedly insisted before the grand jury that he was innocent and that he pleaded his Fifth Amendment privilege solely on the advice of counsel.

"Second, the Fifth Amendment claim was made before a grand jury where Halperin was a compelled, and not a voluntary witness; where he was not represented by counsel; where he could summon no witnesses; and where he had no opportunity to cross-examine witnesses testifying against him. These factors are crucial in weighing whether a plea of the privilege is inconsistent with later exculpatory testimony on the same questions, for the nature of the tribunal which subjects the witness to questioning bears heavily on what inferences can be drawn from a plea of the Fifth Amendment. See Griswold, supra, at 62. Innocent men

To repeat, whether innocent or guilty with respect to the major questions, as long as he had any reason whatever to avoid revealing some "incriminating" matter he could not have replied to even the most outrageous question in the same general area. This was a matter his investigators knew well and played to the hilt, making the grossest allegations (and, it seems quite likely in retrospect, largely in the interest of publicity.)

When Irving Peress discovered, as he put it, that Senator McCarthy was concerned with inquiring into his "political beliefs" he said that he would continue to decline to answer any such questions under the protection offered to him by the Fifth Amendment. Then, upon being lectured by McCarthy to the effect that he (Peress) was before the Army-McCarthy hearings solely in regard to the part that he had played "while an officer in the United States Army in the conspiracy designed to destroy this nation," Peress responded with a statement as to his own beliefs, and also a statement as to how his "promotion" had been effected (a statement which McCarthy had earlier denied him the opportunity to make).

From the record: *

* Hearings on S. Res. 301, Pt. 1, pp. 217-218 (picked up from the Army-McCarthy hearings.)

---

are more likely to plead the privilege in secret proceedings, where they testify without advice of counsel and without opportunity for cross-examination, than in open court proceedings, where cross-examination and judicially supervised procedure provide safeguards for the establishing of the whole, as against the possibility of merely partial, truth.

"We need not tarry long to reiterate our view that, as the two courts below held, no implication of guilt could be drawn from Halperin's invocation of his Fifth Amendment privilege before the grand jury. Recent re-examination of the history and meaning of the Fifth Amendment has emphasized anew that one of the basic functions of the privilege is to protect *innocent* men. Griswold, The Fifth Amendment Today, 9-30, 53-82. "Too many, even those who should be better advised, view this privilege as a shelter for wrongdoers. They too readily assume that those who invoke it are either guilty of crime or commit perjury in claiming the privilege." Ullmann v. United States, 350 U.S. 422, 426, 76 S.Ct. 497, 500, 100 L. Ed. 511. See also Slochower v. Board of Higher Education, 350 U.S. 551 at pages 557-558, 76 S.Ct. 637, at page 641, 100 L. Ed. 692, when at the same Term, this Court said: "The privilege serves to protect the innocent who otherwise might be ensnared by ambiguous circumstances."

Justice Black in a concurring opinion made this statement: ". . . I can think of no special circumstances that would justify use of a constitutional privilege to discredit or convict a person who asserts it. The value of constitutional privileges is largely destroyed if persons can be penalized for relying on them. It seems peculiarly incongruous and indefensible for courts which exist and act only under the Constitution to draw inferences of lack of honesty from invocation of a privilege deemed worthy of enshrinement in the Constitution. . . ."

This case follows other decisions made earlier by the Supreme Court.

Mr. Peress: From my earliest schooling I have been taught that the United States Constitution is the highest law of our land and that one of the strongest provisions is the protection afforded to all persons of the privilege under the fifth amendment. My education has also taught me that anyone, even a United States Senator, who would deny this constitutional protection to any individual or who under his cloak of his immunity would draw inferences therefrom, and publicly announce such inferences, is subversive. I use that word advisedly. By subversive I mean anyone who would undermine the strength of the Constitution and thereby weaken our democratic form of Government. When I appeared before you, Senator McCarthy, on January 30, 1954, at an executive session of your committee, you, acting as a committee of one, made certain charges concerning my promotion in rank and pending honorable discharge. Just to make the record clear, I was promoted and honorably discharged under Public Law 84 of the 83rd Congress, which incidentally was passed when you, Senator McCarthy, were a member of the Senate. In recognition of my honest and faithful service to my country I was awarded an honorable discharge on February 2, 1954. In the period of my service, no one either within or without found it necessary to question my loyalty.

Another bit of schooling which I had as a Jew was a study of the Old Testament, which I highly recommend to you, Senator, and your counsel, and particularly Book 7 of the Psalms, which reads:

> His mischief shall return upon his own head and his
> violence shall come down upon his own pate.

The record shows that McCarthy ignored these remarks completely.

To keep the record straight, it should be recalled that McCarthy requested the Army not to discharge Major Peress from the Army but to court martial him. The Army said it could not do this because it had insufficient reasons to sustain a court martial decision. The cases cited, although some are of a later date, support one of the purposes of the Fifth Amendment, that to claim its protection is not a crime. I have no doubt that Military Appeals Court would have reversed a court martial judgement against Peress, if the Army had court martialed him.

QUESTION NO. 2: What authority does the Senate have to discipline its members? How is that power executed?

ANSWER: The Constitution (Art. 1, Sec. 5) provides that "Each House

---

The following are cases of the Military Appeals Court which are to the same effect as the Supreme Court ruling previously recited:

United States v. Stegar, 16 USCMA 569, 37 CMR 189
United States v. Kavula, 16 USCMA 468, 37 CMR 88
United States v. Kowert, 7 USCMA 678, 23 CMR 142
United States v. Workman, 15 USCMA 228, 35 CMR 200
United States v. Brooks 12 USCMA 423, 31 CMR 9

may determine the rules of its proceedings, punish members for disorderly behavior and, with the concurrence of two-thirds, expel a member." Even without this Section 5, the Congress as the Supreme legislative body of the Nation is said to have the inherent power of all legislative bodies to control the conduct of its members. (See Cushing, *Law and Practice of Legislative Assemblies,* p. 258).

Also, the Constitutional provision in Article 1, Section 5, clause 1, provides that each house shall be the judge of the qualifications of its members.

The Senate has adopted the practice of instituting proceedings for censure, and for expulsion by the introduction of a resolution authorizing the selection of a committee to hold hearings, make investigations, and report to the Senate its findings so that final action can be taken on the resolution. This was the procedure used in the McCarthy proceedings.

QUESTION NO. 3:   What, if any, Senate rules apply to censure or condemnation proceedings?

ANSWER: The rules of the Senate which have been adopted are compiled in a volume designated "Senate Procedure" and annotated by the late Charles L. Watkins, Senate Parliamentarian for many years, and Floyd M. Riddick, Assistant Parliamentarian.

QUESTION NO. 4:   Who can vote on censure resolutions?

Answer: All members of the Senate, except possibly the Senator who is the subject of the censure proceeding. It has never been determined whether or not the Senator, the subject of the resolution, has the right to vote.

As a matter of practice the subject Senator does not vote. (See "Senate Procedure," page 126.)

QUESTION NO. 5:   What standing has a Senate resolution of censure with relation to any other business?

ANSWER: A resolution proposing the censure of a Senator is privileged business and a motion to proceed to its consideration when submitted, without reference to a committee, is in order. (See "Senate Procedure," page 126.)

QUESTION NO. 6:   Did the Select Committee have the authority, without further action by the Senate, to consider additional charges against Senator McCarthy? Could and did the Senate itself consider additional charges and evidence against McCarthy prior to the censure vote?

ANSWER: The answer to the first question is no. The Select Committee was confined strictly to the charges set forth in Senate Resolution 301 and in the amendments thereto. Actually, there were some 45 charges that were submitted to the Committee for investigation and study.

My answer to the second question is that the Senate, acting under powers granted in the Constitution, did consider and adopt additional charges not mentioned in Resolution 301. That Resolution as finally adopted contained new and additional charges and findings against McCarthy. This is described—and the wording of the amendment is given—in Chapter 16. Readers may well wish to read again the words and actions of Senator McCarthy which the Senate of the United States deemed censurable. Section 2 of the Censure Resolution, which is the amendment adopted on motion of my colleague, Senator Wallace F. Bennett, contained these new charges.

Since McCarthy's conduct toward me and other members of the Select Committee and to the Senate, so thoroughly demonstrated the character of the man, his determination to continue along the same lines for which he was being investigated, and the utter contempt he showed his fellow Senators and the Senate itself, I believe that this amendment and its adoption by the Senate to be among the most significant actions of the entire censure proceedings.

If McCarthy's case had been heard before a court of law, it would have been recognized that he could not have done these things with impunity. There is no question that he would have been silenced immediately by the court and probably punished for contempt. While the Senate is essentially a legislative body, it can on occasion (and this was one of those occasions) sit as a semi-judicial body. The Senate, therefore, did in fact consider McCarthy's words and actions toward me (as Chairman of the Select Committee) and its members and to the Senate, to be contemptuous . . . and condemned him for these reasons, among others.

QUESTION NO. 7: **Why did the Select Committee refuse to permit Senator McCarthy to insert in the hearings record all the material that he offered? Did Senator McCarthy get a chance to defend himself—that is, to be heard—before the Select Committee?**

ANSWER: The Select Committee, having taken judicial notice of Senator McCarthy's conduct before other committees, made the ruling that it would consider only material that was germane and relevant to the charges it was instructed by the Senate to investigate. Senator McCarthy would have filled the record with extraneous and irrelevant material, such as (for example) about Communism (a matter not concerned with the charges against Senator McCarthy) except as he tried to bring it up as part of his defense.

McCarthy, of course, had every opportunity to be heard by the Select Committee. In the main, however, McCarthy chose to make his defense through the press and before the TV camera, and—as he said—take his case to the people of the country.

QUESTION NO. 8: **Did the Select Committee really have authority to "Try" Senator McCarthy or merely to make an investigation? What was the principal function of the Committee?**

ANSWER: While the functions of the Select Committee were not clear to the general public at the time, it should be clear now that—as in all similar cases—the Senate appoints a committee to inquire into the charges, the facts of the case, and to make recommendations to the Senate (which, of course, leaves the Senate free to take any action it wishes). The Senate of the United States, sitting in a judicial mood and capacity, tried Senator McCarthy and gave its judgment. The Committee had no authority to try him. It was, simply stated, a gatherer of facts and the precedents and the law involved which would aid the Senate in making its decision.

QUESTION NO. 9: Why did not the Select Committee investigate Senators Flanders, Fulbright, and Morse for things they said about McCarthy, and recommend their censure?

ANSWER. The Select Committee could function only within the limits of its assignment, that is to investigate McCarthy. There were no formal charges against these other Senators nor was the Select Committee asked by the Senate to inquire into these matters. If the Senate had directed the Select Committee to investigate and report on these three Senators, it would have done so.*

QUESTION NO. 10: Senator McCarthy claimed that it was not necessary to appear before the Gillette Committee because he had not been subpoenaed. Is this a correct interpretation?

ANSWER: No, for in effect Senator McCarthy *was* subpoenaed by the Committee. The expression: ". . . to require by subpoena or *otherwise*" (emphasis supplied) is overlooked in the Legislative Reorganization Act of 1945, Public Law 601 by many. This reads: "Each standing committee of the Senate, including any subcommittee of any such committee, is authorized to hold such hearings, to sit and act at such times and places during the Session's recesses, and adjourned periods of the Senate, to require by subpoena or otherwise, the attendance of such witnesses, and the production of such correspondence, books, papers, and documents, to take such testimony and to make such expenditures . . . as it deems advisable. Each such committee may make investigations into any matter within its jurisdiction, may report such hearings as may be had by it. . . ."

It may be noted that the word "otherwise" comprehends lesser and more informal methods of summoning or directing a witness to appear. The provisions of R.S. 102 and 104 (U.S.C. 2; Sections 192 and 194) provide for the prosecution of witnesses refusing to testify and refer to ". . . every person who having been summoned . . ." The Senate Judiciary Committee in the 81st Congress took the position, clearly supported by the above references, that it is not necessary to issue a subpoena, but that adequate notice by registered mail, telegram, publication, or other reasonable method is sufficient, and in fact would be enough to form the basis for contempt proceedings, Senate Report 2639, 81st Congress.

But the Select Committee also came to the conclusion that under the circum-

* I received many letters from across the country urging that the Select Committee censure the Senators above named. In fact one member of the Senate asked me the same question.

stances of this case, it became the duty and responsibility of Senator McCarthy to appear and cooperate with the committee, independent of whether he had been subpoenaed. See page 27, Select Committee Report, in Appendix B.

QUESTION NO. 11: Wasn't McCarthy censured in part for what he said about other Senators, and this in violation of his Constitutional Right to free speech in the Senate?

ANSWER: There are two Constitutional provisions which bear on this matter. It is true that the Constitution says that Senators and Representatives have certain privileges. It says, in fact, that ". . . for any speech or debate in either house, they shall not be questioned in any other place." Note the key words "in any other place." The Constitution also provides that "Each house may determine the rules of its proceedings, punish its members for disorderly behavior, and, with the concurrence of two-thirds, expel a member." Only the House and Senate may discipline their respective members for actions therein, which is precisely what the Senate was doing in investigating and censuring Senator McCarthy for his abuse of fellow Senators and his contempt for the Senate.

Senator McCarthy said that the Senate was trying to establish a new rule in saying that a Senator could not criticize a committee of the Senate. This is, of course, nonsense. McCarthy was censured among other things, for his *abuse* of Senators on the Gillette and Select Committees, but not for criticizing them. There is a world of difference, which should not require extensive elaboration.

He said they had no jurisdiction over him, that they were dishonest in many of the committee activities. He never would have been permitted to make his charges against the committee from the Senate floor. These charges would have violated Rule XIX.

QUESTION NO. 12: Why did the Select Committee refuse to let Senator McCarthy attack the qualifications of some members of the Select Committee, on the ground that they were biased and prejudiced against him? (As for example, referring to the news story in which Senator Edwin C. Johnson of Colorado was quoted as saying there wasn't a Democrat in the Senate who didn't loath Senator McCarthy.)

ANSWER: For one reason, McCarthy violated the rules which he and his attorney had agreed to follow. If Mr. Williams, McCarthy's attorney, raised a question or made a statement, then McCarthy was not to take part, and if the Senator began a statement or asked a question, Mr. Williams was to refrain from participating. This rule was intended to prevent another Army-McCarthy type of circus. On the Senator Johnson news story, McCarthy (in attempting to speak) was out of order and it was incumbent upon me as Chairman to hold him to the rules.

With respect to the argument in general, the Select Committee had been given a specific job to do and that was to hold hearings and to obtain evidence which could be supplied the Senate. It was clearly out of the Committee's jurisdiction to hear or determine charges against its own members. McCarthy should have raised his questions about Committee members before the Senate itself, which is what he ultimately did. See Chapter 15.

QUESTION NO. 13: Since the hearings of the Select Committee were open to the public, and newspaper reporters were permitted to attend, why was direct TV and Radio broadcasting not permitted from the Hearing Room?

ANSWER: While this is explained more fully in Chapter 21, the reason is traditional. Such distracting influences as direct TV, news photography and radio broadcasting may adversely affect the course of an investigation (through "grandstanding" of witnesses, improper emphasis on matters which may be sketchily and inadequately reported, and the commotion within the hearings room.) It was our effort to establish and maintain a *judicial* atmosphere rather than the atmosphere of the usual *legislative* committee hearing. With respect to this matter we adopted the same rules which govern the sessions of the Senate. With one or two exceptions both Federal and State courts of the United States follow the same practice. McCarthy's attorney Mr. Williams agreed with this item of procedure.

QUESTION NO. 14: What was the effect of the Hayden Resolution, No. 300, with respect to the jurisdiction of the Gillette Committee and the honesty of its members?

ANSWER: As described in Chapter 7, and elsewhere in this volume, the unanimous vote of the Senate on this matter had the effect of upholding the right or jurisdiction of the Gillette Committee to inquire into McCarthy's behavior and also that its members were honest in their activities. Therefore, the Select Committee had no right to reopen the issues into which the Gillette Committee had inquired. Our responsibility was to inquire, among other things, into Senator McCarthy's conduct *toward* the Gillette Committee and not to hear the evidence, or make inquiry on Benton's charges against McCarthy. We would have violated our own assignment had we attempted to reopen matters which the Senate had decided. The Senate had found that the Gillette Committee had the exclusive jurisdiction over the Benton charges and it found the Committee and its members were honest. This decision was conclusive on McCarthy and the Select Committee and it was Res Adjudicata—as would be said in a legal case. Senator McCarthy had an opportunity to oppose the Hayden Resolution, but he supported it instead.

QUESTION NO. 15: If it was true—as Senator McCarthy said— that Senators Hendrickson, Hennings, and Hayden really believed that McCarthy was unfit to serve in the United States Senate (on the basis of the report of the Gillette-Hennings Committee), why didn't they

move—as McCarthy suggested—to keep him from being seated in the 83rd Congress?

ANSWER: Obviously, I do not know what was in the minds of the Senators mentioned so I cannot speak for them. However, I suggest this might have been their answer:

Expulsion charges were already pending before the Gillette-Hennings Subcommittee against McCarthy and Benton. The hearings had not been concluded, but were in suspension because of the failure of the Senator to cooperate. I doubt that the Committee had decided to recommend to the Senate that McCarthy be expelled even though McCarthy's conduct, to say the least, had been downright insulting and unfair to the Committee.

Also, the debate on a motion to deny him his seat would have tied up the Senate in the very beginning for a considerable period of time. I believe the Committee felt there was a hope that a reprimand would bring McCarthy to his senses and then it would not be necessary to impose a drastic penalty such as denying him a seat in the Senate, or expelling him. I knew all three of the Senators mentioned in the question. I found them to be kindly, fair-minded gentlemen. I believe they also felt such a countermove as suggested would be in a way and to a small degree, an admission that they were guilty of the charges McCarthy had made against the Gillette-Hennings Committee. Namely, that they were prejudiced, dishonest, and opposed to him solely becase of his anticommunism activities. He made the charge that anyone opposed to him was in the same class as the *Daily Worker* (an avowed communist newspaper).

QUESTION NO. 16: To what extent, if at all, was McCarthy's fight against Communism involved in the Select Committee's recommendations?

ANSWER: None, except as McCarthy brought it in. He did so, apparently, as a defense for his methods. The seriousness of his charges about communist subversion, he implied, justified the things he said and did.

McCarthy begged the question. He wasn't fighting communism when he attacked the Gillette Subcommittee. Senator Benton's charges against McCarthy had to do with his personal conduct, alleged conflict of interests, financial irregularities, and violation of State and Federal laws involving receipt of funds, and diverting to his own use funds donated for the fight against communism. This was described in Chapter 7 of this volume, and in the Report of the Select Committee which is included in this book as Appendix B.

In the General Zwicker matter the Committee's recommendation was that McCarthy be censured for his insulting language spoken to the General because the officer could not answer certain questions (for the reason he was under orders from his superiors not to answer them). Zwicker was opposed to communism just as much as was Senator McCarthy, a fact well known to McCarthy.

REPORT

OF THE

SELECT COMMITTEE TO STUDY CENSURE CHARGES
UNITED STATES SENATE
EIGHTY-THIRD CONGRESS
SECOND SESSION
PURSUANT TO THE ORDER ON

S. Res. 301
AND AMENDMENTS

A RESOLUTION TO CENSURE THE SENATOR FROM WISCONSIN, MR. McCARTHY

NOVEMBER 8, 1954.—Ordered to be printed

UNITED STATES
GOVERNMENT PRINTING OFFICE
42008 WASHINGTON : 1954

SELECT COMMITTEE TO STUDY CENSURE CHARGES

ARTHUR V. WATKINS, Utah, *Chairman*

EDWIN C. JOHNSON, Colorado, *Vice Chairman*

JOHN C. STENNIS, Mississippi   FRANCIS CASE, South Dakota

FRANK CARLSON, Kansas   SAM J. ERVIN, JR., North Carolina

E. WALLACE CHADWICK, *Counsel*

GUY G. DE FURIA, *Assistant Counsel*

JOHN M. JEX, *Clerk*

JOHN W. WELLMAN, *Staff Member*

FRANK I. GINSBURG and R. RAY MCGUIRE, *Members of Senator Watkins' Staff on Loan to the Committee*

II

REPORT ON RESOLUTION TO CENSURE

NOVEMBER 8, 1954—Ordered to be printed

Mr. WATKINS, from the Select Committee To Study Censure Charges, submitted the following

REPORT

[To accompany S. Res. 301]

The Select Committee To Study Censure Charges, consisting of—

Arthur V. Watkins (chairman)

Edwin C. Johnson (vice chairman)

John C. Stennis   Francis Case

Frank Carlson   Sam J. Ervin, Jr.

to which was referred the resolution (S. Res. 301) and amendments, having considered the same, reports thereon and recommends that the resolution be adopted with certain amendments.

INTRODUCTION

On August 2 (legislative day, July 2), 1954, Senate Resolution 301, to censure the Senator from Wisconsin, Mr. McCarthy, submitted by Senator Flanders on July 30, and amendments proposed thereto, was referred to a select committee to be composed of 3 Republicans and 3 Democrats and named by the Vice President. By said order the select committee was authorized—

(1) To hold hearings;

(2) To sit and act at such times and places during the sessions, recesses, and adjourned periods of the Senate;

(3) To require by subpena or otherwise the attendance of such witnesses and the production of such correspondence, books, papers, and documents, and to take such testimony as is deemed advisable.

The select committee was instructed to act and to make a report to the Senate prior to the adjournment sine die of the Senate in the 2d session of the 83d Congress.

The order of the Senate is set forth in the hearing record, page 1 et seq.

1

The Vice President, on August 5, 1954, acting on the recommendations of the majority leader and the minority leader, made the following appointments of members of the select committee: From the majority, the Senator from Utah (Mr. Watkins), the Senator from Kansas (Mr. Carlson), and the Senator from South Dakota (Mr. Case). From the minority, the Senator from Colorado (Mr. Johnson), the Senator from Mississippi (Mr. Stennis), and the Senator from North Carolina (Mr. Ervin). The select committee chose the Senator from Utah (Mr. Watkins) as chairman, and the Senator from Colorado (Mr. Johnson) as vice chairman.

The select committee, on August 24, 1954, served upon the junior Senator from Wisconsin, and other interested persons, a notice of hearings, setting forth 5 categories containing 13 specifications of charges from certain of the proposed amendments, establishing the general procedural rules for the hearings before the select committee, and formally requesting the appearance of Senator McCarthy. The notice of hearings will be found in the hearing record, page 8.

All testimony and evidence taken and received by the select committee was at public hearings attended by Senator McCarthy and his counsel, except the opinion of the Senate Parliamentarian which was obtained pursuant to Senator McCarthy's request.

The public hearings were held in accordance with said notice of hearings, on August 31, September 1, 2, 7, 8, 9, 10, 11, and 13, 1954. The entire testimony, evidence, and proceedings at said public hearings are in the printed record of the hearings.

At the commencement of the hearings, on August 31, 1954 (p. 11 of the hearings), the chairman stated:

STATEMENT OF PURPOSES OF COMMITTEE MADE AT COMMENCEMENT OF HEARING

Now, at the outset of this hearing, the committee desires to state in general terms what is involved in Senate Resolution 301 and the Senate order on it, which authorized the appointment of the select committee to consider in behalf of the Senate the so-called Flanders resolution of censure, together with all amendments proposed in the resolution.

The committee, in the words of the Senate order was "authorized to hold hearings, to sit and act at such times and places during the sessions, recesses, and adjourned periods of the Senate, to require by subpena, or otherwise, the attendance of such witnesses and the production of such correspondence, books, papers, and documents, and to take such testimony as it deems advisable, and that the committee be instructed to act and make a report to this body prior to the adjournment sine die of the Senate in the second session of the 83d Congress."

That is a broad grant of power, carrying with it a heavy responsibility— a responsibility which the committee takes seriously. In beginning its duties, the committee found few precedents to serve as a guide. It is true that there had been other censure resolutions before the Senate in the past, but the acts complained of were, for the most part, single occurrences which happened in the presence of the Senate or one of its committtees. Under such circumstances, prolonged investigations and hearings were not necessary.

It should be pointed out that some forty-and-odd alleged instances of misconduct on the part of Senator McCarthy referred to this committee are involved and complex, both with respect to matters of fact and law. With reference to the time element, the incidents are alleged to have happened within a period covering several years. In addition, 3 Senate committees already have held hearings on 1 or more phases of the alleged incidents of misconduct. Obviously, with all this in mind, the committee had good reason for concluding it faced an unprecedented situation which would require adoption of procedures, all within the authority granted it in the Senate order, that would enable it to perform the duties assigned within the limited time given by the Senate.

The committee interprets its duties, functions, and responsibilities under the Senate order to be as follows:

1. To analyze the charges set forth in the amendments and to determine—

    (a) If there were duplications which could be eliminated.

    (b) If any of the charges were of such a nature that even if the allegations were established as factually true, yet there would be strong reasons for believing that they did not constitute a ground for censure.

2. To thoroughly investigate all charges not eliminated under No. 1 in order to secure relevant and material facts concerning them and the names of witnesses or records which can establish the facts at the hearings to be held.

In this connection the committee believes it should function as an impartial investigating agency to develop by direct contacts in the field and by direct examination of Senate records all relevant and material facts possible to secure.

When Senate Resolution 301 and amendments offered were referred to the committee, the committee interprets this action to mean that from that time on the resolution and charges became the sole responsibility of the Senate. To state it another way, the Senator, or Senators, who offered Resolution 301, and proposed amendments thereto, have no legal responsibility from that point on for the conduct of the investigations and hearings authorized by the order of the Senate. The hearings are not to be adversary in character. Under this interpretation, it became the committee's duty then to get all the facts and material relevant to the charges irrespective of whether the facts sustained the charges or showed them to be without foundation.

The foregoing statement seems to be necessary in view of a widespread misunderstanding that the Senator who introduced the resolution of censure into the Senate and the Senators who offered amendments thereto, setting up specific charges against the Senator from Wisconsin, are the complaining witnesses, or the parties plaintiff, in this proceeding. That is not true, as has been explained. However, because of the fact that they had made some study of the situation, the committee did give them an opportunity to submit informational documentation of the charges they had offered. Also they were asked to submit the names of any witnesses who might have firsthand knowledge of the matters charged and who could give relevant and material testimony in the hearings.

Since matters of law also will be involved in reaching evaluation of the facts developed, pertinent rules of the Senate and sections of law, together with precedents and decisions by competent tribunals, should be briefed and made a part of the hearing record, the committee believes.

3. To hold hearings where the committee can present witnesses and documentary evidence for the purpose of placing on record, for later use by the Senate, the evidence and other information gathered during the preliminary investigation period, and for the development of additional evidence and information as the hearings proceed.

The resolution of censure presents to the Senate an issue with respect to the conduct and possible punishment of one of its Members. The debate in the Senate preceding the vote to refer the matter to a select committee made it abundantly clear that the proceedings necessary to a proper disposal of the resolution and the amendments proposed, both in the Senate and in the select committee, would be judicial or quasi-judicial in nature, and for that reason should be conducted in a judicial manner and atmosphere, so far as compatible with the investigative functions of the committee in its preliminary and continuing search for evidence and information bearing on all phases of the issues presented.

Inherent in the situation created by the resolution of censure and the charges made, is the right of the Senator against whom the charges were made to be present at the hearings held by the select committee. He should also be permitted to be represented by counsel and should have the right of cross-examination. This is somewhat contrary to the practice by Senate committees in the past, in hearings of this nature, but the present committee believes that the accused Senator should have these rights. He or his counsel, but not both, shall be permitted to make objections to the introduction of testimony, but the argument on the objections may be had or withheld at the discretion of the chairman. The Senator under charges should be permitted to present witnesses and documentary evidence in his behalf, but, of course, this should be done in compliance with the policy laid down by the committee in its notice of hearing, which is a part of this record.

In general, the committee wishes it understood that the regulations adopted are for the purpose of insuring a judicial hearing and a judicial atmosphere as befits the importance of the issues raised. For that reason, and in accordance with the order the committee believes to be the sentiment of the Senate, all activities which are not permitted in the Senate itself will not be permitted in this hearing.

4. When the hearings have closed, to prepare a report and submit it to the Senate. Under the order creating this committee, this must be done before the present Senate adjourns sine die.

By way of comment, let me say that the inquiry we are engaged in is of a special character which differentiates it from the usual legislative inquiry. It involves the internal affairs of the Senate itself in the exercise of a high constitutional function. It is by nature a judicial or semijudicial function, and we shall attempt to conduct it as such. The procedures outlined are not necessarily appropriate to congressional investigations and should not, therefore, be construed as in any sense intended as a model appropriate to such inquiries. We hope what we are doing will be found to conform to sound senatorial principles and traditions in the special field in which the committee is operating.

It has been said before, but it will do no harm to repeat, that the members of this committee did not seek this appointment. The qualifications laid down by the Senate order creating the commission, said the committee should be made up of 3 Democrat Senators and 3 Republican Senators. This was the only condition named in the order. However, in a larger sense the proper authorities of the Senate were charged with the responsibility of attempting to choose Members of the Senate for this committee who could and would conduct a fair and impartial investigation and hearing. Members of the committee deemed their selection by the Senate authorities as a trust.

We realize we are human. We know, and the American people know, that there has been a controversy raging over the country through a number of years in connection with the activities of the Senator against whom the resolution is directed. Members of this committee have been conscious of that controversy; they have seen, heard, and read of the activities, charges, and countercharges, and being human, they may have at times expressed their impressions with respect to events that were happening while they were happening.

However, each of the Senators who make up this special select committee are mature men with a wide background of experience which should enable them to disregard any impressions or preconceived notions they may have had in the past respecting the controversies which have been going on in public for many years.

We approach this matter as a duty imposed upon us and which we feel that we should do our very best to discharge in a proper manner. We realize the United States Senate, in a sense, is on trial, and we hope our conduct will be such as to maintain the American sense of fair play and the high traditions and dignity of the United States Senate under the authority given it by the Constitution.

As the investigations and the hearings progressed, the committee found that the period of time allotted to perform the task assigned would not be sufficient if all the charges were given thorough investigation and hearings were held thereon. The committee also was aware of the practical situation that required that its task be completed sufficiently early to permit the Senate to consider its report before that body must adjourn sine die.

PROCEDURE FOR COMMITTEE HEARINGS ESTABLISHED IN NOTICE OF HEARINGS

All testimony and evidence received in the hearings shall be such as is found by the select committee to be competent, relevant, and material to the subject matters so under inquiry, with the right of examination and cross-examination, in general conformity to judicial proceedings and in accordance with said order of the Senate.

The select committee will admit, subject to said order, as competent testimony for the record, so far as material and relevant, the official proceedings and pertinent actions of the Senate and of any of its committees or subcommittees, taking judicial notice thereof, and using official reprints when convenient. Following

Senate tradition, witnesses may be examined by any member of the committee, and they may be examined or cross-examined for the committee by its counsel. Witnesses may be examined or cross-examined either by Senator McCarthy or his counsel, but not by both as to the same witness.

Senator McCarthy was permitted to and made an opening statement in his own behalf at the commencement of the first hearing, on condition that it be relevant and material, and not to be received as testimony (hearing record, p. 14).

By unanimous vote of the members of the select committee taken after the issuance of the notice of hearings, it was decided to proceed with hearings only upon the 13 specifications set forth in the 5 categories contained in the notice of hearings, to which reference is hereby made (hearing record, p. 8).

I

CATEGORY I. INCIDENTS OF CONTEMPT OF THE SENATE OR A SENATORIAL COMMITTEE

A. GENERAL DISCUSSION AND SUMMARY OF EVIDENCE

The evidence on the question whether Senator McCarthy was guilty of contempt of the Senate or a senatorial committee involves his conduct with relation to the Subcommittee on Privileges and Elections of the Senate Committee on Rules and Administration. An analysis of the three amendments referring to this general matter (being amendment (3) proposed by Senator Fulbright, amendment (a) proposed by Senator Morse, and amendment (17) proposed by Senator Flanders) reveals these specific charges:

(1) That Senator McCarthy refused repeated invitations to testify before the subcommittee.

(2) That he declined to comply with a request by letter dated November 21, 1952, from the chairman of the subcommittee to appear to supply information concerning certain specific matters involving his activities as a Member of the Senate.

(3) That he denounced the subcommittee and contemptuously refused to comply with its request.

(4) That he has continued to show his contempt for the Senate by failing to explain in any manner the six charges contained in the Hennings-Hayden-Hendrickson report, which was filed in January 1953.

We have decided to consider and discuss in our report under this category the incident with reference to Senator Hendrickson, since the conduct complained of is related directly to the fact that Senator Hendrickson was a member of the Subcommittee on Privileges and Elections. This incident is referred to in the amendment proposed by Senator Flanders (30), the specific charge being:

(5) That he ridiculed and defamed Senator Hendrickson in vulgar and base language, calling him: "A living miracle without brains or guts."

The report referred to as the Hennings-Hayden-Hendrickson report is the report of the Subcommittee on Privileges and Elections to the Committee on Rules and Administration, pursuant to Senate Resolution 187, 82d Congress, 1st session, and Senate Resolution 304, 82d Congress, 2d session, filed January 2, 1953, and appears in part II of the hearing record. The select committee admitted in evidence the Hennings-Hayden-Hendrickson report for the limited purposes of showing the nature of the charges before that subcommittee, as bearing upon the question of jurisdiction of that subcommittee, and what was the subject matter of the investigation (pp. 55, 121, and 524 of the hearings).

As stated by the chairman (p. 17 of the hearings), the select committee did not construe this category as involving in any way the truth or falsity of any of the charges against Senator McCarthy considered by that subcommittee. These charges, as shown by its report and as stated briefly by the chairman, Senator Hennings, in a letter to Senator McCarthy under date of November 21, 1952 (Hennings-Hayden-Hendrickson report, p. 98), were:

Pursuant to your request, as transmitted to us through Mr. Kiermas, we are advising you that the subcommittee desires to make inquiry with respect to the following matters:

(1) Whether any funds collected or received by you and by others on your behalf to conduct certain of your activities, including those relating to "communism," were ever diverted and used for other purposes inuring to your personal advantage.

(2) Whether you, at any time, used your official position as a United States Senator and as a member of the Banking and Currency Committee, the Joint Housing Committee, and the Senate Investigations Committee to obtain a $10,000 fee from the Lustron Corp., which company was then almost entirely subsidized by agencies under the jurisdiction of the very committees of which you were a member.

(3) Whether your activities on behalf of certain special interest groups, such as housing, sugar, and China, were motivated by self-interest.

(4) Whether your activities with respect to your senatorial campaigns, particularly with respect to the reporting of your financing and your activities relating to the financial transactions with, and subsequent employment of, Ray Kiermas involved violations of the Federal and State Corrupt Practices Acts.

(5) Whether loan or other transactions which you had with the Appleton State Bank, of Appleton, Wis., involved violations of tax and banking laws.

(6) Whether you used close associates and members of your family to secrete receipts, income, commodity, and stock speculation, and other financial transactions for ulterior motives.

The evidence taken by the select committee under this category consisted of letters and documents, oral testimony by Senator McCarthy and oral testimony by Senator Hayden, and by the Parliamentarian. As to the statement regarding Senator Hendrickson, there is the testimony of a reporter. There is no material contradiction in any of the testimony relating to this category. The sending and receipt of the correspondence is admitted. There is no contradiction of the verbal testimony of Senator McCarthy with reference to his conversations with Chairman Gillette, or of that of Chairman Hayden with reference to the constitution of the Subcommittee on Privileges and Elections and the filing of its report, or of that of Parliamentarian Watkins, discussed fully hereinafter.

The evidence shows that the Subcommittee on Privileges and Elections was proceeding to investigate and report on Senate Resolution 187; that Senator McCarthy was invited to appear to testify before the subcommittee on five separate occasions extending from September 25, 1951, to November 7, 1952, and formally requested to appear by letter and telegram of November 21, 1952; that Senator McCarthy could not appear at the times specified in the request because of his absence in Wisconsin; that Senator McCarthy did not appear before the subcommittee in answer to the matters under investigation regarding his own conduct, but did appear on one occasion in support of his Senate Resolution 304 directed against Senator Benton; that Senator McCarthy accused the subcommittee of acting without power and beyond its jurisdiction, of wasting vast amounts of public money for improper partisan purposes, of proceeding dishonestly, of aiding the cause of communism, and that these accusations were directed toward an official subcommittee of the Senate. The uncontradicted testimony further shows that Senator McCarthy directed and gave to the press an abusive and insulting statement concerning Senator Hendrickson, calculated to wound a colleague, solely because Senator Hendrickson was a member of the subcommittee and performing services required by the Senate.

Senate Resolution 187, introduced by Senator Benton, was not voted upon by the Senate, but when the jurisdiction of the Subcommittee on Privileges and Elections and the integrity of its members was attacked, the Senate by its vote of 60 to 0 in Senate Resolution 300, affirmed and ratified both.

Counsel for Senator McCarthy advanced the contention that these specifications relating to "Incidents of contempt of the Senate or a senatorial committee" were legally insufficient on their face as a predicate for the censure of Senator McCarthy because (1) there has never been a case of censure upon a Member of Congress for conduct antedating the inception of the Congress which is hearing the censure charges (p. 18 of the hearings), and (2) because the subcommittee acted unlawfully and beyond its jurisdiction (pp. 53 to 58 of the hearings).

B. FINDINGS OF FACT

From the evidence and testimony taken with reference to the first category, the select committee finds the following facts:

1. On August 6, 1951, Senate Resolution 187, 82d Congress, 1st session, was introduced by Senator Benton and referred to the Committee on Rules and Administration (p. 20 of the hearings).

2. In turn, this resolution was referred by the Committee on Rules and Administration to its Subcommittee on Privileges and Elections (p. 280 of the hearings).

3. This resolution provided, inter alia, that whereas "any sitting Senator, regardless of whether he is a candidate in the election himself, should be subject to expulsion by action of the Senate, if it finds such Senator engaged in practices and behavior that make him, in the opinion of the Senate, unfit to hold the position of United States Senator,": Therefore be it

Resolved, That the Committee on Rules and Administration of the Senate is authorized and directed to proceed with such consideration of the report of its Subcommittee on Privileges and Elections with respect to the 1950 Maryland senatorial general election, which was made pursuant to Senate Resolution 250, 81st Congress, April 13, 1950, and to make such further investigation with respect to the participation of Senator Joseph R. McCarthy in the 1950 senatorial campaign of Senator John Marshall Butler, and such investigation with respect to his other acts since his election to the Senate, as may be appropriate to enable such committee to determine whether or not it should initiate action with a view toward the expulsion from the United States Senate of the said Senator Joseph R. McCarthy.

It will be noted that this proposed resolution authorized and directed such investigation as may be appropriate "with reference to his other acts since his election to the Senate."

4. Senator McCarthy was elected to the Senate in the fall of 1946, and took his seat in January 1947.

5. Among the charges pending before and investigated by that Subcommittee on Privileges and Elections, charges (1), (2), (3), and (4) related to matters since Senator McCarthy's election to the Senate in 1946, and charges (5) and (6) may or may not have referred to matters since his election to the Senate, or to matters both before and after his election.

6. Senator Guy M. Gillette was chairman of that Subcommittee on Privileges and Elections until his resignation on September 26, 1952 (p. 22 of the hearings).

7. By letter of Senator McCarthy to Chairman Gillette dated September 17, 1951, Senator McCarthy stated that he intended to appear to question witnesses and that the subcommittee, without authorization from the Senate was undertaking to conduct hearings in the matter (p. 280 of the hearings).

8. By letter of September 25, 1951, Chairman Gillette notified Senator McCarthy that the Benton resolution (S. Res. 187) would be taken up by the subcommittee on September 28, 1951, and that Senator McCarthy could be present to hear Senator Benton in executive session and make his own statement also, if time permitted (p. 23 of the hearings).

9. Senator McCarthy did not reply to this letter.

10. By letter of October 1, 1951, Chairman Gillette advised Senator McCarthy that Senator Benton had appeared and presented a statement in support of his resolution looking to action pertaining to the expulsion of Senator McCarthy from the Senate, that the subcommittee had taken action to accord to Senator McCarthy the opportunity to appear and make any statement he wished to make concerning the matter, and that the subcommittee "will be glad to hear you at an hour mutually convenient," before the 10th of October, if Senator McCarthy desired to appear (p. 23 of the hearings).

11. Under date of October 4, 1951, Senator McCarthy wrote to Chairman Gillette, in reply to the latter's letter of October 1, 1951, that "I have not and do not even intend to read, much less answer, Benton's smear attack" (p. 23 of the hearings).

12. By letter of December 6, 1951, Senator McCarthy advised Chairman Gillette (p. 24 of the hearings).

(a) That the "Elections Subcommittee, unless given further power by the Senate, is restricted to matters having to do with elections.

(b) That "a horde of investigators hired by your committee at a cost of tens of thousands of dollars of taxpayers' money, has been engaged exclusively in trying to dig up on McCarthy material covering periods of time long before he was even old enough to be a candidate for the Senate—material which can have no conceivable connection with his election or any other election."

(c) That the "obvious purpose is to dig up campaign material for the Democrat Party for the coming campaign against McCarthy.

(*d*) That "when your Elections Subcommittee, without Senate authorization, spends tens of thousands of taxpayers' dollars for the sole purpose of digging up campaign material against McCarthy, then the committee is guilty of stealing just as clearly as though the Members engaged in picking the pockets of the taxpayers and turning the loot over to the Democrat National Committee."

(*e*) That "if one of the administration lackies were chairman of this committee, I would not waste the time or energy to write and point out the committee's complete dishonesty."

(*f*) That instead of obtaining the necessary power from the Senate, "your committee decided to spend tens of thousands of dollars of taxpayers' money to aid Benton in his smear attack upon McCarthy."

(*g*) That "I cannot understand your being willing to label Guy Gillette as a man who will head a committee which is stealing from the pockets of the American taxpayer tens of thousands of dollars and then using this money to protect the Democrat Party from the political effect of the exposure of Communists in Government."

(*h*) That "to take it upon yourself to hire a horde of investigators and spend tens of thousands of dollars without any authorization from the Senate is labeling your Elections Subcommittee even more dishonest than was the Tydings committee."

13. Chairman Gillette replied to Senator McCarthy by letter of December 6, 1951 (p. 26 of the hearings), stating that the subcommittee did not seek its unpleasant task, but that since Senate Resolution 187 was referred by the Senate to the Committee on Rules and Administration, and by it to its Subcommittee on Privileges and Elections, its duty was clear and would be discharged "in a spirit of utmost fairness to all concerned and to the Senate."

14. In the same letter, Chairman Gillette informed Senator McCarthy, "your information as to the use of a large staff and the expenditure of a large sum of money in investigations relative to the resolution is, of course, erroneous."

15. By letter from Senator McCarthy to Chairman Gillette dated December 7, 1951, information was requested of the number and salaries of employees of the subcommittee (p. 26 of the hearings).

16. Chairman Gillette gave this information to Senator McCarthy under date of December 11, 1951 (p. 27 of the hearings).

17. Under date of December 19, 1951, Senator McCarthy wrote to Chairman Gillette stating that: "the full committee appointed you chairman of an Elections Subcommittee, but gave you no power whatsoever to hire investigators and spend vast amounts of money to make investigations having nothing to do with elections. Again, may I have an answer to my questions as to why you feel you are entitled to spend the taxpayers' money to do the work of the Democratic National Committee" (p. 27 of the hearings).

18. In the same letter, Senator McCarthy stated: "You and every member of your subcommittee who is responsible for spending vast amounts of money to hire investigators, pay their traveling expenses, etc., on matters not concerned with elections, is just as dishonest as

though he or she picked the pockets of the taxpayers and turned the loot over to the Democratic National Committee."

19. In the same letter, Senator McCarthy stated: "I wonder if I might have a frank, honest answer to all the questions covered in my letter of December 7. Certainly as a member of the Rules Committee and as a Member of the Senate, I am entitled to this information. Your failure to give this information highlights the fact that your subcommittee is not concerned with dishonestly spending the taxpayers' money and using your subcommittee as an arm of the Democratic National Committee" (p. 28 of the hearings).

20. On December 21, 1951, Chairman Gillette wrote Senator McCarthy, advising him as follows:

(*a*) "I shall be very glad to give you such information as I have or go with you, if you so desire, to the rooms occupied by the subcommittee and aid you in securing any facts that are there available, relative to the employees of the subcommittee or their work," and stating further that:

(*b*) Previous correspondence had been printed in the public press, even before receipt by Chairman Gillette.

(*c*) That it was improper to discuss matters pertaining to pending litigation in the public press.

(*d*) That a meeting of the subcommittee was being called for January 7, 1952, to consider the Benton resolution.

(*e*) That if Senator McCarthy cared to appear before the subcommittee, he would be glad to make the necessary arrangements as to time and place.

(*f*) That he would be glad to confer with Senator McCarthy personally as to matters concerning the staff and the work of the subcommittee.

(*g*) That neither the Democratic National Committee nor any person or group other than an agency of the United States Senate has had or will have any influence on his duties and actions as a member of the subcommittee, and that no other member of the subcommittee has been or will be so influenced (p. 28 of the hearings).

21. Senator McCarthy wrote to Chairman Gillette on January 4, 1952, asking: "the simple question of whether or not you have ordered the investigators to restrict their investigation to matters having to do with elections, or whether their investigations extend into fields having nothing whatsoever to do with either my election or the election of any other Senator" (p. 29 of the hearings).

22. Chairman Gillette replied to Senator McCarthy by letter dated January 10, 1952, informing him that the staff of the subcommittee had just submitted a report on the legal question raised by Senator McCarthy, that this was being studied, and the subcommittee would then determine what action, if any, they would take (p. 29 of the hearings).

23. Because Senator McCarthy questioned the jurisdiction of the subcommittee, the subcommittee adopted a resolution, approved by a majority of the Committee on Rules and Administration, that Senator McCarthy be requested to bring to the floor of the Senate a motion to discharge the Subcommittee on Privileges and Elections (p. 30 of the hearings).

24. Senator Hayden, chairman of the Committee on Rules and Administration, informed Senator McCarthy that the purpose would

be to test the jurisdiction and integrity of the members of the subcommittee (p. 30 of the hearings).

25. Under date of March 21, 1952, Senator McCarthy wrote to Senator Hayden, chairman of the parent Committee on Rules and Administration, that he thought it improper to discharge the subcommittee for the following reasons:

The Elections Subcommittee unquestionably has the power and, when complaint is made, the duty to investigate any improper conduct on the part of McCarthy or any other Senator in a senatorial election.

The subcommittee has spent tens of thousands of dollars and nearly a year making the most painstaking investigation of my part in the Maryland election, as well as my campaigns in Wisconsin. The subcommittee's task is not finished until it reports to the Senate the result of that investigation, namely, whether they found such misconduct on the part of McCarthy in either his own campaigns or in the Tydings campaign to warrant his expulsion from the Senate.

I note the subcommittee's request that the integrity of the subcommittee be passed upon. As you know, the sole question of the integrity of the subcommittee concerned its right to spend vast sums of money investigating the life of McCarthy from birth to date without any authority to do so from the Senate. However, the vote on that question cannot affect the McCarthy investigation, in that the committee for a year has been looking into every possible phase of McCarthy's life, including an investigation of those who contributed to my unsuccessful 1944 campaign.

As you know, I wrote Senator Gillette, chairman of the subcommittee, that I considered this a completely dishonest handling of taxpayers' money. I felt that the Elections Subcommittee had no authority to go into matters other than elections unless the Senate instructed it to do so. However, it is obvious that insofar as McCarthy is concerned this is now a moot question, because the staff has already painstakingly and diligently investigated every nook and cranny of my life from birth to date. Every possible lead on McCarthy was investigated. Nothing that could be investigated was left uninvestigated. The staff's scurrilous report, which consisted of cleverly twisted and distorted facts, was then "leaked" to the left-wing elements of the press and blazoned across the Nation in an attempt to further smear McCarthy.

A vote of confidence in the subcommittee would be a vote on whether or not it had the right, without authority from the Senate, but merely on the request of one Senator (in this case Senator Benton) to make a thorough and complete investigation of the entire life of another Senator. A vote to uphold the subcommittee would mean that the Senate accepts and approves this precedent and makes it binding on the Elections Subcommittee in the future.

A vote against the subcommittee could not undo what the subcommittee has done in regard to McCarthy. It would not force the subcommittee members to repay into the Treasury the funds spent on this investigation of McCarthy. A vote against the subcommittee would merely mean that the Senate disapproves what has already been done insofar as McCarthy is concerned, and therefore, disapproves an investigation of other Senators like the one which was made of McCarthy. While I felt the subcommittee exceeded its authority, now that it has established a precedent in McCarthy's case, the same rule should apply to every other Senator. If the subcommittee brought up this question before the investigation had been made, I would have voted to discharge it. Now that the deed is done, however, the same rule should apply to the other 95 Senators.

For that reason, I would be forced to vigorously oppose a motion to discharge the Elections Subcommittee at this time.

I hope the Senate agrees with me that it would be highly improper to discharge the Gillette-Monroney subcommittee at this time, thereby, in effect, setting a different rule for the subcommittee to follow in case an investigation is asked of any of the other 95 Senators (p. 30 of the hearings).

26. In view of Senator McCarthy's refusal to make the requested motion in the Senate, Chairman Hayden, of himself, and for the other four members of the Subcommittee on Privileges and Elections (Senators Gillette, Monroney, Hennings, and Hendrickson), submitted Senate Resolution 300, 82d Congress, 2d session, on April 8, 1952 (p. 31 of the hearings).

27. Senate Resolution 300 provided that whereas Senator McCarthy in a series of communications addressed to Chairman Gillette between December 6, 1951, and January 4, 1952, had charged that the subcommittee lacked jurisdiction to investigate such acts of Senator McCarthy as were not connected with election campaigns, and attacked the honesty of the members of the subcommittee, charging that in their investigation of such other acts, the members were improperly motivated and were guilty of stealing just as clearly as though the members engaged in picking the pockets of the taxpayers, and whereas the subcommittee adopted a motion, as the most expeditious parliamentary method of obtaining an affirmation by the Senate of its jurisdiction of this matter and a vote on the honesty of its members, that Senator McCarthy be requested to raise the question of jurisdiction and of the integrity of the members of the Subcommittee on Privileges and Elections, by making a formal motion on the floor of the Senate to discharge the committee, and that unless Senator McCarthy did so, the chairman of the Committee on Rules and Administration or the chairman of the subcommittee would present such a motion, and since Senator McCarthy in effect had declined so to do, therefore, to determine the proper jurisdiction of the Committee on Rules and Administration and to express the confidence of the Senate in its committee in their consideration of Senate Resolution 187, be it resolved that the Committee on Rules and Administration be, and it hereby is, discharged from the further consideration of Senate Resolution 187 (p. 31 of the hearings).

28. The Senate voted upon this resolution on April 10, 1952, and the resolution was rejected by a vote of 0 to 60, with 36 Members not voting (p. 32 of the hearings).

29. Senator McCarthy is recorded as not voting but he stated in the Senate that he could not wait for the vote and if present would have voted against the discharge of the subcommittee (p. 378 of the hearings).

30. Chairman Gillette wrote to Senator McCarthy on May 7, 1952, fixing May 12, 1952, as the time for public hearing on Senate Resolution 187, informing him that the first charge to be heard would be the matter concerning the Lustron Corp. booklet, and extending to Senator McCarthy "the opportunity to appear at the hearings for the purpose of presenting testimony relating to this charge. The hearings in this case will probably continue for several days, and we shall make whatever arrangements for your appearance as are most convenient for you" (p. 32 of the hearings).

31. Under date of May 8, 1952, Senator McCarthy wrote to Chairman Gillette, acknowledging receipt of the letter of May 7, 1952, asking on what point the subcommittee desired information, and giving a statement of facts with reference to the Lustron Corp. booklet, in argumentative fashion, and charging the subcommittee with knowingly allowing itself to serve the Communist cause, and stating:

The Communists will have scored a great victory if they can convince every other Senator or Congressman that if he attempts to expose undercover Communists, he will be subjected to the same type of intense smear, even to the extent of using a Senate committee for the purpose. They will have frightened away from this fight a vast number of legislators who fear the political effect of being inundated by the Communist Party line sewage.

If you have evidence of wrongdoing on McCarthy's part, which would justify removal from the Senate or a vote of censure by the Senate, certainly you have the obligation to produce it. However, as you well know, every member of your committee and staff privately admits that no such evidence is in existence. It is an evil and dishonest thing for the subcommittee to allow itself to be used for an evil purpose. Certainly the fact that the Democrat Party may temporarily benefit thereby is insufficient justification. Remember the Communist Party will benefit infinitely more (p. 32 of the hearings).

32. Senator McCarthy again wrote to Chairman Gillette on the same day, May 8, 1952, demanding expeditious action in the Benton case (p. 35 of the hearings).

33. Chairman Gillette wrote to Senator McCarthy under date of May 10, 1952, informing him that the subcommittee had concluded to take testimony on May 12, 1952, and that it was the courteous thing to do to invite him to attend, to present evidence in refutation or explanation, and that the opportunity would continue to be that of Senator McCarthy to present such matter as he might wish in connection with the hearing and to attend if he so desired (p. 43 of the hearings).

34. On May 11, 1952, Senator McCarthy wrote to Chairman Gillette, Senator Monroney, and Senator Hennings jointly, a sarcastic letter, the meaning and intention of which can be understood only by reading it in its entirety (p. 43 of the hearings).

35. The chief counsel for the subcommittee wrote to Senator McCarthy on November 7, 1952, inviting Senator McCarthy to appear before a subcommittee in executive session, in connection with Senate Resolution 187, during the week of November 17, 1952, and asking to be advised of the date of Senator McCarthy's appearance (p. 44 of the hearings).

36. The administrative assistant to Senator McCarthy replied for Senator McCarthy by letter of November 10, 1952, stating that Senator McCarthy was away and that he did not know when he would return to Washington, stating, however, that if the subcommittee would let him know what information was desired, he would be glad to try to be of help (p. 45 of the hearings).

37. Chairman Hennings, of the subcommittee, then wrote a letter to Senator McCarthy under date of November 21, 1952, which because of its importance is set forth in full:

DEAR SENATOR McCARTHY: As you will recall on September 25, 1951, May 7, 1952, and May 10, 1952, this subcommittee invited you to appear before it to give testimony relating to the investigation pursuant to Senate Resolution 187.

Under date of November 7, 1952, the following communication was addressed to you:

"DEAR SENATOR McCARTHY: In connection with the consideration by the Subcommittee on Privileges and Elections of Senate Resolution No. 187, introduced by Senator Benton on August 6, 1951, as well as the ensuing investigation, I have been instructed by the subcommittee to invite you to appear before said subcommittee in executive session. Insofar as possible, we would like to respect your wishes as to the date on which you will appear. However, the subcommittee plans to be available for this purpose during the week beginning November 17, 1952.

"It will be appreciated if you will advise me at as early a date as possible of the day you will appear, in order that the subcommittee may arrange its plans accordingly.

"Very truly yours,

"PAUL J. COTTER, *Chief Counsel.*"

On November 14, 1952, the subcommittee received the following communication, dated November 10, 1952:

"DEAR MR. COTTER: Inasmuch as Senator McCarthy is not now in Washington, I am taking the liberty of acknowledging receipt of your letter of November 7. "I have just talked to the Senator over the telephone and he does not know just when he will return to Washington. It presently appears that he will not be available to appear before your committee during the time you mention. However, he did state that if you will let him know just what information you desire, he will be glad to try to be of help to you.
       "Sincerely yours,

                                              "RAY KIERMAS,'"
                    "Administrative Assistant to Senator McCarthy."

The subcommittee is grateful for your offer of assistance, and we want to afford you with every opportunity to offer your explanations with reference to the issues involved. Therefore, although the subcommittee did make itself available during the past week in order to afford you an opportunity to be heard, we shall be at your disposal commencing Saturday, November 22, through but not later than Tuesday, November 25, 1952.

This subcommittee has but one object, and that is to reach an impartial and proper conclusion based upon the facts. Your appearance, in person, before the subcommittee will not only give you the opportunity to testify as to any issues of fact which may be in controversy, but will be of the greatest assistance to the subcommittee in its effort to arrive at a proper determination and to embody in its report an accurate representation of the facts.

Pursuant to your request, as transmitted to us through Mr. Kiermas, we are advising you that the subcommittee desires to make inquiry with respect to the following matters:

(1) Whether any funds collected or received by you and by others on your behalf to conduct certain of your activities, including those relating to "communism," were ever diverted and used for other purposes inuring to your personal advantage.

(2) Whether you, at any time, used your official position as a United States Senator and as a member of the Banking and Currency Committee, the Joint Housing Committee, and the Senate Investigations Committee, to obtain a $10,000 fee from the Lustron Corp., which company was then almost entirely subsidized by agencies under the jurisdiction of the very committees of which you were a member.

(3) Whether your activities on behalf of certain interest groups, such as housing, sugar, and China, were motivated by self-interest.

(4) Whether your activities with respect to your senatorial campaigns, particularly with respect to the reporting of your financing and your activities relating to the financial transactions with and subsequent employment of Ray Kiermas, involved violations of the Federal and State Corrupt Practices Acts.

(5) Whether loan or other transactions which you had with the Appleton State Bank, of Appleton, Wis., involved violations of tax and banking laws.

(6) Whether you used close associates and members of your family to secrete receipts, income, commodity and stock speculation and other financial transactions for ulterior motives.

We again assure you of our desire to give you the opportunity to testify, in executive session of the subcommittee, as to the foregoing matters. The 82d Congress expires in the immediate future and the subcommittee must necessarily proceed with dispatch in making its report to this Congress. To that end, we respectfully urge you to arrange to come before us on or before November 25, and thus enable us to do our conscientious best in the interests of the Senate and our obligation to complete our work. We would thank you to advise us immediately, so that we may plan accordingly.

This letter is being transmitted at the direction and with the full concurrence of the membership of this subcommittee.
       Sincerely yours,

                                THOMAS C. HENNINGS, Jr., Chairman.

(P. 45 of the hearings.)

38. This letter was delivered by hand to the office of Senator McCarthy in Washington on November 21, 1952 (p. 47 of the hearings).

39. On the same day, November 21, 1952, Chairman Hennings sent the following telegram addressed to Senator McCarthy at Appleton, Wis.:

Today you were advised by letter delivered by hand to your office of the principal matters which the subcommittee desires to interrogate you in furtherance of your express desire transmitted to the committee by your administrative assistant, Mr. Ray Kiermas, under date of November 10. The subcommittee appreciates your willingness to help in the completion of the work in connection with the investigation of Resolution 187 and the investigations predicated thereon. Your prompt appearance before the subcommittee can save the Government much effort and expense. We are sure that you want to be of help to us in arriving at a proper determination of the issues in controversy. We are therefore at your disposal in executive session and for your convenience suggest that the subcommittee is available to you commencing with tomorrow, Saturday, November 22, but not later than Tuesday the 25th, to enable the committee to hear you and allow time thereafter to prepare the subcommittee report.

Senator Benton has also been notified to appear by similar communication. This action is being taken at the direction and with the full concurrence of the committee members (p. 47 of the hearings).

40. The copy of the telegram in the H-H-H Report, designated "Exhibit No. 42" at page 99 thereof, was not sent to Senator McCarthy and was inserted as an exhibit by error in place of the foregoing telegram of November 21, 1952, as shown by the fact it is not dated and as appears in the index of appendix, page 55, wherein exhibit No. 42 is described as "Telegram dated Nov. 21, 1952, from Senator Hennings to Senator McCarthy . . . . Page 99" (p. 51 of the hearings).

41. On November 21, 1952, Senator McCarthy was deer hunting in northern Wisconsin (p. 298 of the hearings).

42. Senator McCarthy wrote to Chairman Hennings on November 28, 1952, stating that he had just received the wire of November 22, and that, as Senator Hennings had been previously advised, Senator McCarthy was not expected to return to Washington until November 27, on which date he did return (p. 49 of the hearings).

43. Senator McCarthy did not see the letter or telegram dated November 21, 1952, until November 28, 1952 (p. 299 of the hearings)

44. Senator McCarthy wrote to Chairman Hennings under date of December 1, 1952, stating as follows:

Senator THOMAS C. HENNINGS, Jr.,
    Chairman, Subcommittee on Privileges and Elections,
        Senate Office Building.

DEAR MR. HENNINGS: This is to acknowledge receipt of yours of November 21 in which you state that your object is to reach an "impartial and proper conclusion based upon the facts" in the Benton application which asks for my removal from the Senate.

I was interested in your declaration of honesty of the committee and would like to believe that it is true. As you know, your committee has the most unusual record of any committee in the history of the Senate. As you know two members of your staff have resigned and made the public statement that their reason for resignation was that your committee was dishonestly used for political purposes. Two Senators have also resigned. One, Senator Welker, in the strongest possible language indicted your committee for complete dishonesty in handling your investigation. Senator Gillette also resigned without giving any plausible reason for his resignation from the committee. Obviously, he also couldn't stomach the dishonest use of public funds for political purposes. For that reason it is difficult for me to believe your protestations of the honesty of your committee.

I would, therefore, ordinarily not dignify your committee by answering your letter of November 21. However, I decided to give you no excuse to claim in your report that I refused to give you any facts. For that reason you are being informed that the answer to the six insulting questions in your letter of November 21 in "No." You understand that in answering these questions I do not in any way approve of nor admit the false statements and innuendoes made in the questions.

I note with some interest your reference to my "activities on behalf of certain special-interest groups, such as housing, sugar, and China." I assume you refer to my drafting of the comprehensive Housing Act of 1946, which was passed without a single dissenting vote in the Senate, either Democrat or Republican. Neither you nor any other Senator has attempted to repeal any part of that Housing Act. Or perhaps you refer to the slum-clearance bill which I drafted and introduced in 1948, which slum-clearance bill was adopted in toto by the Democrat-controlled Senate in 1949.

When you refer to sugar, I assume you refer to my efforts to do away with your party's rationing of sugar, as I promised the housewives I would during my 1946 campaign. If that were wrong, I wonder why you have not introduced legislation in the Democrat-controlled Senate to restore sugar rationing. You have had 2 years to do so.

I thought perhaps the election might have taught you that your boss and mine—the American people—do not approve of treason and incompetence and feel that it must be exposed.

You refer to the above as "special interests." I personally feel very proud of having drafted the Housing Act in 1948 which passed the Congress without a single dissenting vote—a Housing Act which contributed so much toward making it possible for veterans and all Americans in the middle- and low-income groups to own their own home. Likewise, I am proud of having been able to fulfill my promise to American housewives to obtain the derationing of sugar. I proved at the time that rationing was not for the benefit of the housewives but for the commercial users.

I likewise am double proud of the part I played in alerting the American people to your administration's traitorous betrayal of American interests throughout the world, especially in China and Poland.

You refer to such activities on my part as "activities for special interests." I am curious to know what "special interests" you mean other than the special interest of the American people.

This letter is not written with any hope of getting an honest report from your committee. It is being written merely to keep the record straight.

Sincerely yours,

JOE MCCARTHY.

(P. 51 of hearings.)

45. Senator McCarthy appeared before the Subcommittee on Privileges and Elections once only, on July 3, 1952, in connection with his charges against Senator Benton under Senate Resolution 304, without requiring a subpena (pp. 52, 290, and 375 of hearings).

46. Senator McCarthy did not appear before that subcommittee, at any other time, nor make any explanation in defense, except as shown in the foregoing correspondence, in connection with the charges pending against him, either before or after the Senate action in Senate Resolution 300 (pp. 52 and 375 of hearings).

47. Senator McCarthy did make an explanation of the Lustron matter on the floor of the Senate, on August 2, 1954 (p. 53 of hearings).

48. Senate Resolution 187, introduced by Senator Benton, was not voted upon by the Senate, although it was considered by the Senate in its vote on April 10, 1952, upon Senate Resolution 300 to test the jurisdiction of the subcommittee and the integrity of its members.

49. The vote of the Senate upon Senate Resolution 300 notwithstanding any previous question of the jurisdiction of the Hennings subcommittee, was a grant of authority to that subcommittee to proceed with its investigation of the charges pending against Senator McCarthy, since his election to the Senate.

50. Senate Resolution 187, introduced by Senator Benton, confined the subcommittee to activities of Senator McCarthy subsequent to his election in 1946.

51. Senator McCarthy's position was that he would not appear before the Hennings subcommittee upon the charges pending against him unless he was ordered to appear (p. 288 of hearings).

52. Senator McCarthy did not say in any of the correspondence relating to the hearings and his appearance, that he would not appear before the subcommittee unless he was ordered to do so, but testified that he so notified Chairman Gillette orally (p. 288 of hearings).

53. Senator McCarthy advised Chairman Gillette that unless he was given the right to cross-examine, that he had no desire to appear before the subcommittee but that he would appear if ordered to do so (p. 288 of hearings).

54. At the hearings before the select committee, Senator McCarthy testified that the subcommittee knew that a witness was mentally incompetent "and they were going to call him solely for the purpose of doing a smear job" (p. 296 of hearings).

55. At the hearings before the select committee, Senator McCarthy testified that the insertion of the undated telegram, exhibit No. 42 in the Hennings report (found by this select committee to be a clerical error), "was completely dishonest," insisting upon this conclusion when the chairman asked whether it could not have been a mistake (pp. 299, 384, and 385 of hearing record).

56. Senator McCarthy told Chairman Gillette "that I would not appear unless I was ordered to appear or subpenaed. I forget which word I used. I told him I had no desire to appear before that committee and that his extending an opportunity meant nothing to me" (p. 305 of the hearing).

57. The report of the Subcommittee on Privileges and Elections was filed January 2, 1953 (p. 306 of the hearings).

58. On that day, Senator McCarthy, according to his own testimony, called Senator Hendrickson, a member of that subcommittee, by telephone and told him that it was completely dishonest to sign a report that was factually wrong (p. 306 of the hearings).

59. That evening Senator McCarthy gave a statement to the press regarding Senator Hendrickson, a member of that subcommittee, stating:

"This report accuses me either directly or by innuendo and intimation of the most dishonest and improper conduct.

"If it is true, I am unfit to serve in the Senate. If it is false, then the three men who joined in it—namely, Hendrickson, Hennings, and Hayden—are dishonest beyond words.

"If those 3 men honestly think that all of the 4 things of which they have accused me, they have a deep, moral obligation tomorrow to move that the Senate does not seat me as a Senator.

"If they think the report is true, they will do that. If they know the report is completely false and that it has been issued only for its smear value, then they will not dare to present this case to the Senate.

"This committee has been squandering taxpayers' money on this smear campaign for nearly 18 months. If they feel that they are honest and right, why do they fear presenting their case to the Senate?

"I challenge them to do that. If they do not, they will have proved their complete dishonesty.

"I can understand the actions of the leftwingers in the administration, like Hennings and Hayden. As far as Hendrickson is concerned, I frankly can bear him no ill will.

"Suffice it to say that he is a living miracle in that he is without question the only man in the world who has lived so long with neither brains nor guts" (pp. 67 and 68 of hearing record).

60. By letter of September 10, 1952, Chairman Gillette of the subcommittee wrote to Chairman Hayden, of the Committee on Rules and Administration, suggesting that the membership of the subcommittee be reduced from 5 members to 3, as it was originally, to facilitate the work of the subcommittee (p. 294 of the hearings).

61. Senator Welker resigned as a member of the subcommittee on September 9, 1952 (p. 291 of the hearings).

62. Chairman Gillette resigned as a member of the subcommittee on September 26, 1952 (p. 294 of the hearings).

63. After consultation with the Parliamentarian, Senator Hayden, chairman of the parent Committee on Rules and Administration, decided it was unnecessary to appoint 2 Members of the Senate to take the places of those who had resigned, because it was a committee of 5 with a majority of 3, and because the Senate not being in session, it was very difficult to obtain Senators who were members of the Committee on Rules and Administration (p. 361 of the hearings).

64. Senator Monroney, who was in Europe, resigned as a member of the subcommittee, on November 20, 1953 (p. 361 of the hearings).

65. On November 20, 1952, Senator Hayden made it a matter of record by writing to the clerk of the Committee on Rules and Administration that he was appointing himself a member of the Subcommittee on Privileges and Elections in place of Senator Monroney (p. 362 of the hearings).

66. The subcommittee, with Senator Hennings as chairman, and Senators Hendrickson and Hayden as members, continued to function until January 16, 1953 (pp. 362 and 367 of the hearings).

67. Since January 1953 the Subcommittee on Privileges and Elections has had but three members (p. 362 of the hearings).

68. The suggestion of Senator Gillette that the membership of the subcommittee be reduced to three members was given consideration by both the Committee on Rules and Administration and the subcommittee (p. 362 of the hearings).

69. Senators Hennings, Hayden, and Hendrickson signed the subcommittee report pursuant to Senate Resolution 187 and Senate Resolution 304 (p. 363 of the hearings).

70. It was the opinion of Chairman Hayden, of the Committee on Rules and Administration, that without reducing the subcommittee to 3 members, the subcommittee could continue to function as a committee of 5 with but 3 members (p. 365 of the hearings).

71. It was the opinion of Chairman Hayden, that the Senate not being in session, it was not necessary for him as chairman of the parent committee to obtain confirmation by the parent committee of appointments to the subcommittee (p. 365 of the hearings).

72. Chairman Hayden testified that there was immediate important work for the subcommittee to do and that there was no one other than himself on the Committee on Rules and Administration who could be appointed to the subcommittee (p. 365 of the hearings).

73. This manner of conducting the Subcommittee on Privileges and Elections was consistent with its practice since before the 81st Congress and did not violate any rule of the parent committee (p. 366 of the hearings).

74. Chairman Hayden continued as chairman of the Committee on Rules and Administration, and Chairman Hennings of the Subcom-

mittee on Privileges and Elections continued in office until about January 16, 1953 (pp. 367 and 369 of the hearings).

75. At the hearings before the select committee, Senator McCarthy testified when asked whether he had any evidence to support his written statements that the subcommittee was spending tens of thousands of dollars and as guilty as though engaged in picking the pockets of the taxpayers to turn the loot over to the Democrat National Committee, that he had produced this evidence in letters to the subcommittee (p. 377 of the hearings).

76. No such evidence appears in the letters.

77. When asked whether he had any evidence that the subcommittee had spent tens of thousands of dollars illegally, Senator McCarthy testified that, "They were spending a vast amount of money illegally, I don't know the exact figure" (p. 378 of the hearings).

78. When asked whether he knew that the matters pending before the subcommittee reflected seriously upon his character and activities and were of sufficient moment ordinarily to justify making some reply, Senator McCarthy testified that: "They were six insulting questions asked by the committee—by a Senator, not by a legal committee. I answered his questions. I told him the answer was 'No'." (p. 383 of the hearings). (But note that the above answer was contained in a letter from Senator McCarthy to Senator Hennings dated December 1, 1952, addressed to the latter as chairman of the Subcommittee on Privileges and Elections) (pp. 51–52 of the hearings).

79. At page 384 of the hearings, Senator McCarthy was asked whether it was his position that when matters of that serious nature are pending against a Member of the United States Senate, instead of appearing and making an answer, he can call them "insulting" and need not appear, and Senator McCarthy testified in reply that: "They are no more 'matters' than the 46 statements made by Senator Flanders."

80. On January 2, 1953, Senator McCarthy bitterly criticized Senator Hendrickson with reference to the latter's work with the Subcommittee on Privileges and Elections, and then gave to the press a statement that Senator Hendrickson was "a living miracle in that he is without question the only man who has lived so long with neither brains nor guts" (pp. 66 and 425 of the hearings). (See also Finding of Fact No. 59.)

81. At the hearings before the select committee, when given the opportunity by Senator Case to withdraw or modify his remarks about Senator Hendrickson, a member of the subcommittee, Senator McCarthy indicated he had no desire to change his position (p. 425 of the hearings).

C. LEGAL QUESTIONS INVOLVED IN THIS CATEGORY

Several legal questions are involved and were considered in this part of the inquiry. They may be stated briefly as follows:

1. Is the Senate a continuing body?
2. Does the Senate have the power to censure a Senator for conduct occurring during his prior term as Senator?
3. Was it necessary for Senate Resolution 187 to be adopted by the Senate?

4. Was the Gillette-Hennings subcommittee acting beyond its power and jurisdiction?

5. Was it a lawfully constituted subcommittee?

6. Was it necessary for that subcommittee to subpena Senator McCarthy?

7. Was Senator McCarthy repeatedly invited to appear?

8. Was it the duty of Senator McCarthy to appear without an order or subpena to appear and was his failure to appear obstructive?

9. Was the request to Senator McCarthy to appear a legal basis for contempt, and was his reply contumacious?

10. Was Senator McCarthy's conduct toward that subcommittee contemptuous, independently of his failure to appear?

11. Did Senator McCarthy "denounce" the subcommittee?

12. Has the conduct of Senator McCarthy been contumacious toward the Senate by failing to explain the six charges contained in the subcommittee's report?

13. Did the reelection of Senator McCarthy in 1952 make these matters moot?

DISCUSSION OF LEGAL QUESTIONS

1. The Senate is a continuing body

The fact that the Senate is a continuing body should require little discussion. This has been uniformly recognized by history, precedent, and authority. While the rule with reference to the House, whose Members are elected all for the period of a single Congress may be different, the Senate is a continuing body, whose Members are elected for a term of 6 years, and so divided into classes that the seats of one-third only become vacant at the end of each Congress. Senate Document No. 99, 83d Congress, 2d session, Congressional Power of Investigation, page 7.

Senate rule XXV (2) provides that each standing committee shall continue and have the power to act until their successors are appointed. That rule was followed in the case of the committee in question. The testimony taken in the hearings of the select committee shows that Senator Hayden, chairman of the Committee on Rules and Administration in the 82d Congress, certified the payroll for that committee for the first month of the 83d Congress.

The continuity of the Senate was questioned at the beginning of the 83d Congress, and the issue was decided in favor of the precedents. Congressional Record, Senate—January 6, 1953, pages 92–114. For further discussion see Senate Document No. 4, 1953, 83d Congress. The rule that the Senate is a continuing body has been recognized by the Supreme Court, in *McGrain* v. *Daugherty* (273 U. S. 135, 182 (1927)), where the Court said:

This being so, and the Senate being a continuing body, the case cannot be said to have become moot in the ordinary sense.

2. The Senate has the power to censure a Senator for conduct occurring during his prior term as Senator

The contention has been made by Senator McCarthy that since he was reelected in 1952 and took his seat for a new term on January 3, 1953, the select committee lacks power to consider any conduct on his part, occurring prior to January 3, 1953, as the basis for censure. His counsel based this contention on several cases cited as authority for this proposition (p. 19 of the hearings), being *Anderson* v. *Dunn* (6 Wheat. 204) ; *Jurney* v. *McCracken* (294 U. S. 125) ; and *U. S.* v. *Bryan* (339 U. S. 323). The argumentative basis for this contention is that the power to censure is part of the power of the Senate to punish for contempt, and that any limitations on the latter power must necessarily limit the power to censure. This contention is without foundation for at least two reasons: (1) The power to censure is an independent power and may be exercised by the Senate for conduct totally unrelated to any act or acts which may be contemptuous; and (2) even assuming that the power to censure is limited to the extent of the power to punish for contempt, the authorities cited do not sustain the proposition advanced.

The case of *Anderson* v. *Dunn* (6 Wheat. 204 (1821)) was an action in trespass for an assault and battery and false imprisonment against the Sergeant at Arms of the House of Representatives. The Supreme Court held that the defendant Sergeant at Arms had a proper and lawful defense by showing that he acted under the orders of the Speaker and had taken the plaintiff into custody for a high contempt of the dignity of the House. The only possible relevancy of the opinion to the matters now pending before the select committee appears in the opinion by Mr. Justice Johnson, at page 231, that the duration of the imprisonment for contempt of the House is limited when the legislative body ceases to exist on the moment of its adjournment, and the imprisonment must terminate with that adjournment. It is clear that this was dictum, applies to the House and not to the Senate, does not involve a case of censure of a Member of the Senate, and was the law only until Congress by statute made contempt of either House a criminal offense.

In the case of *Jurney* v. *MacCracken* (294 U. S. 125 (1935)) the defendant, a lawyer, was arrested by the Sergeant at Arms of the Senate, pursuant to a resolution of the Senate, for contempt in failing to produce and permitting the removal and destruction of certain papers, after they had been subpenaed by the special Senate committee investigating ocean and airmail contracts. The Supreme Court affirmed the dismissal of the defendant's writ of habeas corpus holding that where the offending act was of a nature to obstruct the legislative process, the fact that the obstruction has since been removed or that its removal has become impossible is without significance; that the enactment of Revised Statute 102 did not impair the right of Congress to punish for contempt; and that whether a recalcitrant witness has purged himself of contempt is for Congress to decide and cannot be inquired into by a court by a writ of habeas corpus. It is evident that this case does not deal with any question of censure or punishment of a Member of the Senate. MacCracken did contend that the Senate was absolutely without power itself to impose punishment for a past act, and that such punishment must be inflicted by the courts, as for other crimes, and under the safeguard of all constitutional provisions, but this contention was dismissed by the opinion of the Supreme Court, delivered by Mr. Justice Brandeis, at page 149.

The case of *United States* v. *Bryan* (339 U. S. 323 (1950)) involved a criminal trial for contempt of the House Committee on Un-American Activities, and the refusal of the defendant to produce certain records under subpena from that committee. In the opinion of the

Supreme Court, by Mr. Chief Justice Vinson, mention is made of Revised Statutes, section 102 (2 U. S. C., sec. 192), enacted in 1857.   It is clear that one of the purposes of the act was to permit the imprisonment of a contemnor beyond the expiration of the current session of Congress.   The Supreme Court states unequivocally that the judicial proceedings under the statute are intended as an alternative method of vindicating the authority of Congress to compel the disclosure of facts which are needed in the fulfillment of the legislative function.   The select committee was advised by its counsel that this case has no apparent bearing upon the contention of Senator McCarthy in these proceedings with reference to his failure to appear before the Gillette-Hennings subcommittee.   Counsel further advised that it is inappropriate to cite cases of criminal contempt as the basis for the law of censure by the Senate of one of its Members.

It seems clear that if a Senator should be guilty of reprehensible conduct unconnected with his official duties and position, but which conduct brings the Senate into disrepute, the Senate has the power to censure.   The power to censure must be independent, therefore, of the power to punish for contempt.   A Member may be censured even after he has resigned (2 Hinds' Precedents 1239, 1273, 1275 (1907)).   Precedents in both the Senate and House for expulsion or censure for conduct occurring during a preceding Congress may be found in Hinds (op. cit., 1275 to 1289).   Precedents in the House cannot be considered as controlling because the House is not a continuing body.

In this connection, it must be remembered that the report of the Subcommittee on Privileges and Elections was filed on January 2, 1953, and since the new Congress convened the next day, there was not time for action in the prior session.

While it may be the law that one who is not a Member of the Senate may not be punished for contempt of the Senate at a preceding session, this is no basis for declaring that the Senate may not censure one of its own Members for conduct antedating that session, and no controlling authority or precedent has been cited for such position.

The particular charges against Senator McCarthy, which are the basis of this category, involve his conduct toward an official committee and official committee members of the Senate.

The reelection of Senator McCarthy in 1952 was considered by the select committee as a fact bearing on this proposition.   This reelection is not deemed controlling because only the Senate itself can pass judgment upon conduct which is injurious to its processes, dignity, and official committees.

In the Senate on April 8, 1952 (Congressional Record, Senate, April 8, 1952, p. 3753), at the request of Senator Hayden, there were ordered printed Senate Expulsion, Exclusion, and Censure Cases Unconnected with Elections, 1871–1951.

A résumé of precedents on expulsion, exclusion, and censure cases since the organization of the Committee on Privileges and Elections is printed at page 73 of the Hennings-Hayden-Hendrickson report.   Another collection of Senate precedents appears in the Congressional Record, Senate, August 2, 1954, page 12361, being a study prepared by William R. Tansill, of the Government Division of the Legislative Reference Service of the Library of Congress, printed on motion of Senator Morse. In election cases, the Senate, of course, considers conduct occurring before the commencement of the term of the Senator involved. Senator Morse, in the same day, had printed in the same Congressional Record at page 12371 certain pertinent material from Hinds' Precedents, and at page 12373 certain pertinent material from Cannon's Precedents.

From an examination and study of all available precedents, the select committee is of the opinion that the Senate has the power, under the circumstances of this case, to elect to censure Senator McCarthy for conduct occurring during his prior term in the Senate, should it deem such conduct censurable.

3. It was not necessary for Senate Resolution 187 to be adopted by the Senate

Senate Resolution 187, introduced by Senator Benton on August 6, 1951, was not actually a resolution for the expulsion of Senator McCarthy. In the resolution paragraph, the Committee on Rules and Administration is authorized to make an investigation—

as may be appropriate to enable such committee to determine whether or not it should initiate action with a view toward the expulsion from the United States Senate of the said Senator, Joseph R. McCarthy.

In the regular order of Senate business, after this resolution was introduced, it was referred by the President of the Senate, without a vote by the Senate, to the Committee on Rules and Administration.

The Legislative Reorganization Act of 1946, in section 102, which incorporates rule XXV of the Standing Rules of the Senate, provides that among the standing committees to be appointed at the commencement of each Congress, with leave to report by bill or otherwise, there shall be a Committee on Rules and Administration, to which committee shall be referred all proposed legislation, messages, petitions, memorials, and other matters relating to * * * credentials and qualifications. By section 134-A of the same act, each standing committee of the Senate, including any subcommittee of such committee, is authorized to hold such hearings, to sit and act at such times and places during the sessions and adjourned periods of the Senate, to require by subpena or otherwise the attendance of such witnesses * * * as it deems advisable. It is further provided in the same section that each such committee may make investigations into any matter within its jurisdiction and report such hearings as may be had by it.

As stated by Senator Case (at p. 61 of the hearings) reference is made on page 71 of the Hennings report, being the report of the Subcommittee on Privileges and Elections to the Committee on Rules and Administration pursuant to Senate Resolutions 187 and 304, that investigations with reference to alleged misconduct by a Senator may be undertaken by the Subcommittee on Privileges and Elections with or without specific Senate authorization or direction. That report states at the page indicated:

The old Committee on Privileges and Elections was presented with five cases of expulsion or exclusion unconnected with an election. In three of these cases, those of Smoot, Burton, and Gould, the Senate adopted resolutions directing an investigation of the charges against the respective Senators. In the other two cases, those of La Follette and Langer, the petitions and protests of private citizens were referred by the presiding officer to the Committee on Privileges and Elections, which then conducted investigations without obtaining resolutions of authorization from the Senate.

These precedents indicate that the legal power of the subcommittee to conduct investigations of its own motion is not subject to question; and, also, that the subcommittee may act under a resolution formally adopted by the Senate.

It is the opinion of the select committee, in addition to the conclusion made evident by the foregoing precedents, that the vote of the Senate on April 10, 1952, upon Senate Resolution 300, 82d Congress, 2d session, introduced by Senator Hayden for himself and Senators Gillette, Monroney, Hennings, and Hendrickson, to obtain the sense of the Senate upon the right and power of the Committee on Rules and Administration and its Subcommittee on Privileges and Elections to proceed with the investigation of Senator McCarthy under Senate Resolution 187, and to obtain a vote of confidence from the Senate in the integrity of the committee members, carried all the implications, and was to the same effect, as if the Senate by vote had directed that committee and subcommittee, on August 6, 1951, to proceed with the investigation sought by Senate Resolution 187.

It is, therefore, the opinion of the select committee that it was not necessary for Senate Resolution 187 to have been adopted by the Senate.

4. The Gillette-Hennings Subcommittee on Privileges and Elections was not acting beyond its power or jurisdiction

The action of the Senate upon Senate Resolution 300 must be considered as an affirmance that as of April 10, 1952, when the actions of the Subcommittee on Privileges and Elections and the integrity of its members were ratified and approved by a vote of 60 to 0, the committee and subcommittee were acting within its power and jurisdiction.

The jurisdiction of the Subcommittee on Privileges and Elections was not limited to the conduct of Senator McCarthy connected with elections only but extended to acts totally unconnected with election matters, but which were relevant in inquiries relating to expulsion, exclusion, and censure. The debate in the Senate and the vote of the Senate makes this abundantly clear. (See Congressional Record, Senate, April 8, 1952, pp. 3701, 3753–3756.) One of the principal purposes of the introduction of Senate Resolution 300 was to affirm or deny the contention of Senator McCarthy that the Subcommittee on Privileges and Elections lacked jurisdiction to investigate such acts as were not connected with elections and campaigns. Senate Resolution 187, introduced by Senator Benton, provided for an investigation with reference to the other acts of Senator McCarthy since his election to the Senate (in the fall of 1946), as might be appropriate to carry out the purposes of the resolution. It is clear, therefore, that the subcommittee had the right and power to investigate the acts of Senator McCarthy at least since January 1947. While Senate Resolution 187 did not itself specify any charges against Senator McCarthy, the charges pending upon the Subcommittee on Privileges and Elections were known to Senator McCarthy and were disclosed to him in detail in the correspondence between him and the chairman of the subcommittee. Most of the six charges referred clearly to activities of Senator McCarthy after January 1947. It may be, although this select committee is not in a position to so decide, that some parts of the investigations and proceedings of the Subcommittee on Privileges and Elections were concerned with matters arising before January 1947, but it is the judgment of this select committee that this extension of power and authority did not ipso facto nullify the power and jurisdiction of that subcommittee to proceed with its lawful duties and powers.

It is, therefore, the judgment of the select committee that for purposes of the present inquiry, it can be stated that the Gillette-Hennings Subcommitee on Privileges and Elections was not acting beyond its power and jurisdiction so far as forming a basis for the possible censure of Senator McCarthy by reason of his conduct in relation with and toward that subcommittee.

5. The Gillette-Hennings Subcommittee on Privileges and Elections was a lawfully constituted committee

As shown by the testimony taken in this proceeding, the subcommittee originally had five members. After the resignations of Senators Welker and Gillette, and the reduction of the number of acting members to 3, Senator Hayden, chairman of the Committee on Rules and Administration, the parent committee, decided that it was not necessary to fill the 2 vacancies, and that the work of the subcommittee would be better performed by the smaller number. After that time, Senator Monroney resigned, and Senator Hayden then appointed himself to that vacancy, so that the subcommittee continued with three members.

Senator Hayden testified that there was no rule of the parent committee or subcommittee which was contrary to the procedure adopted in this case, and that the procedure was consonant with the practice both before and after 1952. As a matter of fact, the subcommittee since 1952 has consisted of three members.

With the approval of Senator McCarthy and his counsel, testimony was taken from Charles L. Watkins, the Senate Parliamentarian, upon the status and legality of the Gillette-Hennings subcommittee. This testimony appears on page 535 of the hearings, and may be epitomized as follows:

1. The three-member subcommittee, as constituted by Senator Hayden, after the resignation of Senator Monroney, by appointing himself as the third member, was a legal committee for the discharge of regular business under the rules and precedents of the Senate.

2. There was no mandatory requirement for a chairman to fill a vacancy on a subcommittee.

3. Chairman Hayden of the parent Committee on Rules and Administration had the right to appoint himself a member of the Subcommittee on Privileges and Elections, without submitting the appointment to the Committee on Rules and Administration, for prior approval or subsequent ratification.

4. This was particularly true when the Senate was not in session.

5. Chairman Hayden had the right to recognize Senator Hennings as chairman of the Subcommittee on Privileges and Elections, and had the right to appoint the chairman of the subcommittee.

6. The subcommittee of 3 members had the right to designate 1 member as a legal quorum for the purpose of taking testimony.

7. The subcommittee of 3 members was authorized and had the duty to make a report to the full committee, signed by its 3 members, Senators Hennings, Hayden, and Hendrickson, and file the report with the full Committee on Rules and Administration, with Senator Hayden as chairman.

8. In a quasi-judicial proceeding such as an expulsion matter, although 3 of the original 5 members of the Subcommittee on Privileges and Elections have resigned, although 2 of the vacancies have not been filled, and the chairman of the Committee on Rules and Administration has appointed himself to the third vacancy on the subcommittee, that subcommittee of 3 members had the right to file a valid legal report with the parent committee, when less than half of its original 5 members have heard the evidence.

6. It was not necessary for the subcommittee to subpena Senator McCarthy

A question has been raised in these proceedings whether it was necessary for the Subcommittee on Privileges and Elections to subpena Senator McCarthy to appear before it.

According to his testimony, he had no desire to appear before the subcommittee and advised the chairman that he would not appear before it to answer the charges made against him and pending before that subcommittee, unless he was ordered so to do. The provisions of the Legislative Reorganization Act, above referred to, make it clear that the subcommittee had the power and right to require the attendance of Senator McCarthy for purposes of investigation and examination "by subpena or otherwise." It can be stated, therefore, categorically, that it was not necessary for the subcommittee to issue its subpena for him. Section 134-A of the Legislative Reorganization Act does refer to "requiring" the attendance of witnesses, and the select committee is of the opinion that an invitation to appear, is not such action indicating a requirement to appear as is contemplated by the act. It is the opinion of the select committee that a request to appear, such as the letter and telegram from the subcommittee to Senator McCarthy dated November 21, 1952, was sufficient (aside from any question whether Senator McCarthy received them in time) to meet the requirements of the law. The related questions whether Senator McCarthy was repeatedly invited to appear, and whether he should have appeared even without invitation and without request or subpena, are considered hereinafter.

7. Senator McCarthy was repeatedly invited to appear

The select committee has carefully considered all the letters in evidence between Senator McCarthy and the Subcommittee on Privileges and Elections, and all the testimony relating to his appearance before the subcommittee. The facts relating to whether or not Senator McCarthy was repeatedly invited to appear before that subcommittee in order to make answer to the very serious charges against his character and his activities in the Senate have already been found by the select committee and incorporated hereinabove as finding of fact. This evidence and this testimony, upon analysis, has convinced the select committee that Senator McCarthy was invited by that subcommittee to appear before it in order to aid its investigation and to give answer to the charges made against him and pending before that subcommittee. It must be remembered that Senator McCarthy wrote to Chairman Gillette under date of September 17, 1951, stating that he intended to appear to question witnesses (see finding of fact No. 7). Senator McCarthy was invited to appear before the subcommittee by letter of September 25, 1951 (finding of fact No. 8), by letter of October 1, 1951 (finding of fact No. 10), by letter of December 21, 1951 (finding of fact No. 20), by letter of May 7, 1952 (finding of fact No. 30), by letter of May 10, 1952 (finding of fact No. 33), and by letter of November 7, 1952 (finding of fact No. 35).

8. *It was the duty of Senator McCarthy to accept the repeated invitations by the subcommittee and his failure to appear was obstructive of the processes of the Senate, for no formal order or subpena should be necessary to bring Senators before Senate committees when their own honor and the honor of the Senate are at issue*

The matters against Senator McCarthy under investigation by the Gillette-Hennings subcommittee were of a serious nature. Apparently, Senator McCarthy knew the nature of these matters since he testified:

I know all about this matter: I have been living with it. It had been underway. They had been going far beyond the resolution, investigating things they had no right to investigate; going back beyond the time that I was even old enough to run for Senator, investigating the income-tax returns of my father, who died before I was elected. So I knew those facts (p. 385 of the hearings).

Furthermore, Chairman Gillette specified one of the matters against Senator McCarthy (that of the Lustron payment), in his letter of May 7, 1952, to Senator McCarthy (p. 32 of the hearings), and Chairman Hennings specified all six of the matters in his letter to Senator McCarthy of November 21, 1952 (p. 45 of the hearings).

The mere reading of these matters (p. 46 of the hearings) without deciding or attempting to decide whether they are true or not, makes it clear that the honesty, sincerity, character, and conduct of Senator McCarthy were under inquiry. It is the opinion of the select committee that when the personal honor and official conduct of a Senator of the United States are in question before a duly constituted committee of the Senate, the Senator involved owes a duty to himself, his State, and to the Senate, to appear promptly and cooperate fully when called by a Senate committee charged with the responsibility of inquiry. This must be the rule if the dignity, honor, authority, and powers of the Senate are to be respected and maintained. This duty could not and was not fulfilled by questioning the authority and jurisdiction of the subcommittee, by accusing its members of the dishonest expenditure of public funds, or even by charging that the subcommittee was permitting itself to be used to serve the cause of communism. When persons in high places fail to set and meet high standards, the people lose faith. If our people lose faith, our form of Government cannot long endure.

The appearance which we believe was necessary was before a subcommittee of the Senate itself, to which subcommittee the Senate, through its normal processes, had confided a matter affecting its own honor and integrity. In such a case legal process was not and should not be required.

*9. The request of November 21, 1952, to Senator McCarthy to appear
did not form a legal basis for contempt, but his reply of December
1, 1952, was, in itself, contumacious in character*

As appears from the findings of fact, Senator McCarthy was formally requested to appear by letter and by telegram from Subcommittee Chairman Hennings, dated November 21, 1952. The request was that he appear before the subcommittee between November 22 and November 25, 1952 (p. 46 of the hearings).

Senator McCarthy testified that he was in Wisconsin, on a hunting trip, and that he did not see the letter or telegram until November 28, 1952 (p. 298 of the hearings). The select committee accepts this testimony as true.

Considering this request as a formal request, and Senator McCarthy being unable to appear in the dates fixed because he did not know of the request in time, we believe that this request, considered independently, would not be contempt in the ordinary legal sense, but we think the letter which he wrote in reply to the request was contumacious in its entire form and manner of expression when directed at a committee of the Senate seeking to act upon a matter referred to it (p. 51 of the hearings).

10. The conduct of the junior Senator from Wisconsin toward the Subcommittee on Privileges and Elections was contemptuous, independently of his failure to appear

We have considered carefully all of the correspondence and all the conduct, relation, and attitude of Senator McCarthy toward the Subcommittee on Privileges and Elections. We believe it fair to say on the evidence in this record that the junior Senator from Wisconsin did not intend to appear before that subcommittee for examination.

He first questioned the jurisdiction of the subcommittee to inquire into any but election charges. Later he contended that the subcommittee was investigating conduct preceding his election to the Senate, and that, therefore, its activities were illegal.

He also stated that he would not appear unless he were given the right to cross-examine witnesses. We feel that this right should have been accorded to him and that upon proper request, either to the Committee on Rules and Administration, of which Senator McCarthy was a member (p. 27 of the hearings), or to the Senate itself, he could have obtained this right, but that in any event, this cannot be a justification for contemptuous conduct.

The letters of Senator McCarthy to the respective chairmen of the subcommittee dated December 6, 1951 (p. 24 of the hearings), December 19, 1951 (p. 27 of the hearings), March 21, 1952 (p. 30 of the hearings), May 8, 1952 (p. 32 of the hearings), May 8, 1952 (p. 35 of the hearings), May 11, 1952 (p. 44 of the hearings), and December 1, 1952 (p. 51 of the hearings), are clearly contemptuous, disregarding entirely his duty to cooperate, ridiculing the subcommittee, accusing these committee officers of the Senate with dishonesty and impugning their motives, and making it impossible for them to proceed in orderly fashion, or to complete their duties.

The same attitude was expressed in the statement given to the press by Senator McCarthy on January 2, 1953 (p. 68 of the hearings).

The letters to Senator McCarthy from Chairman Gillette, later from Chairman Hennings, and the letter from Chairman Hayden, were uniformly courteous and cooperative, as one Senator should have the right to expect from colleagues.   There is no justification in this record for the harsh criticisms directed by Senator McCarthy to the subcommittee, in letters apparently sometimes given to the press before receipt by the person to whom directed (p. 27 of the hearings).

It is the opinion of the select committee that this conduct of Senator McCarthy was contemptuous, independently of his failure to appear before the subcommittee.

11. The junior Senator from Wisconsin did "denounce" the Senate Subcommittee on Privileges and Elections without justification

We feel that the fact that Senator McCarthy denounced the Subcommittee on Privileges and Elections is established by reference to a few of the letters in the exchange of correspondence. In his letter of December 6, 1951 (p. 24 of the hearings), to Chairman Gillette, Senator McCarthy states that when the subcommittee, without Senate authorization, is "spending tens of thousands of taxpayers' dollars for the sole purpose of digging up campaign material against McCarthy, then the committee is guilty of stealing just as clearly as though the members engaged in picking the pockets of the taxpayers and turning the loot over to the Democrat National Committee." Such language directed by a Senator toward a committee of the Senate pursuing its authorized functions is clearly intemperate, in bad taste, and unworthy of a Member of this body.

These accusations by Senator McCarthy are continued and repeated in his letter to Chairman Gillette dated December 19, 1951 (p. 27 of the hearings). Under date of March 21, 1952 (p. 30 of the hearings), Senator McCarthy wrote to Senator Hayden, chairman of the parent Committee on Rules and Administration that: "As you know, I wrote Senator Gillette, chairman of the subcommittee, that I consider this a completely dishonest handling of taxpayers' money." Similar language is used in Senator McCarthy's letters down to the last dated December 1, 1952 (p. 51 of the hearing).

If Senator McCarthy had any justification for such denunciation of the subcommittee, he should have presented it at these hearings. His failure so to do leaves his denunciation of officers of the Senate without any foundation in this record.

The members of the subcommittee were Senators representing the people of sovereign States. They were performing official duties of the Senate. Every Senator is understandably jealous of his honor and integrity, but this does not bar inquiry into his conduct, since the Constitution expressly makes the Senate the guardian of its own honor.

It is the opinion of the select committee that these charges of political waste and dishonesty for improper motives were denunciatory and unjustified.

In this connection, attention is directed to the charges referred to this committee relating to words uttered by the junior Senator from Wisconsin about individual Senators.

It has been established, without denial and in fact with confirmation and reiteration, that Senator McCarthy, in reference to the official actions of the junior Senator from New Jersey, Mr. Hendrickson, as a member of the Subcommittee on Privileges and Elections, questioned both his moral courage and his mental ability.

His public statement with reference to Senator Hendrickson was vulgar and insulting. Any Senator has the right to question, criticize, differ from, on condemn an official action of the body of which he is a Member, or of the constituent committees which are working arms of the Senate in proper language. But he has no right to impugn the motives of individual Senators responsible for official action, nor to reflect upon their personal character for what official action they took.

If the rules and procedures were otherwise, no Senator could have freedom of action to perform his assigned committee duties. If a Senator must first give consideration to whether an official action can be wantonly impugned by a colleague, as having been motivated by a lack of the very qualities and capacities every Senator is presumed to have, the processes of the Senate will be destroyed.

12. The conduct of Senator McCarthy has been contumacious toward the Senate by failing to explain three of the questions raised in the subcommittee's report

The report of the subcommittee was filed on January 2, 1953. Since that time Senator McCarthy has given to the Senate, on the Senate floor, an explanation of the Lustron matter only. Of the other 5 matters, mentioned in the November 21, 1952, letter by Chairman Hennings, 3 are of a serious nature, reflecting upon Senator McCarthy's character and integrity, and have not been answered either before the Senate or before any of its committees.

It is our opinion that the failure of Senator McCarthy to explain to the Senate these matters: (1) Whether funds collected to fight communism were diverted to other purposes inuring to his personal advantage; (2) whether certain of his official activities were motivated by self-interest; and (3) whether certain of his activities in senatorial campaigns involved violations of the law; was conduct contumacious toward the Senate and injurious to its effectiveness, dignity, responsibilities, processes, and prestige.

13. The reelection of Senator McCarthy in 1952 did not settle these matters

This question is answered in part by our conclusions that the Senate is a continuing body and has power to censure a Senator for conduct occurring during his prior term as Senator, and in part by the fact that some of the contumacious conduct occurred after his reelection, notably the letter of December 1, 1952. The Senate might have proceeded with this matter in 1953 or earlier in 1954 had the necessary resolution been proposed.

Some of the questions, notably the use for private purposes of funds contributed for fighting communism, were not raised until after the election. The people of Wisconsin could pass only upon what was known to them.

Nor do we believe that the reelection of Senator McCarthy by the people of Wisconsin in the fall of 1952 pardons his conduct toward the Subcommittee on Privileges and Elections. The charge is that Senator McCarthy was guilty of contempt of the Senate or a senatorial committee. Necessarily, this is a matter for the Senate and the Senate alone. The people of Wisconsin can only pass upon issues before them; they cannot forgive an attack by a Senator upon the integrity of the Senate's processes and its committees. That is the business of the Senate.

D. CONCLUSIONS

It is therefore, the conclusion of the select committee that the conduct of the junior Senator from Wisconsin toward the Subcommittee on Privileges and Elections, toward its members, including the statement concerning Senator Hendrickson acting as a member of the subcommittee, and toward the Senate, was contemptuous, contumacious, and denunciatory, without reason or justification, and was obstructive to legislative processes. For this conduct, it is our recommendation that he be censured by the Senate.

II

CATEGORY II. INCIDENTS OF ENCOURAGEMENT OF UNITED STATES EMPLOYEES TO VIOLATE THE LAW AND THEIR OATHS OF OFFICE OR EXECUTIVE ORDERS

A. SUMMARY OF EVIDENCE

The committee, pursuant to the category 2, "Incidents of encouragement of United States employees to violate the law and their oaths of office or Executive orders," received evidence and took testimony regarding:

1. Amendment proposed by Mr. Fulbright to the resolution (S. Res. 301) to censure the Senator from Wisconsin, Mr. McCarthy, viz:

(5) The junior Senator from Wisconsin openly, in a public manner before nationwide television, invited and urged employees of the Government of the United States to violate the law and their oath of office.

2. Amendment proposed by Mr. Morse to the resolution (S. Res. 301) to censure the Senator from Wisconsin, Mr. McCarthy, viz:

(e) Openly invited and incited employees of the Government to violate the law and their oaths of office by urging them to make available information, including classified information, which in the opinion of the employees could be of assistance to the junior Senator from Wisconsin in conducting his investigations, even though the supplying of such information by the employee would be illegal and in violation of Presidential order and contrary to the constitutional rights of the Chief Executive under the separation-of-powers doctrine.

This category involves alleged statements of Senator McCarthy made at and during the hearings before the Special Subcommittee on Investigations for the Committee on Government Operations of the United States Senate pursuant to Senate Resolution 189, and reveals the following specific charges:

1. That Senator McCarthy openly, in a public manner before nationwide television, invited, urged, and incited employees of the Government to violate the law and their oaths of office.
2. That he invited, urged, and incited such employees to give him classified information.
3. That the supplying of such classified information by such employees would be illegal, in violation of Presidential orders and contrary to the constitutional rights of the Chief Executive.

The committee received documentary evidence in the form of excerpts from the printed record of the testimony taken and published by the Special Subcommittee on Investigations for the Committee on Government Operations, oral testimony by Senator McCarthy in his own behalf, and received documentary evidence offered by him from the reports of the Internal Security Subcommittee and the Committee on the Judiciary of the Senate wherein Government workers were invited to supply certain information to congressional committees.

From the aforementioned relevant and competent evidence and testimony so adduced, the select committee regards the following as having been established:

That at the hearings of the Permanent Subcommittee on Investigations for the Committee on Government Operations, following an attempt by Senator McCarthy to question Secretary Stevens about the "2½-page document," and following questioning by certain members of that subcommittee, relative to the legality of his receiving and using the document, the Senator made the replies or statements which are the subject of this category of charges.

At those hearings Senator McCarthy took the position that:

* * * I would like to notify those 2 million Federal employees that I feel it is their duty to give us any information which they have about graft, corruption, communism, treason, and that there is no loyalty to a superior officer which can tower above and beyond their loyalty to their country * * * (hearing record, p. 87).

Again, I want to compliment the individuals who have placed their oaths to defend the country against enemies—and certainly Communists are enemies—above and beyond any Presidential directive * * * (hearing record, p. 87).

* * * I think that the oath which every person in this Government takes, to protect and defend this country against all enemies, foreign and domestic, that oath towers far above any Presidential secrecy directive. And I will continue to receive information such as I received the other day * * * (hearing record, p. 87).

* * * that I have instructed a vast number of these employees that they are dutybound to give me information even though some little bureaucrat has stamped it "secret" to protect himself (hearing record, p. 87).

I don't think any Government employee can deny the people the right to know what the facts are by using a rubber stamp and stamping something "secret" (hearing record, p. 89).

* * * while I am chairman of the committee I will receive all the information I can get about wrongdoing in the executive branch (p. 89 of the hearings).

I think that oath to defend our country against all enemies foreign and domestic, towers above and beyond any loyalty you might have to the head of a bureau or the head of a department (p. 90 of the hearings).

I am an authorized person to receive information in regard to any wrongdoing in the executive branch. When you say "classified documents," Mr. Symington, certainly I am not authorized to receive anything which would divulge the names of, we will say, informants, of Army Intelligence, anything which would in any way compromise their investigative technique, and that sort of thing. * * * (p. 91 of the hearings).

* * * no one can deny us information by stamping something "classified" (p. 92 of the hearings).

Any committee which has jurisdiction over a subject has the right to receive the information. The stamp on the document, I would say, is not controlling * * * (p. 92 of the hearings).

* * * anyone who has evidence of wrongdoing, has not only the right but the duty to bring that evidence to a congressional committee (p. 92 of the hearings).

That the Senator, at the hearings of the select committee, admitted making some of the foregoing statements charged against him (pp. 261–263 of the hearings), and did not deny having made the others.   At these hearings, Senator McCarthy took an affirmative position relative to the following question of Senator Ervin:

Senator, when you made the statement which Mr. de Furia characterized as an invitation to the employees of the executive departments, did you mean to invite those employees to bring to you, as chairman of the investigating sub-committee, information relating to corruption, wrongdoing, communism, or trea-son in Government, even though such employees could find such information only in documents marked "classified" by the department in which such employees were working?

By Senator McCarthy.   Yes (hearing record p. 417).

In addition to the foregoing, which the committee believes to have been established, the select committee received the following addi-tional evidence and testimony:

Senator McCarthy testified in his own behalf that—

* * * I was not asking for general classified information.   I was only asking for evidence of wrongdoing.   I was asking these people to conform with the crimi-nal code which requires they give that evidence (p. 262 of the hearings).

* * * When I invited them to give the chairman of that committee evidence of wrongdoing, I am inviting them not to violate their oath of office but to conform to their oath of office * * *" (pp. 263 and 264 of the hearings).

I confined this information with regard to illegal activities on the part of Federal employees.   It did not include general classified material * * * that as chairman of the Government Operations Committee and the investigation committee, if I did not try to get that information, then I should be subject to censure (p. 265 of the hearings).

* * * I feel very strongly that if someone in the executive knows of wrong-doing, of a crime being committed, and they do not bring it to someone who will act on it they are almost equally guilty * * * and let me emphasize again I am not asking for general classified information; I am merely asking for evidence of wrongdoing.   I maintain that you cannot hide wrongdoing by using a rubber stamp, stamping "Confidential," "Secret," or "Top Secret"—I don't care what classification they stamp upon it—as long as it is evidence of wrongdoing (p. 266 of the hearings).

I am referring here, obviously, to valid information (p. 394 of the hearings).

The Senator contended that the following statutes permitted, even imposed a duty upon, Federal employees to give to him the informa-tion so requested:

Title V, United States Code, section 652 (d) (p. 264 of the hearings).
Title XVIII, United States Code, section 4 (p. 265 of the hearings).
Title XVIII, United States Code, section 798 (p. 395 of the hearings).

Senator McCarthy further stated that the position which he took was not new or unprecedented, but that the Vice President (then Con-gressman), Nixon, took a position much stronger, and the then Senator Hugo Black in 1934 took a similar position to the one presently taken by him (p. 267 of the hearings).   He introduced into the record ex-cerpts from a report of the Committee on the Judiciary, 1951.   "Sub-versive and Illegal Aliens in the United States," wherein the subcom-mittee invited the employees of the Immigration and Naturalization Service to report to the subcommittee laxity in enforcement of immi-gration laws or other matters affecting national security; and also parts of a report of the Internal Security Subcommittee, "Interlock-ing Subversion in Government Departments," wherein Government workers were invited to supply information of subversion to the Fed-eral Bureau of Investigation or the congressional committees (pp. 418 and 419 of the hearings).

B. LEGAL ISSUE INVOLVED

The select committee believes that the charges in this category, and the evidence and testimony thereunder adduced, give rise to the following legal or quasi-legal question:

Whether Senator McCarthy openly invited, incited, and urged employees of the Government of the United States to report to him information coming to their attention without disinction to whether or not contained in a classified document; and thereby to violate (a) their oath of office, (b) the law of the United States, (c) Executive orders and directives.

Senator McCarthy contended at the hearings of the select committee, and by a brief submitted to the committee by his counsel, that he had not requested "classified" information, but only information relating to "graft, corruption, Communist infiltration and espionage" and that such information "could not be insulated from exposure by a rubber stamp." He asserts that by statute (U. S. C., title V, sec. 652 (9)) Federal employees are not precluded from furnishing such information to a Member of Congress; indeed, by virtue of United States Code, title XVIII, section 4, such employees have a duty to give such information. He further contends that as chairman of the Committee on Government Operations, a duty is imposed upon him by the Senate itself to get such information, and that in seeking this information he was doing no more than had been done in the past by other Senators and senatorial committees.

The committee believes that from a reading of the entire section 652 of title V, it will appear that this portion of the Civil Service Act of 1912 does no more than affirm that Federal employees do not lose or forfeit any of their rights merely be virtue of their Federal employment. A study of title XVIII, section 4, by the committee leads it to the conclusion that it applies only to persons possessing actual personal knowledge of the actual commission of a felony, as distinguished from information obtained by reviewing files.

As to the alleged precedents of other Senators and senatorial committees, the committee has taken note of the statements contained in the reports of certain senatorial committees cited by Senator McCarthy, as expressing the official opinion of the members of such committees. The committee was of the opinion that any similar statements of other Senators are expressions of individuals and do not establish senatorial precedent unless confirmed by official action.

The charges contained in this category involve the right of the legislative branch of the Government to investigate the executive branch and to be informed of the operations of that branch. This committee believes that the principles, frequently enunciated by the Senate and its committees, sustaining the right of the Congress to be informed of all pertinent facts with respect to the operations of the executive branch should not be relaxed; and any contrary view is hereby disavowed. These principles certainly embrace information of wrongdoing in the executive branch of a general nonclassified nature, and the right of employees to inform the Congress of the same.

The precedents do show with certitude, however, that the Congress has the constitutional power to investigate activities in the executive branch to determine the advisability of enacting new laws directed to such activities, or to determine whether existing laws directed to such activities are being executed in accordance with the congressional intent. To these ends, the Congress may make investigations into allegedly corrupt or subversive activities in executive agencies or departments. The power to investigate such activities necessarily carries with it the power to receive information relating to such activities.

By the Reorganization Act of 1946, the Congress conferred upon the Senate Committee on Government Operations express authority to study "the operation of Government activities at all levels with a view to determining its economy and efficiency," and also that "Each such (standing) committee may make investigations into any matter within its jurisdiction."

In so doing, Congress delegated, in part, to the Senate Committee on Government Operations its constitutional power to make investigations into alleged corruption or subversion in executive agencies or departments. The Senate Committee on Government Operations elected to exercise this delegated power through its Permanent Subcommittee on Investigations, whose chairman was Senator McCarthy.

The committee is immediately concerned with the conduct of Senator McCarthy rather than with the conduct of employees of the executive branch. The President no doubt has power to safeguard from public dissemination, by Executive order or otherwise, information affecting, for example, the national defense, notwithstanding that the regulations might indirectly interfere with any secret transmission line between the executive employees and any individual Member of the Congress. But the President, we think, cannot (nor do we believe he has sought by any order or directive called to our attention) deny to the Congress, or any duly organized committee or subcommittee thereof, and particularly the Committee on Government Operations of the Senate, any information, even though classified, if it discloses corruption or subversion in the executive branch.

This, we think, is true on the simple basis that the Congress is entitled to receive such information in the exercise of its investigatory power under the Constitution. The Congress, too, is charged with the responsibility for the welfare of the Nation.

What the executive branch may rightfully expect is that the coequal legislative branch, or its authorized committees, will inform the President, or his specially designated subordinate (ultimately the Attorney General) of the request, and that the desired information will be supplied subject to the protectives customarily thrown around classified documents by such committees.

In receiving such information, however, the Congress should refrain from thwarting or impeding the proper efforts of executive agencies, charged with duties incident to discovering, prosecuting, or punishing corruption or subversion in Government, or charged with safeguarding secrets involving the national defense.

However, the committee is equally of the view that the manner of approaching this important aspect of investigation in the light of the peculiar dangers of this hour, must be taken into account. The executive branch is initially peculiarly charged with inquiry into and suppression of insidious infiltrations of subversives into its own departments and agencies; this responsibility is a delicate and necessarily confidential one, because it involves the clearing of loyal personnel as well as the identification and elimination of disloyal em-

ployees. It also involves techniques of investigation which must be
kept secret to be effective.

For this reason, there has been developed, under pressure of necessity, a system by which certain information, involving the national
security, is protected in the executive branch by a machinery of classification, to insure that such information will remain confidential, as
against unauthorized revelation or publication by employees, officers,
or other agents of the executive branch.

If this system, which has expanded during recent years to keep step
with the danger, were to be presented to the Congress as an iron curtain, denying to properly authorized agencies or persons (in which
class the Congress and its committees are to be placed first) any right
of access, a situation would be presented against which this committee
would protest with all its power, as other committees have protested
in the past. This we would regard as a challenge to the coequal
powers of the legislative branch.

If on the other hand the Executive has recognized the prerogatives
of the Congress, and incidentally other agencies of Government, even
in the executive department itself, to be informed of classified material
or information, by orderly and formal application to responsible heads
of departments or to the Presidential office itself, then the committee
believes another problem of orderly constitutional government may
be presented, and that the Senate itself would be the first to respect the
necessary right of the Executive to protect its special functions, so
long as the equally important powers of the legislative branch are not
unduly impeded thereby.

We would be of the view that for the executive department, even
the President himself, to deny to a properly constituted committee or
subcommittee of the Senate or any Senator operating with authority
in the matter, facts involving wrongdoing in any executive department, might well offer a proper ground for challenging such decision,
on the broadest and soundest constitutional grounds. But by the same
token, a failure of the Congress or any Member to adapt itself or himself, to reasonable regulations by the President or his authorized department heads (for example, the Department of Defense or the Federal Bureau of Investigation), with respect to matters involving national security, might readily expose the Congress to an equally sound
criticism.

In this connection, it is apparent that Congress itself, by specific
legislation, has expressed an intent to protect documents relating to
national security, and to prevent unauthorized disclosures of such
information contained therein. At the same time, the executive
branch, by departmental orders and Presidential directives ("not inconsistent with law") has expressed a cooperative attitude, by providing an orderly method of disclosing such information to proper
authorities, including, of course, the Congress, in a reasonable pre-
scribed manner, not harmful to the Nation's interest.

(For a further consideration and discussion of these authorities by
this committee, reference is made to the legal discussion contained in
pt. III, category III–B of this report.)

If the invitation of Senator McCarthy to the Federal employees is
a mere solicitation of general information of wrongdoing, this committee would believe that he was within his senatorial prerogative, as

there appears to be no law or Presidential order prohibiting employees of the Federal Government from giving such information to the Congress or members thereof. Indeed, there is law which affirmatively imposes a duty upon such employees to disclose to proper authorities any actual knowledge of the commission of a felony.

A more difficult legal question is presented if the invitation of the Senator goes beyond general information of wrongdoing, and includes within its scope classified information and documents, such as the 2¼ page document and the information contained therein. The law hereinbefore mentioned and Presidential orders would seem to prevent the receipt or disclosure of such information or documents except through established orderly procedures.

The task of considering the allegations embodied in category II is a perplexing one because of the ambiguity of the statements made by Senator McCarthy as well as because of the difficulty of distinguishing between the constitutional power of the Congress to investigate the executive branch and the constitutional power of the President to withhold information from the Congress.

The statements of Senator McCarthy are susceptible of alternative constructions.

The first construction is that Senator McCarthy merely invited employees of the executive branch to bring to him as chairman of the Senate Committee on Government Operations and as chairman of its Permanent Subcommittee on Investigations, information acquired by them in the ordinary course of their employment having a logical tendency to disclose corrupt or subversive activities in governmental areas.

The second construction is that Senator McCarthy in effect urged employees of the executive branch to ransack confidential files of executive agencies or departments regardless of whether they had lawful access to those files, and bring to him classified documents the confidential retention of which in those files was necessary to enable the executive agencies charged with such duties to discover, prevent, or bring to justice persons guilty of corrupt or subversive activities in governmental areas.

If his statements were susceptible of the second construction alone, Senator McCarthy might well merit the censure of the Senate upon the allegations embodied in category II, for the conduct reflected by the second construction would evince an irresponsibility unworthy of any Senator and particularly of a Senator occupying the chairmanship of the Senate Committee on Government Operations and its Permanent Subcommittee on Investigations.

Since his statements admit of the alternative construction set out above, however, the select committee feels justified in giving Senator McCarthy the benefit of the first or more charitable construction.

In receiving information relating to corruption or subversion in the executive branch under the circumstances delineated in the first construction, that is, without irregular and possibly illegal use of classified documents, the chairman of the Senate Committee on Government Operations and of its Permanent Subcommittee on Investigations would be exercising the investigatory power vested in the Congress by the Constitution. This would be true even though employees of the executive branch should communicate such information to him in disobedience to Presidential orders.

The committee does not overlook the allegation that the statements of Senator McCarthy were tantamount to incitement to employees of the executive branch to violate the provisions of the Espionage Act embraced in 18 United States Code 793 (d) (e), which are couched in this language:

(d) Whoever having lawful possession of * * * any * * * information relating to the national defense which information the possessor has reason to believe could be used to the injury of the United States * * *, willfully communicates * * * the same to any person not entitled to receive it * * * shall be fined not more than $10,000 or imprisoned not more than 10 years, or both.

(e) Whoever having unauthorized possession of * * * any * * * information relating to the national defense which information the possessor has reason to believe could be used to the injury of the United States * * *, willfully communicates * * * the same to any person not entitled to receive it * * * shall be fined not more than $10,000 or imprisoned not more than 10 years, or both.

These statutory provisions do not define who is entitled to receive information relating to the national defense. Moreover, the code leaves to conjecture the question whether the definition embodied in 18 United States Code 798 (b) applies to 18 United States Code 793 (d) (e). Since it is a cardinal rule of statutory construction that statutes defining crimes are to be construed strictly against the Government and it does not appear that the chairman of the Senate Committee on Government Operations and its Permanent Subcommittee on Investigations is a "person not entitled to receive" information relating to the national defense, within the purview of 18 United States Code 793 (d) (e), the select committee is of the opinion that the statements of Senator McCarthy cannot assuredly be deemed, under all the facts before us, to constitute an incitement to employees of the executive branch to violate the provisions of the Espionage Act embraced in 18 United States Code 793 (d, (e).

C. FINDINGS OF THE COMMITTEE

After carefully considering, evaluating, and weighing the evidence and testimony presented at the hearings, and construing the applicable legal principles involved, the select committee is of the opinion—

1. That insofar as Senator McCarthy invited Federal employees to supply him with general information of wrongdoing, not of a classified nature, he was acting within his prerogative as a United States Senator and as head of an investigative arm of the United States Senate, and was not inviting such employees to violate their oath of office, Presidential orders, or any law.

2. That the invitation of Senator McCarthy, made during the hearings before the Special Subcommittee on Investigations of the Committee on Government Operations, and affirmed and reasserted at the hearings before the select committee, is susceptible to the interpretation that it was sufficiently broad by specific language and necessary implication to include information and documents properly classified by executive department heads as containing information affecting the national security.

3. However, the select committee is convinced that the invitation so made, affirmed, and reasserted by Senator McCarthy was motivated by a sense of official duty and not uttered as the fruit of evil design or wrongful intent.

4. That were the invitation as made, affirmed, and reasserted to be acted upon by the Federal employees, as to classified material affecting the national security, the orderly and constitutional functioning of the executive and legislative branches of the Government would be unduly disrupted and impeded, and this select committee warns such employees that such conduct involves the risk of effective penalties.

D. CONCLUSIONS

The select committee feels compelled to conclude that the conduct of Senator McCarthy in inviting Federal employees to supply him with information, without expressly excluding therefrom classified documents, tends to create a disruption of the orderly and constitutional functioning of the executive and legislative branches of the Government, which tends to bring both into disrepute. Such conduct cannot be condoned and is deemed improper.

However, the committee, preferring to give Senator McCarthy the benefit of whatever doubts and uncertainties may have confused the issue in the past, and in recognition of the Senator's responsibilities as chairman of the Committee on Government Operations and its Permanent Subcommittee on Investigations, does not feel justified in proposing his acts in this particular to the Senate as ground for censure.

The committee recommends that the leadership of the Senate endeavor to arrange a meeting of the chairman and the ranking minority members of the standing committees of the Senate with responsible departmental heads in the executive branch of the Government in an effort to clarify the mechanisms for obtaining such restricted information as Senate committees would find helpful in carrying out their duly authorized functions and responsibilities.

III

CATEGORY III. INCIDENTS INVOLVING RECEIPT OR USE OF CONFIDENTIAL OR CLASSIFIED DOCUMENT OR OTHER CONFIDENTIAL INFORMATION FROM EXECUTIVE FILES

A. SUMMARY OF EVIDENCE

The evidence adduced before this committee relating to this charge was evolved from the testimony before the Special Subcommittee on Investigations for the Committee on Government Operations (Mundt committee), together with some testimony taken at hearings of this select committee.

The charge is based upon the specifications contained in amendment (d) proposed by Senator Morse (hearing record, p. 3) and amendment (13) proposed by Senator Flanders (hearing record, p. 6).

The charge or charges inherent in these specifications are—

1. That Senator McCarthy received and used confidential information unlawfully obtained from an executive department classified document, and failed to restore the document.

2. That in so doing he was in possible violation of the Espionage Act.

3. That he offered such information to a Senate subcommittee in the form of a spurious document.

The evidence supporting these charges was in part derived in documentary form from the record of the Mundt subcommittee hearings held in April, May, and June 1954 and in part oral testimony presented before the select committee.

It is the opinion of the select committee that competent, relevant, and material testimony has been submitted before the committee to support the charge that Senator McCarthy, before the Mundt subcommittee, produced what purported to be a copy of a letter from J. Edgar Hoover, Director of the Federal Bureau of Investigation, to Major General Bolling, Assistant Chief of Staff, G2, Army, bearing the typed words "Personal and Confidential via Liaison," asserting it had been in the Army files (hearing records, pp. 95 and 96) and suggesting this was one of a series of letters from the FBI to the Army complaining "about the bad security setup at" the Fort Monmouth Signal Corps Laboratory, and giving information on certain individuals (hearing record, p. 96); that Mr. Hoover, after examining the "letter," which was dated January 26, 1951, declared that the "letter" was not a carbon copy or a copy of any communication prepared or sent by the FBI to General Bolling (hearing record, p. 99) but that "the letter" contained information identical in some respects with that contained in a 15-page interdepartmental memorandum from the FBI to General Bolling of the Army, dated January 26, 1951, marked "Confidential via Liaison"; also that Mr. Hoover had stated that "confidential" was the highest classification that could be put on a document by the FBI (hearing record, p. 110). *It is also established that Senator McCarthy urged that the document, 2¼ pages in length, which he had received from an Army Intelligence officer be made available to the public (hearing record, p. 111).*

It is further established that Attorney General Brownell on May 13, 1954, advised Chairman Mundt by letter that the 2¼-page document was not authentic; that portions of the 2¼-page document which were taken verbatim from the 15-page interdepartmental memorandum are classified "confidential" by law; this means they must not be disclosed "in the best interests of the national security * * *. It would not be in the public interest to declassify the document or any part of it at the present time" (hearing record, p. 116). The Attorney General further stated that "if the 'confidential' classification of the FBI reports and memoranda is not respected, serious and irreparable harm will be done to the FBI" (hearing record, p. 116).

Despite the fact that the Attorney General had ruled that the document was a classified document, Senator McCarthy insisted that all security information had been deleted from it, and a request was made by his attorney as follows:

Mr. WILLIAMS. I want to read it, sir, because there is no security information in it.

The CHAIRMAN. Are you offering it in evidence?

Mr. WILLIAMS. Yes (p. 314 of the hearings).

but Senator McCarthy suggested that the names contained in the document be deleted (p. 326 of the hearings). This committee received the document into the possession of the chairman, without making public the contents (p. 327 of the hearings) upon the advice of the Attorney General that the document was a security document and could not be declassified (p. 327 of the hearings). This committee thereupon ruled that the 2¼-page document is a security document and that the information contained in it should be kept classified (p. 328 of the hearings).

Clifford J. Nelson, of the Internal Security Division of the Department of Justice, testified that in January 1951 the word "confidential" was the only classification officially recognized by the FBI (p. 510 of the hearings); and that there was no regulation requiring any particular way of imprinting the classification designation on the document or paper (p. 511 of the hearings); and that it was not necessary for Government agencies "to go through their files and * * * declassify restricted information" when a new classification order was promulgated (p. 513 of the hearings).

Senator McCarthy's position was that the names contained in the document were not security information (p. 389 of the hearings); he requested that, in accordance with the rule of his committee, the names be deleted if the document be made public, "unless * * * the individual named can appear * * * and answer the charges against him" (p. 389 of the hearings). His position also was that he had presented the document to the Mundt committee in good faith believing it was a copy of a letter in the Army files, it being self-evident that certain information had been deleted (pp. 397 and 417 of the hearings). Finally he insisted that the document and the information contained therein were not classified until Attorney General Brownell "classified it during the McCarthy hearings"; and "that it was not classified from the time I received it until the time that Brownell either classified it or attempted to classify it" (p. 432 of the hearings); "It did not disclose any secrets of our national defense of any kind" (p. 433 of the hearings).

B. LEGAL ISSUES INVOLVED

1. What were the statutes, Executive orders, and directives applicable to the 2¼-page letter or document?

2. Was the 2¼-page letter or document or the information therein classified?

3. Was it proper for Senator McCarthy to attempt to make the 2¼-page letter or document public?

Congress has long recognized the need for providing legislation authorizing the heads of executive departments to make regulations relative to records and papers within their departments. As early as the act of June 22, 1874 (R. S., sec. 161, U. S. C., title 18, sec. 22), the Congress authorized the heads of executive departments to prescribe regulations, not inconsistent with law, controlling the conduct of its officers and clerks, and the custody, use, and preservation of its records and papers.

This early act is cited by the Department of Justice Order No. 3229, filed May 2, 1946 (11 Fed. Reg. 4920, 18 Fed. Reg. 1368), protecting official files, documents, records, and information in the offices of the Department, including the Federal Bureau of Investigation, as "confidential," by providing that "no officer or employee may permit the disclosure or use of the same for any purpose except in the discretion of the Attorney General."

To the same effect, Presidential directive of March 13, 1948, 13 Federal Register 1359, which was apparently in effect in May and June 1953; and the subsequent Executive Order No. 10290 of September 24, 1951, setting up a system of classification "to the extent not inconsistent with law." The regulations promulgated by such order expressly apply only to classified security information, which term is restricted to official information which requires safeguarding in the interest of national security. It restricts the dissemination of classified information outside the executive branch, but authorizes the Attorney General on request to interpret such regulations, in connection with any problem arising thereunder.

Of particular import is the Department of Justice order of April 23, 1948, directed to the "Heads of all Government Departments, Agencies and Commissions" (see testimony of Clifford J. Nelson, of the Department of Justice, hearing record, p. 512) providing as follows:

As you are aware, the Federal Bureau of Investigation from time to time makes available to Government departments, agencies and commissions information gathered by the Federal Bureau of Investigation which is of interest to such departments, agencies or commissions. These reports and communications are confidential. All such reports and communications are the property of the Federal Bureau of Investigation and are subject at all times to its control and to all privileges which the Attorney General has as to the use or disclosure of documents of the Department of Justice. Any department, agency or commission receiving such reports or communications is merely a custodian thereof for the Federal Bureau of Investigation, and the documents or communications are subject to recall at any time.

Neither the reports and communications nor their contents may be disclosed to any outside person or source without specific prior approval of the Attorney General or of the Assistant to the Attorney General or an Assistant Attorney General acting for the Attorney General.

Should any attempt be made, whether by request or subpena or motion for subpena or court order, or otherwise, to obtain access to or disclosure of any such report or communication, either separately or as a part of the files and records of a Government department, agency or commission, and reports and communications involved should be immediately returned to the Federal Bureau of Investigation in order that a decision can be reached by me or by my designated representative in each individual instance as to the action which should be taken.

This order, providing that all reports and communications are confidential and shall remain the property of and in the control of the FBI, was effective in January of 1951.

Executive Order 10501, dated November 5, 1953, also undertakes to safeguard official information in the interest of national defense, and also commits to the Attorney General the interpreting of the regulations in connection with the problems arising out of their administration.

We mention in this connection the Espionage Act of June 25, 1948 (ch. 645, 62 Stat. 736; 18 U. S. C., secs. 793 (d) and (e); also ch. 645, 62 Stat. 736, 18 U. S. C. 792; also 18 U. S. C. sec. 4, ch. 645, 62 Stat. 684; also ch. 645, 62 Stat. 811, amended May 24 1949, ch. 139, sec. 46, 69 Stat. 96, 18 U. S. C. 2387). (a) (1) (2) and (b) (cited in the brief of committee counsel, supplement to the record, p. 545 of hearing record) as showing a legislative intent to protect documents relating to national security, to prevent concealment of felonies; to forbid publications or disclosures not authorized by law by any officer or employee of the United States of information coming to him in the course of his employment or official duty.

These statutes are referred to here as affirmative evidence of congressional cooperation with the Executive, in a common effort to discourage unauthorized disclosures of confidential documents or information relating to the national defense, or obtained in the course of official duties; and to prevent interference with or impairment of the loyalty or discipline of the Armed Forces.

All the cited statutes, Executive orders and directives are applicable to the 2¼-page letter or document.

In determining whether the letter or document was classified or contained classified information, reference must be made to the facts which have been established that the contents of this letter or document were taken from the 15 page interdepartmental memorandum dated January 15, 1951, from the FBI to the Army marked and classified confidential; that the letter or document in some respects contained identical language with that of the 15-page memorandum; and that Senator McCarthy knew in May of 1953 when he acquired the 2¼-page letter or document that it had been in part extracted from a document containing security information and, therefore, a classified document. It must be admitted, and in fact was so admitted by Senator McCarthy's counsel, that the material copied from a classified document retains the same classification as the document from which it is copied (hearing record, p. 753). It follows that the 2¼-page document retains the character of a classified document. While Senator McCarthy contends that the deletion of certain information from the 2¼-page document renders it an unclassified document, this position overlooks the legal necessity that declassification can only be effected by a legally constituted authority. Furthermore, the Attorney General has formally ruled that the document still contains security information. The committee, after examining the document, likewise has agreed that the 2¼-page document contains security information.

Apart from these considerations, the established facts show that Senator McCarthy attempted to make public over nationwide television the contents of a document which he believed emanated from the Federal Bureau of Investigation to the Intelligence Department of the Army regarding possible espionage in a defense installation and which bore a classified or confidential marking. This conduct on his part shows a disregard of the evident purpose to be served by such a document and overlooks the serious import which attaches to a document affecting the national defense, and the dangers flowing from causing such information to become public knowledge. This transgression is nonetheless grave even though the Senator personally may have been, as he contends, of the opinion that the document did not contain security information. This disposition on the part of Senator McCarthy to determine for himself what is or is not security information regardless of the evident classified marking on a document, confirmed by the opinion of a duly constituted agency authorized to make such a ruling, evidences a lack of regard for responsibility to the laws and regulations providing for orderly determination of such matters. This conduct on the part of Senator McCarthy is all the more serious when considered in the light of the act of June 25, 1948 (ch. 645, 62 Stat. 736, title 18, sec. 793 (d) and (e)) which provides that whoever having lawful or unauthorized possession of any document relating to national defense or information relating to the national defense which information the possessor has reason to believe could be used to the injury of the United States, attempts to communicate the same to persons not entitled to receive it, is an offender against the criminal laws of the country.

We believe under the facts and our conception of the law that the 2¼-page document was a legally classified document entitled to the protection and respect legally surrounding such a document, and binding on all civil and military officers of the Government, as well as on all employees of the Government.

Such a conclusion is not inconsistent with the further view that representatives of the legislative branch have a complete legal right to obtain access to such documents by using the methods available to them to get such information by formal request to the classifying agency or to the Attorney General or to the President himself. It is only when such orderly methods are rebuffed that an issue between two coequal branches of the Government can or should develop.

It follows that any attempt to make public the contents or any portion of this 2¼-page document, affecting national security, would be a transgression upon authority. When Senator McCarthy offered to make public this document, which he knew involved information irregularly obtained and which on its face carried a classification of "confidential" by the FBI, it was an assumption of authority which itself is disruptive of orderly governmental processes, violative of accepted comity between the two great branches of our Government, the executive and legislative, and incompatible with the basic tenets of effective democracy.

C. FINDINGS OF THE COMMITTEE

1. During the hearings before the Permanent Subcommittee on Investigations of the Committee on Government Operations, Senator McCarthy, in the course of the development of his defense, offered to make public the contents of a document bearing the markings of the Federal Bureau of Investigation, "Personal and Confidential via Liaison," which contained classified information relating to the national defense. This offer was not accepted by the committee.

2. In offering to make the contents of the document public, Senator McCarthy acted in the bona fide belief that the document was a valid rather than a spurious instrument and offered it in evidence as such.

D. CONCLUSIONS

The committee concludes that in offering to make public the contents of this classified document Senator McCarthy committed grave error. He manifested a high degree of irresponsibility toward the purposes of the statutes and Executive directives prohibiting the disclosure to unauthorized persons of classified information or information relating to the national defense. He should have applied in advance to the Attorney General for express permission to use the document in his defense under adequate safeguards, or to the committee to receive its contents in evidence in an executive rather than an open session. The committee recognizes, however, that at the time in question Senator

McCarthy was under the stress and strain of being tried or investigated by the subcommittee. He offered the document in this investigation, which was then being contested at every step by both sides. The contents of the document were relevant to the subject matter under inquiry, in our opinion.

These mitigating circumstances are such that we do not recommend censure on the specifications included in category III.

It is the opinion of this committee that it will not serve the necessary purposes of this inquiry to make public the 2¼-page document or any part of the contents thereof. If the committee had been of different opinion, the chairman would have been authorized, in light of the opinions of the Attorney General, still adhered to by the latter officer (p. 116 of the hearings), to direct a request to the President for authority to declassify the same. Pending the final action of the Senate in this matter, the committee has directed its chairman to retain physical possession of this document, in confidence. Unless the Senate otherwise directs, it will be surrendered to the Federal Bureau of Investigation for such disposition as shall be proper after the Senate has concluded its consideration of Senate Resolution 301.

IV

Category IV. Incidents Involving Abuses of Colleagues in the Senate

A. GENERAL DISCUSSION AND SUMMARY OF EVIDENCE

Pursuant to the category designated by the select committee, "Incidents Involving Abuses of Colleagues in the Senate," it received evidence and took testimony relating to—

Amendment proposed by Mr. Flanders to the resolution (S. Res. 301) to censure the Senator from Wisconsin, Mr. McCarthy, viz:

(30) He has ridiculed his colleagues in the Senate, defaming them publicly in vulgar and base language (regarding Senator Hendrickson—"a living miracle without brains or guts"; on Flanders—"Senile—I think they should get a man with a net and take him to a good quiet place").

Amendment proposed by Mr. Morse to the resolution (S. Res. 301) to censure the Senator from Wisconsin, Mr. McCarthy, viz:

(b) Unfairly accused his fellow Senators Gillette, Monroney, Hendrickson, Hayden, and Hennings of improper conduct in carrying out their duties as Senators.

The alleged abuses of senatorial colleagues, considered in this category, result from certain oral and written statements of Senator McCarthy directed by him to and about certain fellow Members of the Senate, and center around the following specific charges:

1. That Senator McCarthy publicly ridiculed and defamed Senator Hendrickson in vulgar and base language by calling him " * * * a living miracle without brains or guts."

2. That Senator McCarthy publicly ridiculed and defamed Senator Flanders in vulgar and base language by saying of him, "Senile—I think they should get a man with a net and take him to a good quiet place."

3. That Senator McCarthy unfairly accused Senators Gillette, Monroney, Hendrickson, Hayden, and Hennings of improper conduct in carrying out their senatorial duties.

As relating to this category, the select committee received documentary evidence in the form of correspondence between Senator McCarthy and the Subcommittee on Privileges and Elections, testimony taken before and published by the Permanent Subcommittee on Investigations of the Committee on Government Operations, being part of the Army-McCarthy hearings, the testimony of two reporters, certain other record evidence, and the testimony of Senator McCarthy in his own behalf.

We point out that for convenience, and by reason of related subject matter, the select committee has already considered and disposed of two of the charges contained in this category, being the charge that Senator McCarthy publicly ridiculed and defamed Senator Hendrickson, in vulgar and base language, being No. 1 above-mentioned, and the charge that Senator McCarthy unfairly accused Senators Gillette, Monroney, Hendrickson, Hayden, and Hennings of improper conduct in carrying out their senatorial duties, being No. 3 above-mentioned. These two charges have already been considered and reported upon in this report under I—"Incidents of Contempt of the Senate or a Senatorial Committee." The discussion under this category IV, therefore, will be restricted to the one charge contained in the amendment proposed by Senator Flanders (30), that Senator McCarthy publicly ridiculed and defamed Senator Flanders, in vulgar and base language, by calling him "senile."

The evidence shows that on June 11, 1954, Senator Flanders walked into the Senate caucus room where Senator McCarthy was testifying before a vast television audience in the Army-McCarthy hearings, and unexpectedly gave Senator McCarthy notice of an intended speech attacking Senator McCarthy which he proposed forthwith to deliver on the Senate floor; that shortly thereafter Senator McCarthy was asked by the press to comment on Senator Flanders' intended speech; that Senator McCarthy thereupon made this remark concerning Senator Flanders:

I think they should get a man with a net and take him to a good quiet place;

and that on occasions prior to that time Senator Flanders made provocative speeches in respect to Senator McCarthy on the Senate floor.

B. CONCLUSIONS

The remarks of Senator McCarthy concerning Senator Flanders were highly improper. The committee finds, however, that they were induced by Senator Flanders' conduct in respect to Senator McCarthy in the Senate caucus room, and in delivering provocative speeches concerning Senator McCarthy on the Senate floor. For these reasons, the committee concludes the remarks with reference to Senator Flanders do not constitute a basis for censure.

V

CATEGORY V: INCIDENT RELATING TO RALPH W. ZWICKER, A GENERAL OFFICER OF THE ARMY OF THE UNITED STATES

A. GENERAL DISCUSSION AND SUMMARY OF EVIDENCE

This category refers to the question whether Senator McCarthy should be censured for his treatment of Gen. Ralph W. Zwicker, in connection with General Zwicker's appearance before the Senator as a witness.

The pertinent proposed amendments are that of Senator Fulbright:

(4) Without justification, the junior Senator from Wisconsin impugned the loyalty, patriotism, and character of General Ralph Zwicker;

and that of Senator Morse:

(c) As chairman of a committee, resorted to abusive conduct in his interrogation of Gen. Ralph Zwicker, including a charge that General Zwicker was unfit to wear the uniform, during the appearance of General Zwicker as a witness before the Permanent Subcommittee on Investigations of the Senate Committee on Government Operations on February 18, 1954;

and that of Senator Flanders:

(10) He has attacked, defamed, and besmirched military heroes of the United States, either as witnesses before his committee or under the cloak of immunity of the Senate floor (General Zwicker, General Marshall).

The select committee restricted its hearings to the case of General Zwicker. Its reasons for not inquiring into the case of remarks made against General Marshall appear in part VI of this report.

In his capacity as chairman on the Permanent Subcommittee on Investigations, Senator McCarthy held hearings to determine whether there were espionage activities in the radar laboratory at Fort Monmouth. General Zwicker was summoned as a witness and appeared on February 18, 1954, at a hearing held in New York, N. Y.

The evidence on this phase consisted of the records of both a public and executive hearing, the testimony of William J. Harding, Jr., who was a spectator at the public hearing, the testimony of Senator McCarthy and of General Zwicker, the testimony of Gen. Kirke B. Lawton, and of Capt. William J. Woodward, a medical officer who accompanied General Zwicker to the hearings, and of James M. Juliana and C. George Anastos, of the staff of the Permanent Subcommittee on Investigations.

There is no dispute concerning the reported testimony of General Zwicker and the questions, statements, and comments of Senator McCarthy during the hearings. General Zwicker attended a public hearing, as a spectator, in the morning of February 18, 1954, and testified as a witness at an executive session late that afternoon. There is dispute as to the attitude and truthfulness of General Zwicker, the statements made to and about him by Senator McCarthy at the conclusion of the executive session, and concerning alleged utterances of General Zwicker prior to his testimony.

Gen. Kirke B. Lawton testified to a conversation which he had with General Zwicker at Camp Kilmer sometime before General Zwicker was called as a witness. It was charged that General Lawton was "gagged" by his military superiors, but after General Lawton testified, it became clear that his inability to give details of his conversation with General Zwicker was not the result of any military secrecy order but was the result of his inability to remember any of the details of the conversation. General Lawton testified that General Zwicker gave him the impression of being generally opposed to Senator McCarthy or the Senator's method in investigation. He could not remember any words used by General Zwicker but was permitted to testify to his general impression and conclusion as to the effect of General Zwicker's remarks.

William J. Harding, Jr., who was a spectator at the morning public session of the hearing held by Senator McCarthy in New York on February 18, 1954, testified that he was seated near General Zwicker. In the morning session, General Zwicker also was a spectator. Mr. Harding stated that Senator McCarthy addressed a question to General Zwicker, who was then seated in the audience, and that General Zwicker replied to the question. As General Zwicker seated himself, after replying to the Senator's question, Mr. Harding testified that the general muttered under his breath the letters "S. O. B." with reference to Senator McCarthy.

James M. Juliana and C. George Anastos, members of the staff of the Permanent Subcommittee on Investigations, were called as witnesses by the select committee. Mr. Juliana testified that he saw General Zwicker at Camp Kilmer on February 13, 1954, 5 days before the appearance of General Zwicker as a witness before Senator McCarthy in New York. On February 13, 1954, Mr. Juliana received from General Zwicker a copy of the Army order directing the honorable discharge of Maj. Irving Peress. In the New York hearing, Senator McCarthy tried to establish who was responsible for the advancement of Peress from captain to major, and who was responsible for his separation and discharge from the military service, the latter having occurred after he had claimed the protection of the fifth amendment as to his Communist connections and activities, at a hearing before Senator McCarthy. (The separation order was read into the record at these hearings before the select committee.) Mr. Juliana also testified that his copy of the Peress separation order was produced at the hearing of February 18, 1954, and handed by him either to Senator McCarthy, or to Roy M. Cohn, counsel for the subcommittee.

Under examination by counsel for Senator McCarthy, Mr. Juliana stated that when he talked to General Zwicker, General Zwicker said that he had been in contact with Washington, prior to discharging Major Peress on February 2, 1954, relative to the Peress matter, and that he, Mr. Juliana, had so informed Senator McCarthy prior to February 18, 1954.

C. Georges Anastos testified that he talked with General Zwicker about the Peress case, by telephone on January 22, 1954. General Zwicker gave him the name of Peress, and stated that the file showed there was information that Peress and his wife were or had been Communists, and that in August 1953 Peress had refused to answer a loyalty questionnaire. There was reference made also, according to Mr. Anastos, to an Army effort to get Peress out of the service. This testimony is in contrast with that of General Zwicker that he did not give to Mr. Anastos any information contained in the Peress classified personnel file. The next day, according to Mr. Anastos, General

Zwicker called him voluntarily and told him of the Peress separation order.

Major Peress was examined by Chairman McCarthy on January 30, 1954. He had been promoted on November 2, 1953. He received an honorable discharge on February 2, 1954.

It was the contention of Senator McCarthy that General Zwicker was most arrogant, very irritating, and evasive, that he was untruthful in his testimony, and that he was "covering up" for his superiors. General Zwicker stood upon his testimony and contended that he had been truthful in all respects and as frank as he could be in view of the military restrictions upon his testimony. General Zwicker also contended that Senator McCarthy had full knowledge of General Zwicker's attitude and conduct with reference to the Peress case, and that this made Senator McCarthy's treatment of him unjustified and unwarranted. General Zwicker appeared as a witness at the invitation of the select committee.

B. FINDINGS OF FACT

From the evidence and testimony taken with reference to this fifth category, the select committee finds the following facts:

1. In connection with this incident, Senator McCarthy was acting as chairman of the Senate Committee on Government Operations and chairman of its Permanent Subcommittee on Investigations (pp. 69 and 182 of the hearings).

2. Ralph W. Zwicker is a brigadier general of the Army of the United States, a graduate of West Point Military Academy, and an Army officer since 1927 (p. 80 of the hearings).

3. From July 1953 to August 1954, General Zwicker was the commanding officer at Camp Kilmer, an Army separation center (pp. 70 and 81 of the hearings).

4. Senator McCarthy began looking into the Peress matter in November 1953 (p. 182 of the hearings).

5. In late November or December 1953, General Zwicker had a conversation with Gen. Kirke B. Lawton, and gave General Lawton the impression that he was antagonistic toward Senator McCarthy (p. 438 of the hearings).

6. On January 22, 1954, C. George Anastos, a member of the staff of the Permanent Subcommittee on Investigations, talked to General Zwicker by telephone; the general gave him the name of Peress and made some reference to the latter's Communist connections (p. 519 of the hearings).

7. This information was reported to Roy Cohn and Frank Carr of the subcommittee staff (p. 519 of the hearings).

8. On February 13, 1954, General Zwicker talked to James C. Juliana, another member of the subcommittee's staff, and gave to Mr. Juliana a copy of the Peress separation order (p. 515 of the hearings).

9. This copy was available to Senator McCarthy at the New York hearing of February 18, 1954 (pp. 79, 515, and 516 of the hearings).

10. On the same date, General Zwicker also told Mr. Juliana that he was opposed to giving Peress an honorable discharge and had been in touch with Washington about the matter (p. 517 of the hearings).

11. This was reported by Mr. Juliana to Senator McCarthy some days before February 18, 1954 (pp. 188, 189, 333, and 517 of the hearings).

12. Major Peress was summoned to appear before the permanent subcommittee by request made on January 26, 1954, and appeared on January 30, 1954 (p. 183 of the hearings).

13. Senator McCarthy and General Zwicker met for the first time on February 18, 1954 (p. 330 of the hearings).

14. They had a pleasant social conversation during the lunch intermission (p. 456 of the hearings).

15. There was a public hearing during the morning of February 18, 1954, attended by General Zwicker as a spectator (p. 455 of the hearings).

16. During this morning session, William J. Harding, Jr., testified, after General Zwicker had answered a question of Senator McCarthy, that he heard General Zwicker mutter under his breath, "You S. O. B.," and (turning to his companions) said, "You see. I told you what we'd get" (p. 179 of the hearings).

17. General Zwicker testified he had no recollection of and knew of no reason for making such an utterance (p. 456 of the hearings).

18. Senator McCarthy did not know of the Harding incident when he examined General Zwicker (p. 204 of the hearings).

19. General Zwicker was called as a witness at an executive session before Senator McCarthy, sitting as a subcommittee of one, about 4 : 30 p. m. on February 18, 1954 (pp. 69 and 190 of the hearings).

20. At the beginning of the hearing, under examination by Mr. Cohn, General Zwicker testified that if he were in a position to do so, that he would be glad to tell what steps he took "and others took at Kilmer to take action against Peress a long time before action was finally forced by the committee," and that the information would not reflect unfavorably on General Zwicker or "on a number of other people at Kilmer and the First Army (p. 70 of the hearings).

21. Senator McCarthy then took over the examination of General Zwicker in an effort to bring out that the general's information, if given in evidence, "would reflect unfavorably on some of them, of course" (p. 70 of the hearings).

22. Senator McCarthy then ordered the witness to reply to the question whether somebody kept Peress on, knowing he was a Communist, and General Zwicker responded that he respectfully declined to answer since he was not permitted to do so under the Presidential directive (p. 70 of the hearings).

23. General Zwicker tried unsuccessfully to have this Presidential directive read at the hearing before Senator McCarthy (p. 354 of the hearings).

24. Senator McCarthy stated that he was familiar with the provisions of the Presidential directive (p. 354 of the hearings).

25. The Presidential directive of March 13, 1948, provided:

* * * in order to insure the fair and just disposition of loyalty cases * * * reports rendered by the Federal Bureau of Investigation and other investigative agencies of the executive branch are to be regarded as confidential * * * and files relative to the loyalty of employees * * * shall be maintained in confidence * * *.—HARRY S. TRUMAN.

(P. 457 of the hearings.)

26. Senator McCarthy then asked General Zwicker whether he knew on the day an honorable discharge was signed for Peress that Peress had refused to answer certain questions before the subcommittee, and General Zwicker replied : "No, sir ; not specifically on answer-

ing any questions, I knew he had appeared before your committee" (p. 70 of the hearings).

27. When asked whether he "knew generally that he (Peress) had refused to tell whether he was a Communist," General Zwicker replied: "I don't recall whether he refused to tell whether he was a Communist" (p. 71 of the hearings).

28. General Zwicker testified that he had read the press releases about Peress, and knew that Peress had taken refuge in the fifth amendment, but that he did not know specifically that Peress had refused to answer questions about his Communist activities (p. 71 of the hearings).

29. Senator McCarthy then told the witness: "General, let's try and be truthful. I am going to keep you here as long as you keep hedging and hemming" (p. 71 of the hearings).

30. The following then occurred:

General Zwicker. I am not hedging.

The Chairman. Or hawing.

General Zwicker. I am not hawing, and I don't like to have anyone impugn my honesty, which you just about did.

The Chairman. Either your honesty or your intelligence; I can't help impugning one or the other, when you tell us that a major in your command who was known to you to have been before a Senate committee, and of whom you read the press releases very carefully—to now have you sit here and tell us that you did not know whether he refused to answer questions about Communist activities. I had seen all the press releases, and they all dealt with that. So when you do that, General, if you will pardon me, I cannot help but question either your honesty or your intelligence, one or the other. I want to be frank with you on that.

Now, is it your testimony now that at the time you read the stories about Major Peress, that you did not know that he had refused to answer questions before this committee about his Communist activities?

General Zwicker. I am sure I had that impression.

The Chairman. Were you aware that the major was being given an honorable discharge * * *.

The Chairman. Did you also read the stories about my letter to Secretary of the Army Stevens in which I requested or, rather, suggested that this man be court-martialed, and that anyone that protected him or covered up for him be court-martialed?

General Zwicker. Yes, sir. (Pp. 71 and 72 of the hearings.)

31. As to the Peress discharge, General Zwicker testified:

The Chairman. Who ordered his discharge?

General Zwicker. The Department of the Army.

The Chairman. Who in the Department?

General Zwicker. That I can't answer.

Mr. Cohn. That isn't a security matter?

General Zwicker. No. I don't know. Excuse me.

Mr. Cohn. Who did you talk to? You talked to somebody?

General Zwicker. No; I did not.

Mr. Cohn. How did you know he should be discharged?

General Zwicker. You also have a copy of this. I don't know why you asked me for it. This is the order under which he was discharged, a copy of that order.

And also:

The Chairman. Did you take any steps to have him retained until the Secretary of the Army could decide whether he should be court-martialed?

General Zwicker. No, sir.

The Chairman. Did it occur to you that you should?

General Zwicker. No, sir.

The Chairman. Could you have taken such steps?

General Zwicker. No, sir.

The Chairman. In other words, there is nothing you could have done; is that your statement?

General Zwicker. That is my opinion (p. 72 of the hearings).

32. The Peress discharge order was dated January 18, 1954, was received by General Zwicker on January 23, 1954, and provided:

a. That Peress be relieved from active duty and honorably discharged.
b. That this be at the desire of Peress "but in any event not later than 90 days from date of receipt of this letter" (p. 454 of the hearings).

33. Major Peress asked for his discharge on February 1, 1954, and he was discharged the next day (p. 483 of the hearings).

34. Senator McCarthy had read the Peress discharge order, and knew about it on February 2, 1954 (pp. 199 and 333 of the hearings).

35. Senator McCarthy then examined General Zwicker as follows:

The CHAIRMAN. Let me ask this question. If this man, after the order came up, after the order of the 18th came up, prior to his getting an honorable discharge, were guilty of some crime—let us say that he held up a bank or stole an automobile—and you heard of that the day before—let's say you heard of it the same day that you heard of my letter—could you then have taken steps to prevent his discharge, or would he have automatically been discharged?

General ZWICKER. I would have definitely taken steps to prevent discharge.

The CHAIRMAN. In other words, if you found that he was guilty of improper conduct, conduct unbecoming an officer, we will say, then you would not have allowed the honorable discharge to go through, would you?

General ZWICKER. If it were outside the directive of this order?

The CHAIRMAN. Well, yes; let's say it were outside the directive.

General ZWICKER. Then I certainly would never have discharged him until that part of the case——

The CHAIRMAN. Let us say he went out and stole $50 the night before.

General ZWICKER. He wouldn't have been discharged.

The CHAIRMAN. Do you think stealing $50 is more serious than being a traitor to the country as part of the Communist conspiracy?

General ZWICKER. That, sir, was not my decision.

The CHAIRMAN. You said if you learned that he stole $50, you would have prevented his discharge. You did learn something much more serious than that. You learned that he had refused to tell whether he was a Communist. You learned that the chairman of a Senate committee suggested that he be court-martialed. And you say if he had stolen $50 he would not have gotten the honorable discharge. But merely being a part of the Communist conspiracy, and the chairman of the committee asking that he be court-martialed, would not give you grounds for holding up his discharge. Is that correct?

General ZWICKER. Under the terms of this letter, that is correct, Mr. Chairman.

The CHAIRMAN. That letter says nothing about stealing $50, and it does not say anything about being a Communist. It does not say anything about his appearance before our committee. He appeared before our committee after that order was made out.

Do you think you sound a bit ridiculous, General, when you say that for $50, you would prevent his being discharged, but for being a part of the conspiracy to destroy this country you could not prevent his discharge?

General ZWICKER. I did not say that, sir.

The CHAIRMAN. Let's go over that. You did say if you found out he stole $50 the night before, he would not have gotten an honorable discharge the next morning?

General ZWICKER. That is correct.

The CHAIRMAN. You did learn, did you not, from the newspaper reports, that this man was part of the Communist conspiracy, or at least that there was strong evidence that he was. Didn't you think that was more serious than the theft of $50?

General ZWICKER. He has never been tried for that, sir, and there was evidence, Mr. Chairman——

The CHAIRMAN. Don't you give me that doubletalk. The $50 case, that he had stolen the night before, he has not been tried for that.

General ZWICKER. That is correct. He didn't steal it yet.

The CHAIRMAN. Would you wait until he was tried for stealing the $50 before you prevented his honorable discharge?

General ZWICKER. Either tried or exonerated.

The CHAIRMAN. You would hold up the discharge until he was tried or exonerated?

General ZWICKER. For stealing the $50; yes.

The CHAIRMAN. But if you heard that this man was a traitor—in other words, instead of hearing that he had stolen $50 from the corner store, let's say you heard that he was a traitor, he belonged to the Communist conspiracy; that a Senate committee had the sworn testimony to that effect. Then would you hold up his discharge until he was either exonerated or tried?

General ZWICKER. I am not going to answer that question, I don't believe, the way you want it, sir.

The CHAIRMAN. I just want you to tell me the truth.

General ZWICKER. On all of the evidence or anything that had been presented to me as Commanding General of Camp Kilmer, I had no authority to retain him in the service.

And also:

The CHAIRMAN. You say that if you had heard that he had stolen $50, then you could order him retained. But when you heard that he was part of the Communist conspiracy, that subsequent to the time the orders were issued a Senate committee took the evidence under oath that he was part of the conspiracy, you say that would not allow you to hold up his discharge?

General ZWICKER. I was never officially informed by anyone that he was part of the Commmunist conspiracy, Mr. Senator.

The CHAIRMAN. Well, let's see now. You say that you were never officially informed?

General ZWICKER. No.

The CHAIRMAN. If you heard that he had stolen $50 from someone down the street, if you did not hear it officially, then could you hold up his discharge? Or is there some peculiar way you must hear it?

General ZWICKER. I believe so, yes, sir, until I was satisfied that he had or hadn't, one way or the other.

The CHAIRMAN. You would not need any official notification so far as the 50 bucks is concerned?

General ZWICKER. Yes.

The CHAIRMAN. But you say insofar as the Communist conspiracy is concerned, you need an official notification?

General ZWICKER. Yes, sir; because I was acting on an official order, having precedence over that.

The CHAIRMAN. How about the $50? If one of your men came in a half hour before he got his honorable discharge and said, "General, I just heard downtown from a police officer that this man broke into a store last night and stole $50," you would not give him an honorable discharge until you had checked the case and found out whether that was true or not; would you?

General ZWICKER. I would expect the authorities from downtown to inform me of that or, let's say, someone in a position to suspect that he did it.

The CHAIRMAN. Let's say one of the trusted privates in your command came in to you and said, "General, I was just downtown and I have evidence that Major Peress broke into a store and stole $50." You wouldn't discharge him until you had checked the facts, seen whether or not the private was telling the truth and seen whether or not he had stolen the $50?

General ZWICKER. No; I don't believe I would. I would make a check, certainly, to check the story (pp. 73–74 of the hearings).

36. The examination then proceeded on a further hypothetical basis as follows:

The CHAIRMAN. Do you think, General, that anyone who is responsible for giving an honorable discharge to a man who has been named under oath as a member of the Communist conspiracy should himself be removed from the military?

General ZWICKER. You are speaking of generalities now, and not on specifics— is that right, sir, not mentioning about any one particular person?

The CHAIRMAN. That is right.

General ZWICKER. I have no brief for that kind of person, and if there exists or has existed something in the system that permits that, I say that that is wrong.

The CHAIRMAN. I am not talking about the system. I am asking you this question, General, a very simple question: Let's assume that John Jones, who is a major in the United States Army——

General ZWICKER. A what, sir?

The CHAIRMAN. Let's assume that John Jones is a major in the United States Army. Let's assume that there is sworn testimony to the effect that he is part of the Communist conspiracy, has attended Communist leadership schools. Let's assume that Maj. John Jones is under oath before a committee and says, "I cannot tell you the truth about these charges because, if I did, I fear that might tend to incriminate me." Then let's say that General Smith was responsible for this man receiving an honorable discharge, knowing these facts. Do you think that General Smith should be removed from the military, or do you think he should be kept on in it?

General ZWICKER. He should be by all means kept if he were acting under competent orders to separate that man.

The CHAIRMAN. Let us say he is the man who signed the orders. Let us say General Smith is the man who originated the order.

General ZWICKER. Originated the order directing his separation?

The CHAIRMAN. Directing his honorable discharge.

General ZWICKER. Well, that is pretty hypothetical.

The CHAIRMAN. It is pretty real, General.

General ZWICKER. Sir, on one point; yes. I mean, on an individual; yes. But you know that there are thousands and thousands of people being separated daily from our Army.

The CHAIRMAN. General, you understand my question——

General ZWICKER. Maybe not.

The CHAIRMAN. And you are going to answer it.

General ZWICKER. Repeat it.

The CHAIRMAN. The reporter will repeat it.

(The question referred to was read by the reporter.)

General ZWICKER. That is not a question for me to decide, Senator.

The CHAIRMAN. You are ordered to answer it, General. You are an employee of the people.

General ZWICKER. Yes, sir.

The CHAIRMAN. You have a rather important job. I want to know how you feel about getting rid of Communists.

General ZWICKER. I am all for it.

The CHAIRMAN. All right. You will answer that question, unless you take the fifth amendment. I do not care how long we stay here, you are going to answer it.

General ZWICKER. Do you mean how I feel toward Communists?

The CHAIRMAN. I mean exactly what I asked you, General; nothing else. And anyone with the brains of a 5-year-old child can understand that question.

The reporter will read it to you as often as you need to hear it so that you can answer it, and then you will answer it.

General ZWICKER. Start it over, please.

(The question was reread by the reporter.)

General ZWICKER. I do not think he should be removed from the military.

The CHAIRMAN. Then, General, you should be removed from any command. Any man who has been given the honor of being promoted to general and who says "I will protect another general who protected Communists," is not fit to wear that uniform, General. I think it is a tremendous disgrace to the Army to have this sort of thing given to the public. I intend to give it to them. I have a duty to do that. I intend to repeat to the press exactly what you said. So you know that. You will be back here, General (pp. 75 and 76 of the hearings).

37. At page 77 of the hearings, the following occurred:

The CHAIRMAN. Did you at any time ever object to this man being honorably discharged?

General ZWICKER. I respectfully decline to answer that, sir.

The CœAIRMAN. You will be ordered to answer it.

General ZWICKER. That is on the grounds of this Executive order.

The CHAIRMAN. You are ordered to answer. That is a personnel matter.

General ZWICKER. I shall still respectfully decline to answer it.

The CHAIRMAN. Did you ever take any steps which would have aided him in continuing in the military after you knew that he was a Communist?

General ZWICKER. That would have aided him in continuing, sir?

The CHAIRMAN. Yes.

General ZWICKER. No.

The CHAIRMAN. Did you ever do anything instrumental in his obtaining his promotion after knowing that he was a fifth-amendment case?

General ZWICKER. No, sir.

The CHAIRMAN. Did you ever object to his being promoted?

General ZWICKER. I had no opportunity to, sir.

The CHAIRMAN. Did you ever enter any objection to the promotion of this man under your command?

General ZWICKER. I have no opportunity to do that.

The CHAIRMAN. You say you did not; is that correct?

General ZWICKER. That is correct.

The CHAIRMAN. And you refuse to tell us whether you objected to his obtaining an honorable discharge?

General ZWICKER. I don't believe that is quite the way the question was phrased before.

The CHAIRMAN. Well, answer it again, then.

General ZWICKER. I respectfully request that I not answer that question.

The CHAIRMAN. You will be ordered to answer.

General ZWICKER. Under the same authority as cited before, I cannot answer it.

38. At the hearings before the select committee, Senator McCarthy testified that General Zwicker was evasive (p. 193 of the hearings), that he changed his story (p. 192 of the hearings), that he was difficult to examine (p. 192 of the hearings), that it was "a long, laborious truth-pulling job," and that he was "most arrogant" (pp. 193 and 204 of the hearings).

39. As stated by the chairman and other members of the select committee, these were matters of argument (p. 195 of the hearings).

40. The transcript of the New York hearing shows that Senator McCarthy said to General Zwicker: "Then, General, you should be removed from any command. Any man who has been given the honor of being promoted to general and who says, 'I will protect another general who protected Communists', is not fit to wear that uniform, General," and Senator McCarthy testified he was referring to the uniform of a general (pp. 202 and 332 of the hearings).

41. General Zwicker did not make any such statement.

42. Senator McCarthy testified that General Zwicker had said in effect: "It is all right to give Communists honorable discharges" (p. 202 of the hearings).

43. There is no testimony in this record which justifies such a conclusion.

44. When asked to give the facts on which he based his testimony that General Zwicker was an unwilling witness, arrogant and evasive, Senator McCarthy reiterated his conclusion that: "All I can say is the full attitude was one of complete arrogance, complete contempt of the committee" (p. 204 of the hearings).

45. Senator McCarthy testified that he was justified in his treatment of General Zwicker solely by the latter's conduct at the hearing in New York (p. 330 of the hearings).

46. He testified further that he had not criticized General Zwicker and it was: "just a method of cross-examination, trying to get the truth" (p. 331 of the hearings).

47. Senator McCarthy refused to draw any inference but that General Zwicker was not telling the truth (specifically excluding perjury, p. 337 of the hearings), as follows:

Mr. DE FURIA. Now, assuming, Senator, that for the sake of this question, anyhow, that General Zwicker did testify in what we might call a stilted fashion, don't you think that the fair inference, rather than to say that the general was deliberately telling an untruth, or stalling, or distorting facts, that the fair, judicious inference was that he couldn't do very much else in the face of the Presidential orders and the other orders of his superiors; isn't that the fair way to look at it, Senator?

Senator McCarthy. No, Mr. de Furia. When a general comes before me first says, "I didn't know this man refused to answer any questions," then after he is pressed under cross-examination. he says, "Yes, I knew he refused to answer questions. but I didn't know he refused to answer questions about Communist activities"—then, after further cross-examination, he says, "Yes, I know that he refused to answer questions about Communist activities"—I can't assume that is the result of any Presidential directive. We cannot blame the President for that.

48. Before examining General Zwicker, Senator McCarthy knew that General Zwicker was opposed to giving Peress an honorable discharge (p. 342 of the hearings) and Senator McCarthy had received a long letter from the Secretary of the Army giving a full explanation of the Peress case (pp. 459 and 462 of the hearings):

49. Senator McCarthy contended at the hearings before the select committee that matters in the Peress personnel file could be revealed by General Zwicker (p. 344 of the hearings) and that General Zwicker was not relying on any Presidential order (p. 344 of the hearings).

50. Later, Senator McCarthy testified that General Zwicker was relying on Presidential and Executive orders, and that he, Senator McCarthy, had copies of them (pp. 347 and 354 of the hearings)ₛ

51. Immediately after General Zwicker had testified in New York, Senator McCarthy gave to the press his version of what had occurred at the executive hearing (p. 348 of the hearings).

52. Senator McCarthy could not recall whether he told the press that the Zwicker hearing had been held principally for the benefit of Secretary of the Army Stevens, did not think so, was reasonably certain he had not said so (p. 348 of the hearings).

53. On his right to reveal to the press what had been testified to at the Zwicker executive hearing, Senator McCarthy testified:

Mr. de Furia. Senator, were you authorized by either the major committee or your Subcommittee on Permanent Investigations to reveal what transpired at the Zwicker executive hearing?

Senator McCarthy. I discussed the matter with the representatives of the two Senators who were present and we agreed, in view of the Stevens' statement, it should be released.

Mr. de Furia. You say you discussed it with the representatives of the two Senators?

Senator McCarthy. That is correct.

Mr. de Furia. In spite of the rules of your own committee that all testimony taken in executive session shall be kept secret and will not be released or used in public session without the approval of the majority of the subcommittee?

Senator McCarthy. I felt that the two men who were present were representing the Senators and they constituted a majority. There were only four Senators on the committee at that time.

Mr. de Furia. In a matter involving a general of the United States, then, you permitted an administrative assistant to exercise the prerogatives of the United States Senate?

Senator McCarthy. I think I have recited the facts to you (pp. 349 and 350 of the hearings).

And also:

Senator McCarthy. May I say further, Mr. de Furia, in answer to your question, that General Zwicker had already released a distorted version of the testimony, through Bob Stevens, in affidavit form. I felt under the circumstances that the correct version should be released.

Mr. de Furia. Why, Senator, you released this first 2 or 3 minutes after your hearing concluded, did you not?

Senator McCarthy. No; I did not. It was the transcript.

Mr. de Furia. You called in the press, did you not, right away?

Senator McCarthy. I did not.

Mr. de Furia. To tell them what had happened in the executive session?

Senator McCarthy. Mr. de Furia, if you want to know what the practice was here, and what the practice is——

Mr. de Furia. I do not want the practice.

Senator McCarthy. I did not release the transcript.

Mr. de Furia. I am not talking about the transcript. But you did tell the press what happened in the closed executive session, within a few minutes after that session ended?

Senator McCarthy. I gave them a résumé of the testimony; yes.

Mr. de Furia. Sir, I am asking you, upon what authority, or by what right, you did that?

Senator McCarthy. Because that has been our practice.

Mr. de Furia. In spite of the rule of your own committee?

Senator McCarthy. That has been the practice of the committee.

Mr. de Furia. General Zwicker's affidavit was not made until 2 days later; isn't that right, Senator? It is dated February 20.

Senator McCarthy. I don't know what date it is dated, but the transcript was not released until after the distorted version of the testimony given by Zwicker.

Mr. Williams. Do you have the rule, there, Mr. de Furia?

Mr. de Furia. Yes, I have the rule, and I would like to have it in evidence, if the chairman please.

The Chairman. It will be received (p. 350 of the hearings).

54. The rules of the Senate Committee on Government Operations, adopted January 14, 1953, provided:

6. All testimony taken in executive session shall be kept secret and will not be released or used in public session without the approval of a majority of the subcommittee (p. 352 of the hearings).

55. At that time the subcommittee consisted of seven members (p. 353 of the hearings).

56. During the executive session, Senator McCarthy said with reference to General Zwicker: "This is the first fifth-amendment general we've had before us" (p. 451 of the hearings).

57. After the executive session, Senator McCarthy said to General Zwicker:

General, you will be back on Tuesday, and at that time I am going to put you on display and let the American public see what kind of officers we have (p. 451 of the hearings).

58. The facts concerning Peress' Communist connections were known to General Zwicker's superior officers when he was directed to discharge Peress (p. 492 of the hearings).

59. General Zwicker was not responsible in any way for promoting or discharging Peress and was very much opposed to both (pp. 505 and 506 of the hearings).

60. Major Peress was not in a sensitive position so far as intelligence, or classified information or material was concerned (p. 505 of the hearings).

C. LEGAL QUESTIONS INVOLVED IN THIS CATEGORY

The legal questions arising with reference to the incident relating to General Zwicker may be stated briefly as follows:

1. Is there any evidence that General Zwicker was not telling the truth in testifying before Chairman McCarthy?

2. Is there any evidence that General Zwicker was intentionally irritating or evasive or arrogant?

3. What is the law governing the treatment of witnesses before congressional committees?

4. Was the conduct of Senator McCarthy toward General Zwicker proper under the circumstances?

1. There is no evidence that General Zwicker was not telling the truth in testifying before Chairman McCarthy

We have analyzed carefully the testimony of General Zwicker, of Senator McCarthy, and of the other witnesses relating to this question. We have concluded that General Zwicker, when he appeared as a witness before Senator McCarthy, on February 18, 1954, was a truthful witness. We feel that it was evident that his examination was unfair, and that General Zwicker testified as fully and frankly as he could do, in view of the Presidential and Army directives which restricted his freedom of expression. These directives were known to his examiners, and however much they may have been out of sympathy with the directives, the fact remains that this was no excuse for berating General Zwicker and holding him up to public ridicule.

General Zwicker testified before the select committee. He underwent a vigorous and taxing cross-examination from Senator McCarthy's counsel. A reading of his testimony and examination makes it clear that in no material respect was it necessary for General Zwicker to modify or change his testimony from that given on February 18, 1954, and that the double exposure of his evidence under searching examination revealed no distortion of fact or untruth.

2. There is no evidence that General Zwicker was intentionally irritating, evasive, or arrogant

General Zwicker was initially examined at the New York hearing by Mr. Cohn, counsel for the subcommittee. It is evident that this examination was mutually courteous and satisfactory. Mr. Juliana and Mr. Anastos, of the staff of the subcommittee, both found General Zwicker to be cooperative and helpful. Even in his examination by Senator McCarthy, the record shows that the general was courteous and respectful throughout the hearing. We find in the record no single instance which supports the conclusion that he was intentionally irritating. Some questions General Zwicker refused to answer and in his answers to some of the questions, apparently, he meticulously sought to avoid the disclosure of material or information in the classified personnel file of Peress, or involving intra-Army discussions and policies, which he was under orders not to reveal. It should not have been difficult to meet this situation in a fair and reasonable way. Senator McCarthy said he was familiar with the Presidential order and the Army directives. A few moments could have been taken to analyze them, and so frame the questions propounded to the witness as to avoid any difficulty. The insistence that the witness answer long hypothetical questions and questions that are not clear even upon careful inspection and reflection, was much more the source of any resulting irritation on the part of the examiner than any conduct on the part of the witness.

Moreover, when he was before this committee, General Zwicker was subjected to a long and vigorous cross-examination and manifested great patience and candor and a complete lack of any tendency toward arrogance or irritability.

3. The law governing the treatment of witnesses before congressional committees

The law and precedent on this subject has been stated many times. Senate Document No. 99, 83d Congress, 2d session, 1954, on Congressional Power of Investigation gives an excellent summary of the law and procedure. Pertinent articles in current legal literature on the subject may be found in American Bar Association Journal, September 1954 at page 763, The Investigating Power of Congress: Its Scope and Limitations; Ohio Bar, August 9, 1954, at page 607, A Comparison of Congressional Investigative Procedures and Judicial Procedures With Reference to the Examination of Witnesses; and Federal Bar Journal, April–June 1954, page 113, Executive Privilege and the Release of Military Records. These articles are mentioned only as source material and do not necessarily express or contain the views of the select committee.

There are no statutes and few court decisions bearing on the subject (Dimock, Congressional Investigation Committees, p. 153 (1929)). There are few safeguards for the protection of the witness. His treatment usually depends and must depend upon the skill and attitude of the chairman and the members. Since an investigation by a committee is not a trial, the committee is under no compulsion to make the hearing public.

We call attention to three cases in the Federal courts discussing this subject. *Barksy* v. *United States* (167 F. (2d) 241 (1948)) was a prosecution for failure to produce records before a congressional committee pursuant to subpena. The court stated at page 250:

(14–17) Appellants press upon us representations as to the conduct of the Congressional committee, critical of its behavior in various respects. Eminent persons have stated similar views. But such matters are not for the courts. We so held in *Townsend* v. *United States*, citing *Hearst* v. *Black*. The remedy for unseemly conduct, if any, by the Committees of Congress is for Congress, or for the people; it is political and not judicial. "It must be remembered that legislatures are ultimate guardians of the liberties and welfare of the people in quite as great a degree as the courts." The courts have no authority to speak or act upon the conduct by the legislative branch of its own business, so long as the bounds of power and pertinency are not exceeded, and the mere possibility that the power of inquiry may be abused "affords no ground for denying the power." The question presented by these contentions must be viewed in the light of the established rule of absolute immunity of governmental officials, Congressional and administrative, from liability for damage done by their acts or speech, even though knowingly false or wrong. The basis of so drastic and rigid a rule is the overbalancing of the individual hurt by the public necessity for untrammeled freedom of legislative and administrative activity, within the respective powers of the legislature and the executive.

In *Townsend* v. *U. S.* (95 F. (2d) 352 (1938)), the defendant was convicted of failure to appear before a congressional committee. In affirming the conviction, the court said at page 361:

(14–17) A legislative inquiry may be as broad, as searching, and as exhaustive as is necessary to make effective the constitutional powers of Congress. *McGrain* v. *Daugherty* (273 U. S. 135, 47 S. Ct. 319, 71 L. Ed. 580, 50 A. L. R. 1). A judicial inquiry relates to a case, and the evidence to be admissible must be measured by the narrow limits of the pleadings. A legislative inquiry anticipates all possible cases which may arise thereunder and the evidence admissible must be responsive to the scope of the inquiry, which generally is very broad. Many a witness in a judicial inquiry has, no doubt, been embarrassed and irritated by questions which to him seemed incompetent, irrelevant, immaterial, and impertinent. But that is not a matter for a witness finally to decide. Because a witness could not understand the purpose of cross-examination, he would not be justified in leaving a courtroom. The orderly processes of judicial determination do not permit the exercise of such discretion by a witness. The orderly processes of legislative inquiry require that the Committee shall determine such questions for itself. Within the realm of legislative discretion, the exercise of good taste and good judgment in the examination of witnesses must be entrusted to those who have been vested with authority to conduct such investigations. *Hearst* v. *Black*, 66 App. D. C. 313, 87 F. 2d 68.

Under these authorities, the Senate alone can review this record and determine, in justice to itself and to General Zwicker, whether the bounds of propriety, consonant with the lawful purpose of the subcommittee's investigation and fair and reasonable standards of senatorial conduct, were transgressed by Senator McCarthy in his examination of the general at New York on February 18, 1954, and later in his testimony before this committee.

The select committee is of the opinion that the very fact that "the exercise of good taste and good judgment" must be entrusted to those who conduct such investigations places upon them the responsibility of upholding the honor of the Senate. If they do not maintain high standards of fair and respectful treatment the dishonor is shared by the entire Senate.

4. The conduct of Senator McCarthy toward General Zwicker was not proper under the circumstances

In the opinion of this select committee, the conduct of Senator McCarthy toward General Zwicker was not proper. We do not think that this conduct would have been proper in the case of any witness, whether a general or a private citizen, testifying in a similar situation.

Senator McCarthy knew before he called General Zwicker to the stand that the Judge Advocate General of the Army, who was the responsible person under the statutes, had given the opinion that a court-martial of Major Peress would not stand under the applicable regulations and that General Zwicker had been directed by higher authority to issue an honorable discharge to Peress upon his application.

Senator McCarthy knew that General Zwicker was a loyal and outstanding officer who had devoted his life to the service of his country, that General Zwicker was strongly opposed to Communists and their activities, that General Zwicker was cooperative and helpful to the staff of the subcommittee in giving information with reference to Major Peress, that General Zwicker opposed the Peress promotion and opposed the giving to him of an honorable discharge, and that he was testifying under the restrictions of lawful Executive orders.

Under these circumstances, the conduct of Senator McCarthy toward General Zwicker in reprimanding and ridiculing him, in holding him up to public scorn and contumely, and in disclosing the proceedings of the executive session in violation of the rules of his own committee, was inexcusable. Senator McCarthy acted as a critic and judge, upon preconceived and prejudicial notions. He did much to destroy the effectiveness and reputation of a witness who was not in any way responsible for the Peress situation, a situation which we do not in any way condone. The blame should have been placed on the shoulders of those culpable and not attributed publicly to one who had no share in the responsibility.

D. CONCLUSIONS

The select committee concludes that the conduct of Senator McCarthy toward General Zwicker was reprehensible, and that for this conduct he should be censured by the Senate.

VI

CHARGES NOT INCLUDED IN THE PUBLIC HEARINGS

Senate Resolution 301 provides that the committee—

shall be authorized to hold hearings, to sit and act at such times and places during the sessions, recesses, and adjourned periods of the Senate, to require by subpena or otherwise the attendance of such witnesses and the production of such correspondence, books, papers, and documents, and to *take such testimony as it deems advisable,* and that the committee be instructed to act and *make a report * * *"*

At the outset of our deliberations, the committee decided, preliminarily, that it was advisable to proceed with hearings upon 13 of the charges in the various proposed amendments, classified into the 5 major categories outlined in the notice of hearing. The other charges, however, remained pending before the committee and its staff. We have studied them in the light of the law and testimony developed in the hearings and have also investigated the evidence suggested in the charges. The committee thereafter confirmed its tentative decision not to conduct hearings on these other items. The committee believes it desirable under the resolution from which its powers and duties stem, to express its reasons for determining that formal hearings need not be conducted on these remaining charges.

The committee eliminated some of the charges for reasons of legal insufficiency, having concluded that the particular conduct charged was not in its judgment a proper basis for Senate censure. The determination of what constituted "legal insufficiency" in the context of a charge intended to support a proposed motion to censure a Member of the United States Senate was the most difficult task imposed upon this committee. No precedents found by the committee were particularly helpful in connection with this task. The path is narrow and the guideposts few.

Only three Senators have previously been censured by the Senate. Two, Senators McLaurin and Tillman, in 1902, for abusive and provocative language and engaging in a physical altercation on the floor of the Senate. The third, Senator Hiram Bingham, was censured in 1929 for having brought into an executive session of the Finance Committee's meeting on the tariff bill, as his aide, the assistant to the president of the Connecticut Manufacturers Association. The Senate found this action by Senator Bingham, "while not the result of corrupt motives" to be "contrary to good morals and senatorial ethics * * * (tending) * * * to bring the Senate into dishonor and disrepute * * *". The very paucity of precedents tends to establish the importance placed by the Senate on its machinery of censure.

Obviously, with such limited precedents the task of this committee in undertaking to determine what is and what is not censurable conduct by a United States Senator was indeed formidable. Individuals differ in their view and sensitivities respecting the propriety or impropriety of many types of conduct. Especially is this true when the conduct and its background present so many complexities and shadings of interpretations. Moreover, it is fairly obvious that conduct may be distasteful and less than proper, and yet not constitute censurable behavior.

We begin with the premise that the Senate of the United States is a responsible political body, important in the maintenance of our free institutions. Its Members are expected to conduct themselves with a proper respect for the principles of ethics and morality, for senatorial customs based on tradition, and with due regard for the importance of maintaining the good reputation of the Senate as the highest legislative body in the Nation, sharing constitutional responsibilities with the President in the appointment of officials and judges through advice and confirmation and participating in the conduct of foreign affairs through the ratification of treaties.

At the same time we are cognizant that the Senate as a political body imposes a multitude of responsibilities and duties on its Members which create great strains and stresses. We are further aware that individual Senators may, within the bounds of political propriety, adopt different methods of discharging their responsibilities to the people.

We did not, and clearly could not, undertake here to establish any fixed, comprehensive code of noncensurable conduct for Members of the United States Senate. We did apply our collective judgment to the specific conduct charged, and in some instances to the way a charge was made and the nature of the evidence preferred in support of it. And on the basis of the precedents and our understanding of what might be deemed censurable conduct in these circumstances, we determined whether, if a particular charge were established, we would consider it conduct warranting the censure of the Senate.

In concluding that certain of the charges dropped were legally insufficient for Senate censure, we do not want to be understood as saying that this committee approves of the conduct alleged. Yet disapproval of conduct does not necessarily call for official Senate censure.

The decision to eliminate any of the charges was arrived at only following extremely careful and thorough consideration. Unquestionably, one consideration underlying the elimination of these charges was the overall time factor. Under Senate Resolution 301 the select committee was directed by the Senate to hold its hearings and file its report prior to the sine die adjournment of the Senate in the 2d session of the then 83d Congress. And it was expressly contemplated that the Senate should be able to meet and consider such report at an appropriate time prior to such adjournment.

In order to abide by this direction and conform to such purpose it was necessary to narrow and confine the scope of its deliberations, and particularly of its formal hearings. The committee's study developed 12 major reasons which, singly or cumulatively, led to the elimination of these other charges from the committee's formal hearings. Only a few of these reasons, in addition to the ground of legal insufficiency, involved the passing of judgment upon the merits of any particular charge. The other reasons deal with the feasibility of the committee's attempting to investigate, document, and receive suitable testimonial evidence upon such specifications.

We set forth here the 12 general grounds upon which the other charges were dropped. Following that will be set forth, and appropriately identified, each charge eliminated, with the reasons for the omission of that particular charge indicated by a number or numbers in the right margin of the page. The numbers in the right margin correspond to the numbers of the 12 reasons for eliminating charges.

The 12 reasons applied as appropriate for eliminating particular charges are—

1. Charges which, even if fully supported and established, would not in the judgment of the committee constitute censurable conduct.

2. Charges which, even if fully supported and established after investigation, would in the judgment of the committee be of doubtful validity as a basis for censure.

3. Charges which are too vague and uncertain, or which were too broad in apparent scope to justify formal hearings by the committee.

4. Charges reflecting largely personal opinion rather than delineating specific, concrete conduct upon which a judgment of censure could properly be based.

5. Charges which, in order to determine properly, would have required more time to investigate, document, and take testimony upon, than was practically available to this committee.

6. Charges which were substantially covered or duplicated by other charges upon which the committee actually held hearings and received evidence.

7. Charges concerning statements made on the floor of the Senate about public officials, with which statements we may disagree, but which, if held censurable, would tend to place unwarranted limitations on the freedom of speech in the Senate of the United States.

8. Charges involving such matters as the receipt by a member of a committee of payments not corresponding to the value of services rendered, from persons subject to the jurisdiction of such committee (which might be reprehensible if true, because of some implication of improper influence), but which the committee believed were not susceptible of satisfactory proof in this forum.

9. Charges of improper treatment of a particular committee witness who is presently undergoing confidential security investigation by the executive department.

10. Charges involving misconduct of the staff of a standing committee of the Senate, over which that committee as a whole has jurisdiction and primary responsibility.

11. Charges concerning matters over which other committees have already acquired jurisdiction.

12. Charges on which no substantial evidence was submitted and none could be found by the committee.

Reason why eliminated

The charges eliminated, and the reasons therefor, are:

Amendments proposed by the Senator from Arkansas, Mr. Fulbright:

(1) The junior Senator from Wisconsin, while a member of the committee having jurisdiction over the affairs of the Lustron Co., a corporation financed by Government money, received $10,000 without rendering services of comparable value.   8

(2) In public hearings, before the Senate Permanent Investigations Subcommittee, of which he was chairman, the junior Senator from Wis-   9

consin strongly implied that Annie Lee Moss was known to be a member
of the Communist Party and that if she testified she would perjure her-
self, before he had given her an opportunity to testify in her own behalf.

(6) The junior Senator from Wisconsin in a speech on June 14, 1951,   7
without proof or other justification made an unwarranted attack upon
Gen. George C. Marshall.

Amendments proposed by the Senator from Oregon, Mr. Morse:

(*f*) Attempted to invade the constitutional power of the President   2, 5
of the United States to conduct the foreign relations of the United States
by carrying on negotiations with certain Greek shipowners in respect to
foreign trade policies, even though the executive branch of our Government had a few weeks previously entered into an understanding with
the Greek Government in respect to banning the flow of strategic ma-
terials to Communist countries; and

(*g*) Permitted and ratified over a period of several months in 1953 and   10
1954 the abuse of senatorial privilege by Mr. Roy Cohn, chief counsel to
the Permanent Investigations Subcommittee of the Senate Committee on
Government Operations of which committee and subcommittee the junior
Senator from Wisconsin is chairman. Mr. Cohn's abuse having been
directed toward attempting to secure preferential treatment for Pvt.
David Schine by the Department of the Army, at a time when the Army
was under investigation by the committee.

Amendments proposed by the Senator from Vermont, Mr. Flanders:

(1) He has retained and/or accredited staff personnel whose reputa-   4, 5
tions are in question and whose backgrounds would tend to indicate un-
trustworthiness (Surine, Lavinia, J. B. Matthews).

(2) He has permitted his staff to conduct itself in a presumptuous   4, 5, 10
manner. His counsel and his consultant (Messrs. Cohn and Schine)
have been insolent to other Senators, discourteous to the public, and dis-
creditable to the Senate. His counsel and consultant traveled abroad
making a spectacle of themselves and brought discredit upon the Senate
of the United States, whose employees they were.

(3) He has conducted his committee in such a slovenly and unpro-   3, 4, 10
fessional way that cases of mistaken identities have resulted in grievous
hardship or have made his committee, and thereby the Senate, appear
ridiculous. (Annie Lee Moss, Lawrence W. Parrish, subpenaed and
brought to Washington instead of Lawrence T. Parish.)

(4) He has proclaimed publicly his intention to subpena citizens of   1
good reputation, and then never called them. (Gen. Telford Taylor,
William P. Bundy, former President Truman, reporters Marder, Joseph
Alsop, Friendly, Bigrant, Phillip Potter.)

(5) He has repeatedly used verbal subpenas of questionable legality.   2, 5
(Tried to prevent State Department granting visa to William P. Bundy
on ground that he was under "oral subpena.")

(6) He has attempted to intimidate the press and single out indi-   4, 5
vidual journalists who have been critical of him or whose reports he has
regarded with disfavor, and either threatened them with subpena or
forced them to testify in such a manner as to raise the possibility of a
breach of the first amendment of the Constitution. (Murray Marder of
Washington Post, the Alsops, James Wechsler.)

(7) He has attempted "economic coercion" against the press and   2, 3, 5
radio, particularly the case of Time magazine, the Milwaukee Journal,
and the Madison Capital Times. (On June 16, 1952, McCarthy sent
letters to advertisers in Time magazine, urging them to withdraw their
advertisements.)

(8) He has permitted the staff to investigate at least one of his fellow   4, 10
Senators (Jackson) and possibly numerous Senators. Such material
has been reserved with the obvious intention of coercing the other Senator or Senators to submit to his will, or for the purpose of inhibiting
them from expressing themselves critically. (Cohn said he would "get"
Senator Jackson.)—Washington News, June 14, 1954.

(9) He has posed as savior of his country from communism, yet the   1
Department of Justice reported that McCarthy never turned over for
prosecution a single case against any of his alleged "Communists." (The
Justice Department report of December 18, 1951.) Since that date not
a single person has been tried for Communist activities as a result of
information supplied by McCarthy.

(11) He has used distortion and innuendo to attack the reputations   3, 4, 5
of the following citizens: Former President Truman, Gen. George Marshall, Attorney General Brownell, John J. McCloy, Ambassador Charles
E. Bohlen, Senator Raymond Baldwin, former Assistant Secretary of
Defense Anna Rosenberg, Philip Jessup, Marquis Childs, Richard L.
Strout of the Christian Science Monitor, Gen. Telford Taylor, and the
three national press associations.

(12) He has disclosed restricted security information in possible vio-   4, 6, 12
lation of the espionage laws. (McCarthy has made public portions of
an Army Intelligence study, Soviet Siberia, which compelled the Army to
declassify and release the entire document.)

(15) He has used his official position to fix the Communist label upon   3, 4, 5
all individuals and newspapers as might legitimately disagree with him
or refuse to acknowledge him as the unique leader in the fight against
subversion. (Deliberate slips such as calling Aldai Stevenson "Alger";
saying that the American Civil Liberties Union had been "listed" as
doing the work of the Communist Party; calling the Milwaukee Journal
and Washington Post local "editions of the Daily Worker.")

(16) He has attempted to usurp the functions of the executive   2, 3, 5
department by having his staff negotiate agreements with a group
of ship owners in London; and has infringed upon functions of the
State Department, claiming that he was acting in the "national interest."

(18) He has made false claims about alleged wounds which in fact   1
he did not suffer. (Claims he was a tailgunner when, in fact, he was a
Marine Air Force Ground Intelligence officer * * * claims he entered
as buck private, when he entered as commissioned officer.)

(19) His rude and ruthless disregard of the rights of other Senators   2
has gone to the point where the entire minority membership of the Permanent Investigating Subcommittee resigned from the committee in protest
against his highhandedness (July 10, 1953).

(20) He has intruded upon the prerogative of the executive branch,   5
violating the constitutional principles of separation of powers. (Within
a single week (February 14–20, 1953) McCarthy's activities against the
Voice of America forced the State Department three times to reverse
administrative decisions on matters normally considered internal operating procedures:

((1) The Department had authorized the use of certain writings by
pro-Communist authors as part of their program to expose Communist
lies and false promises. McCarthy compelled the State Department to
discontinue this practice; (2) the Department authorized its employees to
refuse to talk with McCarthy's staff in the absence of McCarthy himself.
It was compelled to cancel this directive; and (3) John Matson, a departmental security agent who had "cooperated" with McCarthy, was trans-
ferred so as to be put out of reach of the Department's confidential files.
McCarthy compelled the Department to return Matson to his original
position.)

(21) He has infringed upon the jurisdiction of other Senate com-   1, 3
mittees, invading the area of the Internal Security Subcommittee and
other committees of the Congress.

(22) He has failed to perform the solid and useful duties of the   3
Government Operations Committee, abandoning the legitimate and vital
functions of this committee.

(23) He has held executive sessions in an apparent attempt to   3, 4, 5
prevent the press from getting an accurate account of the testimony of
witnesses, and then released his own versions of that testimony, often
at variance with the subsequently revealed transcripts, and under circumstances in which the witness had little opportunity to correct or object
to his version.

Reason why eliminated

(24) He has questioned adverse witnesses in public session in such a manner as to defame loyal and valuable public servants, whose own testimony he failed to get beforehand, and whom he never provided a comparable opportunity for answering the charges. — 3, 5

(25) He has barred the press and general public from executive sessions and then permitted unauthorized persons whom his whim favored to attend, in one case, a class of schoolgirls, thus holding the very principle of executive sessions up to ridicule. — 3

(26) His conduct has caused and permitted his subcommittee to be incomplete or incapacitated in its normal work for approximately 40 percent of the time that he has been its chairman. (During his 19 months as chairman of the subcommittee, his refusal to recognize their rights—later acknowledged by him—caused the minority members to leave the subcommittee on July 10, 1953, and they did not return until January 25, 1954. His personally motivated quarrel with the United States Army necessitated the interruption of the subcommittee's work and its exclusive preoccupation with the Army-McCarthy hearings from April 22, 1954, to June 17, 1954.) — 2, 4, 10

(27) He has publicly threatened publications with the withdrawal of their second-class mailing privilege because he disagreed with their editorial policy. (Washington Post, Wall Street Journal, Time magazine.) Letter to Postmaster General Summerfield made public August 22, 1953. See Washington Post, August 23, 1953. — 12

(28) He has exploited his committee chairmanship to disseminate fantastic and unverified claims for the obvious purpose of publicity. (McCarthy's hint that he was in secret communication with Lavrenti P. Beria and would produce him as a witness when Beria was on the verge of execution in Moscow.) Washington News, September 21, 1953 (announcement of plan to subpena Beria). — 2

(29) He has denied Members of Congress access to the files of the committee, to which every Member of Congress is entitled under the Reorganization Act (title II, sec. 202, par. d). — 3, 11

(31) He has announced investigations prematurely, subsequently dropping these investigations so that the question whether there was ever any serious intent to pursue them may be justifiably raised, along with the inevitable conclusion that publicity was the only purpose. (Central Intelligence Agency, Beria, and so forth.) — 3

(32) Checking through hearings, one will note that favorable material submitted by witnesses will usually have the notation "May be found in the files of the subcommittee," whereas unfavorable material is printed in the record. — 3, 4, 5

(33) He has permitted changing of committee reports and records in such a way as to substantially change or delete vital meanings. (Senator Margaret Chase Smith felt compelled to object to the filing of his 1953 subcommittee reports without their first being sent through the full committee.) — 3

VII

Bush Amendment

Senate Resolution 301 submitted to the select committee for consideration contains not only the charges for censure, but also contains the amendment proposed by the Senator from Connecticut, Mr. Bush, in regard to proposed changes in rules and procedure for Senate committees.

The select committee is aware of the fact that the Subcommittee on Rules of the Senate Committee on Rules and Administration has held extensive hearings on this subject.

Many witnesses appeared before that subcommittee, including Senator Bush, and we are advised that this committee expects to have a report ready for the opening of the next session of Congress.

It is the firm conviction of the select committee that this is a subject which requires much study before affirmative action is taken on a general change in the rules and procedure of committees and subcommittees of the Senate. However, after hearing the evidence and the testimony presented at the hearing before our committee, we are of the opinion that had certain rules of committee procedure been in effect, much of the criticism against investigative committee hearings would have been avoided. For this reason, we report a separate resolution on the subject of the Bush amendment, to read as follows:

Resolved, That subsection 3 of rule XXV of the Standing Rules of the Senate is amended by adding at the end thereof the following:

"(c) No witness shall be required to testify before a committee or subcommittee with less than two members present, unless the committee or subcommittee by majority vote agrees that one member may hold the hearing, or the witness waives any objection to testifying before one member.

"(d) Committee interrogation of witnesses shall be conducted only by members and authorized staff personnel of the committee and no person shall be employed or assigned to investigate activities until approved by the committee.

"(e) No testimony taken or material presented in an executive session shall be made public, either in whole or in part or by way of summary, unless authorized by majority vote of the committee.

"(f) Vouchers covering expenditures of any investigating committee shall be accompanied by a statement signed by the chairman that the investigation was duly authorized and conducted under the provisions of this rule."

And we recommend that this amendment to the rules be approved by the Senate to be effective January 3, 1955.

VIII

RECOMMENDATIONS OF SELECT COMMITTEE UNDER SENATE ORDER PURSUANT TO SENATE RESOLUTION 301

For the reasons and on the facts found in this report, the select committee recommends:

1. That on the charges in the category of "Incidents of Contempt of the Senate or a Senatorial Committee," the Senator from Wisconsin, Mr. McCarthy, should be censured.

2. That the charges in the category of "Incidents of Encouragement of United States Employees To Violate the Law and Their Oaths of Office or Executive Orders," do not, under all the evidence, justify a resolution of censure.

3. That the charges in the category of "Incidents Involving Receipt or Use of Confidential or Classified or Other Confidential Information From Executive Files," do not, under all the evidence, justify a resolution of censure.

4. That the charges in the category of "Incidents Involving Abuse of Colleagues in the Senate," except as to those dealt with in the first category, do not, under all the evidence, justify a resolution of censure.

5. That on the charges in the category of "Incident Relating to Ralph W. Zwicker, a general officer of the Army of the United States," the Senator from Wisconsin, Mr. McCarthy, should be censured.

6. That with reference to the amendment to Senate Resolution 301 offered by the Senator from New Jersey, Mr. Smith, this

report and the recommendations herein be regarded as having met the purposes of said amendment.

7. That with reference to the amendment to Senate Resolution 301 offered by the Senator from Connecticut, Mr. Bush, that an amendment to the Senate Rules be adopted in accord with the language proposed in part VII of this report.

The chairman of the select committee is authorized in behalf of the committee to present to the Senate appropriate resolutions to give effect to the foregoing recommendations.

INDEX

69

O

Appendix C   Official United States Army statement, released November 3, 1954

DOCTOR IRVING R. PERESS, FORMER MAJOR U. S. ARMY

The Department of the Army announced today that exhaustive investigations have conclusively established that there was no collusion, conspiracy, or preferential treatment with respect to any of its actions in the case of Doctor Irving R. Peress. The evidence shows clearly that it was the system which was at fault. Accordingly, the inference which has been made repeatedly during the past several months that these actions provide tangible evidence of "coddling of Communists" by the Army is completely false.

As the Secretary of the Army has previously stated, the comprehensive investigation by The Inspector General of the Army of all actions taken in the case was directed at determining, among other things, whether there had been any collusion or conspiracy which might have been inspired by subversive interests, or whether the personnel actions involved were taken in a routine manner under policies and regulations in existence at the time. The report of this investigation reveals that the latter was true in each instance and that there was no semblance of disloyalty or pro-Communist influence reflecting on the loyalty, integrity, or patriotism of any of the officers or civilians who were involved in the processing of the personnel actions in the case. This was confirmed by a similar investigation conducted by the Department of Defense. Immediate action was taken to correct procedural deficiencies which were discovered during the course of the investigations.

By letter of 23 June 1954, Secretary Stevens furnished this information—in addition to the previously furnished list of names of Army personnel, who, in the course of their official duties, took some type of administrative action in the case—to Senator Mundt, in his capacity as Temporary Chairman, Permanent Subcommittee on Investigations, U.S. Senate.

A brief chronology of the significant events in the case, as developed by these investigations, follows:

Doctor Peress registered with his local draft board early in 1951, as was required by Public Law 779, 81st Congress (the so-called Doctor Draft Act). In May of 1952, he completed DD Form 390 (Initial Data for Classification and Commissioning in Medical Services for Medical, Dental, and Veterinary Corps) which was a statement of professional qualifications and an application for a commission. On this form he certified that he was not and had not been a member of any subversive group. Subsequently, he was designated by his local board as available for service in the Armed Forces.

From the information furnished it appeared that he possessed all of the necessary qualifications for a commission and he was so appointed. The three copies of the DD Form 390 which Doctor Peress had completed in May of 1952, having served their initial purpose in connection with his appointment were distributed in accordance with the then established procedure—one copy to the local draft board, one to The Surgeon General for a worksheet, and one was retained in Headquarters, First Army.

In October of 1952 Doctor Peress was appointed in the grade of Captain, USAR, and took the oath of office on the 15th of that month. It is emphasized that at this stage of the processing, there was nothing in the record to distinguish this case from that of hundreds of other doctors and dentists being commissioned for service during the Korean emergency.

At the time that Doctor Peress was furnished his letter of appointment he was also supplied with other forms which were to be completed by him and returned within 15 days. On 28 October 1952 he completed DD Forms 398 (Personal History Statement) and DD Form 98 (Loyalty Certificate) wherein for the first time he claimed Federal Constitutional privilege in answering questions concerning membership in subversive organizations.

(At that time regulations provided that these forms might be completed after appointment by persons being commissioned under the Doctor Draft Act, while all other personnel were required to complete the forms prior to appointment. The following considerations led to the promulgation, and later the recission, of these regulations. Doctors were needed immediately in large numbers to provide adequate care of the wounded in Korea, and their procurement was expedited by permitting the tendering of commissions to them without requiring the prior accomplishment of the normal administrative forms, including the Loyalty Certificate. In November of 1952, however, after the fighting in Korea had stabilized, and the urgent need for doctors and dentists had decreased, and upon review of the case of a Communist lieutenant among this group, these regulations were rescinded. Thereafter special registrants were required to complete Loyalty Certificates before being commissioned the same as all others.)

While Doctor Peress was in the process of completing these forms, arrangements were being made to call him and a number of new appointees to active duty. He was ordered to duty as of 1 January 1953 and was assigned to Brooke Army Medical Center to attend a medical service officers training course. His call to duty was not delayed by virtue of qualification of his Loyalty Certificate in accordance with regulations then in force which provided that individuals subject to the draft would not be deferred until they had been investigated and the results determined to warrant removal from the service. Had the rule been otherwise, any individual could have dodged service by a claim of Constitutional privilege. Peress requested a delay of 15 days in order to conclude his business affairs, but this request was refused.

Upon completion of 4 weeks of training at Brooke Army Medical Center, Captain Peress was ordered to proceed to Fort Lewis, Washington, for further assignment to the Far East Command. He was given the normal 7 days leave.

On the day he reported to Fort Lewis for shipment to the Far East, a message was received at Fort Lewis from the American Red Cross in New York City, reporting that his wife and daughter were ill and undergoing medical treatment. Emergency leave was suggested in the message as a means of temporary relief. A 15-day emergency leave was granted. Concurrently Captain Peress wrote to The Adjutant General requesting cancellation of his oversea orders and compassionate reassignment to a station near his home and family. He inclosed letters from two physicians and a copy of the Red Cross report in support of his request.

This request, together with the letters and the Red Cross report, was considered by a board of officers which recommended deferment from overseas assignment to Camp Kilmer because of its proximity to his home. Accordingly, The Adjutant General revoked the overseas orders and assigned Captain Peress to Camp Kilmer. Upon reporting to this station, he was assigned duties as a Dental Officer which did not involve access to classified information. Based on the evidence furnished, there was nothing unusual in the approval of this compassionate reassignment.

On 29 June 1953, Public Law 84, 83rd Congress, the amendment to the so-called Doctor Draft Act under which the rank of Captain Peress was later adjusted to that of major, was passed. It required that persons who had been ordered to active duty under the Doctor Draft Act would be reappointed in the rank commensurate with their professional education and experience.

On 7 October the Department of Defense issued a directive implementing the law and prescribing criteria for determining appropriate grade adjustments. Accordingly, the Army moved promptly to carry out the provisions of the law as directed by the Department of Defense. The Surgeon General, as head of the medical services of the Army screened the qualification records of all officers of the Medical, Dental, and Veterinary Corps for medical professional qualifications only.

On 14 October 1953, exactly one week after the issuance of the Department of Defense directive, a list of 538 medical officers, 125 dental officers, and 18 veterinary officers was forwarded by The Surgeon General to The Adjutant General, the Army's principal administrative officer, for automatic adjustment in rank as the law required. Captain Peress' name was on that list. Based upon it, new letters of appointment were issued, and under his letter of appointment Captain Peress' rank was adjusted to that of major on 2 November 1953. The Department of the Army acknowledges that thorough coordination through security channels was not effected on all such readjustments. However, changes in procedure have since been made so that under the present system, administrative or personnel files are flagged and checked to preclude adjustment of rank, promotion, or any other favorable personnel action on any individual against whom an investigation has been directed.

On 30 December 1953, the Department of the Army determined on the basis of an investigation which had been initiated in February of 1953 that Major Peress should be separated from the service by reason of his subversive connections prior to entering the Service. It is significant to note at this juncture that up to this time no one outside the Department of the Army had manifested any interest in or concern over Peress. Three possible courses of action were considered—(1) court-martial, (2) appearance before a board of officers to show cause why he should not be eliminated from the service, and (3) discharge under the program then in effect to reduce the number of officers serving on active duty.

The first alternative was rejected as it appeared then that he had done nothing during his military service which was an offense against military law. Since the DD Form 390, upon which he had denied membership in any subversive organization, was not in the personnel and intelligence files being reviewed in connection with this action, the possibility of his being tried by courtmartial for fraudulent procurement of a commission was not considered. Subsequent to his discharge, however, this possibility was given careful study. It was concluded that the available evidence which could have been used in such a court-martial action was not sufficient to prove actual membership in a subversive organization. Thus, a conviction on this ground could not have been sustained. The entire case has, however, been forwarded to the Department of Justice for study and decision as to whether action under criminal law is appropriate.

The second alternative was rejected because such proceedings are lengthy, voluminous, time-consuming, and expensive.

The third alternative, that of effecting most expeditiously his discharge, was elected as the means of separating him from the service. Consideration in making this election was given to the fact that it would result in the revocation of his commission in the Army Reserve, as well as his release from active duty, and would return him to a purely civilian status in the shortest possible time. Such action was permitted by the Officer Personnel Act of 1947 and Public Law 84, 83rd Congress; however, the discharge had to be one under honorable conditions. It was also consistent with instructions issued personally by the Secretary of the Army on 9 September 1953 that, in connection with the reduction-in-force program, the Army would give first attention to those officers found to be unsatisfactory. In the absence of a resignation for the good of the service, a discharge of any other type could only be awarded pursuant to an approved sentence of a court-martial or to the approved findings and recommendations of a board of officers. Again, the investigation revealed that all actions in connection with the discharge of Peress were taken in good faith and were in strict accord with the laws, policies, and regulations in force at that time. Peress was then notified that he would be separated from the service under the reduction-in-force program and that his commission would be terminated—an action which would completely sever his connections with the military service.

Under the reduction-in-force program, all officers were given 90 days' notice of the decision to effect their separation, unless they elected to be separated at an earlier date. Peress initially selected 31 March 1954 as the date upon which to be released. However, on Monday, 1 February 1954, following his appearance the preceding Saturday before a subcommittee of the United States Senate in New York City, he asked to be discharged as soon as possible. Consistent with the decision reached on 30 December to get him out of the service as quickly as possible, his request was accepted and he was discharged the following day. At the same time, action was taken to insure that he is never again commissioned or accepted in the Armed Services in any capacity.

In conclusion, the Department of the Army acknowledges that there was undue delay in the investigation, processing, and adjudication of this affair. His compassionate reassignment within the Zone of the Interior was in accord with the policies and regulations then in effect. Public law 84, 83d Congress, and Department of Defense instructions were interpreted as a mandate to effect the readjustment in grade of officers inducted under the Doctor Draft Act. This resulted in the readjustment in grade of Peress. It is also true that the DD Form 390 (a form primarily designed to list professional qualifications) upon which he had initially denied past or present membership in any subversive organizations was held, in accordance with the then established procedure, in technical channels until after he had been discharged. Thus it was not in the official personnel file for consideration by personnel involved in determining the most appropriate method of terminating his commission. The Department of the Army has amended its procedure to require that a copy of DD Form 390 be incorporated in the official personnel file of each individual to preclude any similar oversight in the future.

Again, the Department of the Army emphasizes that exhaustive investigation of this case established clearly that there was no collusion, conspiracy, or "coddling of Communists" on the part of any of the personnel involved in any of the actions taken. Appropriate changes have been made to correct weaknesses discovered in policies and procedures with respect to the handling of cases of this nature. These changes have been published in Department of Defense directives and Department of the Army regulations.

Index